LANGUAGE AND STYLE

LANGUAGE AND STYLE

Collected Papers by

STEPHEN ULLMANN
Ph.D., D.Litt.

Professor of Romance Philology
University of Leeds

NEW YORK

BARNES & NOBLE, INC.
Publishers · Booksellers · Since 1873

FIRST PUBLISHED 1964

*Published in the United States
in 1964
by Barnes & Noble, Inc.
105 Fifth Avenue, New York 3*

PRINTED IN GREAT BRITAIN

TO MY WIFE

PREFACE

The present volume contains eleven papers written during the last eight years. Four of these (chapters 4, 6, 10 and 11) are printed here for the first time; two others (chapters 1 and 2) were published in journals; the rest appeared in proceedings of congresses and conferences, which are not always easily accessible. All the papers have been revised, modified and brought up to date, and some of them have been considerably expanded: chapter 8, for example, has grown from five pages to nineteen. Papers in French have been translated into English.

In order to give some shape and unity to the volume, the articles have been grouped around three main themes: meaning, style, and the influence of language upon thought. Each of the three sections starts with a general survey of the field, followed by one or more chapters on particular problems. The various papers have also been integrated as far as possible: repetitions and overlaps have been eliminated, numerous cross-references have been added, and material has been transferred, wherever necessary, from one chapter to another.

The eleven papers were based, wholly or partly, on the following:

(1) 'Semantics at the Cross-Roads', *Universities Quarterly*, xii (1958), pp. 250–60.

(2) 'The Concept of Meaning in Linguistics', *Archivum Linguisticum*, viii (1956), pp. 12–20.

(3) 'Sémantique et étymologie', *Cahiers de l'Association Internationale des Etudes Françaises*, xi (1959), pp. 323–35.

(4) 'Synchronie et diachronie en sémantique', paper read at the Tenth International Congress of Romance Linguistics (Strasbourg, April 1962).

(5) 'Semantic Universals', in *Universals of Language*, edited by Joseph H. Greenberg (Cambridge, Mass., The M.I.T. Press, 1963), pp. 172–207.

(6) This chapter is based on lectures given in various universities and societies; it also uses some of the material which appeared in the introduction ('Language and Style') to my book, *Style in the French Novel* (Cambridge University Press, 1957; Blackwell, 1963). Many of the examples contained in the same book and its sequel, *The Image in the Modern French Novel* (Cambridge University Press, 1960; Blackwell, 1963), are also quoted in other chapters of this volume, especially in chapters 7–9.

(7) 'Choix et expressivité', in *Actes du IXᵉ Congrès International de Linguistique Romane* (Lisbon, Centro de Estudos Filológicos, 1961), vol. II, pp. 217–26.

(8) 'Un Problème de reconstruction stylistique', in *Atti dell'VIII Congresso Internazionale di Studi Romanzi* (Florence, Sansoni, 1959), vol. II, part 1, pp. 465–9.

(9) 'L'Image littéraire. Quelques questions de méthode', in *Langue et littérature. Actes du VIIIᵉ Congrès de la Fédération Internationale des Langues et Littératures Modernes* (Bibliothèque de la Faculté de Philosophie et Lettres de l'Université de Liège, fasc. clxi; Paris, Les Belles Lettres, 1961), pp. 41–59.

(10) 'Le Vocabulaire, moule et norme de la pensée', paper read at a 'Colloque sur les problèmes de la personne' (Royaumont, September–October 1960), organized by the 'Ecole Pratique des Hautes Etudes, VIᵉ Section: Centre de Recherches de Psychologie Comparative'.

(11) 'Latinisme et hellénisme dans le vocabulaire de la Renaissance', lecture given in July 1961 at the 'Centre d'Etudes Supérieures de la Renaissance de Tours'.

I am most grateful to the Editors, Secretaries or other officials of the institutions concerned for authorizing me to use this material. My sincere thanks are also due to the following colleagues for bibliographical and other information as well as for advice on the translation of difficult passages: Dr. T. V. Benn, Professor G. T. Clapton and Mlle Marie-Louise Thyss. More specific debts have been acknowledged in the footnotes.

The fact that essays on linguistic and stylistic themes are published here under the same cover is intended to emphasize the indissoluble unity of these two disciplines. As the Editor of a recent Dutch symposium on the subject has put it, 'the *rapprochement* between linguistics and literature, leading to the stylistic study of literary works, is one of the most important achievements of the last thirty years'.[1] It is hoped that the new 'Language and Style' series, of which this book forms the first volume, will contribute to the further development of research in this field.

LEEDS, 1963   STEPHEN ULLMANN

---

[1] *Style et littérature*, The Hague, 1962, p. 7.

CONTENTS

PART I

PROBLEMS OF MEANING

CHAPTER I

SEMANTICS AT THE CROSS-ROADS

JUST over eighty years ago, a new term was introduced into linguistic studies. In 1883, the French philologist Michel Bréal published an article on what he called the 'intellectual laws' of language. In this he argued that, alongside of phonetics and morphology, the study of the formal elements of human speech, there ought also to be a science of meaning, which he proposed to call *la sémantique*, by a word derived from the Greek σῆμα 'sign' (cf. *semaphore*).[1] The branch of study advocated in this article was not entirely new;[2] yet it was mainly Bréal's generation, and in the first place Bréal himself, who established semantics as a discipline in its own right. In 1897 he published his *Essai de sémantique* which saw many subsequent editions and is still widely read. It is interesting to note that one of the most language-conscious poets of our time, Paul Valéry, had great admiration for this book and reviewed it in the *Mercure de France*.[3] Three years after its publication, Bréal's *Essai* was translated into English under the title *Semantics: Studies in the Science of Meaning*, and although the term had been used in English a few years earlier, this translation played a decisive role in the diffusion of the new science and its name.

Semantics ought to set an example to other sciences in the avoidance of ambiguity, and it is somewhat paradoxical that the term itself has become highly ambiguous in recent years. Since the 1920s the philosophers have acquired their own brand, or brands, of semantics, which have very little in common with the homonymous science practised by philologists. Philosophical semantics in the more esoteric sense of the term is a branch of the 'theory of signs', dealing with relations between signs and what they stand for. In its more popular sense, philosophical semantics is a study of the misuse of abstractions, and of other shortcomings of language. The campaign against these abuses was launched in 1933 by A. Korzybski in his monumental *Science and Sanity*, and is still being vigorously pursued by the writers grouped around the journal *Etc*. Neither of these movements has made any notable contribution to lin-

---

[1] 'Les lois intellectuelles du langage', published in *L'Annuaire de l'Association pour l'encouragement des études grecques en France*. Quoted by A. W. Read, 'An Account of the Word *Semantics*', *Word*, iv (1948), pp. 78–97.
[2] See below, ch. III.
[3] See F. Scarfe, *The Art of Paul Valéry*, London, 1954, pp. 56 f.

guistic semantics,[1] and such impulses as have been received from philosophers came from other sources, as will be seen in the second chapter of this book.

At the time when semantics appeared on the scene, the science of language was an exclusively historical discipline. Semantics whole-heartedly accepted this orientation, and for the first half-century of its existence it remained a purely historical study. Its prime purpose was the classification of changes of meaning according to logical, psychological or sociological criteria, and the discovery of any abiding tendencies—misleadingly called 'semantic laws'—which governed these changes. This phase found its crowning achievement in Gustaf Stern's *Meaning and Change of Meaning, with Special Reference to the English Language*,[2] which was published in 1931 and contained the first scheme of classifica-tion based on an extensive collection of concrete data. Meanwhile, however, far-reaching changes had taken place in general linguistics, as a result of which semanticists were soon faced with a dilemma which remains unresolved to this very day.

In the early years of the present century, linguistics underwent what has been rightly described as a 'Copernican revolution'. This revolution, which was ushered in by the posthumous publication, in 1916, of Fer-dinand de Saussure's *Cours de linguistique générale*,[3] showed itself in two main ways. Firstly, the historical bias of nineteenth-century philology gave way to a broader view which admitted the existence of two ap-proaches to language, one descriptive or 'synchronic', the other historical or 'diachronic', and boldly proclaimed the primacy of the descriptive method because it is more akin to the attitude of the ordinary speaker. The second great change concerned the way in which the tasks of des-criptive linguistics were conceived. Language came to be viewed, not as an aggregate of discrete elements but as an organized totality, a *Gestalt*, which has a pattern of its own and whose components are interdependent and derive their significance from the system as a whole. In Saussure's famous simile, language is like a game of chess: you cannot add, remove or displace any element without affecting the entire field of force. In the United States, thinking about the fundamental structure of language developed on similar lines; the new approach was codified with remarkable precision and rigour in Leonard Bloomfield's book *Language* (1933),

---

[1] A useful, though rather biased, survey of these various trends will be found in A. Schaff, *Introduction to Semantics*, English transl., Oxford, etc., 1962. See also H. Gipper, *Bausteine zur Sprachinhaltsforschung*, Düsseldorf, 1963.
[2] *Göteborgs Högskolas Arsskrift*, vol. XXXVIII.
[3] 5th ed., Paris, 1955; English transl. by Wade Baskin, London, 1960.

which, second only to Saussure's *Cours*, is easily the most influential work on linguistics published so far in this century.

The new conception of language, which has come to be known by the name of '*structuralism*', has sometimes been carried to unreasonable lengths. To assert, as has often been done, that language is a system where everything hangs together—'un système où tout se tient'—is obviously unrealistic. The late Professor Entwistle was nearer the mark when he wrote: 'I do not find language either systematic or wholly unsystematic, but impressed with patterns, generally incomplete, by our pattern-making minds'.[1] Be that as it may, the idea of an underlying pattern has proved an extremely fruitful working hypothesis. It has been applied with conspicuous success to the phonological side of language where it has yielded the invaluable concept of 'phoneme' or 'distinctive sound'. From phonology, there has been a gradual shift of interest to morphological structure where the theory has produced another useful though more controversial concept: that of the 'morpheme' or 'minimum significant unit of language'—a diverse category which comprises simple words, prefixes and suffixes, inflexions, non-independent roots and other elements, including even the intonation of the sentence.[2] The structuralist theory has also made an impact on syntax where it has given rise, during the last few years, to an entirely new and promising technique known as 'transformational grammar'.[3] Even the reconstruction of extinct languages has benefited by the advent of the structural approach. Semantics, too, has felt the need to align itself with the rest of linguistics by adopting structuralist viewpoints, but these attempts have so far met with less success than in other branches of language study.

The reasons for this discrepancy are not far to seek: they lie in the very nature of the subject. Whereas the phonological and even the grammatical resources of a language are closely organized and limited in number, the vocabulary is a loose assemblage of a vast multitude of elements. The numerical contrast is striking: a recent authority states that there are forty-four or forty-five phonemes in English while on the other hand the Oxford Dictionary is said to contain over 400,000 words:[4] a ratio of nearly 1 to 10,000! But there is an equally sharp contrast in cohesion and stability. The phonological and grammatical system, though

[1] W. J. Entwistle, *Aspects of Language*, London, 1953, p. viii.
[2] See on these problems C. F. Hockett, *A Course in Modern Linguistics*, New York, 1958, ch. XIV. Cf. below, p. 65.
[3] See N. Chomsky, *Syntactic Structures*, The Hague, 1957. On structural syntax, see two recent review articles by R. H. Robins (*Archivum Linguisticum*, xiii, 1961, pp. 78–89) and P. H. Matthews (ibid., pp. 196–209).
[4] S. Potter, *Modern Linguistics*, London, 1957, pp. 40 and 101.

subject to long-term changes, is relatively stable at a given moment, whereas the vocabulary is in a perpetual state of flux. New words are continuously formed or borrowed from outside sources to fill a genuine gap or to suit the whims of the speaker; new meanings are attached to old words; existing terms are dropped and others are unexpectedly revived, as Horace already knew:

> Multa renascentur quae iam cecidere, cadentque
> Quae nunc sunt in honore vocabula, si volet usus,
> Quem penes arbitrium est et ius et norma loquendi.[1]

It is clear, then, that the vast, unstable and loosely organized congeries of words which we call vocabulary cannot be analysed with the same scientific rigour and precision as the phonological and grammatical system of a language. This does not mean, however, that words are not amenable to any kind of structural treatment. It is here rather than in other sectors of language that we are likely to find the incomplete patterns envisaged in Entwistle's formula. In the search for such patterns, some linguists and other scholars have evolved, since the early 'thirties, a number of different techniques from which a new, structurally oriented semantics has begun to emerge. These experiments fall into three main groups: those which aim at a statistical analysis of word-frequency and other lexical features; those which seek to identify the characteristic tendencies of a language; lastly, those which are concerned with the way the vocabulary is built up, with the principles and the hierarchy of values which underlie its structure.

1. The *statistical* approach has become of late very popular in linguistics, not only because of the precision and objectivity which it is held to guarantee, but also because language is a mass phenomenon *par excellence*, which seems to invite this kind of treatment.[2] In semantics, one of the boldest attempts to introduce statistical methods was made by the late G. K. Zipf in his book, *Human Behaviour and the Principle of Least Effort* (1949), and in other writings. Zipf's analysis was based on the assumption that words work like ordinary tools and are subject to the same laws which govern the use of tools. The analogy between words and

---

[1] 'Many a term which has fallen from use shall have a second birth, and those shall fall that are now in high honour, if so Usage shall will it, in whose hands is the arbitrament, the right and the rule of speech' (*Ars Poetica*, ll. 70 ff.; transl. from *The Oxford Dictionary of Quotations*, 2nd impr., 1942, p. 541).

[2] For a general survey see P. Guiraud, *Problèmes et méthodes de la statistique linguistique*, Dordrecht, 1959. Cf. also H. Mitterand, *Les Mots français*, Paris, 1963.

tools was by no means new, but Zipf pursued it to its ultimate implications. He argued that, just as there is a direct relationship between the frequency of the use of a tool and the diversity of the uses to which it is put, in the same way 'we may expect to find a direct relationship between the number of different meanings of a word and its relative frequency of occurrences'.[1] He even found a mathematical formula for this relationship: with the possible exception of the few dozen most frequent words of a language, 'different meanings of a word will tend to be equal to the square root of its relative frequency'.[2]

The ordinary linguist is here on unfamiliar ground; yet he cannot help feeling somewhat alarmed at the very precision of the result. His experience with word-meanings has taught him that they are seldom as precise, as sharply delimited, as Zipf's formula would suggest. He has come to view with some scepticism the dictionary method—inevitable but none the less misleading—of setting up the various meanings of a word as so many independent entities; he knows that, more often than not, these meanings have no clear-cut demarcation lines but rather a kind of hazy fringe through which they imperceptibly merge into each other; they are, as Wittgenstein once put it, 'concepts with blurred edges'.[3] Zipf was no doubt on the right track when he discerned a correlation between word frequency and diversity of meaning; but he built on insecure foundations when he tried to give his findings, based on dictionary data, a mathematical formulation to which the material just does not lend itself.

As will be seen in Chapter V and elsewhere in this book, there are many ways in which statistical methods can be usefully applied to semantic problems. In recent years there have also been hopeful signs of co-operation between semantics and communication theory; a leading authority on cybernetics actually went so far as to claim that there is no 'fundamental opposition between the problems of our engineers in measuring communication and the problems of our philologists'.[4] At a practical level, electronic computers and other mechanical devices have

[1] 'The Repetition of Words, Time-Perspective, and Semantic Balance', *The Journal of General Psychology*, xxxii (1945), pp. 127–48: p. 144.
[2] 'The Meaning-Frequency Relationship of Words', ibid., xxxiii (1945), pp. 251–6; cf. J. Whatmough, *Language. A Modern Synthesis*, London, 1956, p. 73.
[3] *Philosophical Investigations*, Oxford, 1953, p. 34.
[4] Norbert Wiener, *Journal of the Acoustical Society of America*, xxii (1950), p. 697; quoted by R. Jakobson, 'Linguistics and Communication Theory', *Structure of Language and its Mathematical Aspects* (Proceedings of Symposia in Applied Mathematics, vol. XII, 1961), pp. 245–52: p. 245. On contacts between linguistics and communication theory, see C. Cherry, *On Human Communication*, New York — London, 1957, and other works mentioned in my *Semantics. An Introduction to the Science of Meaning*, Oxford, 1962, p. 18, nn. 3 and 4.

B

already been applied with good effect to a wide variety of lexical data.[1] At the same time, these new contacts, however valuable, are bound to create serious problems of communication. The situation was neatly summed up a quarter of a century ago by one of the champions of mathematical linguistics: '... both philology and mathematics are essentially esoteric subjects, the latter more so than the former. This means that the mathematics will not be intelligible to someone who is not a mathematician and the philology will, at the best, be difficult for someone who is not a philologist'.[2] Unfortunately, these difficulties are only too often disregarded by mathematicians and even by mathematically minded linguists. 'Flaunting mathematical formulae before a linguistic audience or in a linguistic publication', writes Professor A. Martinet, 'is either grossly misinterpreting the needs and capacities of one's audience or readers, or else trying to bully them into accepting one's views by claiming for these the support of a science they tend to respect as the most exact of all sciences, but whose data they are not in a position to verify. We need more and more rigour in linguistics, but our own brand'.[3]

2. A second avenue of approach to structural semantics is through what is sometimes called 'idiomatology': the study of the unique and idiosyncratic structure of a language.[4] As far back as 1921, one of the pioneers of structural linguistics, Edward Sapir, wrote these prophetic words:

'It must be obvious to anyone who has thought about the question at all or who has felt something of the spirit of a foreign language that there is such a thing as a basic plan, a certain cut, to each language. This type or plan or structural "genius" of the language is something much more fundamental, much more pervasive, than any single feature of it that we can mention, nor can we gain an adequate idea of its nature by a mere recital of the sundry facts that make up the grammar of a language.'[5]

Sapir's words refer in the first place to grammatical structure, but it seems intrinsically probable that the vocabulary too, if properly explored,

---

[1] Cf. J. B. Carroll, *The Study of Language. A Survey of Linguistics and Related Disciplines in America*, Cambridge, Mass., 1953, pp. 61 ff.; P. Guiraud, *Les Caractères statistiques du vocabulaire*, Paris, 1954; B. Quemada, 'La technique des inventaires mécanographiques', *Lexicologie et lexicographie françaises et romanes*, Paris, 1960, pp. 53–63. See also the *Bulletin d'Information du Laboratoire d'Analyse Lexicologique*, published by the 'Centre d'Etude du Vocabulaire Français' at Besançon. Work on mechanical translation and on such projects as 'le français élémentaire' also has important semantic implications.

[2] A. S. C. Ross, 'Philologica Mathematica', *Časopis pro Moderní Filogii*, xxxi (1937), p. 16 of offprint.

[3] 'The Unity of Linguistics', *Word*, x (1954), pp. 121–5: p. 125.

[4] H. A. Hatzfeld, *A Critical Bibliography of the New Stylistics Applied to the Romance atures, 1900–1952*, Chapel Hill, 1953, ch. X.

[5] *Language. An Introduction to the Study of Speech*, New York, repr. 1949, p. 120.

will reveal some idiosyncratic tendencies, some characteristic preferences and aversions for certain modes of expression. These tendencies vary from language to language and may even change within the history of the same idiom. Some of them are capable of a strictly statistical formulation; others are less sharply defined, but stand out all the same very clearly.[1] A good example in point is the ratio of *transparent and opaque terms* in a particular language. Greek philosophers were already divided into two camps in their views on the origin and nature of words: some regarded them as purely conventional symbols, while others believed in an intrinsic connexion between sound and meaning—a connexion which may have lost its transparency in the course of time. Modern linguists know that there are both transparent and opaque words in any language, and they seek to determine the factors which govern the dosage of the two elements. It has been found, for example, that English and French often have opaque, unanalysable names for objects and ideas which are denoted in German by transparent, self-explanatory terms. There are several symptoms of this relative opacity of English and French. A foreigner hearing the English word *thimble* or the French *dé* for the first time will have to memorize them as they contain no clue to their meaning. But the corresponding German term, *Fingerhut*, is immediately understood if you know its two components, and it is also easy to remember because of the graphic metaphor which lies at its root: a hat put on a finger. The same may be said of English *glove* and French *gant* versus German *Handschuh* ('hand' + 'shoe'), or of English *skate* and French *patin* versus German *Schlittschuh* ('sledge' + 'shoe'). The ease with which compounds are formed in German can be seen from cases like the following:

German *Nilpferd* ('Nile' + 'horse')	*hippopotamus*, French *hippopotame* (from Greek *hippos* 'horse' + *potamos* 'river')[2]
German *Bildhauer* ('image' + 'hewer')	*sculptor*, French *sculpteur*
German *Lautlehre* ('sound' + 'lore')	*phonetics*, French *phonétique*
German *Fernsehen* ('far' + 'seeing')	*television*, French *télévision*

Except for speakers with a sound classical background, these English and French words are opaque, whereas the German ones are self-explanatory, motivated within the language itself.

German also possesses many derivatives, formed by means of pre-

---

[1] See below, ch. V, section (A).

[2] Cf. Norwegian *flodhest* (*flod* 'river' + *hest* 'horse') and Hungarian *víziló* (*vízi* 'watery' + *ló* 'horse').

fixes and suffixes, where English and French have to use Greek or Latin formations. From the noun *Stadt* 'town', German can derive the adjective *städtisch*, while English and French have the hybrid pairs *town—urban*, *ville—urbain*. In the same way, *bishop* is flanked by the learned adjective *episcopal* (French *évêque—épiscopal*) whereas German has *Bischof—bischöflich*, and there are many similar pairs. But it should be noted that English does not go as far as French in its predilection for the opaque. English *week* has a derived adjective, *weekly*, but in French nothing can be formed from *semaine*: the corresponding adjective is the awkward Greek word *hebdomadaire* (cf. Italian *settimana—settimanale*, and Spanish *semana—semanal*). Similarly we have *month—monthly*, but *mois—mensuel*; *room—roomy*, but *espace—spacieux*; *head—heady*, but *tête—capiteux*; *water—watery*, but *eau—aqueux*; *soot—sooty*, but *suie—fuligineux*, etc. The prevalence of opaque terms in English and French throws an additional burden on the memory of foreigners learning these languages, though this will often be compensated by the international character of many English and French words which in German have more parochial equivalents.[1] Among native speakers, the use of so many learned Greek and Latin terms tends to erect what has been called a 'language bar' between different sections of the population according to their educational background, a problem which does not exist in Germany in such an acute form.[2]

The contrast between transparent and opaque words is only one criterion in the study of semantic tendencies. There are other criteria which are perhaps of even greater importance: preference for particular or generic terms, the distribution and organization of synonymic resources, the various types of ambiguity and their remedies, etc. Further progress along these lines may lead to a new typology of languages on semantic grounds, as will be seen in a later chapter of this book.[3]

3. Attempts have also been made to identify and describe the various *lexical structures* into which our words are organized. These inquiries, which are still at a tentative stage, are being conducted at three superimposed levels: that of single words, that of conceptual spheres, and that of the vocabulary as a whole.

(*a*) At the level of single words, the most useful concept that has

---

[1] Cf. the situation in Serbo-Croat where the international term *theatre* has two local equivalents: it is called *pozorište* in Belgrade and *kazalište in* Zagreb (A. Meillet, *Linguistique historique et linguistique générale*, 2 vols., Paris, repr. 1948–52, vol. II, p. 38).

[2] V. Grove, *The Language Bar*, London, 1949. For further details on these problems, see my *Semantics*, pp. 106 ff.

[3] See below, pp. 80 f.

emerged so far is that of the *'associative field'*.[1] Every word is surrounded by a network of associations which connect it with other terms related to it in form, in meaning, or in both; as Saussure graphically put it, it is 'like the centre of a constellation, the point where an indefinite number of co-ordinated terms converge'.[2] To take a very simple example, the verb *to write* stands at the point of intersection of three associative series: (1) derivatives formed from the same stem: *writing, writer, underwrite, writ*, etc.; (2) words of similar or related meaning: *scribble, scrabble, scrawl; letter, script, pen, print; read, say, speak*, etc.; (3) homonymous words: *wright, rite, right*. In (1) the association is based on both sound and sense, in (2) on sense alone, and in (3) on a chance identity of sound.

The associative field of a word is an unstable and highly variable structure: it differs from one speaker to another, from one social group to another, and possibly even from one situation to another. It has been described as a 'halo which surrounds the sign and whose outer fringes merge into their environment'.[3] In spite of its vagueness and its lack of sharp contours, it is a linguistic reality which can be studied by psychological as well as philological methods.[4] To give an approximate idea of the size of such a field, it may be mentioned that a French linguist has fully investigated the associative field of the word *chat* 'cat' and has found that it comprises about 2000 terms which, by various criteria, can be reduced to a hard core of 300.[5]

The importance of associative fields lies in the changes, formal as well as semantic, which they may initiate. As will be seen in a later chapter, this concept plays a vital part in historical semantics and in etymological research.[6] At the same time many formal changes which are usually put down to analogy appear in an entirely new light when set against the wider background of associations surrounding the term in question. To mention but one example, which links up with the associative field of 'writing', the French *écrire* 'to write' comes from Latin *scribere* and originally had the form *escrivre*; subsequently it was altered to *escrire*, later *écrire*, under the influence of two verbs belonging to the same associative field: *dire* 'to say' and *lire* 'to read'. *Lire* in its turn has been

[1] The term 'associative field' was coined by Ch. Bally in his article, 'L'arbitraire du signe', *Le Français Moderne*, viii (1940), pp. 193–206: pp. 195 f.
[2] Op. cit., 4th ed., 1949, p. 174.
[3] Bally, loc. cit.
[4] T. Cazacu, 'La "structuration" dynamique des significations', *Mélanges linguistiques publiés à l'occasion du VIIIᵉ Congrès International des Linguistes*, Bucharest, 1957, pp. 113–27; O. Ducháček, 'Les relations sémantiques des mots', *Kwartalnik Neofilologiczny*, ix (1962), pp. 27–34.
[5] P. Guiraud, 'Les champs morpho-sémantiques', *Bulletin de la Société de Linguistique de Paris*, lii (1956), pp. 265–88: p. 286.
[6] See below, ch. III.

influenced by *dire* in several of its forms.[1] The morphological development of languages is full of interferences of this kind.

(*b*) Between the associative fields of single words and the vocabulary in its entirety, there is an intermediate level which has attracted much attention in recent years: that of conceptual spheres or '*lexical fields*'. The concept of lexical field first arose in the 1920s and was developed by Professor Jost Trier in his famous monograph on German terms for intellectual qualities.[2] Trier's view of language has been described as 'neo-Humboldtian', and it certainly has many affinities with the ideas of Humboldt and other German thinkers, in particular E. Cassirer; but it is essentially an application of Saussurean principles to problems of lexical structure. Close study of the history of intellectual terminology in Old and Middle High German convinced Trier that it was fundamentally wrong to consider words in isolation: they must be viewed within the context of the lexical field to which they belong. A lexical field is a closely organized sector of the vocabulary, whose elements fit together and delimit each other like pieces in a mosaic. In each field some sphere of experience is analysed, divided up and classified in a unique way. In this sense, the vocabulary of every language embodies a peculiar vision of the universe; it implies a definite philosophy of life and hierarchy of values which is handed down from one generation to another.

How differently the raw material of experience is elaborated by various languages can be seen even in such a pre-eminently concrete field as the scale of *colours*. The spectrum is a continuous band, without any sharp boundaries; the number and nature of colour distinctions is therefore largely a matter of habit and convention. The Greeks and Romans had a poorer palette than our modern languages; there was, for example, no generic term for 'brown' or 'grey' in Latin: modern Romance forms like French *brun* and *gris* are borrowings from Germanic. There is no single word for 'grey' in modern Lithuanian either; different words are used to denote the grey colour of wool, of horses, cows or human hair. Colour terms employed in other languages will often appear more differentiated, or less differentiated, than our own, although it would be more correct to say that the field is divided up on different principles. Thus Russian distinguishes between *sinij* 'dark blue' and *goluboj* 'sky-blue'; conversely,

---

[1] M. K. Pope, *From Latin to Modern French*, Manchester, 1934, §§928, 936, 940.

[2] *Der deutsche Wortschatz im Sinnbezirk des Verstandes. Die Geschichte eines sprachlichen Feldes, I: Von den Anfängen bis zum Beginn des 13. Jh.* (Heidelberg, 1931). For detailed references, see my *Semantics*, pp. 243 ff. See now also L. Weisgerber, *Grundzüge der inhaltbezogenen Grammatik*, 3rd ed., Düsseldorf, 1962; Id., *Die sprachliche Gestaltung der Welt*, 3rd ed., Düsseldorf, 1962; A. A. Ufimtseva, *Opyt Izuchenija Leksiki kak Sistemy*, Moscow, 1962.

the Greek γλαυκός has a wide range of applications, some with and some without a notion of colour: 'gleaming, silvery; bluish-green, light blue, grey'.[1] Oddly enough, there is a somewhat similar accumulation of meanings in a Japanese colour adjective, *awo*, which can mean 'green', 'blue' and 'dark'; it can be used when speaking of 'green vegetables', the 'blue sea', or 'dark clouds'.[2] Elsewhere, the discrepancies are even more marked. The Navaho Indians, for example, 'have two terms corresponding to "black", one denoting the black of darkness, the other the black of such objects as coal. Our "grey" and "brown", however, correspond to a single term in their language, and likewise our "blue" and "green" '.[3]

It might be argued that language may have an important part to play in the analysis of a continuum, but that fields of experience where there are discrete elements will everywhere have the same linguistic structure. A glance at *kinship* terms in various languages shows that this is not so. It is, for example, surprising to learn that Hungarian had no term for 'brother' or 'sister' till the middle of the nineteenth century; it had instead, and still has, separate words for 'elder' and 'younger brother' and 'elder' and 'younger sister'. Malay has again a different arrangement: it has a generic term for 'sibling or cousin' and more specialized ones for 'elder' and 'younger sibling or cousin', the latter being further subdivided into male and female.[4] Other family relations show the same diversity. In Swedish there is no single word for 'grandfather' and 'grandmother', only separate ones for 'father's father', *farfar*, 'mother's father', *morfar*, and for the two kinds of grandmother: *farmor* amd *mormor*. Several languages also distinguish between two kinds of uncle and aunt; in Latin, for example, there were four terms, only two of which have survived: *avunculus* 'mother's brother', which has given English *uncle*, and *amita* 'father's sister', which is the origin of English *aunt*. There are even greater variations when one compares languages with a totally different social and cultural background; in Dravidian, for instance, there is an intricate hierarchy of kinship terms based on four sets of distinctions: sex, generation, alliance and age, of which the third, the only non-biological one, is the most important.[5]

[1] *An Intermediate Greek-English Lexicon Founded upon the Seventh Edition of Liddell and Scott's Greek-English Lexicon*, Oxford, 1955 impression.
[2] H. Yamaguchi, *Essays towards English Semantics*, Tokyo, 1961, pp. 41 f.
[3] P. Henle (Ed.), *Language, Thought, and Culture*, Ann Arbor, 1958, p. 7. On the relativity of colour terms in general, see esp. I. Meyerson (Ed.), *Problèmes de la couleur*, Paris, 1957. Cf. recently Weisgerber, op. cit., *passim*.
[4] I am indebted to Professor H. C. Conklin, of Columbia University, for this information.
[5] L. Dumont, 'The Dravidian Kinship Terminology as an Expression of Marriage', *Man*, liii

In the sphere of *abstract thought*, the organizing role of language is even more evident since abstract concepts could not possibly exist without the words in which they are clothed. Trier's study of intellectual terms has been particularly revealing in this respect; it has uncovered, in the heyday of Middle High German literature, a system of concepts and values which is totally alien to the modern mind. A German around 1200 had no name for a quality which we would regard as of crucial importance: that of cleverness. He had, however, two special words, *kunst* and *list*, for courtly and non-courtly, chivalric and non-chivalric skills, and also a comprehensive term, *wîsheit*, for any form of knowledge or wisdom, whether courtly or non-courtly, mundane or divine. Such inquiries are directly relevant to a problem which will be examined in the third part of this book: the influence of language upon thought.

Starting from rather different premises, the French linguist G. Matoré has evolved a field concept closely akin to Trier's, but marked by a strong sociological bias. In his book, *La Méthode en lexicologie* (1953), he has outlined a technique for studying the structure of the vocabulary as a reflection of the structure of society. His conceptual spheres are mapped out on the basis of sociological criteria, and organized around two types of important words: *mots-témoins* ('witness-words'), which occupy a prominent place in the hierarchy, and *mots-clés* ('key-words'), which epitomize the leading ideals of each generation. M. Matoré has given an illustration of his procedure in his remarkable monograph on vocabulary and society in the age of Louis-Philippe.[1]

(*c*) Some linguists believe that the structural approach, which has been tried out so successfully at the level of single words and conceptual spheres, can be extended to embrace the entire *vocabulary* of a language. To this end, R. Hallig and W. von Wartburg have devised a general classification of concepts which, in their view, is both broad and flexible enough to be applied to any idiom.[2] In this scheme, which springs basically from the same idea as Roget's *Thesaurus*, concepts are divided into three groups, each of them with numerous subdivisions: the Universe, Man, and Man and the Universe. The aim is to provide a uniform framework

---

(1953), pp. 34–9. For other systems, see e.g. F. G. Lounsbury, *Language*, xxxii (1956), pp. 158–94, and W. H. Goodenough, ibid., pp. 195–216. Cf. also the *Preprints of Papers for the Ninth International Congress of Linguists*, Cambridge, Mass., 1962, pp. 436–41 (M. Ayoub) and pp. 583–8 (F. G. Lounsbury).

[1] *Le Vocabulaire et la société sous Louis-Philippe*, Geneva – Lille, 1951.

[2] *Begriffssytem als Grundlage für die Lexikographie. Versuch eines Ordnungsschemas*, Abhandlungen der deutschen Akademie der Wissenschaften zu Berlin, Klasse für Sprachen, Literatur und Kunst, Heft 4, 1952. Further details in my *Semantics*, pp. 254 ff. Cf. E. Wüster, 'Die Struktur der sprachlichen Begriffswelt und ihre Darstellung in Wörterbüchern', *Studium Generale*, xii (1959), pp. 615–27.

for lexicological studies of different languages and different periods of the same language, so that the results should be readily comparable with each other. Without claiming any special virtues for this scheme, which is only one of many possible arrangements, the adoption of a common framework offers obvious practical advantages, and a beginning has already been made in applying it in lexicological inquiries.

It can be seen from the foregoing that considerable progress has been made, during the last three decades, in the introduction of structural viewpoints into semantics. It is indeed symptomatic of current interest in these problems that structural semantics appeared on the agenda of the last two international congresses of linguistics, held at Oslo in 1957 and at Cambridge, Massachusetts, in 1962. All this makes it surprising and regrettable that many structuralists should still feel disinclined to handle problems of meaning. As a leading American linguist once put it, 'for many linguistic students the word *meaning* itself has almost become anathema'.[1] It has even been suggested that language could be defined in such a way that semantic problems would lie outside the purview of linguistics proper.[2] As Professor W. S. Allen pertinently remarked in his recent inaugural lecture at Cambridge: 'Meaning, as at least one linguist has expressed it, has become a "dirty word"; but if the name tends to be avoided, there is no doubt that every linguist employs the concept, though some would be unwilling to admit to such improper thoughts'.[3] At the London congress of linguistics in 1952, the term *crypto-semantics* was coined to describe this paradoxical attitude.[4]

Some of this reluctance to deal with semantic problems undoubtedly started as a reaction against the indiscriminate use of the term *meaning* and other 'mentalistic' abstractions; but this is surely no sufficient reason for excluding the semantic side of language from the field of linguistics. As an acute critic of the excesses of structuralism points out, 'it is true that many crimes have been committed in the name of meaning, and by professed linguists as well as linguistic philosophers; but this is not a situation in which sin can be prevented by abolishing the occasion for sin, for without meaning there can be no language and no linguistics'.[5]

Another reason for the avoidance of semantics by many linguists is the widespread belief that structural viewpoints are inapplicable to

---

[1] C. C. Fries, 'Meaning and Structural Analysis', *Language*, xxx (1954), pp. 57–68: p. 58.
[2] See Hockett, op. cit., p. 138.
[3] *On the Linguistic Study of Languages*, Cambridge, 1957, p. 22.
[4] *Proceedings of the Seventh International Congress of Linguists*, London, 1956, p. 197 (O. Funke, quoting L. C. Wrenn).
[5] T. B. W. Reid, *Historical Philology and Linguistic Science* (Inaugural Lecture), Oxford, 1960, p. 18.

problems of meaning. In the light of recent developments in semantics, this position is, as we have seen, no longer tenable—unless, of course, the term *structure* is equated with 'formal structure', as is only too often the case.[1]

But there is an even deeper cause for the structuralists' refusal to tackle problems of meaning. For the reasons mentioned earlier on in this chapter, semantic phenomena cannot usually be described with the same scientific rigour as the formal elements of language, and to many linguists scientific rigour is the supreme test of scholarship, even where the subject-matter would invite a different method of approach. This attitude explains why, not so long ago, semantics was virtually ostracized by extreme structuralists. The last few years have witnessed a spectacular change of climate in linguistics, but one still has the impression that many structuralists are merely paying lip-service to a study which has become more respectable.[2] If this formalistic bias were to be perpetuated, linguistics would develop into a strangely unbalanced discipline and would lose much of its humanistic content. It would become an esoteric study, unable to contribute to the solution of the great problems of our time, some of which are closely bound up with the nature of our words. In this sense, not only semantics but linguistics at large is at the cross-roads, and the direction it will take may determine its future for a long time to come.

[1] For a different view on structural semantics, see L. J. Prieto's review of the 2nd edition of my *Principles of Semantics*, in *Romance Philology*, xiv (1960), pp. 162 ff. Cf. L. Hjelmslev, 'Some Reflexions on Practice and Theory in Structural Semantics', in *Language and Society. Essays Presented to A. M. Jensen*, Copenhagen, 1961, pp. 55–63; Y. Ikegami, 'Structural Semantics; its Assumptions and Problems', *The Tsuda Review*, vii (1962); pp. 1–15; M. Leroy, 'Le Renouveau de la sémantique', *II. Fachtagung für Indogermanische und Allgemeine Sprachwissenschaft*, Innsbruck, 1962, pp. 95–106; A. A. Ufimtseva, *Voprosy Jazykoznanija*, 1962, no. 4, pp. 36–46; A. I. Kuznetsova, *Ponjatie Semanticheskoj Sistemy i Metody ee Issledovanija*, Moscow, 1963; J. J. Katz-J. A. Fodor, 'The Structure of a Semantic Theory', *Language*, xxxix (1963), pp. 170–210.

[2] The following statement, made recently by a philosopher, has therefore a somewhat Utopian ring: 'the majority of works on general linguistics treat semantic problems as being their focal problems' (Schaff, op. cit., p. 5).

CHAPTER II

THE CONCEPT OF MEANING IN LINGUISTICS[1]

THE definition of meaning is the central problem of all semantic studies. It is fundamental to the analysis of any symbol, linguistic or otherwise, and the philologist cannot hope to solve it by his own efforts. Although contemporary linguistics tends to rely increasingly on 'immanent' criteria derived exclusively from language itself, in this particular field many useful suggestions have been received from neighbouring disciplines: from psychology and neurology, philosophy, anthropology and social science. Naturally, non-linguistic viewpoints have not been applied mechanically to the facts of language; they have been tested for their linguistic relevance, adapted to the techniques of structural analysis, and checked in the light of empirical data.

Among the definitions of meaning evolved outside linguistics proper, two lines of thought have proved particularly fruitful in their application to language: the analytical and the operational approach to the problem.[2]

A. ANALYTICAL DEFINITIONS OF MEANING

The analytical type of definition resolves words, or any other symbols, into their constitutive elements. The best-known modern attempt at this

---

[1] This paper was originally part of a discussion on 'Language' in the Psychology Section of the British Association (Bristol, September 1955). A summary of the whole discussion will be found in G. P. Meredith, 'Language, Meaning and Mind', *Nature*, clxxvi (1955), pp. 673–4. The present paper, in its original form, and two others (G. P. Meredith, 'Semantics in Relation to Psychology', and Sir Russell Brain, 'The Semantic Aspect of Aphasia') were subsequently published in *Archivum Linguisticum*, viii (1956), pp. 1–27, under the title 'Semantics: a Symposium'.

[2] The analytical approach to meaning is also known as 'referential', whereas the operational theory is often referred to as 'contextual', and sometimes as 'functional' or 'instrumental'. A more detailed account of these and other theories will be found in my *Semantics*, ch. III. See also the following: L. Antal, *Questions of Meaning*, The Hague, 1963; R. Brown, *Words and Things*, Glencoe, repr. 1959, ch. III; W. L. Chafe, 'Phonetics, Semantics, and Language', *Language*, xxxviii (1962), pp. 335–44; L. J. Cohen, *The Diversity of Meaning*, London, 1962, esp. section 7; W. Coutu, 'An Operational Definition of Meaning', *Quarterly Journal of Speech*, xlviii (1962), pp. 59–64; J. Deese, 'On the Structure of Associative Meaning', *Psychological Review*, lix (1962), pp. 161–75; K. A. Levkovskaya, 'Nekatorye Zarubezhnye Jazykovedcheskie Teorii i Ponjatie Slova', *Voprosy Teorii Jazyka v Sovremennoj Zarubezhnoj Lingvistike*, Moscow, 1961, pp. 64–89; W. V. O. Quine, 'The Problem of Meaning in Linguistics', *From a Logical Point of View*, Cambridge, Mass. 1953, pp. 47–64; Schaff, op. cit., esp. Part II, ch. III; W. Schmidt, 'Lexikalische und aktuelle Bedeutung', *Zeitschrift für Phonetik, Sprachwissenschaft und Kommunikationsforschung*, xiv (1961), pp. 231–43; A. I. Smirnitskij, 'Znachenie Slova', *Voprosy Jazykoznanija*, 1955, no. 2, pp. 79–89; Yamaguchi, op. cit., pp. 13–21; P. Ziff, *Semantic Analysis*, Ithaca, 1960, esp. ch. V.

kind of analysis is the so-called 'basic triangle' put forward by Ogden and Richards in their *Meaning of Meaning*.[1] The authors posit a tripartite relationship between three terms which, by simplifying their terminology, we shall call the 'name', the 'sense' and the 'thing'. 'Name' means here the sound, the phonetic word; the 'sense' is the information conveyed by the name; the 'thing' is the non-linguistic phenomenon to which the word refers.[2] These three terms stand at the three apices of the triangle, but the name and the thing are connected by a dotted line: there is no short cut, no direct relation between them; as the medieval Schoolmen put it, 'Vox significat mediantibus conceptibus':

SENSE

NAME   THING

This diagram offers too little and too much to the linguist. On the one hand, he can safely dispense with the 'thing' and confine his attention to the other two terms; he is not concerned with the non-linguistic world as such, only with those aspects of it which are relevant to, and embodied in, language. Thus the tripartite relationship is reduced to a binary one between name and sense. On the other hand, it is vitally important for the understanding of semantic processes that the relation between name and sense is reciprocal and reversible. For the speaker, the sense precedes the name; he will, for example, think of a pencil and thereupon articulate the word *pencil*. At the hearer's end, the sequence is reversed: he will first perceive the name, which in its turn will make him think of a pencil. Nothing short of a cataclysm, such as the brain lesions studied by the neurologist, will sever this link between name and sense. It is this reciprocal and reversible relationship which we might call the *'meaning'* of the word, though it is ultimately immaterial what terms we choose.[3] Indeed, the diversity of conflicting and overlapping terminologies conceals here a wide area of agreement among linguists, stretching from the more

[1] 4th ed., London, 1936, p. 11.

[2] In Ogden-Richards's terminology, the 'name' is called 'symbol', the 'sense' 'thought or reference', and the 'thing' 'referent'.

[3] 'Experience shows that it is not profitable to begin the study of a subject by trying to define the popular or technical terms that are connected with it. It is much better simply to examine the object of one's curiosity and then, when one comes across some feature which seems to deserve a name, to assign to this feature a familiar term which seems roughly to fit the case. Or else, we may prefer to invent some new word to name the feature we have seen' (L. Bloomfield, 'Meaning', *Monatshefte für deutschen Unterricht*, xxxv (1943), pp. 101–6: p. 101). On semantic terminology, see L. Rosiello, 'La Semantica; note terminologiche ed epistemologiche', *Archivio Glottologico Italiano*, xlvii (1962), pp. 32–53; on the problem of definition in general, see R. Robinson, *Definition*, Oxford, 1950.

orthodox schools to the Danish glossematists, with their distinction between 'expression' and 'content'. It is perhaps worth noting that at a small conference on semantics held at Nice in March 1951, this relational definition of meaning was one of the few basic principles on which there was fairly general agreement.[1]

In recent years, three major objections have been advanced against this conception of meaning. Perhaps the least serious of the three concerns the position of the 'thing', the *referent* in Ogden-Richards's terminology. The fear has been expressed that by excluding the referent, semantics 'would fall prey to an extreme esoteric formalism'.[2] But it should be borne in mind that all linguistically relevant features of the referent will enter, *via* the sense, into the constitution of the word and will thus come within the purview of semantic analysis. As Bloomfield pertinently warns us, 'we must discriminate between *non-distinctive* features of the situation, such as the size, shape, colour, and so on of any particular apple, and the *distinctive*, or *linguistic meaning* (the *semantic* features) which are common to all the situations that call forth the utterance of the linguistic form, such as the features which are common to all the objects of which English-speaking people use the word *apple*' (*Language*, p. 141).

The difference between thing and sense, between the referent and our awareness of it, can be illustrated by the change of meaning which the word *atom* has undergone in recent years. The atom itself, the referent, has not changed, but our conception of it has been so revolutionized that it has come to belie its etymology: it is no longer ἄτομος, 'indivisible'.

A second and more dangerous criticism calls into doubt the *dichotomy* between name and sense. According to some linguists, this distinction implies a dualism modelled on the metaphysic of body and soul. 'As, in a human person, a soul or mind is supposed to accompany the body and its overt behaviour, so in a linguistic sign, a meaning is supposed to accompany the form in its various occurrences. The linguistic sign is supposed to emerge from a correspondence, a kind of psycho-physical parallelism, between a form and a meaning.'[3] This criticism seems to be

---

[1] G. Devoto, 'La "Conferenza di semantica" di Nizza (26–31 marzo 1951)', *Archivio Glottologico Italiano*, xxxvi (1951), pp. 82–4.

[2] H. Werner, *Language*, xxviii (1952), p. 255.

[3] W. Haas, 'On Defining Linguistic Units,' *Transactions of the Philological Society*, 1954, pp. 54–84: p. 71. Cf. also J. R. Firth, *Papers in Linguistics, 1934–1951*, London — New York — Toronto, 1957, pp. 19 and 227; Id., 'A Synopsis of Linguistic Theory, 1930–1955', *Studies in Linguistic Analysis*, Special Volume of the Philological Society, Oxford, 1957, pp. 1–32; A. W. Read, 'The Term *Meaning* in Linguistics', *Etc.*, xiii (1956), pp. 37–45. It should

based on a misunderstanding suggested by a metaphor which Saussure had already dismissed as unsatisfactory.[1] There is indeed a duality at the root of all analytical definitions of meaning, but it has nothing to do with the metaphysic of body and soul: it is the duality inherent in any kind of sign or symbol, from traffic-lights to the most recondite images of the poet. All signs have this in common that they point beyond themselves, to something other than themselves, and words are no exception to the rule.

The most damaging criticism levelled at the analytical conception of meaning is directed against what we have called the *sense* of the word. Many modern linguists are anxious to avoid any 'mentalistic' assumptions; they are reluctant to operate with nebulous mental entities and to postulate that, 'prior to the utterance of a linguistic form, there occurs within the speaker a non-physical process, a *thought, concept, image, feeling, act of will,* or the like, and that the hearer, likewise, upon receiving the sound-waves, goes through an equivalent or correlated mental process'.[2] The crux of this criticism is that such mental phenomena are purely subjective and thus inaccessible to scientific analysis; they can be observed only by the doubtful method of introspection. As one critic of the analytical theory tersely put it, 'an empirical science cannot be content to rely on a procedure of people looking into their minds, each into his own'.[3]

In view of these criticisms, which have done much to bring semantics into disrepute,[4] special importance attaches to a recent American publication which bears the ambitious title: *The Measurement of Meaning.*[5] The method expounded in this book is based on a simple device, called the 'semantic differential'. This consists of a number of scales, each with seven divisions, whose poles are formed by pairs of opposite adjectives, and the subjects are asked to enter each concept in the division which

be noted that this criticism is directed against all 'correspondence theories' of meaning, including even such purely structuralist experiments as the glossematists' distinction between 'expression' and 'content', and the 'distributional analysis' of meaning advocated by Z. S. Harris in *Methods in Structural Linguistics*, Chicago, 1951; cf. Haas, loc. cit., pp. 72 ff.

[1] Op. cit., p. 145.
[2] Bloomfield, *Language*, p. 142. On the same scholar's definition of the meaning of a linguistic form as 'the situation in which the speaker utters it and the response which it calls forth in the hearer' (ibid., p. 139), see my *Semantics*, pp. 59 ff., and R. H. Robins, 'A Problem in the Statement of Meanings', *Lingua*, iii (1952–53), pp. 119–37.
[3] Haas, loc. cit., p. 74. Cf. now A. Reichling, 'Meaning and Introspection', *Lingua*, xi (1962), pp. 333–9.
[4] See above, pp. 15 f.
[5] C. E. Osgood, G. J. Suci, P. H. Tannenbaum, *The Measurement of Meaning*, Urbana, 1957.

they find most appropriate. Here, as an example, is part of the test for the word *lady*:

LADY

rough	——	——	——	——	——	——	——	smooth
fair	——	——	——	——	——	——	——	unfair
active	——	——	——	——	——	——	——	passive

Taking the last line as an example, the seven divisions mean, from left to right: 'extremely active; quite active; slightly active; neither active nor passive, equally active and passive; slightly passive; quite passive; extremely passive'. The various adjectival scales, which were obtained by careful sampling, were subsequently subjected to factor analysis, carried out with the aid of an electronic computer, and this revealed that they fell into three broad categories: evaluation (*good—bad*), potency (*hard—soft*), and activity (*active—passive*). In this way a three-dimensional 'semantic space' was obtained in which each concept could be given its place after subjecting the answers of a large number of persons to statistical analysis.

As the critics have not been slow to point out, the new method suffers from one inherent weakness: it does not measure 'meaning' in any of the accepted senses of that overworked term.[1] This was admitted by the authors themselves with disarming candour: 'It is certain that we are not providing an index of what signs refer to, and if reference or designation is the *sine qua non* of meaning, as some readers will insist, then they will conclude that this book is badly mistitled' (p. 325). But it is equally clear that what the semantic differential does measure is an important component of meaning, usually referred to as 'affective meaning'[2] or 'emotive connotation'. Whatever the initial crudities of the experiment, it is a valuable achievement to have reduced one of the basic aspects of meaning to numerical analysis. Such a method, if properly developed and extended to other components of meaning, would go a long way to rid semantics of that element of vagueness and subjectivity which had hitherto seemed inescapable. To quote the authors once more: 'It may be argued that the data with which we deal in semantic measurement are entirely subjective—introspections about meanings on the part of subjects—and that all we have done is to objectify expressions of these

[1] For criticisms of the new technique, see e.g. J. B. Carroll, *Language*, xxv (1959), pp. 58–77; J. J. Gumperz, *Romance Philology*, xv (1961), pp. 63–9; R. Wells, 'A Mathematical Approach to Meaning', *Cahiers Ferdinand de Saussure*, xv (1957), pp. 117–36; U. Weinreich, 'Travels through Semantic Space', *Word*, xiv (1958), pp. 346–66; cf. also Osgood's rejoinder in *Word*, xv (1959), pp. 192–200.
[2] Cf. Weinreich, loc. cit.

subjective states. This is entirely true, but it is no criticism of the method. Objectivity concerns the role of the observer, not the observed. Our procedures completely eliminate the idiosyncrasies of the investigator in arriving at the final index of meaning, and this is the essence of objectivity' (pp. 125 f.).

At the Eighth International Congress of Linguists, held at Oslo in 1957, the forthcoming publication of *The Measurement of Meaning* raised high hopes for revolutionary progress in semantics. 'Dramatic developments in the study of meaning', it was claimed, 'have opened vistas for semantic description undreamed of a few years ago'.[1] Since then, the initial enthusiasm has been somewhat damped, but it would be wrong to underestimate the potential importance of the experiment. Further progress on these lines would have a most fruitful effect on lexicography. In the authors' own words, 'one can envisage the gradual construction of a functional dictionary of connotative meaning—a quantized Thesaurus—in which the writer would find nouns, adjectives, verbs and adverbs (all lexical items) listed according to their locations in the semantic space, as determined from the judgments of representative samples of the population'.[2] This in turn would have significant repercussions in many spheres; early applications of the technique cover fields as diverse as politics, aesthetics, advertising and psychotherapy. As regards semantic theory, which primarily concerns us here, the new approach, if successfully developed, would inevitably strengthen the analytical definition of meaning at the very point which has always been its heel of Achilles: it would transform the 'sense' from an elusive and intangible mental entity into a scientific concept amenable to precise and objective criteria.

Apart from the three objections which have just been discussed, the analytical theory of meaning has two further weaknesses which have to be corrected before it can furnish a workable basis for semantics. One such weakness is that the analysis is too simple: it is applicable only to ideal situations where one name and one sense are involved, and does not provide for more complex structures. The semanticist will therefore distinguish between '*simple*' and '*multiple*' meaning. The latter has two

---

[1] U. Weinreich, 'Research Frontiers in Bilingualism Studies', *Proceedings of the Eighth International Congress of Linguists*, Oslo, 1958, p. 790.

[2] *The Measurement of Meaning*, p. 330. Cf. J. J. Gumperz's comments: 'The advantages of quantified semantic analysis are readily apparent. It enables the investigator not only to determine whether or not two concepts differ, but also to measure the extent of this difference and break it down into its components. Furthermore, cultural meanings of a concept within a social group are calculable from the individual numerical scores by averaging across subjects, and the average scores across concepts provide an estimate of the total factor structure for a particular individual' (loc. cit., p. 64). Cf. recently K. F. Riegel-R. M. Riegel, 'An Investigation into Denotative Aspects of Word-Meaning', *Language and Speech*, vi (1963), pp. 5–21.

cardinal forms: several names may be linked with one sense, and several senses with one name. Within these two basic categories, the linguist may have to introduce supplementary distinctions imposed by his material; he will, for example, distinguish between different meanings of one word and different words identical in form, between 'polysemy' and homonymy. The ambiguity of a term like *act*—'action', 'Act of God', 'Act of Parliament', 'division of a play'—and that arising out of the chance coincidence of two words like *'page* boy' and *'page* of a book', are quite distinct both linguistically and psychologically, even though they belong to the same variety of multiple meaning.

Another weakness of the analytical definition is the danger of atomism. Words do not live isolated within the vocabulary; the relation between name and sense must be supplemented by other relations connecting each word with its neighbours. As we saw in the previous chapter (pp. 11 f.), every word has its own *associative field*; the whole vocabulary is intersected by associations between names and between senses. This twofold associative network, unstable, highly subjective but none the less real, underlies all changes of meaning; it also enables us to describe the vocabulary in structural terms.

With these two correctives, the analytical definition of meaning can serve, and has actually served, as a basis for a comprehensive system of semantics, descriptive as well as historical.[1] Naturally, there will always be border-line cases, but such empirical data as we already possess can, on the whole, be accommodated smoothly within the general framework.

B. Operational Definitions of Meaning

The second school of thought approaches the problem of meaning from an entirely different angle. It endeavours to grasp it by studying words in action and surveying the combinations into which they enter and the uses to which they are put. An important factor in the rise of this theory was P. W. Bridgman's book, *The Logic of Modern Physics*, in which he emphasized the purely operational character of such scientific concepts as length, time and energy. According to Bridgman, 'in general, we mean by any concept nothing more than a set of operations; *the concept is synonymous with the corresponding set of operations*. If the concept is physical, as of length, the operations are actual physical operations,

---

[1] See e.g. G. Stern's *Meaning and Change of Meaning* and my *Précis de sémantique française* and *The Principles of Semantics*. A brief survey of the various systems will be found in P. Guiraud, *La Sémantique*, Paris, 1955. See also C. E. Kany, *American-Spanish Semantics*, Berkeley — Los Angeles, 1960.

C

namely, those by which length is measured; or if the concept is mental, as of mathematical continuity, the operations are mental operations, namely those by which we determine whether a given aggregate of magnitudes is continuous'.[1] This led Bridgman to his often-quoted axiom: 'the true meaning of a term is to be found by observing what a man does with it, not by what he says about it'.[2] In his posthumous *Philosophical Investigations*, Ludwig Wittgenstein went even further; in his view, the meaning of a word is not merely *ascertained* by its use: the meaning of a word *is* its use in the language.[3] Perhaps the formula is too categorical; Wittgenstein himself seems to have had some doubts about it and allowed for certain exceptions.[4] It is as if he felt that there was in the meaning of a word something more than its use, but that this extra something defied analysis. But even if one hesitates to equate 'meaning' with 'use', this will not affect the substance of the operational doctrine.

Before exploring the relevance of this doctrine to linguistics, it might be well to examine its relation to the analytical theory of meaning. At first sight the two might seem to be diametrically opposed to each other; yet, on closer inspection, they turn out to be merely complementary. The procedure followed in the compilation of a major dictionary will elucidate the point. The lexicographer's first task is to observe each word in operation, i.e. to collect a representative selection of contexts. From these he will then abstract the highest common factor and record it as the meaning, or one of the meanings, of the word. In the first phase he is applying the operational method, in the second the analytical. The succession of the two phases has been admirably summed up by Bertrand Russell: 'A word has a meaning, more or less vague; but the meaning is only to be discovered by observing its use; the use comes first, and the meaning is distilled out of it'.[5] Fundamentally we have to do here with

---

1 *The Logic of Modern Physics*, New York, 1927, p. 5.
2 Ibid., p. 7. Cf. S. Chase, *The Tyranny of Words*, London, 1938, p. 7; L. J. Cohen, op. cit., pp. 167 ff; Schaff, op. cit., pp. 252 ff.
3 'For a *large* class of cases—though not for all—in which we employ the word "meaning" it can be defined thus: the meaning of a word is its use in the language' (p. 20). In his essay, 'The Theory of Meaning' (in C. A. Mace (ed.), *British Philosophy in the Mid-Century*, London, 1957, pp. 239–64), Professor Gilbert Ryle has coined several illuminating formulas to bring out the operational nature of meaning: 'Word-meanings do not stand to sentence-meanings as atoms to molecules or as letters of the alphabet to the spellings of words, but more nearly as the tennis-racket stands to the strokes which are or may be made with it' (p. 249); 'Learning the meaning of an expression is more like learning a piece of drill than like coming across a previously unencountered object' (pp. 256 f.); 'the meaning of an expression is not an entity denoted by it, but a style of operation performed with it, not a nominee but a rôle' (p. 262).
4 Ibid., pp. 53 and 215.
5 Quoted from *Logic and Knowledge* by Schaff, op. cit., p. 255.

the two facets of linguistic activity: the difference between language and speech, between the virtual and the actual, between a code and the encoding of particular messages.[1]

The operational concept of meaning has not yet been tested on a large scale for its applicability to semantic problems, but some of its advantages are apparent even at this early stage. At more than one point it shows a remarkable affinity with the general trend of contemporary linguistic thought. It will commend itself first of all by its salutary reliance on *context*. It cannot be sufficiently emphasized that language is a high-order abstraction which is accessible to us only when clothed in particular utterances. The full significance of a word can be grasped only in the light of the context in which it occurs, with reference to the situation in which it is spoken, and, ultimately, within the framework of the whole culture of which it forms part.[2] A contextual theory of meaning will therefore appeal to all empiricists—and most linguists are empiricists, by training and by temperament.

Another interesting feature of the doctrine is that it pictures words as if they were *tools*. 'Language', says Wittgenstein, 'is an instrument. Its concepts are instruments'.[3] Elsewhere he elaborates the same analogy: 'Think of the tools in a tool-box: there is a hammer, pliers, a saw, a screw-driver, a rule, a glue-pot, glue, nails and screws. The functions of words are as diverse as the functions of these objects'.[4] Although this simile, as we shall see presently, is not entirely appropriate, it is illuminating in one respect: as already noted (pp. 6 f.), statistical investiga-

---

[1] On the Saussurean distinction between language and speech, *langue* and *parole*, which is one of the main moot points of contemporary linguistics, see recently E. Coseriu, *Sistema, Norma y Habla*, Montevideo, 1952, and N. C. W. Spence, 'A Hardy Perennial: the Problem of *la Langue* and *la Parole*', *Archivum Linguisticum*, ix (1957), pp. 1–27. On the application of the distinction to semantic problems, see A. Gill, 'La Distinction entre *langue* et *parole* en sémantique historique', *Studies in Romance Philology and French Literature Presented to John Orr*, Manchester, 1953, pp. 90–101. The same duality reappears in W. Coutu's distinction between 'sign-potential' and 'stimulus-value' (loc. cit., pp. 62 f.).

[2] 'The conception of context must burst the bonds of mere linguistics and be carried over into the analysis of the general conditions under which a language is spoken ... The study of any language, spoken by a people who live under conditions different from our own and possess a different culture, must be carried out in conjunction with the study of their culture and of their environment' (B. Malinowski, 'The Problem of Meaning in Primitive Languages', Supplement I to Ogden-Richards's *The Meaning of Meaning*, p. 306). In the same way, Professor Firth advocates a 'serial contextualization of our facts, context within context, each one being a function, an organ of the bigger context and all contexts finding a place in what may be called the context of culture' (*Papers in Linguistics*, p. 32). On the whole problem of context in language, see now T. Slama-Cazacu, *Langage et contexte*, The Hague, 1961; cf. my *Semantics*, pp. 48 ff. Cf. also E. R. Kurilowich, 'Zametki o znachenii slova', *Voprosy Jazykoznanija*, 1955, no. 3, pp. 73–81.

[3] Op. cit., p. 151.

[4] Ibid., p. 6. On this conception see recently G. P. Meredith, 'Words as Instruments', *Proceedings of the Aristotelian Society*, New Series, lxii (1962), pp. 241–60.

tions have revealed that in some ways our words behave exactly like tools: just as there is a direct relationship between the frequency and the diversity of a tool's usage, there seems to be a direct relationship between the frequency of a word and the diversity of its meanings.

The operational approach is also in harmony with modern linguistics when it seeks to identify the meaning of words by *substituting* them for each other. Thus, the different meanings of the verb *is* in the two sentences: 'The rose *is* red—Twice two *is* four', are revealed by a simple substitution test: in 'Twice two *is* four', the verb can be replaced by the sign of equality, whereas in 'The rose *is* red' it cannot.[1] It is by a similar procedure that the linguist identifies phonemes and other distinctive features. If, by substituting one sound for another, we obtain a different meaning we have to do with two distinctive units; thus, |k| and |g| are distinctive in English because, by replacing |k| by |g|, we obtain different words: *came* becomes *game, coat goat, crow grow*, etc. The same is true if we substitute one word for another in a phrase or sentence. As far back as 1935, the late Professor J. R. Firth described words as 'lexical substitution-counters',[2] and it is interesting to note that Macaulay had defined synonymy in closely similar terms: 'Change the structure of the sentence; substitute one synonym for another; and the whole effect is destroyed'.[3] The substitution test which underlies all these pronouncements is one of the fundamental techniques in the structural analysis of language.

In a more general way, the operational concept of meaning inevitably leads to a structural view which regards language as a highly integrated totality made up of interdependent elements. According to Saussure's famous simile, which was mentioned in the last chapter (p. 4), language is like a game of *chess* where no unit can be added, shifted or removed without altering the entire field of force. Wittgenstein too was intensely interested in language games, and it is not surprising to find him echoing, no doubt unwittingly, the same simile when he likens a word to a piece in chess and when he declares: 'It is the field of force of the word which is decisive.'[4]

All these are solid advantages and suggest that the operational concept of meaning is more amenable to structural treatment than the

---

[1] Ibid., p. 149. Cf. also the following passage: 'How do I find the "right" word? How do I choose among words? Without doubt it is sometimes as if I were comparing them by fine differences of smell: *That* is too … , *that* is too … , — *this* is the right one' (p. 218).

[2] *Papers in Linguistics*, p. 20; cf. Haas, loc. cit., p. 80.

[3] See the *NED, s.v. synonym*.

[4] Op. cit., pp. 47, 150, 219.

analytical theory. It must, however, be stated that no major attempt has yet been made to build an orderly and comprehensive system of semantics around the operational definition, nor is it at the moment easy to see how such an attempt could succeed. For the time being, at least, the older formula seems to lend itself better to the classification and explanation of semantic phenomena.[1]

The operational definition of meaning also raises certain specific difficulties, one or two of which may be mentioned here. As a recent critic of the theory rightly points out, 'the use of a word depends on many factors many of which have nothing to do with questions of meaning'.[2] The rules governing the use of the word *ūtor* in Latin, for example, are not confined to the fact that it is a verb occurring in contexts where its English equivalent would be 'use, employ, enjoy, profit by, be in possession of, etc.'; before we know how to use *ūtor* we must also be told that it is a deponent and that it takes the ablative, neither of which rules has anything to do with the meaning of the word. It is clear, therefore, that the meaning of a term in a given language is not co-extensive with its use.

Another point made by the same critic is that not all uses of a word can provide a safe guide to its meaning. 'In order to discover the intension of a term it is necessary to examine not its purported extension but its actual or correct extension; e.g. if one attempts to grasp the intension of the term *cups* and mistakenly takes the extension of the term to include such things as cans and pots, then one will fail to grasp the correct intension . . . Misuses of words occur. One cannot find out what a word means by examining its actual usage unless one can recognize misuses and deviant uses.'[3] As can be seen, the theory raises the whole vexed question of standards of correctness in language. Here we come up against the limitations of the parallel between words and tools. 'The trouble with this analogy', writes another of Wittgenstein's critics, 'is partly that in reality words are not artifacts, to be operated in accordance with craft-rules or manufacturers' instructions, and that speech is not exactly a technique, but rather something that can itself be either technical or non-technical. By treating speech as a technique the tool-use analogy encourages a nor-

[1] For some suggestions about the application of Wittgenstein's formula to linguistic problems, see R. Wells, 'Meaning and Use', *Word*, x (1954), pp. 235–50. Cf. Haas, loc. cit., p. 81, n., his paper, 'Semantic Value', in the *Preprints* of the Ninth International Congress of Linguists, pp. 425–30, and his recent article, 'The Theory of Translation', *Philosophy*, xxxvii (1962), pp. 208–28, which also contains an interesting restatement of the contextualist position. Cf. also R. H. Robins, 'Considerations on the Status of Grammar in Linguistics', *Archivum Linguisticum* xi (1959), pp. 91–114: p. 95, n. 3.
[2] Ziff, op. cit., p. 158.
[3] Ibid., p. 70.

mative attitude to language, when philologists themselves have long since abandoned any such attitude in order to do justice to all social levels of speech'.[1]

These debates on fundamentals, and their repercussions in linguistics, serve once again as a reminder that the linguist cannot afford to ignore what is happening in neighbouring fields. Whether he likes it or not, a process of cross-fertilization is in progress. The disappearance of traditional boundaries may in time lead to closer integration of all the manifold interests converging on language. There are already some indications that the importance of co-ordinated efforts and of a reasonable division of labour is being recognized, and the many conferences and symposia which bring together representatives of various disciplines will play a valuable part in further progress along these lines.

---

[1] L. J. Cohen, op. cit., p. 53. Mr. Cohen also makes the interesting suggestion that 'the sentences of a language, not the words, are like tools in being either the stock means to certain frequently desired ends or the *ad hoc* means, especially constructed, to ends that may or may not be so frequently desired' (ibid.). Cf. also pp. 123 ff. On these problems see recently G. Ryle-J. N. Findlay, 'Use, Usage and Meaning', *The Aristotelian Society*, Supplementary Vol. xxxv (1961), pp. 223–42.

CHAPTER III

SEMANTICS AND ETYMOLOGY

ETYMOLOGY is one of the oldest branches of linguistics; semantics is one of the youngest. In Greece, speculation on language started with etymological theories on the origin of words, the famous controversy between naturalists and conventionalists, which found its classic expression in Plato's *Cratylus*; in Rome, the grammarian Varro set up etymology as one of the three main divisions of linguistic study, the other two being morphology and syntax.[1] Semantics, on the other hand, did not emerge as an independent discipline until the beginning of the nineteenth century. It was ultimately to the Romantic Movement, with its absorbing interest in the past and its cult of the word, of its powers of suggestion and its magic potencies, that the new science owed its existence. A passage from Balzac's novel *Louis Lambert* enables the modern student to recapture something of the intellectual climate in which semantics took shape:

'Quel beau livre ne composerait-on pas en racontant la vie et les aventures d'un mot? Sans doute il a reçu diverses impressions des événements auxquels il a servi; selon les lieux, il a réveillé des idées différentes ... Tous sont empreints d'un vivant pouvoir qu'ils tiennent de l'âme, et qu'ils lui restituent par les mystères d'une action et d'une réaction merveilleuse entre la parole et la pensée ... Par leur seule physionomie, les mots raniment dans notre cerveau les créatures auxquelles ils servent de vêtement ... Mais ce sujet comporte peut-être une science tout entière'.[2]

Unbeknownst to Balzac, the science he foreshadowed in this passage had actually come into existence a few years before, in a more modest and less poetical form, in the lectures on Latin philology which the German

---

[1] See R. H. Robins, *Ancient and Mediaeval Grammatical Theory in Europe*, London, 1951, p. 53. Cf. P. Zumthor, 'Fr. *Etymologie*. Essai d'histoire sémantique', in *Etymologica. W. v. Wartburg zum 70. Geburtstag*, Tübingen, 1958, pp. 873–93.

[2] 'What a fine book one could write by relating the life and adventures of a word! It has no doubt received various impressions from the events in which it was used; it has evoked different ideas in different places ... All words are impressed with a living power which they derive from the mind and which they return to it through the mysteries of a miraculous action and reaction between speech and thought ... By their very appearance, words awaken in our minds the creatures whose garments they are ... But this subject would perhaps require an entire science to itself' (ed. M. Lévy, p. 4).

scholar C. Chr. Reisig had been giving in Halle since about 1825.[1] In these lectures he spoke of the need to evolve a new branch of linguistic studies, 'semasiology', which would explore the principles governing the evolution of word-meanings. He did not, however, develop the idea in detail, and his lectures, published after his death, were known only to a small circle of specialists. If Reisig was the Moses of the Promised Land of semantics, Michel Bréal was its Joshua. It was Bréal who gave it the name by which it is still best known; it was he who established the theoretical foundations of the new science and ensured its international diffusion.[2]

We saw in the first chapter that Bréal and his contemporaries conceived of semantics as of a purely historical study and that their ideas held sway for many decades, but have been radically modified during the last thirty years or so, as a result of the penetration of structuralist methods into semantics. The reorientation of semantic research is bound to have important implications for etymological studies. There are three points in particular where recent progress in semantics seems to be of direct relevance to etymology: the distinction between descriptive and historical viewpoints; the way in which the structure of the vocabulary is visualized in modern linguistics; lastly, the new approach to the perennial problem of the motivation of words.[3]

A. Towards a 'Static' Etymology

As will be seen at greater length in the next chapter, the distinction between 'synchronic' and 'diachronic' linguistics was fundamental to the teaching of Ferdinand de Saussure. He never tired of emphasizing the need for a strict and consistent separation of the two approaches. As his most outstanding disciple, Charles Bally, wittily put it, a linguist who tried to mingle the two methods would be like a painter making a composite portrait after photographs taken at different periods, where the mouth of an infant was combined with the beard of an adult and the wrinkles of an old man. In recent years, this antinomy has been somewhat

---

[1] See H. Kronasser, *Handbuch der Semasiologie*, Heidelberg, 1952, pp. 29 ff., and K. Baldinger, *Die Semasiologie*, Berlin, 1957, pp. 4 ff.

[2] See above, p. 3.

[3] On the problems and methods of etymological research, see esp. K. Baldinger, 'L'Etymologie hier et aujourd'hui', *Cahiers de l'Association Internationale des Etudes Françaises*, xi (1959), pp. 233–64; Y. Malkiel, 'The Place of Etymology in Linguistic Research', *Bulletin of Hispanic Studies*, xxxi (1954), pp. 78–90; Id., 'A Tentative Typology of Etymological Studies', *International Journal of American Linguistics*, xxiii (1957), pp. 1–17; Id., 'Etymology and General Linguistics', *Word*, xviii (1962), pp. 198–219; A. S. C. Ross, *Etymology, with Especial Reference to English*, London, 1958.

relaxed since it was found that certain phenomena, such as for example conflicts between homonyms, can be handled only by a judicious combination of descriptive and historical viewpoints. On the other hand, the separation of the two approaches has proved particularly helpful in dealing with a semantic problem which closely concerns the etymologist as well as the lexicographer: the question whether, in certain cases, one has to do with one word or with two.

Let us take some specific examples. Are there in French two homonymous verbs *voler*, one meaning 'to fly', the other 'to steal', or is this a case of polysemy, of one word having two different senses? The answer will depend on the point of view one adopts. For synchronic semantics they are two different words since the gap in meaning is too wide for any connexion to be felt by the ordinary speaker. A descriptive dictionary of modern French will therefore record them as two separate terms, in accordance with the attitude of the average Frenchman who is unaware of the etymological background. In the words of Saussure, it is only by 'abolishing the past' ('en supprimant le passé') that synchronic linguistics can penetrate into the consciousness of the ordinary speaker (op. cit., p. 117).

The answer of a historical linguist, such as the author of an etymological dictionary, will be entirely different. For him the two verbs *voler* are not two separate terms but one 'fissiparous' word which, in the course of its history, has split in two. *Voler*, derived from the Latin *volare* 'to fly', has retained its original meaning to this very day, but, since the sixteenth century, it has also acquired another sense, 'to steal', which first took shape in the language of falconry, in idioms like 'le faucon *vole* la perdrix' 'the hawk *flies at* the partridge' (Bloch-Wartburg). A historical or etymological dictionary will therefore have only one entry for *voler*, indicating the chronology and filiation of its meanings. The same may be said of many other pairs of words which now look homonymous but which were originally one and the same term: English *pupil* 'scholar' and *pupil* 'apple of the eye', *arch-*, prefix, and *arch* 'mischievous', *sole* of the foot and *sole*, name of a fish; or, with modifications in spelling, English *flower* and *flour*, French *boîte* 'box' and *il boite* 'he limps', *conter* 'to tell, to relate' and *compter* 'to count', etc. In all these cases, polysemy has given rise to homonymy: two meanings of the same word developed on diverging lines until eventually the link between them snapped and they came to be regarded as two independent terms identical in sound.

But if the etymologist has to reunite words which the accidents of history have torn asunder, the converse can also happen: two terms which were originally unconnected may be brought into relation with one another by speakers untutored in the art of etymology. This is what happened in sixteenth-century French when the word *souci* 'marigold' (from Vulgar Latin *solsequia*) was wrongly identified with *souci* 'care' (from Latin *sollicitare*); to make the identification complete, the name of the flower was changed from an earlier *soucie* to its modern form (Bloch-Wartburg). In this case, homonymy has been transformed into polysemy: two separate words have been reinterpreted as if they were one term with two meanings. The same may be said of such pairs as French *flamme* 'flame' and *flamme* 'fleam', English *ear*, name of the organ, and *ear*, 'spike or head of corn', and some others.[1]

These passages from polysemy to homonymy, or vice versa, may face the author of a descriptive dictionary with an awkward problem. Between polysemy and homonymy there exists no sharp line of demarcation; as Bloomfield pertinently remarks, 'the degree of nearness of the meanings is not subject to precise measurement' (*Language*, p. 436). In the last resort, it is a matter of 'linguistic consciousness', of whether the ordinary speaker is (or can be made) aware of any link between the two senses. Unfortunately, 'consciousness' and 'awareness' are vague, unstable and subjective mental conditions to which a rigorously scientific discipline is reluctant to have recourse. Attempts have been made to devise a set of precise criteria for dealing with such border-line cases. Bréal had already drawn attention to the importance of rhyme as an indication of homonymy. Take, for example, these lines from Corneille's *Cinna*, Act IV, scene 3:

> AUGUSTE: Adieu, nous perdons temps.
> LIVIE: Je ne vous quitte *point*,
>   Seigneur, que mon amour n'ait obtenu ce *point*.[2]

For the etymologist, *point* used as a noun and as a negative particle are one and the same word with two different senses and functions; but the fact that Corneille rhymes them with one another on more than one occasion[3] shows that to him they appeared as two separate terms. Another formal criterion is repetition. If, in modern French, there existed any connexion between *pas* 'step' and *pas*, negative particle, one would hardly combine them in expressions like 'une affaire qui ne fait *pas* un

---

[1] For further examples, see my *Semantics*, pp. 164 f.

[2] 'Auguste: Good-bye, we are wasting time. — Livie: I shall not leave you, my Lord, until my love has obtained this point from you.'

[3] Cf. e.g.: 'On les hait; la raison, je ne la connais *point*, Et je ne vois Décie injuste qu'en ce *point*' 'They are hated, I do not know why; this is the only point where I find Decius unjust' (*Polyeucte*, Act IV, scene 6). Cf. Bréal, op. cit., p. 146, n. 2.

pas' 'a matter which is making no progress', or 'cela ne se trouve *pas* dans le *pas* d'un cheval' 'that is not found every day'.[1]

Other scholars have tried to formulate grammatical criteria for the delimitation of homonymy and polysemy. It has been argued, for example, that two forms with different senses must be regarded as two words, not one, if they belong to two different derivational series.[2] On this reading there would be two homonymous adjectives *poli* in French: one of them, meaning 'polished' in the physical sense, belongs to the same series as *polir* 'to polish', *dépolir* 'to take the polish off', *polissage* 'polishing', etc.; the other, which signifies 'polite', forms part of the group *poliment* 'politely', *impoli* 'impolite', *politesse* 'politeness'. This solution is no doubt ingenious, yet it may be doubted whether the existence of two series will in fact destroy the unity of the word in the eyes of ordinary speakers. Quite recently, a Rumanian linguist has underlined the importance of morphological and syntactical criteria (inflexion, gender, word-class) in determining whether we have to do with one word or two.[3] But here again it seems more than doubtful that the following pairs should be regarded as two separate words: *brother: brothers—brethren*; *old: older—elder*; *hang: hanged—hung*; French *aïeul: aïeuls* 'grandfathers' *—aïeux* 'forbears'; *le pendule* 'pendulum'—*la pendule* 'clock'; *marron* 'chestnut'—*des étoffes marron* 'maroon cloths'. Be that as it may, one is still left with a large number of border-line cases where no formal criteria are applicable, and where we have therefore to fall back on linguistic consciousness, on the opinions or the instinctive and subjective reactions of linguistically unsophisticated speakers. Perhaps the best way out of the dilemma is that suggested by an American linguist, namely, that 'social science has workable techniques for studying subjective opinions, which could be applied to homonymy problems (if it is granted that they are a matter of speakers' opinions) as well as to political issues'.[4] We saw in the last chapter that statistical inquiries, if properly conducted, can enable one to measure meaning or at least some components of it; in the same way,

---

[1] There is also the evidence of rhyme; cf. Racine, *Phèdre*, Act II, scene 1: 'Tu vois depuis quel temps il évite nos *pas*, Et cherche tous les lieux où nous ne sommes *pas*' 'You know for how long he has been keeping out of our way and looking for places where we are not'. There are a number of other examples in the same writer.

[2] See R. Godel, 'Homonymie et identité', *Cahiers Ferdinand de Saussure*, vii (1948), pp. 5–15.

[3] P. Diaconescu, 'Omonimia și polisemia', *Probleme de lingvistică generală*, vol. I, Bucharest, 1959, pp. 133–53. Cf. F. Asan, ibid., vol. II, pp. 113–24; M. M. Falkovich, *Voprosy Jazykoznanija*, 1960, no. 5, pp. 85–8; O. Ducháček, 'L'Homonymie et la polysémie', *Vox Romanica*, xxi (1962), pp. 49–56; Ch. Muller, 'Polysémie et homonymie dans le lexique contemporain', *Études de linguistique appliquée*, i (1962), pp. 49–54; W. A. Koch, 'Zur Homonymie und Synonymie', *Acta Linguistica* (Budapest), xiii (1963), pp. 65–91.

[4] U. Weinreich, *Language*, xxxi (1955), pp. 541 f.

one could devise a kind of linguistic Gallup Poll to settle by objective methods these frontier problems between polysemy and homonymy.

The existence of border-line cases must not, however, obscure the basic principle: the need to keep description and history scrupulously apart in etymological studies, since the two approaches may yield diametrically opposite and irreconcilable results: what, to the historian, is a single unit may appear as two or more to the descriptivist, and vice versa. It would seem, therefore, that there are two kinds of etymology, one historical, the other descriptive; the former is concerned with the genealogy of words, the latter with the network of associations, formal, semantic or both, which connect words with each other in a given linguistic system. This realization led the late Professor Vendryes to suggest that, alongside of traditional etymology based on historical evidence, there was need for a strictly synchronic or '*static*' etymology whose programme he summed up in the following terms:

'L'histoire est rigoureusement exclue de l'étymologie statique, dont la tâche est de fixer la valeur sémantique des mots à l'intérieur d'une langue et à un moment donné strictement limité ... Il s'agit de définir la place que tient chaque mot dans l'esprit, d'en circonscrire la significa- tion et l'emploi, d'en calculer la fréquence, d'en apprécier la valeur évocatrice, d'en marquer les rapports qui l'unissent aux autres mots. C'est une sorte d'inventaire du monde intérieur que chacun porte en lui.'[1]

Professor Vendryes also noted that this twofold approach to etymo- logy was foreshadowed by a group of Sanskrit grammarians, the *mīmāṃsā*, who distinguished between *yoga*, the original sense of a term, and *rūdhi*, the meaning in which it is actually used, and claimed that whenever there was any discrepancy between the two, the *rūdhi* ought to prevail—a valuable distinction which was obscured by the exclusively historical orientation of nineteenth-century linguistics.[2]

Within the framework of this theory, a familiar phenomenon, '*popular etymology*', will appear in a new light. Most linguists are unhappy about the term 'popular etymology' since many of the processes involved are anything but popular: they perpetuate mistakes committed not by the

---

[1] 'History is rigorously excluded from static etymology whose task is to determine the semantic value of words within a language and at a given moment strictly limited in time ... We have to define the place which each word occupies in the mind, to delimit its meaning and its use, to calculate its frequency, to estimate its evocative value, to indicate its relations to other words. It is a kind of inventory of the inner world which everybody carries within him' (J. Vendryes, 'Pour une étymologie statique', *Bulletin de la Société de Linguistique de Paris*, xlix (1953), pp. 1–19: p. 7).

[2] Ibid., pp. 5 ff. On the Indian grammarians' approach to semantic problems, see J. Brough, 'Some Indian Theories of Meaning', *Transactions of the Philological Society*, 1953, pp. 161–76.

people but by the learned or semi-learned. Did the 'people' introduce a
g into *sovereign* (from French *souverain*, Medieval Latin *superānus*), to
make it look more like the historically unconnected *reign*, or an *s* into
aisle (from French *aile* 'wing', Latin *ala*), in the erroneous belief that it
was the same word as *isle*?[1] Did the 'people' omit the final *t* in Medieval
French *court* (from Latin *cohortem*) under the influence of *curia*, its
equivalent in contemporary Latin texts?[2] Pope's aphorism: 'A little learning is a dang'rous thing' is applicable to many cases of popular etymology.
But whether the initial error was perpetrated by a medieval scribe, a
Renaissance humanist or ordinary people, whether it was a semi-learned
misinterpretation or a mere malapropism, it had its roots in a purely synchronic association with a word similar in sound, in meaning or in both.
The term 'associative etymology', suggested by Professor Orr over twenty
years ago,[3] would be an admirable description of the mechanism at work.

Quite apart from the misleading nomenclature, there is disagreement
among linguists as to the importance to be attached to popular etymology.
In the first edition of Saussure's *Cours de linguistique générale*, it was
described as a 'pathological phenomenon', and although this expression
was omitted from subsequent editions,[4] it is clear that, for Saussure and
many other linguists, popular etymology is an abnormal process 'which
arises only under special conditions' (ibid., p. 241). In sharp contrast to
this attitude, Gilliéron and his followers maintain that it is a perfectly
normal occurrence which happens far more frequently than one might
think. For contemporary semantics, popular etymology is no more than a
special case of static etymology: it posits connexions which are contra-
dicted by the data of history and which may involve phonetic, orthographical or semantic modifications in the words concerned. If historical
and static etymology, *yoga* and *rūdhi* coincide, there is no problem; if they
differ and the synchronic associations prevail, then we have a case of
popular etymology.[5]

B. ETYMOLOGY AND STRUCTURAL LINGUISTICS

As we saw in the first chapter (pp. 10 ff.), modern semantics is becoming increasingly interested in 'associative fields' and, in a more general

---

[1] See the *NED*; cf. also Bloch-Wartburg, *s.v. aile*.
[2] See Bloch-Wartburg, *s.v. cour*.
[3] *Words and Sounds in English and French*, Oxford, 1953, p. 96.
[4] Op. cit., p. 241; cf. I. Iordan-J. Orr, *An Introduction to Romance Linguistics*, London,
1937, p. 173, n. 1.
[5] The difference between the two approaches is well summed up in Professor Orr's
recent article, 'L'Etymologie populaire', *Revue de Linguistique Romane*, xviii (1954), pp.
129–42: 'L'étymologie populaire ... ne diffère pas essentiellement de sa sœur savante,

way, in the structure and organization of the vocabulary. For etymology, the advent of a structurally oriented semantics will mean a considerable widening of horizons. Rather than tracing the history of isolated words, attention will have to be focused henceforth on their environment, on the network of sound and sense associations which surround each term and which may at any moment influence its development. Among present-day etymologists, Professor Wartburg has been particularly emphatic on the need for such a structural approach. 'Quiconque veut écrire aujourd'hui l'étymologie d'un mot', he writes, 'ne doit pas se contenter de constater la disparition d'une signification ou l'adjonction d'une signification nouvelle. Il doit se demander encore quel mot est l'heureux concurrent, héritier de la signification disparue, ou à quel mot il a ravi sa nouvelle signification.' And again: 'La recherche de la racine d'un mot ou d'un groupe de mots n'est plus aujourd'hui l'unique tâche de l'étymologie. Elle doit suivre le groupe à considérer pendant tout le temps où il appartient à une langue, dans toutes ses ramifications et tous ses rapports avec d'autres groupes, sans jamais cesser de se poser les questions qui relèvent de l'étymologie proprement dite.'[1]

The concept of associative fields, and the new vistas which it opens up, will affect the work of the etymologist in three main ways. They will put him on his guard against certain errors of perspective inherent in his data; more positively, they will enable him to solve etymological problems which could not have been tackled on traditional lines, and to give a complete explanation of developments which could only be partially explained by orthodox methods.

1. When a word acquires an entirely new meaning in the course of its history, the etymologist tends to assume that the later sense had developed spontaneously out of the earlier one, whereas in some cases the change may not have not been spontaneous: it may have been induced

l'étymologie des philologues. Plus vivante, plus "opérative" que cette dernière, elle fait instinctivement, intuitivement et du premier jet ce que fait l'autre intentionnellement, à grand renfort de bouquins et de fiches' 'Popular etymology ... does not essentially differ from her learned sister, the etymology of philologists. More vital, more "operative" than the latter, she does instinctively, intuitively and at the first attempt what the other does deliberately, with a great array of books and index cards' (p. 142). For recent work on popular etymology, see my *Semantics*, p. 101, n. 2.

1 'Whoever wishes to write today the etymology of a word must not be content to note the disappearance of a meaning or the addition of a new sense. He must also ask himself which is the lucky rival, the heir to the meaning which has disappeared, or which is the word from which the term in question has taken its new meaning ... To trace the root of a word or a group of words is no longer the only task of etymology. It must follow the group in question throughout the period when it belonged to the language, in all its ramifications and all its relations with other groups, without ever ceasing to ask the questions which pertain to etymology in the proper sense of the term' (*Problèmes et méthodes de la linguistique*, 2nd ed., Paris, 1963, pp. 125 and 130 f.).

by some other term in the same associative field. Professor Orr has coined the term 'pseudo-semantic development' to describe this fallacy.[1] The history of the English noun boon is an example in point. This word, which is of Old Norse origin, meant at first 'prayer, petition, request'. Its modern meaning, 'a blessing, an advantage, a thing to be thankful for', could quite easily have developed from the older sense; it would seem, however, that the change was not spontaneous but was due to confusion with the homonymous adjective boon, the English form of French bon (NED). A somewhat more complex case is the sense-development of French fruste which was borrowed during the Renaissance as an art term from Italian frusto 'worn'. The French adjective originally meant, and still means in some contexts, 'worn, defaced' (coin, statue, etc.); but since 1845 it has acquired the additional sense of 'rough, unpolished, unmannerly'. An etymologist of the old school would no doubt have tried to build a bridge between the two senses by showing the association of ideas which could have led from the old meaning to the new. But such a reconstruction would be purely gratuitous since the later sense did not emerge spontaneously from the earlier one; it was due to the influence of another term in the same associative field: the adjective rustre 'boorish, clownish, loutish'. The fact that fruste occurs once as frustre in the fifteenth century shows that the two phonetically similar adjectives must have been associated with each other almost as soon as the Italian word was introduced into French (Bloch-Wartburg).

2. A striking example of an etymological riddle whose solution lies in the associative field of the word is the history of the French noun maroufle, brilliantly reconstructed by Professor Guiraud.[2] This term appears in three different senses: (a) 'large and fat cat' (now dialectal); (b) 'rogue, scoundrel' (attested since Rabelais); (c) 'strong paste for remounting pictures' (since 1688). The connexion between (a) and (b) is self-evident; but how, if at all, does 'strong paste' fit into the picture? One might be inclined to believe that there is no historical link, that maroufle 'paste' is a chance homonym of the other maroufle. This, however, is intrinsically improbable, in view of the distinctive form of these words; as M. Guiraud rightly notes, 'ces formes si caractéristiques postulent une origine commune, un dénominateur commun'.[3] This common denominator is found, quite unexpectedly, in the word chas

[1] Words and Sounds in English and French, ch. XV.
[2] Bulletin de la Société de Linguistique de Paris, lii (1956), pp. 269 ff.
[3] 'These highly characteristic forms point to a common origin, a common denominator' (ibid., p. 270).

'starch paste, dressing'. By a kind of jocular pun, *maroufle*, a synonym of *chat* 'cat', was used in the sense of *chas*, a homonym of the latter, and the joke was so successful that the new meaning took root, as often happens in the slang of trades and crafts. In M. Guiraud's formula: *chas* = *chat* = *maroufle* = *chat*.

3. Associative fields can also provide a useful *corrective* to etymological solutions which, without being actually wrong, are misleadingly incomplete and oversimplified. A good example of the difference between old and new methods is the semantic history of French *femme*.[1] If one compares the meaning of Latin *fēmina* with that of its French descendant, one notices some significant differences: whereas the Latin term meant 'female of the species', applied to either human beings or animals, *femme* does not refer to the female of an animal but has two main senses: 'woman' and 'wife'. Admittedly, there is nothing very unusual in these shifts of meaning; similar shifts have occurred, for example, in the history of English *wife*. One ought, however, to remember Professor Wartburg's warning, quoted above: the etymologist's work is not finished until he has discovered the word, or words, which *femme* replaced in its new meaning, and also the term which replaced *femme* itself in the sense 'female of an animal'. In other words, we have to glance at the associative field of *fēmina* in Latin. The two key-terms in that field were *mulier* and *uxor*; there were also some subsidiary terms (*conju(n)x, marita*, etc.) which had no influence on Romance developments. *Mulier* meant mainly 'woman' but could also signify 'wife' in certain contexts; *uxor* was reserved for the meaning of 'wife'. Both *uxor* and *mulier* survived in Old French, the former as *oisso(u)r*, the latter as *moillier*; gradually, however, they fell into disuse and were replaced by *femme*. Another word for 'wife', *épouse*, from Latin *spō(n)sa* 'bride' (cf. English *spouse*), belongs to a different stylistic register. As for the meaning 'female of animals', which was vacated by *femme* as the latter became established in its new and wider sphere, this was taken over by *femelle*, from the rare Latin word *fēmella*, a diminutive of *fēmina*, which originally meant 'young female, girl'. It is worth noting that in those Romance languages where *mulier* has survived (Italian *moglie*, Spanish *mujer*), the descendants of *fēmina* did not extend their range in the same way as in French; consequently there was no need in these languages for a new word of the *femelle* type to denote the female of an animal. It is clear, then, that what looked at first like a straightforward shift in meaning was in reality part of a complex chain

---

[1] See Wartburg, *Problèmes et méthodes*, p. 126; cf. also Bloch-Wartburg, *s.v. femme*, and Lewis and Short, *s.v. femella, femina, mulier, uxor*.

of events which can be fully understood only if we follow the transformations of the field as a whole rather than the fate of individual
elements.

As some of these examples show, there are cases where one has to look
beyond a single associative field to find the complete explanation of a
change. Let us assume that the development of word (*a*) is affected at
some stage by modifications in the meaning of an associated term (*b*).
The question now arises as to why (*b*) changed its meaning, and the
answer may lie in the influence of a third term, (*c*), which forms part of
the associative field of (*b*), but not of that of (*a*). An example of such a
complex interplay of interferences is the semantic evolution of French
viande. In accordance with its etymology—it comes from Vulgar Latin
vivenda, derived from *vivere* 'to live'—*viande* meant 'food' in general till
the seventeenth century; since then, however, it has become restricted
to the meaning of 'meat', a secondary sense which it had acquired two
centuries earlier. On the face of it, this looks like a perfectly normal
specialization of meaning, closely parallel to the history of English *meat*.
In French, however, there were special circumstances which explain why
the word should have narrowed its range at that particular time and in
that language alone, whilst retaining its wider sense in Italian, in Spanish,
and in the English *viand(s)*. The immediate explanation of the change in
viande (word *a*) is found in the influence of the associated term *chair*
(word *b*). The latter now means 'flesh', but until the seventeenth century
it also meant 'meat', and still retains that sense in certain expressions as
well as in a variety of dialects. Obviously, *viande* became specialized in
its modern acceptation in the seventeenth century in order to fill the gap
caused by the change in the meaning of *chair*. But we still do not know
how *chair* came to lose the sense of 'meat'. To find the answer to this
further question, we must look round for a word (*c*) in the associative
field of *chair*. We then discover that *chair* (from Latin *caro*, *carnem*)
had a homonym *chère*, a descendant of Graeco-Latin *cara* and the same
word as English *cheer*. This *chère* meant at first 'face, countenance', a
meaning which fell into disuse in the seventeenth century; but it also had
several other senses some of which came perilously near to that of *chair*:
'cheer, fare, living', as in the phrase *faire bonne chère* 'to have a good feed'.
One can well imagine that the homonymy of *chair* and *chère* was bound
to give rise to awkward ambiguities, especially during Lent with its rules
about fasting and meat. As a result of this homonymic clash, people
became increasingly reluctant to use *chair* in the sense of 'meat', and
this in its turn led to the specialization of *viande* in that meaning. It may

D

be added that *chère* itself was considerably weakened in the process and survives now only in a limited number of set phrases.[1]

The impact of semantics on etymological research must be seen against the wider background of the radical reorientation which etymology as a science has undergone in recent years. Traditionally, etymology was conceived of as the study of word-origins; it was concerned with the starting-point and the terminal point in the history of a word, and not with anything that had happened between the two. This narrow view was caricatured in Gilliéron's famous comparison between the etymologist and a literary critic who would summarize Balzac's biography in these two sentences: 'Balzac, sitting in his nurse's lap, wore a blue dress with red stripes. He wrote the *Human Comedy*'.[2] Contemporary etymologists have a far more ambitious view of their task; in the words of Professor Wartburg, 'l'étymologie doit aujourd'hui s'imposer pour tâche essentielle d'observer et de décrire toutes les transformations d'un mot, pour les comprendre ensuite et les expliquer. Elle ne doit plus se contenter du trait insipide qui unit le point de départ au point d'arrivée ... Elle doit au contraire nous dépeindre la vaste fresque des vicissitudes que le mot a traversées, dans les deux mille années de son histoire'.[3] Another leading etymologist has coined the formulae 'étymologie-origine' and 'étymologie-histoire du mot' to bring out the contrast between the two attitudes.[4] It is easy to see why modern semantics, with its strong emphasis on structure and on the interaction of words, will have a vital part to play in the new type of etymological research.

C. ETYMOLOGY AND THE MOTIVATION OF WORDS

As already noted, the etymology of words is closely bound up with their 'motivation': the question whether there is an intrinsic connexion between sound and sense or whether our words are purely conventional symbols, mere 'tokens current and accepted for conceits, as moneys are for values'.[5] The whole problem, which has exercised many philosophers,

---

[1] See Bloch-Wartburg, *s.v. viande, chair, chère*.

[2] See Baldinger, 'L'Etymologie hier et aujourd'hui', p. 239, and Wartburg, *Problèmes et méthodes*, p. 128.

[3] 'Etymology today must regard as its essential task to observe and describe all the transformations of a word, in order to understand them and to explain them. It must no longer be satisfied with the uninteresting line connecting the starting-point with the terminal point ... It should rather paint for us a vast canvas of the vicissitudes through which the word has passed in its two-thousand year old history' (*Problèmes et méthodes*, p. 130). The two thousand years refer of course to Romance etymology; in other branches of linguistics there may be a longer or shorter span of time.

[4] Baldinger, loc. cit., p. 239.

[5] Francis Bacon, *The Advancement of Learning* (quoted by *The Oxford Dictionary of Quotations*).

writers and linguists, has been fully re-examined during the last quarter of a century, and valuable new insights have been gained into the workings of motivation and the principles of word-structure. There are four main points in particular which have been considerably clarified by recent research:[1]

1. We now know that the real issue is not whether words in general are conventional or motivated, opaque or transparent, since both types are present, in varying proportions, in any linguistic system. We also know that motivation itself is a highly complex phenomenon which may work in three different ways:

(a) Onomatopoeic words like *crash, rumble, swish, whizz, zoom* are *phonetically motivated*: there is direct correspondence between the sounds and the sense. The uses of this principle in poetry are innumerable,[2] nor are they by any means confined to the imitation of noises. Sounds may also evoke light and colour, as well as states of mind and moral qualities. In Mallarmé's 'Swan' sonnet ('Le vierge, le vivace et le bel aujourd'hui'), the central impression of whiteness, coldness and purity is powerfully reinforced by the accumulation of *i* sounds:

> *I*l s'*i*mmob*i*l*i*se au songe froid de mépr*i*s
> Que vêt parm*i* l'ex*i*l *i*nut*i*le le Cygne.[3]

Even more significant is the rhyme-scheme of the poem; all fourteen rhymes end in *i* or in a combination culminating in *i: aujourd'hui—ivre—givre — fui — lui — délivre — vivre — ennui — agonie — nie — pris — assigne — mépris — Cygne.*[4]

(b) A great many words are motivated by their *morphological structure*. A compound like *ash-tray* or *motorway*, a derivative like *intake* or *fellowship*, will be readily intelligible to all who know their components. Even such unorthodox formations as *beautility, automation* or *meritocracy* were perfectly comprehensible when we met them for the first time, though some others, such as *beatnik* or *brinkmanship*, whilst transparent in them-

---

[1] For bibliographical references, see my *Semantics*, p. 81, n. 1. Cf. now also R. Engler, 'Théorie et critique d'un principe saussurien: l'arbitraire du signe', *Cahiers Ferdinand de Saussure*, xix (1962), pp. 5–66, and G. C. Lepscky, 'Ancora su "l'arbitraire du signe"', *Annali della Scuola Normale Superiore di Pisa* (Lettere, Storia e Filosofia), Serie II, xxxi (1962), pp. 65–102.

[2] See my *Semantics*, p. 85, nn. 2–5. To the works cited there, one may now add P. Delbouille's important re-examination of the whole problem: *Poésie et sonorités. La critique contemporaine devant le pouvoir suggestif des sons*, Paris, 1961.

[3] 'He comes to a stop in the cold dream of contempt which the Swan puts on in his useless exile.'

[4] On the symbolic value of the vowel i, see most recently M. Chastaing, 'Le Symbolisme des voyelles. Significations des *i*', *Journal de Psychologie*, lv (1958), pp. 403–23, 461–81. See also Id., 'La Brillance des voyelles', *Archivum Linguisticum*, xiv (1962), pp. 1–13.

selves (*beatnik* is obviously based on *sputnik*, *brinkmanship* on *showman-ship*, *penmanship*, etc.), can be fully understood only in the light of the special circumstances which called them into existence.

(*c*) There is also a third type of motivation. If we use a word in a transferred meaning, metaphorical or otherwise, the result will be *semantically motivated*: it will be transparent thanks to the connexion between the two senses. Thus, when we speak of the *root* of an evil, the *branches* of a science, an offensive nipped in the *bud*, the *flower* of a country's manhood, the *fruits* of peace, or a family-*tree*, the use of these botanical terms is not arbitrary, but motivated by some kind of similarity or analogy between their concrete meanings and the abstract phenomena to which they are applied.

Processes (*b*) and (*c*), morphological and semantic motivation, could be bracketed under the more general heading of 'etymological motivation' since they concern words derived from existing elements[1] whereas phonetic motivation involves the creation of completely new forms. This also means that etymological motivation is always 'relative':[2] the result is transparent but the elements themselves are opaque unless they happen to be phonetically motivated. To look again at some of the examples just cited, *ash-tray* is analysable but *ash* and *tray* are not; *fellowship* is motivated but *fellow* and the suffix -*ship* are conventional; 'the *root* of an evil' is a self-explanatory metaphor whereas *root* in the literal sense is opaque. Onomatopoeia alone can provide ultimate motivation in language.

2. A second principle elaborated by semantics is that of the *variability* of motivation. The proportion of transparent and opaque terms in a given language, and the relative frequency of the various types of motivation, depends on a multiplicity of factors; it varies characteristically from one idiom to another and may even differ between successive periods of the same language. We have seen an example of such variations in the first chapter of this book (pp. 9 f.).

3. Another important principle is that of the *mutability* of motivation. A word which was once motivated may seem conventional today; conversely, a term which was originally opaque, or had lost its transparency, may become motivated, or remotivated, at a later stage. Nothing could be less expressive than English *touch* or French *toucher*; yet they go back to Vulgar Latin *toccare*, from the onomatopoeic *toc* 'knock, tap' (Bloch-

---

[1] These elements need not be independent words; motivated terms can also be derived from non-independent stems such as the -*duct* in English *conduct*, *deduct*, *induct*. See on these Hockett, op. cit., pp. 173 and 241.

[2] See already Saussure, op. cit., pp. 180 ff.; cf. recently L. Zawadowski, 'The So-called Relative Motivation in Language', *Omagiu lui Iorgu Iordan*, Bucharest, 1958, pp. 927–37.

Wartburg). The morphological structure of a word may become simi-larly obscured. In English *maintain* and French *maintenir*, the meaning of the two Latin components, *manus* 'hand' and *tenēre* 'to hold', has become totally eclipsed; the present participle of the French verb, *main-tenant*, has moved even farther away from its origins: since the sixteenth century it simply means 'now' (ibid.). Similarly, who would connect *advent* with *adventure* although they come from the same root? Semantic motivation may be lost in the same way, as some of the examples quoted earlier on in this chapter have shown: this is how the link was severed between *pupil* 'scholar' and *pupil* 'apple of the eye', between *flower* and *flour*, the *sole* of a foot and the fish-name *sole*, French *cafard* 'cockroach' and *avoir le cafard* 'to be bored stiff',[1] and many others. At the same time, some words have been given motivations to which they are not historic-ally entitled. Terms which were initially inexpressive have acquired onomatopoeic overtones, as in the case of Graeco-Latin *karebaria* 'heaviness in the head, headache', which has given *charivari* 'din, row, racket' in French.[2] Many unanalysable words have received a spurious morphological motivation through popular etymology; thus the second part of *bridegroom* has historically nothing to do with *groom*: the Old English form was *brȳdguma*, from *brȳd* 'bride' plus the now obsolete *guma* 'man' (*NED*). Semantic motivation can be conferred on a word in a similar manner: witness the identification of the *ear* of corn with the name of the organ, of *souci* 'marigold' with *souci* 'care', and of *flamme* 'fleam' with *flamme* 'flame', which have been discussed above.

4. Yet another fundamental principle is that of the *subjectivity* of these processes. For a creative writer interested in word-origins and sensitive to linguistic nuances, a term may retain its pristine trans-parency, or may even acquire unsuspected powers of evocation and suggestion, where the ordinary reader perceives no trace of motivation. It is in the field of onomatopoeia in particular that writers give free rein to their imagination. As Valéry once said, 'l'accouplement de la variable phonique avec la variable sémantique engendre des problèmes de pro-longement et de convergence que les poètes résolvent les yeux bandés'.[3] For Keats, the word *forlorn* 'is like a bell To toll me back from thee to my sole self' (*Ode to a Nightingale*). The French Romantics' interest

---

[1] On the history of this word see Bloch-Wartburg, *s.v. cafard*.

[2] The retention of the first *i*, which is contrary to normal phonetic development, is pro-bably due to the desire to preserve the expressive force of the word (ibid.).

[3] 'The matching of the phonic variable with the semantic variable raises problems of pro-longation and convergence which the poets solve blindfolded' (*Cours de poétique*, quoted by F. Scarfe, *The Art of Paul Valéry*, p. 81).

in the subject was aroused by Charles Nodier, the linguist of the movement, who actually published a *Dictionnaire des onomatopées*. His comments on the word *catacombes* are symptomatic of his general attitude:
'Il est impossible de trouver une suite de sons plus pittoresques, pour
rendre le retentissement du cercueil, roulant de degrés en degrés sur les
angles aigus des pierres, et s'arrêtant tout à coup au milieu des tombes'.[1]
Balzac was fascinated by the expressive force of the slang term *fafiot*
'bank-note': '*Fafiot!* N'entendez-vous pas le bruissement du papier de
soie?'[2] His speculations on the onomatopoeic significance of the words
vrai 'true' and *vol* 'flight' are even more typical of this new *mystique*:

'N'existe-t-il pas dans le mot VRAI une sorte de rectitude fantastique?
Ne se trouve-t-il pas dans le son bref qu'il exige une vague image de la
chaste nudité, de la simplicité du vrai en toute chose? Cette syllabe respire
je ne sais quelle fraîcheur. J'ai pris pour exemple la formule d'une idée
abstraite, ne voulant pas expliquer le problème par un mot qui le rendît
trop facile à comprendre, comme celui du VOL, où tout parle aux sens'.[3]

Proper names are particularly apt to be caught up in such sound and
sense associations. Some of these may have a private background, as in
the case of the German poet Morgenstern who once declared that all
sea-gulls look as if their name was *Emma*. Elsewhere, the onomatopoeic
motivation may have been suggested by the context. Speaking of the
noises of the *rue Réaumur* ('la rumeur de la rue Réaumur'), Jules Romains
claims that the name itself sounds like a song of wheels and walls, like
the vibration of buildings and the tremor of concrete under the pave-
ment, and like the rumbling of underground trains.[4] It is a safe guess that
the starting-point of this fantasy was the chance similarity of the words
rumeur and *Réaumur*. It may also happen that what looks like genuine
onomatopoeia is ultimately derived from external associations: when

[1] 'It is impossible to find a sequence of more picturesque sounds in order to render the
noise of the coffin rolling from step to step on the sharp corners of the stones, and suddenly
coming to a halt in the midst of the tombs' (quoted by K. Nyrop, *Grammaire historique de la
langue française. IV: Sémantique*, Copenhagen, etc., 1913, p. 7).
[2] '*Fafiot!* Can you not hear the rustle of tissue paper?' (*Splendeurs et misères des courtisanes*,
ed. M. Lévy, p. 401).
[3] 'Is there not a kind of fantastic rectitude in the word VRAI? Is there not, in the brief sound
which it requires, a vague image of the chaste nakedness, of the simplicity of truth in all
things? This syllable breathes an undefinable freshness. I have chosen as an example the
expression of an abstract idea since I did not want to explain the problem by a term which
would make it too easy to understand, such as the word VOL where everything speaks to the
senses' (*Louis Lambert*, p. 4).
[4] 'La rumeur de la rue Réaumur. Son nom même qui ressemble à un chant de roues et
de murailles, à une trépidation d'immeubles, à la vibration du béton sous l'asphalte, au
bourdonnement des convois souterrains' (*Les Amours enfantines*, Paris, Flammarion, p. 302).

Proust described the name *Coutances* as a 'cathédrale normande, que sa diphtongue finale, grasse et jaunissante, couronne par une tour de beurre',[1] there can be little doubt that he was thinking of the butter trade for which that town is famous.

Certain hypersensitive writers seem also to perceive some kind of correspondence between the meaning of a word and its written form. Leconte de Lisle felt that if French *paon* 'peacock' were spelt without an *o* it would not help him to picture the bird with its tail spread out.[2] Among modern poets, Paul Claudel was particularly impressed by the ideographic scripts of the Far East and tried to look on French words in the same way. He thought he could see the two gables of a house in the term *toit* 'roof', and a funnel and wheels in *locomotive*.[3] More elaborately, he suggested that the central theme of Rembrandt's picture 'The Philosopher' was summed up by the three letters of French *SOI* 'self': the *S* indicates a staircase, the *O* a mirror, and the *I* a burning candle.[4]

Some writers are adept at reviving the etymological motivation of words by bringing them back to their origins, whether spurious or real. Shakespeare, for example, was under the impression that the adjective *sand-blind* 'half-blind, dim-sighted, purblind' was connected with *sand*, and reinforced the 'image' by placing it in a suitable combination: 'more than *sand-blind*, high-gravel blind' (*Merchant of Venice*, Act II, scene 2).[5] More discreetly, T. S. Eliot restores the full etymological force of the word *revision* by contrasting it with *vision*:

> And time yet for a hundred indecisions,
> And for a hundred visions and *revisions*.
> *The Love Song of J. Alfred Prufrock*[6]

Similarly, the verb *to express* regains its concrete significance in Emily Dickinson's phrase: 'the attar from the rose Is not *expressed* by suns alone'.

Modern French writers are particularly fond of such 're-motivations'. Valéry, for example, reforges the link between *scrupulus* 'pebble' and *scrupule* 'scruple', when he speaks of *le ruisseau scrupuleux* 'the "scru-

---

[1] 'A Norman cathedral which its fat and yellowing final diphthong [*sic*] crowns with a tower of butter' (*Du Côté de chez Swann*, Paris, 1954 ed., vol. II, p. 222). Cf. J. Pommier, *La Mystique de Marcel Proust*, Paris, 1939, p. 50.

[2] J. Orr, *Words and Sounds in English and French*, p. 27.

[3] Ch. Bally, *Linguistique générale et linguistique française*, 3rd ed., Berne, 1950, p. 133, n. 1.

[4] M.–F. Guyard, 'Claudel et l'étymologie', *Cahiers de l'Association Internationale des Etudes Françaises*, xi (1959), pp. 286–300: p. 297.

[5] *Sand-blind*, now archaic and dialectal, is 'probably a perversion of Old English *samblind*, from *sam-* "half" + *blind*, after *sand*' (*Shorter OED*).

[6] This and the next example are quoted after M. Schlauch, *The Gift of Tongues* (subsequently renamed *The Gift of Language*), London, 1943, pp. 247 f.

pulous" brook'. He also reconnects *contemplate* with *temple* and *consider* with Latin *sidus, sidera* 'star' when he writes: 'En insistant un peu sur les étymologies, on pourrait dire avec une sorte de précision, que le croyant *contemple* le ciel, tandis que le savant le *considère*.'[1] In one of Gide's later novels there is an interesting disquisition on the double meaning of the verb *réfléchir* 'to reflect':

'Toute vraie pensée n'est qu'une *réflexion*, un *reflet*. *Réfléchir*, comme le mot l'indique, c'est *refléter* Dieu ... L'homme qui croit penser par lui-même et qui détourne de Dieu son cerveau-miroir cesse à proprement parler de *réfléchir*. La pensée la plus belle est celle où Dieu, comme dans un miroir, peut proprement se reconnaître.'[2]

The same idea is expressed more tersely by Claudel: '*Réflexion*. Un mot qui nous met soudain à l'arrêt. On dit d'un miroir qu'il *réfléchit* et on dit aussi d'un penseur qu'il *réfléchit*.'[3]

Claudel's life-long interest in etymology is well known. One or two further examples of what has been called his 'etymologitis'[4] may be quoted here:

'Le mot *église* veut dire *assemblement*, le lieu en qui tous les chrétiens réunis se trouvent Assimilés dans l'unité d'un même corps mystique';
' "*Intelligere*", "inlire". "Lire", s'assimiler et le réunir par la prise.'[5]

Nor does he hesitate to invent fanciful motivations which have nothing to do with etymology but which happen to fit his ideas: '*Naître* (avec l'initiale négative), c'est-à-dire être ce qui n'est pas.'[6] His most famous trouvaille of this kind, the reinterpretation of *connaissance* 'knowledge' as *co-naissance* 'being born together', is enshrined in the title of his treatise, 'De la Co-Naissance au Monde et de Soi-même'.

[1] 'By dwelling a little on etymologies one might say, with a kind of precision, that the believer *contemplates* the sky whereas the scientist *considers* it.' This and the preceding example are quoted after M. Wandruszka, 'Etymologie und Philosophie', *Etymologica*, pp. 857–71: p. 865.

[2] 'A true thought is no more than a *reflection*, a *reflex*. To *reflect*, as the word indicates, means *reflecting* God ... A man who believes that he is thinking on his own, and who averts from God the mirror of his brain, ceases to *reflect* in the proper sense of the term. The finest thought is that in which God can actually see Himself as in a mirror' (*Robert*, Paris, 1938 ed., p. 201).

[3] '*Reflection*. A word which suddenly makes you halt. One says of a mirror that it *reflects*, and one also says of a thinker that he *reflects*' (quoted by Guyard, loc. cit., p. 297).

[4] Ibid., p. 296.

[5] 'The word *église* ("church") means "assembly", the place where all Christians, gathered together, are assimilated within the union of a single mystical body';
'*Intelligere*, "to read in". "To read", to assimilate and integrate by one's grasp' (ibid., pp. 288 f.).

[6] '*Naître* ("to be born"), with a negative initial, i.e. to be what does not exist' — a pun on *naître* and *n'être*: *être* 'to be', preceded by the negative particle *n'* (ibid., p. 290). On *connaissance – co-naissance*, see ibid., pp. 288 f.

Examples such as these may warn us against the dangers of this method of 'etymological reduction', as it has been called.[1] Before etymology became a science in the strict sense of the term, it was widely believed that one could find the 'real' or 'proper' meaning of a word by tracing it back to its origins. The term *etymology* itself is derived from the Greek τὸ ἔτυμον 'truth'. In a more sophisticated form, the same idea seems to underlie the etymological lucubrations of writers like Claudel and even those of some professional philosophers. Etymologizing is an important element in the philosophy of Martin Heidegger for whom *Zeichen* 'sign' is connected with *zeigen* 'to show', *hell* 'clear' with *hallen* 'to resound', and who goes so far as to analyse *Entschlossenheit* 'resoluteness' as 'openness, opening up', since it is made up of the privative prefix *ent-* and a derivative of the verb *schliessen* 'to close'. What is disturbing in this procedure is that serious philosophical arguments seem to be suggested by etymological associations; as a recent critic of Heidegger pertinently remarks, 'wide stretches in the development of his ideas are determined by the *figura etymologica* (or *pseudo-etymologica*) whose verbal magic becomes the more inescapable the more persistently it is employed'.[2]

Etymological reduction may also be applied more cynically, as an instrument of political casuistry. In Albert Camus's play, *L'Etat de siège*, the Plague, the symbol of Nazi dictatorship, delights in re-establishing the connexion between *s'exécuter* 'to submit, to comply, to oblige', and the more sinister meaning of the verb:

'L'essentiel n'est pas qu'ils comprennent, mais qu'ils *s'exécutent*. Tiens! C'est une expression qui a du sens, ne trouvez-vous pas? ... Magnifique! On y trouve tout! L'image de l'*exécution* d'abord qui est une image attendrissante et puis l'idée que l'*exécuté* collabore lui-même à son *exécution*, ce qui est le but et la consolidation de tout bon gouvernement!'

And the Plague goes on to apply the same verbal trick to other seemingly harmless words: *to concentrate* suggests, by innuendo, a concentration camp, whereas *to occupy* evokes the idea of foreign occupation:

'Je les ai *concentrés*. Jusqu'ici ils vivaient dans la dispersion et la frivolité, un peu délayés pour ainsi dire! Maintenant ils sont plus fermes,

---

[1] Wandruszka, loc. cit., p. 865.
[2] Ibid., p. 864. All the examples from Heidegger are taken from this article. On Heidegger's excursions into linguistics, see also A. W. H. Adkins, 'Heidegger and Language', *Philosophy*, xxxvii (1962), pp. 229–37.

ils se *concentrent!* ... Ils *s'exécutent,* ils *s'occupent,* ils *se concentrent.* La grammaire est une bonne chose et qui peut servir à tout!'[1]

The examples quoted in this section, which could easily be multiplied, show that etymology is no longer a purely philological occupation; it has become, for ill or well, an important weapon in the armoury of modern writers. It is in France in particular that linguistic sophistication has gone to considerable lengths. This tradition goes back to the Romantic Movement. Some of the etymologies hazarded by Hugo or Balzac in their novels may seem naive to the modern reader,[2] but they are symptomatic of a profound and abiding interest which was bound to colour their whole attitude to language. Théophile Gautier had some fifty dictionaries on his shelves,[3] and Baudelaire has given the following account of his first meeting with the older poet:

'Il (Gautier) me demanda ensuite, avec un œil curieusement méfiant et comme pour m'éprouver, si j'aimais à lire les dictionnaires. Il me dit cela d'ailleurs comme il dit toute chose, fort tranquillement et du ton qu'un autre aurait pris pour s'informer si je préférais la lecture des voyages à celle des romans. Par bonheur, j'avais été pris très jeune de lexicomanie, et je vis que ma réponse me gagnait de l'estime.'[4]

Towards the end of the nineteenth century, the writers' interest in etymologies received a powerful impetus from the publication of Littré's monumental *Dictionnaire de la langue française*. It was in this climate that Mallarmé wrote his curious treatise, *Les Mots anglais*, a mixture of solid philological erudition and of wild speculations on the onomatopoeic significance of English sounds. Valéry's and Claudel's excursions into etymology, some specimens of which have been quoted above, are

1 'The main thing is not that they should understand, but that they should *comply* (*s'exécutent*). Indeed! This is an expression which makes sense, don't you think? ... Splendid! You find everything in it! First of all the image of an *execution*, which is a touching image, and then the idea that the *executed* person co-operates himself in his own *execution*, which is the purpose and consolidation of any good government! ... I have *concentrated* them. Until now they had been living scattered and frivolously, a little diluted, so to speak! Now they are more solid, they *concentrate*! ... They *comply*, they are *occupied*, they *concentrate*. Grammar is a good thing and can serve any purpose!' (Paris, 1948, pp. 117 f. and 121).

2 See some examples in F. Brunot, *Histoire de la langue française*, vol. XII (by Ch. Bruneau), Paris, 1948, pp. 217 and 377.

3 G. Matoré, *Le Vocabulaire et la société sous Louis-Philippe*, p. 157, n. 3.

4 'He (Gautier) then asked me, with a curiously suspicious look, and as if he wanted to test me, whether I liked to read dictionaries. He said it as he says everything, very quietly and in a tone in which someone else would enquire whether I preferred to read travel stories or novels. Fortunately I had been smitten with "lexicomania" since my early youth, and I saw that my answer raised me in his estimation' (quoted ibid., p. 157, from Baudelaire's *L'Art romantique*).

part of the same tradition; so are the long dissertations on word-origins in Proust and, in a different key, the same writer's theories about the magic of proper names, the famous 1.22 train to Balbec, 'magnifiquement surchargé de noms'.[1] Even in such a recent product of the 'anti-roman' movement as Michel Butor's *L'Emploi du temps* (1957), the etymological tradition is still alive: the real protagonist of the novel, Bleston, a large industrial town in the North of England, is given a symbolic etymology: *Bellista, Bella Civitas*.[2] It is also interesting to note that in one of his best-known plays, *La Leçon*, Eugène Ionesco has given a brilliant caricature of philological methods.

At the time when semantics appeared on the scene, etymologists hoped that the new discipline would discover precise laws which would provide them with infallible criteria for their reconstructions. These extravagant hopes have not been fulfilled; nevertheless, semantics has been able to help lexical studies in various ways. It has broadened the traditional field of etymological research by adding to it a new dimension, that of 'static' etymology, and by emphasizing that one cannot write the history of a word without paying attention to its relations with other terms and to its place in the general structure of the vocabulary. It has also deepened our understanding of certain fundamental problems of etymology by analysing the complex factors which govern the motivation of words. In this way, semantics has something to offer not only to the etymologist and the lexicographer, but even to the creative writer interested in the words he uses. When Bréal's book on semantics first appeared, it was, as we have seen (p. 3), enthusiastically reviewed by Paul Valéry. Since then, semantics has made little direct impact on writers, no doubt because it has become a highly specialized academic study, with a technical vocabulary of its own. One may hope, however, that the connexion will one day be re-established, since some familiarity with semantics is bound to have a stimulating effect on writers and to help them in the ambitious task envisaged by Mallarmé: 'Donner un sens plus pur aux mots de la tribu.'[3]

[1] *Du Côté de chez Swann*, vol. II, pp. 243 ff. On Proust's theory of proper names, see J. Vendryes, 'Marcel Proust et les noms propres', *Choix d'études linguistiques et celtiques*, Paris, 1953, pp. 80–8.
[2] L. Spitzer, 'Quelques aspects de la technique des romans de Michel Butor', *Archivum Linguisticum*, xiii (1961), pp. 171–95: p. 180.
[3] 'Give a purer sense to the words of the tribe' (*Le Tombeau d'Edgar Poe*).

CHAPTER IV

DESCRIPTIVE AND HISTORICAL METHODS IN SEMANTICS

THE development of modern linguistics, considered in its broad outlines, seems to fall into three distinct phases which correspond in some ways to the three movements of Hegelian dialectics: thesis, antithesis and synthesis. Until the end of the eighteenth century, linguistic studies had a predominantly descriptive orientation, though description was often vitiated by value-judgments and by the intrusion of normative criteria. In the nineteenth century, there was a vigorous reaction against this attitude: description was replaced by history, and the latter reigned supreme in linguistics right down to the beginning of the present century. Finally, the teaching of Ferdinand de Saussure ushered in the third phase which was to bring about a synthesis of the two approaches. But, by a curious paradox, this synthesis itself assumed the form of a violent antithesis: instead of simply distinguishing between 'synchronic' and 'diachronic' methods,[1] Saussure opposed them to one another and categorically denied any possibility of combining them. When one re-reads the famous first part of the *Cours de linguistique générale,* one cannot help being struck by the intransigent terms in which Saussure formulates the difference between the two viewpoints:

'La multiplicité des signes . . . nous *interdit absolument* d'étudier simultanément les rapports dans le temps et les rapports dans le système';
'Le linguiste qui veut comprendre un état de langue doit *faire table rase* de tout ce qui l'a produit et ignorer la diachronie';
'Vouloir réunir dans la même discipline des faits aussi disparates serait une *entreprise chimérique.*'[2]

In order to bring out the full implications of the contrast, Saussure devised a system of co-ordinates: '1° *l'axe des simultanéités* (AB), concernant les rapports entre choses coexistantes, d'où toute intervention

---

[1] Cf. above, p. 4.
[2] 'The multiplicity of signs *strictly forbids us* to study simultaneously relations in time and relations within the system'; 'The linguist who wishes to understand a given state of the language must *make a clean sweep* of all that has produced that state and disregard the diachronic background'; 'Any attempt to combine such disparate facts within one discipline would be a *chimerical enterprise*' (op. cit., pp. 116 f. and 122; my italics).

50

du temps est exclue, et 2° *l'axe des successivités* (CD), sur lequel on ne peut jamais considérer qu'une chose à la fois, mais où sont situées toutes les choses du premier axe avec leurs changements':[1]

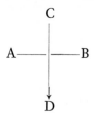

Commenting on this scheme, one of the earliest critics of the *Cours de linguistique générale*, Hugo Schuchardt, wittily remarked that Saussure had tried to 'divide the theory of co-ordinates into a theory of the ordinate and a theory of the abscissa'.[2] In subsequent years, there were many searching discussions on the problem, and Saussure's ban on any combination of descriptive and historical methods was gradually relaxed.[3] Instead of reopening the whole argument I should like, in this chapter, to confine myself to a specific question: how far is the Saussurean principle applicable to semantics, a science which was still in its infancy at the time when the doctrine took shape? As we have seen, the pioneers of modern semantics conceived the latter as a purely historical study. During the last thirty years, however, there has been a remarkable change of perspective: a new, purely descriptive semantics, based on structural methods, has begun to emerge,[4] and its appearance on the scene raises the whole problem of relations between description and history in this part of linguistics. It will be conducive to clarity to distinguish between two types of semantic phenomena: those which require a strict separation of the two approaches, and those which can be tackled only by a judicious combination of descriptive and historical data.

I

There are a number of important semantic problems where the two perspectives have to be kept carefully apart since they yield contradictory

---

[1] '(1) The *axis of simultaneity* (AB), which concerns relations between coexistent things and from which all consideration of time is excluded, and (2) the *axis of succession* (CD), on which one thing only can be considered at a time, but on which are located all the elements of the first axis together with their changes' (ibid., p. 115).

[2] *Hugo Schuchardt-Brevier. Ein Vademecum der allgemeinen Sprachwissenschaft*, ed. L. Spitzer, 2nd ed., Halle a. S., 1928, p. 330.

[3] See esp. W. v. Wartburg, *Problèmes et méthodes de la linguistique*, ch. III, and E. Coseriu, *Sincronía, diacronía e historia. El problema del cambio lingüístico*, Montevideo, 1958.

[4] See above, ch. I.

and irreconcilable results. Best known among these is *popular etymology* which was discussed in the last chapter. Here it is of the utmost importance to bear in mind Saussure's dictum: 'La première chose qui frappe quand on étudie les faits de langue, c'est que pour le sujet parlant leur succession dans le temps est inexistante.'[1] For an ordinary English speaker, *crayfish* is a compound of *cray* and *fish*, whereas the etymologist knows that it comes from Old French *crevice* (Modern French *écrevisse*), and ultimately from the same root as *crab* (*NED*). Similarly, a Frenchman will analyse *choucroute* as *chou* 'cabbage' + *croûte* 'crust', although it is actually derived from *sûrkrût*, the Alsatian form of German *Sauerkraut* (Bloch-Wartburg). In a different sphere, it would be difficult to convince a German that the first syllable of his word for the Flood, *Sündflut*, is not identical with *Sünde* 'sin'; yet the original form of this compound was *sint-vluot* 'universal flood'. The process is too well known to require further illustrations.

Another field where historical and descriptive data have to be scrupulously separated is the problem of *motivation*. Whether the motivation of a word is based on phonetic, morphological or semantic factors, it is, as we have seen,[2] a purely synchronic fact which has nothing to do with historical antecedents. There are even cases where one and the same term exists in the modern language in two forms, one transparent, the other opaque: *housewife* and *hussy* are etymologically the same word, yet the former is motivated and the latter is not. It is interesting to note that Saussure himself, in his anxiety to minimize the importance of onomatopoeia in language, was for once guilty of mixing up the two approaches whose separation he advocated so vigorously. 'Des mots comme *fouet* ou *glas*', he wrote, 'peuvent frapper certaines oreilles par une sonorité suggestive; mais pour voir qu'ils n'ont pas ce caractère dès l'origine, il suffit de remonter à leurs formes latines (*fouet* dérive de *fāgus* "hêtre", *glas* = *classicum*); la qualité de leurs sons actuels, ou plutôt celle qu'on leur attribue, est un résultat fortuit de l'évolution phonétique'.[3] Whether *fouet* 'whip' and *glas* 'knell' are in fact onomatopoeic is perhaps debatable; what is perfectly clear is that their motivation, if it actually exists, is entirely independent of their origin and development.

---

[1] 'The first thing which strikes one when one studies linguistic phenomena is that their succession in time is non-existent for the ordinary speaker' (op. cit., p. 117).

[2] See above, pp. 42 f.

[3] 'Words like *fouet* "whip" or *glas* "knell" may strike some ears by their suggestive sonority; but it is sufficient to go back to their Latin forms (*fouet* comes from *fāgus* "beech", *glas* from *classicum*) to see that they did not originally possess such a quality; the character of their present sounds, or rather the character which is attributed to them, is an accidental result of phonetic development' (op. cit., p. 102).

The same is true of the converse process: the fact that Vulgar Latin *pīpiō, pīpiōnem*, which has given *pigeon* in French and English, has lost its onomatopoeic quality has nothing to do with the expressive force of the word at any particular moment in its history.

It may even happen that a word changes its motivation without actually losing it. The Latin *murmur* was unmistakably onomatopoeic, and so are its modern descendants, French *murmure* and English *murmur*, but they evoke different noises: the French word, with its |y| vowels, suggests lighter and softer sounds than the Latin prototype whose vowel-scheme is expressive of roaring, growling, rumbling, etc.; and the English *murmur*, with its muffled |ə| sounds, has again different overtones. Apart from the vowels, the differences in the pronunciation of the |r| have also affected the onomatopoeic value of the word in the three languages.[1]

A third field where it is imperative to separate description from history is that of *emotive and evocative effects*. These subtle harmonics are even more changeable and evanescent than motivation, and it is often difficult to recapture them without being influenced by our modern reactions. To give but one example of this delicate mechanism of stylistic reconstruction,[2] the French verb *blaguer* 'to joke, to chaff, to banter' is today a harmless colloquialism; yet, just over a century ago, it must have had explosive potentialities; witness the following conversation in one of Balzac's novels where a courtesan reformed by love suddenly relapses into her former way of life and the language that goes with it:

'—J'aurais voulu que Lucien me vît ainsi, dit-elle en laissant échapper un soupir étouffé.—Maintenant, reprit-elle d'une voix vibrante, *blaguons*...

En entendant ce mot, Europe resta tout hébétée, comme elle eût pu l'être en entendant blasphémer un ange.

—Eh bien, qu'as-tu donc à regarder si j'ai dans la bouche des clous de girofle au lieu de dents? Je ne suis plus maintenant qu'une infâme créature, une fille, une *voleuse*, et j'attends milord.'[3]

---

[1] See my *Semantics*, pp. 95 f.

[2] This problem will be more fully discussed in ch. VIII.

[3] 'I should have liked Lucien to see me like this', she said, giving vent to a stifled sigh. 'And now', she went on, in a voice quivering with emotion, 'let's have a crack (*blaguons*)...'
On hearing this word, Europe (the chambermaid) gaped at her as if she had heard an angel blaspheme.
'Well, why are you looking at me as if I had clove in my mouth instead of teeth? All I am now is a vile creature, a tart, a *guttersnipe*, and I am waiting for a money-bags' (*Splendeurs et misères des courtisanes*, p. 186). On the exact value of *blaguer, voleuse* and *milord*, see R. Dagneaud, *Les Éléments populaires dans le lexique de la Comédie Humaine d'Honoré de Balzac*, Quimper, 1954, pp. 81, 86, 98 f.

Without this commentary, the twentieth-century reader would hardly have noticed the intense expressive power of a word which sums up in a nutshell the metamorphosis of a human being.

It should, however, be noted that if most emotive and evocative effects are purely synchronic, there are others which derive their resonance from their past. If a modern writer uses words like *methinks, quoth, verily, whilom, yclad, yclept, yea,* etc., the evocative force of these forms resides precisely in the fact that they are *archaisms,* remnants of earlier stages in the history of the language. The effects they can produce when used in a modern context are manifold. Sometimes they are no more than a mildly humorous witticism: 'The sweet wood *yclept* sassafras' (Charles Lamb);[1] 'qui soulagerait *moult* le trésor public' (Petrus Borel).[2] Elsewhere, an archaism may call forth historical, literary or biblical associations, or may help to create an atmosphere of tradition and antiquity. Sometimes the words themselves need not be archaic; ordinary terms spelt in an old-fashioned way will have the same effect, as on sign-boards like 'Ye Olde Shoppe', or in these lines in T. S. Eliot's *East Coker:*

> The association of man and woman
> In daunsinge, signifying matrimonie—
> A dignified and commodious sacrament.
> Two and two, necessarye coniunction,
> Holding eche other by the hand or the arm,
> Whiche betokeneth concorde.

On a more ambitious scale, archaisms may serve to produce local colour, as in Victor Hugo's evocation of fifteenth-century France in *Notre-Dame de Paris,*[3] or to make a pastiche of the language of an earlier period, as Balzac did in his *Contes drôlatiques.*[4]

A further problem where descriptive and historical data must on no account be intermingled is the border-line between *polysemy* and *homonymy,* the question whether, in certain cases, we have to do with one word or with two. This problem was discussed at length in the last chapter (pp. 31 ff.). As we saw there, it is sometimes very difficult to determine the precise status of such words; but whatever criteria we use, they must be strictly synchronic: the history of the terms in question will throw

---

[1] See the *NED, s.v. yclept.*
[2] 'Which would *greatly* relieve the Treasury' (quoted after F. Brunot, *Histoire de la langue française,* vol. XII, p. 443 (by Ch. Bruneau)).
[3] Cf. my *Style in the French Novel,* pp. 64–73.
[4] Cf. J. Damourette, 'Archaïsmes et pastiches', *Le Français Moderne,* ix (1941), pp. 181–206.

no light on the present position and is in fact more likely to confuse the issue.

II

It is clear, then, that in some branches of semantics we shall have to observe the Saussurean distinction in its full rigour. There are, however, other problems which call for a systematic *combination* of descriptive and historical methods. We shall consider three fields in particular where such combination has proved fruitful. Firstly, certain synchronic conditions can be recognized only after the event, in the light of the diachronic consequences which flowed from them. Secondly, the background of certain semantic changes can be detected only by careful study of the state of the language before the change. Lastly, the combination of the two approaches can have a heuristic value by enabling the student to formulate problems which would otherwise have passed unnoticed.

1. We know since Gilliéron that anything making for instability in a linguistic system, for example conflicts between homonyms, may give rise to certain 'therapeutic' processes: modification or elimination of one of the terms involved, changes in the meaning of the word which is called upon to fill the gap. In a series of remarkable studies, Professor Wartburg has shown the complex interplay of synchronic and diachronic factors set in motion by such a conflict. What particularly interests us here is that these therapeutic processes, which are diachronic events, are more often than not the only *indication* we have of the fact that a homonymic clash had occurred, that, in a previous synchronic state, thousands of speakers had suffered from an awkward ambiguity which had compelled them in the end to abandon a word—sometimes an extremely common word—and to replace it by changing the meaning of another term. To take a concrete example, it is a well-known fact that in Medieval French, the verb for 'swimming', *nouer* (from Latin *natare*, Vulgar Latin **notare*), became homonymous with *nouer* 'to tie' (from Latin *nōdare*). But was this homonymy necessarily intolerable? Was it more serious than the modern homonymy of *louer* 'to praise' and *louer* 'to hire, to let'? Did the two *nouer*-s belong, in Gilliéron's famous formula, to 'the same paths of thought'? It would seem that they did, since *nouer* 'to swim' disappeared and was replaced by *nager* (from Latin *navigare*), which originally meant 'to sail'.[1] In the same way, how can we be sure that the

---

[1] See Wartburg, *Problèmes et méthodes de la linguistique*, pp. 163 ff. As Professor Orr has pointed out (*Words and Sounds in English and French*, p. 104), some of the forms of Old French *noer* 'swim' and *noyer* 'drown' (from Latin *necare*) were homonymous, and this may have been a contributory factor in the obsolescence of the former verb.

E

homonymy, in the south of France, of *claus* 'key' and *claus* 'nail' was felt to be a source of embarrassment? Was this ambiguity more awkward than, say, the double meaning of English *nail* or of German *Nagel* which has the same two senses as the English word? Once again it is the historical consequences of the clash, the disappearance of *claus* 'nail' and its replacement by a diminutive of the *clavellus* type, which show us *ex post facto* that the ambiguity must have been intolerable and must have called for remedial measures.[1]

The same reasoning can be applied to conflicts which arise between different senses of the same word. The French *se passer de* formerly had two contradictory meanings: 'to be content with' and 'to do without'; Molière still wrote in *Don Juan*: 'un homme qui *s'est passé*, durant sa vie, d'une assez simple demeure'.[2] The mere fact that a word has two diametrically opposite senses is by no means unusual: in Latin, the two meanings of *altus*, 'high' and 'deep', coexisted peacefully, and so do those of the French verbs *défendre*, 'to defend' and 'to forbid', and *chasser*, 'to hunt, to pursue' and 'to drive away'; as Nyrop wittily put it, 'on *chasse le gibier* pour s'en emparer; on *chasse un domestique* pour s'en débarrasser'.[3] How do we know, then, that the double meaning of *se passer de* gave rise to frequent and awkward misunderstandings? We know it once again from the diachronic consequences of this ambiguity, from the fact that one of the two senses, that of 'to be content with', gradually fell into disuse. In the same way, *dispenser* once meant both 'to allow to do something' and 'to allow not to do something'; eventually, only the latter sense survived.

Gilliéron was convinced that polysemy is a major cause of the obsolescence of words. 'La collision phonétique (homonymes) et sémantique (hypertrophie)', he wrote, 'a été dans les langues une éternelle menace, une éternelle cause de disparitions lexicales'.[4] It would seem, however, that in ordinary language it is seldom necessary to abandon an ambiguous word altogether; it is usually sufficient to eliminate one or more senses incompatible with the rest. A recent Swedish monograph, where the polysemy of 120 English adjectives is studied in detail, has found no

---

1 See Wartburg, *Problèmes et méthodes de la linguistique*, pp. 166 f.

2 'A man who, throughout his life, *was content* with a fairly simple dwelling' (*Don Juan*, Act III, scene 6, quoted by Nyrop, *Sémantique*, p. 47). On the semantic history of this verb, see J. Orr, 'Le français *s'en passer*', *Revue de Linguistique Romane*, XX (1956), pp. 21–40.

3 'One "*chases*" *game* in order to catch it; one "*chases*" *a servant* to get rid of him' (Nyrop, loc. cit.). On *dispenser*, see ibid.

4 'Phonetic and semantic collision (homonymy and hypertrophy of meaning) has been a perpetual menace in language, a perennial cause of the disappearance of words' (*Généalogie des mots qui désignent l'abeille*, Paris, 1918, p. 157).

more than three cases where a term has completely disappeared from the language because of conflicts between its various senses.[1]

2. A combination of descriptive and historical viewpoints may also enable us to discover the *ultimate causes* of certain semantic changes which look at first sight perfectly straightforward. Semanticists have known for a long time that Leibniz's axiom: 'Natura non facit saltus' ('Nature makes no leaps') is fully applicable to their discipline. All changes of meaning have their roots in some kind of association which may arise between the names or between the senses, and may be based either on similarity or on some other relation.[2] But while traditional semantics pictured these associations as binary relations between two isolated elements, modern research has replaced this 'atomistic' associationism by a more sophisticated structural concept: that of 'associative fields'. The nature of this concept and its importance for etymological studies have already been examined;[3] here we are concerned with its relevance to the problem under discussion: the separation or combination of descriptive and historical data. From this point of view, the associative field of a word, the network of sound and sense associations which surrounds it at a given moment in its history, is a synchronic entity which can be, and has been, studied by descriptive methods, both linguistic and psychological.[4] By the same token, the strains and stresses which exist in such a field, the ambiguities and conflicts in which its elements are involved, are also purely synchronic facts. But when these tensions cause one or more words to change their meaning, we pass from the synchronic to the diachronic plane, and the changes cannot be fully understood unless we are aware of their associative background.

The point will become clearer if we re-examine one of the examples discussed in the last chapter: the sense-change of French *viande*.[5] As we saw there, this word originally referred to food in general, but since the seventeenth century its range has been narrowed to its present meaning of 'meat'. To a semanticist of the older school, this change would have presented no problem at all; he would have dismissed it as a simple case of specialization, a restriction from genus to species, of which there are scores of examples in any language. This is, of course, true as far as it goes; but it is not the whole truth. The real explanation of this

[1] A. Rudskoger, *'Fair, Foul, Nice, Proper': a Contribution to the Study of Polysemy*, Stockholm, 1952, p. 439.
[2] See my *Semantics*, pp. 211 ff.
[3] See above, pp. 10 ff and 35 ff.
[4] Cf. above, p. 11.
[5] See above, pp. 39 f.

deceptively simple change lies in the fact that the associated term *chair* fell into disuse in the sense of 'meat', and this again was due to a homonymic clash between *chair* and *chère*. The close association between *viande* and *chair*, and the conflict between the latter and its homonym, are synchronic facts; their consequences, the changes in the meaning of *viande* and *chair*, are diachronic processes. There could be no clearer example of the interdependence of the two approaches.

3. Description and history may also be combined for '*heuristic*' purposes. If we succeed in transcending the Saussurean duality, we shall notice new and important problems which would otherwise have remained unformulated. This is the great significance, from the point of view of linguistic method, of the theory of '*lexical fields*', which was mentioned in the first chapter (pp. 12 ff.). Such fields, it will be remembered, are highly integrated conceptual spheres whose elements delimit each other and form part of a hierarchical organization. What matters from our point of view is that the theory advocates a combination of descriptive and historical viewpoints, and also that it is more interested in the fields themselves than in their components: it endeavours to follow the transformations of an entire conceptual sphere, of its basic principles, its inner structure and the hierarchy of values which it embodies, rather than tracing piecemeal the evolution of the various words which make up the field.

The chief architect of the field theory, Professor Trier, has given a brilliant demonstration of this technique. By comparing the structure of the sphere of knowledge in Middle High German around 1200, and the shape of the same field a hundred years later, in the mystical writings of Master Eckehart, he was able to identify some significant changes which point to an entirely different mentality, scale of values and social background. As already noted (p. 14) the hard core of the field around 1200 consisted of three key-terms: *wîsheit*, *kunst* and *list*. Relations between these three words were governed by two fundamental principles of medieval civilization: feudalism and a certain catholicity of outlook. The boundary between *kunst* and *list* ran on strictly feudal lines: the former was reserved for courtly and chivalric skills, the latter for non-chivalric accomplishments. *Wîsheit*, on the other hand, was a more comprehensive term: it could act as an alternative for the other two and could also denote wisdom in all its forms, mundane as well as divine.

A mere hundred years later, we find the same field mapped out on entirely different lines. There are still three key-terms, but they are not the same three. *List* has dropped out of the intellectual sphere, because of its pejorative connotations (it means 'cunning, craft, trick' in Modern

German); on the other hand, the substantivized infinitive *wiꝫꝫen* has joined *kunst* and *wîsheit* in the centre of the field. But it is not simply a question of one term replacing another; the whole organization and hierarchy is radically different. With the disintegration of feudal society, there is no longer any need to distinguish between chivalric and non-chivalric attainments; instead, we have the beginnings of a differentiation between *kunst* and *wiꝫꝫen*, which will eventually lead to the modern distinction between 'art' and 'knowledge'. Meanwhile, *wîsheit* has lost the universality which was characteristic of it in the earlier system, and is now reserved for religious and mystical experiences. The bare facts of the transformation, but not its deeper significance, may be summed up in the following two diagrams:[1]

As mentioned in the first chapter (pp. 14. f), some linguists believe that such a 'historico-structural' method may one day be applied to the total vocabulary of a language.

Experiments such as these may be open to criticism on certain points;[2] they show nevertheless that Saussure was too categorical when he opposed descriptive to historical linguistics as two totally disparate studies, the former dealing with systems, the latter with single elements. This opposition was axiomatic to Saussure's whole way of thinking; it is frequently reiterated in his book, underlies his theory of co-ordinates, the distinction between the 'axis of simultaneity' and the 'axis of succession' (see above, p. 51), and is embodied in two famous comparisons. In one of these, descriptive linguistics is likened to a cross-section of the

---

[1] This diagram is taken from P. Guiraud, *La Sémantique*, p. 72. For details see esp. J. Trier, 'Das sprachliche Feld. Eine Auseinandersetzung', *Neue Jahrbücher für Wissenschaft und Jugendbildung*, x (1934), pp. 428–49; cf. also Wartburg, *Problèmes et méthodes de la linguistique*, pp. 169 ff.

[2] For criticisms of the field theory, see recently U. Ricken, 'Onomasiologie oder Feldmethode?', *Beiträge ꝫur Romanischen Philologie*, i (1961), pp. 190–208; W. Rothwell, 'Medieval French and Modern Semantics', *Modern Language Review*, lvii (1962), pp. 25–30; N. C. W. Spence, 'Linguistic Fields, Conceptual Systems and the *Weltbild*', *Transactions of the Philological Society*, 1961, pp. 87–106; cf. also chs. II and VI of the volume *Voprosy Teorii Jaꝫyka*, referred to on p. 17, n. 2. For earlier criticisms see my *Semantics*, p. 249, n. 2.

stem of a plant, and historical linguistics to a longitudinal section: 'La section longitudinale nous montre les fibres elles-mêmes qui constituent la plante, et la section transversale leur groupement sur un plan particulier; mais la seconde est distincte de la première car elle fait constater entre les fibres certains rapports qu'on ne pourrait jamais saisir sur un plan longitudinal.'[1] The contrast is worked out in greater detail in another comparison which has already been mentioned (pp. 4 and 26): the parallel between language and a game of chess:

'Un état du jeu correspond bien à un état de la langue. La valeur respective des pièces dépend de leur position sur l'échiquier, de même que dans la langue chaque terme a sa valeur par son opposition avec tous les autres termes ... Pour passer d'un équilibre à l'autre, ou—selon notre terminologie—d'une synchronie à l'autre, le déplacement d'une pièce suffit; il n'y a pas de remue-ménage général ... Chaque coup d'échecs ne met en mouvement qu'une seule pièce; de même dans la langue les changements ne portent que sur des éléments isolés.'[2]

To this rigid conception, Trier and others have opposed a more flexible model, a structurally oriented history which is more concerned with the evolution of the linguistic system than with the fate of individual units. In this sense, Trier has spoken of a kind of 'comparative statics' where description and history are practised concurrently: 'an account leap-frogging from one cross-section to another, focusing again and again on *the field as a whole*, looking both backward and forward in time'. And Trier, fully aware of the difficult and delicate nature of this operation, wisely adds: 'It will depend on the density of cross-sections how close we can get to the actual drift of linguistic development.'[3]

III

Before drawing some tentative conclusions about the role of description and history in semantic research, there is one further question we shall have to consider: are these two methods the only two ways in which

---

[1] 'The longitudinal section shows us the fibres themselves which form the plant, whereas the cross-section shows their grouping at a particular level; but the latter differs from the former in that it reveals certain relations between the fibres, which could never have been discovered in a longitudinal section' (op. cit., p. 125).

[2] 'The state of the game at a given moment corresponds closely to a state of the language. The value of each piece depends on its position on the chess-board, just as in language each term derives its value from the fact that it is opposed to all other terms ... To pass from one equilibrium to another, or—in our terminology—from one synchronic state to another, it is sufficient to move one piece; there is no general reshuffle ... Each move in chess concerns one piece only; in the same way, changes in language are confined to isolated elements' (ibid., pp. 125 f.).

[3] *Der deutsche Wortschatz im Sinnbezirk des Verstandes*, p. 13.

problems of meaning can be attacked by the linguist, or is there such a thing as a 'universal' or *'panchronic'* semantics? Though it was Saussure himself who introduced the term 'panchronic' into linguistics, he was sceptical about the ultimate value of such an approach (op. cit., pp. 134 f.). In semantics in particular, he was unimpressed by the search for general 'laws'; every change of meaning, he argued, 'is due to special causes' and is 'no more than one accident among all those recorded in the history of a language' (ibid., p. 132). Modern semantics has abandoned the mirage of universally valid laws; at the same time many linguists believe that there are in this field some widespread tendencies whose probability may in certain cases be statistically calculated. The whole problem will be examined in the next chapter.

Even if 'panchronic' semantics were one day to become a reality, would it necessarily do away with the distinction between descriptive and historical data? It seems far more likely that the dichotomy would be applicable even on the panchronic plane. According to the terminology put forward by Professor Sommerfelt a quarter of a century ago, we would have to distinguish between 'pan-synchronic' and 'pan-diachronic' tendencies;[1] the former would include certain general features of semantic structure, for example the relation between polysemy and word-frequency; the latter would comprise certain widely prevalent forms of semantic change, such as anthropomorphic metaphors or transfers from concrete to abstract. Rather than superseding the old duality, panchronic semantics would actually confirm its usefulness by extending it to an entirely new range of problems.

What, then, is the position of the Saussurean doctrine in the present phase of semantic studies? To answer this question, one will have to distinguish between various aspects of the doctrine. In its original form, the theory contained three elements: a distinction, an antinomy, and a methodological principle. Of the three, the *distinction* remains valid, in semantics as elsewhere; as we have just seen, it is even applicable at the panchronic level. As Professor Coseriu pertinently points out, 'language works synchronically and constitutes itself diachronically', and this is bound to be reflected in the organization of linguistic studies.[2]

As regards the *antinomy*, the alleged disparity of the two methods one of which deals with systems and the other with single elements, recent progress in semantics, especially in the study of lexical fields, has clearly

---

[1] A. Sommerfelt, 'Points de vue diachronique, synchronique et panchronique en linguistique générale', *Norsk Tidsskrift for Sprogvidenskap*, ix (1938), pp. 240–9.

[2] *Sincronía, diacronía e historia*, pp. 154 f.

proved that this part of the theory is untenable. Side by side with structural description, there exists also a structural approach to history, in semantics as in other branches of linguistics. These conclusions are closely parallel to those at which Professor Martinet and others have arrived in the sphere of historical phonology.[1]

Finally, the position of the Saussurean doctrine as a *methodological principle* is somewhat paradoxical: we have seen that certain problems of meaning require a strict separation of description and history whereas others can be tackled only if the two approaches are combined. In any case, combination does not mean confusion; even if the two methods are applied concurrently, one must never forget the fundamental duality. Looked at in this way, the Saussurean theory, with the modifications brought about by the passage of time, remains a valuable tool of research in semantics and in linguistics at large, and the fact that it continues to be widely discussed, and even appeared on the agenda of a recent international congress,[2] is striking proof of its vitality.

[1] See esp. A. Martinet, *Economie des changements phonétiques*, Berne, 1955; cf. by the same author, *Eléments de linguistique générale*, Paris, 1960, ch. VI, and *A Functional View of Language*, Oxford, 1962, ch. V. I have discussed these and similar experiments in the chapter 'Phonétique et phonologie' of the second edition of W. v. Wartburg's *Problèmes et méthodes de la linguistique*, pp. 48–61.

[2] The Tenth International Congress of Romance Linguistics, held in Strasbourg in April 1962, at which the original version of this paper was read.

CHAPTER V

SEMANTIC UNIVERSALS

THE quest for universals has played a vital part in the development of semantic studies. The pioneers of modern semantics saw the discovery of general 'laws' as one of the main objectives of the new science. As far back as the 1820s, C. Chr. Reisig had suggested, as we have already seen,[1] that 'semasiology' should investigate 'the principles governing the evolution of meaning'. Half a century later, Michel Bréal was even more categorical. In his article of 1883, in which he launched the term 'semantics', he mentioned among the tasks of the new discipline the study of the 'laws which preside over the transformation of meanings'.[2] Subsequently he showed in his *Essai de sémantique* how this aim could be achieved, and his example was followed by other linguists who put forward a number of 'laws' underlying various types of semantic change. There were some dissentient voices; at the beginning of the present century, a leading French etymologist went so far as to declare: 'There are no laws in semantics, and it is difficult to imagine that there could ever be any.'[3] Yet the quest continued unabated; it was accepted as axiomatic that, as one linguist put it, 'there are universal laws of thought which are reflected in the laws of change of meaning . . . , even if the Science of Meaning . . . has not yet made much advance towards discovering them'.[4] Even today there are some scholars who hold similar views; only a few years ago, a Russian linguist criticized contemporary semantics for having turned away from its principal task: the study of specific laws of linguistic development.[5] Since the early 'thirties, however, there has been a significant shift of emphasis in semantics, as in other branches of linguistics: descriptive and structural problems are at present in the forefront of research, and the traditional study of changes of meaning, though by no means abandoned, has been relegated to the background. This shift of emphasis, the implications of which were discussed in the first chapter, has had an important effect on the search for semantic universals. There

---

[1] See above, p. 30.
[2] See the article referred to in ch. I, n. 1.
[3] A. Thomas, *Nouveaux Essais de philologie française*, Paris, 1904, p. 28.
[4] O. Jespersen, *Mankind, Nation and Individual from a Linguistic Point of View*, Oslo, etc., 1925, p. 212.
[5] V. A. Zvegintsev, *Semasiologija*, Moscow, 1957, p. 46.

is little interest at present in the orthodox type of semantic 'law'; instead, attention is being increasingly focused on synchronic features of general validity, and also on the principles which determine the structure of the vocabulary.

If one surveys the various semantic 'laws' and other universals which have been either implicitly assumed or explicitly formulated in the past, one finds that they have one thing in common: nearly all of them are based on insufficient evidence. Only too often far-reaching conclusions have been drawn from inadequate data collected from a limited number of languages. The alleged universals obtained in this way are in many cases quite plausible, but plausibility is no proof unless the proposition is so self-evident that it becomes truistic and trivial. Besides, by the very nature of things, most semantic universals are no more than statistical probabilities, and the likelihood of their occurring in a given language could be determined only if we possessed far more extensive and representative data than we have at present. What Leonard Bloomfield wrote about general grammar is entirely applicable to semantics and deserves to be quoted in full:

'The only useful generalizations about language are inductive generalizations. Features which we think ought to be universal may be absent from the very next language that becomes accessible ... The fact that some features are, at any rate, widespread is worthy of notice and calls for an explanation; when we have adequate data about many languages, we shall have to return to the problem of general grammar and explain these similarities and divergences, but this study, when it comes, will be not speculative but inductive.'[1]

Since there has been of late a revival of interest in linguistic universals,[2] I shall try to indicate briefly certain semantic features and processes which might repay investigation on an interlinguistic scale. First, however, it will be necessary to define more closely the terms 'semantic' and 'universal'. Throughout this chapter, as elsewhere in this book, 'semantic' will be used solely with reference to *word-meaning*. It has been customary

[1] *Language*, p. 20.
[2] A conference on 'Language Universals', sponsored by the American Social Science Research Council, was held in Dobbs Ferry, New York, in April 1961. The present chapter is based on a paper submitted to that conference and printed in its proceedings (*Universals of Language*, ed. J. H. Greenberg, Massachusetts Institute of Technology, 1963, pp. 172–207); it has benefited by suggestions and criticisms by the following colleagues, to whom I wish to express my gratitude: Professors Harold C. Conklin, Charles F. Hockett, Fred W. Householder and Dell H. Hymes. See also in the same volume an interesting paper on the same subject, but with a different orientation, by Professor Uriel Weinreich (pp. 117–71).

since Aristotle to regard the word as the smallest significant unit of speech.[1] We now know that this is not so: the 'smallest individually meaningful element in the utterances of a language' is the 'morpheme', not the word.[2] The word itself is defined, in Bloomfield's classic formula, as a 'minimum free form'[3] which may consist of one or more morphemes. It follows that semantic problems will arise not only at the word level but also below and above it: below it at the level of 'bound' morphemes (suffixes, prefixes, non-independent roots, etc.), and above it at the level of phrases and the higher combinations into which they enter. No problems of meaning below or above the word level will be considered here; nor shall I deal with the semantics of so-called 'form-words'—pronouns, articles, prepositions, conjunctions, etc.—which, though they behave like words in some respects, have a purely grammatical function and do not therefore belong to the lexical system of a language.[4]

It should also be noted that the word itself is not a linguistic universal in the absolute sense. In the so-called 'polysynthetic' languages, where a whole series of 'bound' forms is combined into a single term, the word will obviously have a structure and status entirely different from, say, English or Chinese, and many of the tendencies discussed below are therefore inapplicable to such languages.

As regards the meaning and implications of the term 'universal', some flexibility will be needed when applying it to semantic phenomena which are often fluid, imprecise and subjective. From the point of view of their validity, the features and processes discussed in this chapter will fall into three broad categories:

1. Some of them may turn out to be *'unrestricted universals'*;[5] even these, however, would be 'unrestricted' only in the sense that they occurred in all the languages examined in a large-scale research programme; we could, of course, never prove conclusively that they are omnipresent—or 'panchronic', in Saussure's terminology[6]—, that they exist in every language at any stage in its development.

[1] See R. H. Robins, *Ancient and Mediaeval Grammatical Theory in Europe*, pp. 20 f.

[2] Hockett, op. cit., p. 123. For a recent critique of this conception, see C. E. Bazell, 'Meaning and the Morpheme', *Word*, xviii (1962), pp. 132–42. Cf. also W. A. Coates in the *Preprints* of the Ninth International Congress of Linguists, pp. 413–8.

[3] *Language*, p. 178. It should be noted that, in Bloomfield's terminology, 'free forms' are forms which occur as sentences; forms which are not used that way are 'bound forms'. On the whole problem, see recently F. Hiorth, 'On Defining "Word"', *Studia Linguistica*, xii (1958), pp. 1–26 and other works listed in my *Semantics*, p. 27, n. 3.

[4] On 'form-words' see ibid., pp. 43–8.

[5] The nomenclature here used is based on the 'Memorandum Concerning Language Universals' submitted by Professors Joseph H. Greenberg, Charles E. Osgood and James J. Jenkins to the conference referred to above, p. 64, n. 2.

[6] See above, p. 61.

2. Most semantic universals are likely to be of the *statistical* variety: they will not be necessarily present in any given language, but one may to some extent predict the probability of their occurrence. It should be noted that certain semantic phenomena are not precise enough to be amenable to rigorously statistical analysis, so that no more than a rough estimate of probabilities can be expected.

3. There is yet another category which has some affinities with universals but is far more restricted in scope: *parallel developments* which occur in a number of different languages but are unknown elsewhere. Many types of metaphor and other forms of semantic change fall within this category: they are too widespread to be due to mere chance, but not widespread enough to be statistically significant. It is, of course, always possible that such a tendency will turn out to be a statistical universal, and will thus pass into the previous category, if the scope of the inquiry is sufficiently widened.

In addition to these general tendencies, attention will also have to be paid to '*typological*' criteria which may enable us to classify languages on semantic grounds.[1] As will be seen, such criteria have close connexions with the problem of universals. Very little work has been done so far on semantic typology;[2] nevertheless, one or two criteria have already been identified, and these will be discussed in the appropriate sections.

In semantics, as in other branches of linguistics, we may expect to find two kinds of universals: *synchronic* features and *diachronic* processes,[3] though in practice it may not always be easy to separate the two. It will also be expedient to distinguish a third class of semantic universals: those which transcend individual words and are bound up with the general structure of the *vocabulary*.

A. Universal Features in Descriptive Semantics

1. *Transparent and opaque words.*—The contrast between these two types of word-structure has already been discussed in some of the previous chapters;[4] here we are concerned only with its relevance to the problem of universals. It seems clear, first of all, that no language is either completely transparent or completely opaque. All of them are likely to contain both conventional, unanalysable terms and self-explanatory, 'motivated'

---

[1] Cf. above, pp. 8 ff.
[2] Cf. my article, 'Descriptive Semantics and Linguistic Typology', *Word*, ix (1953), pp. 225–40. See also Dell H. Hymes, 'On Typology of Cognitive Styles in Language', *Anthropological Linguistics*, iii (1961), pp. 22–54: p. 27; U. Weinreich, loc. cit.; A. Martinet, *A Functional View of Language*, pp. 87 ff.
[3] Cf. pp. 260 ff. of the Memorandum mentioned in p. 64, n. 2. See also above, p. 61.
[4] See above, pp. 9 f.; 40 ff.; 52 f.

ones: it is hard to imagine a language which would have no onomatopoeic words and no metaphors, and equally difficult to conceive of one which would consist solely of transparent forms. The existence of two types of words is thus in all probability a semantic universal. This assumption would, of course, have to be empirically tested, together with some other, more specific aspects of motivation. Three of these may be briefly considered here:

(a) *Three types of motivation.*—In English and many other languages, words can be motivated, as we have seen (pp. 41 f.), in three different ways: phonetically, morphologically or semantically. The question now arises whether these three types of motivation can be regarded as semantic universals. The first and the third type are likely to occur in all languages; the morphological variety, however, will be more restricted in scope since it will depend on the phonological and grammatical structure of each idiom. In a language made up entirely of monosyllabic words,[1] there will be little room for such motivation; on the other hand, some languages exhibit types of morphological structure which English does not possess; thus in Tagalog, a Philippine language, new words can be formed by reduplication and also by adding a so-called 'infix' before the first vowel of the underlying form: from |'suːlat| 'a writing' are derived |suː-'suːlat| 'one who will write' and |suˈmuːlat| 'one who wrote'.[2]

(b) *Relative frequencies.*—The proportion of opaque and transparent terms, and the relative frequency of the various forms of motivation, may provide valuable criteria for the classification of languages. This was adumbrated by Saussure who distinguished between two kinds of idioms: the 'lexicological' type, where opaque words are prevalent, and the 'grammatical' type, which prefers motivated terms. From the examples he gave it is clear that he was thinking primarily in terms of morphological motivation. In his view, Chinese represents the extreme form of opaqueness whereas Proto-Indo-European and Sanskrit tend towards the opposite pole; English is far less transparent than German, while French, compared with Latin, shows a very considerable increase of the opaque element.[3] The examples which were quoted from English, French and German on pp. 9 f.—series like *thimble—dé—Fingerhut, town: urban— ville: urbain—Stadt: städtisch*, etc.—confirm this general impression of

[1] As Professor Hockett points out in a private letter, the term 'monosyllabic', which is usually employed in this context, should, strictly speaking, be replaced by 'monomorphemic', since what matters is not whether a word contains one or more syllables but whether it consists of one or more morphemes.

[2] Bloomfield, *Language*, p. 218.

[3] Saussure, op. cit., pp. 183 f. Cf. Martinet's comments in *A Functional View of Language*, pp. 88 f.

the transparency of German and the opacity of the other two languages. It might be possible to devise some statistical test for these relative frequencies; such a test might be based on samples from dictionaries, on a representative selection of texts, or on both. Such isolated numerical data as are already available seem very suggestive; in Old English, for example, which was a more transparent medium than Modern English, nearly fifty terms derived from *heofon* 'heaven' have been counted, including such picturesque formations as *heofon-candel* 'sun, moon, stars', and *heofon-weard* 'Heaven's keeper, God'.[1] Pending the collection of reliable statistics, the ease with which examples can be multiplied is symptomatic of the preferences of various languages. Naturally, such preferences are merely statistical, and an odd instance can always be found where they do not work, as in the opaque German *Enkel* opposed to the transparent English *grandson* and French *petit-fils*.[2]

Other types of motivation are less suitable for frequency counts since they are more fluid and subjective than morphological structure. It is commonly believed, for example, that German is richer in onomatopoeic formations than French, but it is hard to think of an objective test which might confirm or disprove this impression.

It has also been suggested that there is a kind of equilibrium between morphological and semantic motivation; some languages, it is claimed, will tend to fill gaps in vocabulary by forming new words whereas others will rather add new meanings to existing terms.[3] There may be a grain of truth in this suggestion, but other factors are also involved in the process; if Modern English and Modern French rely far less on morphological motivation than did their older forms, this is due primarily to the introduction of countless foreign words: French and Graeco-Latin into English, mainly Graeco-Latin into French. It would be difficult to prove that semantic motivation, by metaphor or other means, has greatly benefited by the decline of derivation and composition in these languages.

(c) *Patterns of sound-symbolism.*—It is common knowledge that onomatopoeic terms, however conventionalized, often show striking similarities in different idioms; they bear witness, in Schuchardt's famous formula, not to historical connexions but to 'elementary kinship'. Here, then, is a strong *prima facie* case for interlinguistic inquiries looking for universals. Since a great deal has been written on the subject, it might be desirable to start with an extensive inventory of what is already known—sorting

[1] See V. Grove, op. cit., pp. 45 f.
[2] Cf. Weinreich, *Language*, xxxi (1955), p. 538. On the need for statistical data see ibid. and G. Mounin, *Bulletin de la Société de Linguistique de Paris*, lv (1960), p. 50.
[3] Ch. Bally, *Linguistique générale et linguistique française*, p. 343.

out scientifically established facts from dilettantish speculations which at times brought the whole matter into disrepute. It will also be necessary to distinguish between 'primary' and 'secondary' onomatopoeia. Of the two, the primary type, the imitation of sound by sound, is far simpler and less controversial than the secondary type where non-acoustic experiences—movement, size, emotive overtones, etc.—are represented by sounds. It is not surprising that in many cases, though by no means in all, the same noise should be perceived and transcribed in much the same way in different languages. The example of the cuckoo has often been quoted, and it is no doubt significant that the bird should have closely similar, and distinctly onomatopoeic, names not only in many Indo-European languages (English *cuckoo*, French *coucou*, Spanish *cuclillo*, Italian *cuculo*, Rumanian *cucu*, German *Kuckuck*, Greek κόκκυξ, Russian *kukushka*, etc.), but even in some Finno-Ugrian idioms (Hungarian *kakuk*, Finnish *käki*, Zyrian *kök*).[1] Similarly, it is only natural that verbs for 'snoring' should in many languages contain an |r| sound (English *snore*, German *schnarchen*, Dutch *snorken*, Latin *stertere*, French *ronfler*, Spanish *roncar*, Russian *chrapét'*, Hungarian *horkolni*, etc.), and those for 'whispering' an |s|, |ʃ| or |tʃ| (English *whisper*, German *wispern* and *flüstern*, Norwegian *hviske*, Latin *susurrare*, French *chuchoter*, Spanish *cuchichear*, Russian *sheptát'*, Hungarian *súgni, susogni, suttogni*, etc.). Such correspondences are certainly interesting and worth studying on a broader basis, though they are too obvious to throw much light on the fundamental structure of language.

More significant and more delicate are the problems raised by 'secondary' onomatopoeia. In this type, the connexion between sound and sense is less evident than in the previous one; yet even here there exist extensive similarities between various languages. A celebrated example is the 'symbolic value' of the vowel |i| as an expression of smallness.[2] This is found in a number of languages: English *little, slim, thin, wee, teeny-weeny*; French *petit*; Italian *piccolo*; Rumanian *mic*; Latin *minor, minimus*; Greek μικρός; Hungarian *kis, kicsi, pici*, etc. To such adjectives may be added many nouns denoting small creatures or things, such as English *kid, chit, imp, slip, midge, tit, bit, chip, chink, jiffy, pin, pip, tip, whit*, and also such diminutive suffixes as the English *-ie, -kin* and *-ling*.[3] By scrutinizing a wide variety of languages it might be possible to establish

[1] See Z. Gombocz, *Jelentéstan* (Semantics), Pécs, 1926, p. 12.

[2] Cf. recently M. Chastaing's article on this subject, mentioned on p. 41, n. 4.

[3] Cf. O. Jespersen, *Language: its Nature, Development and Origin*, London, repr. 1934, p. 402: Id., 'Symbolic Value of the Vowel *i*', *Linguistica*, Copenhagen—London, 1933, pp. 283–303.

how general this feature is and whether it is formulable in statistical terms. Even then we would, of course, be left with some examples which run counter to the general tendency; indeed, there are pairs of antonyms where the onomatopoeic pattern seems to be reversed, with the |i| sound occurring in the term for 'large' while its opposite has an open vowel: English *big—small*; Russian *velíkij* 'great'—*málen'kij* 'little, small'. The same may be said of German *Riese* 'giant', Hungarian *apró* 'minute', and Latin *parvus*, though in this last case it is perhaps significant that this adjective has not survived in Romance and has been replaced by words whose phonetic structure was better suited to the idea of smallness.

Onomatopoeia is a popular device in poetry, and there is remarkable consistency in the way certain sound-patterns are used for stylistic purposes in different languages. To cite but one example, a sequence of lateral consonants is particularly well fitted to produce an impression of softness, as in Keats's lines:

> Wi*l*d thyme and va*ll*ey-*l*i*l*ies whiter sti*ll*
> Than *L*eda's *l*ove, and cresses from the ri*ll*.
> *Endymion*, Book I.

A famous line in Victor Hugo's poem *Booȝ endormi* is built on the same pattern:

> *L*es souff*l*es de *l*a nuit f*l*ottaient sur Ga*l*ga*l*a.[1]

The same orchestration is used by Goethe in the *West-östlicher Divan*:

> Dir in *L*iedern, *l*eichten, schne*ll*en,
> Wa*ll*et küh*l*e F*l*uth.[2]

The device is very old; it is already found in the *Odyssey*:

> αἰεὶ δὲ μαλακοῖσι καὶ αἱμυλίοισι λόγοισι θέλγει.[3]

It is interesting to find a very similar use of laterals in Finnish and Hungarian poetry:

---

[1] 'The breezes of the night floated over Galgala'.
[2] 'For you the cool waves lap in songs light and nimble' (*An Hafis: 'Hafis, dir sich gleich ȝu stellen . . .'*).
[3] 'And ever with soft and wheedling words she beguiles him' (Book I, ll. 56–7).

Sie*ll*'on *l*apsen *l*ysti o*ll*a,
I*ll*an tu*ll*en tuudite*ll*a.[1]

Ah! *L*ágyan ké*l* az éji szé*l*
Mi*l*ford öbö*l* fe*l*é.[2]

Some at least of these onomatopoeic patterns appear to be deeply rooted in our modes of perception, as has been shown recently by psychological experiments.[3]

It would seem, then, that motivation in its various aspects can suggest several promising lines of research which may well lead to the discovery of linguistic or stylistic universals.

2. *Particular and general terms.*—Some languages are remarkably rich in words with specific meanings, while others prefer to use general terms and to neglect unnecessary details. French is usually regarded as a highly 'abstract' medium,[4] whereas German is fond of 'concrete', particular terms. It may be noted that 'concrete' and 'abstract' are employed in this context not in their usual senses, but as synonyms of 'particular' and 'general'. There are various symptoms of this contrast between French and German word-structure:

(*a*) In some cases, German has three or four specific verbs corresponding to one generic term in French: *gehen* 'to go, to walk', *reiten* 'to ride on horseback', *fahren* 'to drive, to travel by train or car, etc.'— *aller* 'to go'; *stehen* 'to stand (intransitive)', *sitzen* 'to sit', *liegen* 'to lie'— *être* or *se trouver* 'to be'; *stellen* 'to stand (transitive)', *setzen* 'to set', *legen* 'to lay'—*mettre* 'to put'. The detailed particulars expressed by the German verbs will often remain unformulated in French, or will be indicated by the context—unless, of course, there is a specific need to state them, in which case they will be added as supplementary information: *être debout* 'to stand', *aller à cheval* 'to go on horseback', etc.

(*b*) German, which is, as we have noted, a highly motivated language, uses prefixes on a lavish scale in order to specify every aspect of the action expressed by the verb. These subsidiary shades of meaning will normally

---

[1] 'It is pleasant for the child to be there, to swing when the evening comes' (A. Kivi, *Sydämeni Laulu*—My Heart's Song).

[2] 'Oh! the night breeze rises softly towards Milford Haven' (János Arany, *A walesi bárdok*— The Welsh Bards). See I. Fónagy, *A költői nyelv hangtanából* (From the Phonetics of the Language of Poetry), Budapest, 1959, pp. 24 ff. and 71.

[3] See H. Wissemann, *Untersuchungen zur Onomatopoiie*, I, Heidelberg, 1954, and M. Chastaing, *Archivum Linguisticum*, xiv (1962), pp. 1 ff.

[4] V. Brøndal, *Le français, langue abstraite*, Copenhagen, 1936; Bally, *Linguistique générale et linguistique française*, pp. 346 ff.; J. Orr, *Words and Sounds in English and French*, ch. VIII; J. P. Hughes, *The Science of Language*, New York, 1962, p. 12, etc.

F

be neglected in French: *setzen, ansetzen—mettre; schreiben, nieder-schreiben—écrire; wachsen, heranwachsen—grandir.* In English these nuances tend to be expressed by adverbial phrases: *to put on, to write down, to grow up.*

(*c*) French will often use a derivative where German (and English) have a more specific compound: *cendrier—ash-tray, Aschenbecher; théière—teapot, Teekanne; ramoneur—chimney-sweep, Schornsteinfeger.*

(*d*) Outside the lexical sphere proper, there are indications of the same tendency in the German adverbial and prepositional system, such as the distinction between *herein* and *hinein* 'in here—in there', *herunter* and *hinunter* 'down here—down there', etc., according to the speaker's position, and the accumulation of adverbs and prepositions to 'trace the whole trajectory' of an action:[1] 'Wir segelten *vom* Ufer *her über* den Fluss *hin nach* der Insel *zu*' 'We sailed from the bank (here) over the river (there) (on) towards the island'. French and English would leave most of these details unexpressed.

If a sufficient number of languages were examined from this point of view, the relative frequency of particular and general terms might become a useful criterion in linguistic typology, even though it would be difficult to arrive at precise statistical conclusions in this field.

Closely connected with this feature is a problem which has exercised linguists and anthropologists for many years. It has often been asserted that the languages of '*primitive*' races are rich in specific and poor in generic terms. The Tasmanian aborigines, for example, had no single word for 'tree', only special names for each variety of gum-tree and wattle-tree; the Zulus have no term for 'cow': they must specify whether they mean a 'red cow' or a 'white cow', etc.[2] Unfortunately, these reports were based only too often on inadequate evidence such as observations by early missionaries, which were uncritically accepted and reproduced by successive generations of scholars. In this way an American linguist was able, a few years ago, to explode the myth that there is no single term for 'washing' in Cherokee, an American Indian language.[3] Such incidents have brought discredit on the theory of 'prelogical mentality'; at a symposium on relations between language and culture, held in Chicago in 1953, a philosopher noted that 'everyone was apparently quite willing to talk about the primitiveness of a culture but most people

[1] Bally, ibid., p. 350.
[2] See Jespersen, *Language*, p. 429.
[3] A. A. Hill, 'A Note on Primitive Languages', *International Journal of American Linguistics*, xviii (1952), pp. 172–7.

were quite unwilling to talk about the primitiveness of language'.[1] One may wonder, however, whether there is not at least a grain of truth in the old theory. Certain facts in child psychology and in the history of our own languages seem to suggest that there is. The case of the Zulu speaker who has separate words for red and white cow is strangely similar to that of a four-year-old Dutch boy who had special terms for a cow with red spots and one with black spots; it is true that he also possessed a general word for 'cow' *tout court,* which was no doubt due to the influence of his mother tongue.[2] In the same way, the alleged lack of a word for 'tree' in the language of the Tasmanian aborigines reminds one of the history of Latin *planta* and its modern descendants. The Latin word meant 'sprout, slip, cutting'; there was in Latin no generic term for 'plant' in the modern sense: *arbor* and *herba* were the most comprehensive class-concepts in the botanical field. According to a recent inquiry, the modern meaning of 'plant' is first found in Albertus Magnus in the thirteenth century, whereas the French *plante* did not acquire this wider sense until three hundred years later.[3]

It should also be borne in mind that what may seem to us a plethora of specific terms may be due, not to faulty powers of abstraction but to the influence of climate and environment. Thus it is only to be expected that the Eskimos and the Lapps should require a variety of terms to distinguish between different kinds of 'snow'. Similarly, the Paiute, a desert people of the American Indian group, 'speak a language which permits the most detailed description of topographical features, a necessity in a country where complex directions may be required for the location of water holes'.[4] In the words of Edward Sapir, 'language is a complex inventory of all the ideas, interests and occupations that take up the attention of the community'.[5]

In view of the great importance of the problem to linguists and anthropologists alike, it would be most desirable to organize a large-scale research project on the whole question of relations between vocabulary and culture, with special reference to the use of particular and generic terms at different levels of civilization and in different environments. Needless to say, the results of such an inquiry would be of direct relevance

---

[1] A. Kaplan in H. Hoijer (ed.), *Language in Culture. Conference on the Interrelations of Language and Other Aspects of Culture,* Chicago, 1954, p. 219.

[2] See W. Kaper, *Kindersprachforschung mit Hilfe des Kindes,* Groningen, 1959, p. 11.

[3] W. von Wartburg, quoted by K. Baldinger, *Cahiers de l'Association Internationale des Etudes Françaises,* xi (1959), p. 259.

[4] P. Henle, *Language, Thought, and Culture,* p. 5.

[5] Ibid. (quoted from *Selected Writings by Edward Sapir,* ed. D. Mandelbaum, Berkeley, 1949, pp. 90 f.).

to a question which is much discussed nowadays and which will be considered in a later chapter of this book: the influence of language upon thought.

3. *Synonymy.*—In his *Essai de sémantique,* Michel Bréal put forward a linguistic law which he called '*the law of distribution*'. According to this, words which were once synonymous are subsequently differentiated in various ways and will thus cease to be interchangeable.[1] Bloomfield went even further and argued that total synonymy is impossible. 'Each linguistic form', he claimed, 'has a constant and specific meaning. If the forms are phonemically different, we suppose that their meanings also are different—for instance, that each one of a set of forms like *quick, fast, swift, rapid, speedy,* differs from all the others in some constant and conventional feature of meaning. We suppose, in short, that there are no actual synonyms.'[2] In fact it does occasionally happen, in technical nomenclatures, that two synonyms which are completely interchangeable live on side by side for some time, such as for example *spirant* and *fricative* in phonetics, or *caecitis* and *typhlitis* in medicine, both of them denoting an inflammation of the blind gut.[3] Yet it is perfectly true that we automatically tend to discriminate between synonyms, that we tend to assume that two or more words different in form cannot mean exactly the same thing, or cannot mean it in exactly the same manner. Differentiation may work in a variety of ways: it may affect the actual content of the words involved, their emotive overtones, social status or stylistic register. One linguist has counted no less than nine distinct ways in which synonyms can be differentiated.[4] The 'law of distribution' is undoubtedly a widespread tendency, though not necessarily a universal one. In fact there is every reason to believe that differentiation between synonyms is a sophisticated process which appears relatively late in the development of a language. In Old French, for example, a number of synonymous derivatives could be formed from the verb *livrer: livrage, livraison, livrance, livrée, livrement, livreüre.* Subsequently, this superabundance was felt to be a mere *embarras de richesses* and was reduced to one term: *livraison.*[5] Differentiation between synonyms, often on highly artificial grounds, was an important element in the large-scale language reform carried out by Malherbe, Vaugelas and others in the seventeenth

---

[1] *Essai de sémantique,* 6th ed., Paris, 1924, p. 26.

[2] *Language,* p. 145.

[3] Cf. C. Schick, *Il Linguaggio,* Turin, 1960, p. 188.

[4] W. E. Collinson, 'Comparative Synonymics: Some Principles and Illustrations', *Transactions of the Philological Society,* 1939, pp. 54–77.

[5] See F. Brunot-Ch. Bruneau, *Précis de grammaire historique de la langue française,* 3rd ed., Paris, 1949, p. 172.

century; it was suggested, for example, to distinguish between the two words for 'gratefulness', *reconnaissance* and *gratitude*, by using the former when one can return a favour and the latter when one cannot.[1]

Another general principle in the field of synonymy is what might be called '*the law of synonymic attraction*'. It has often been found that subjects which are prominent in the interests and activities of a community tend to attract a large number of synonyms. Some significant concentrations have for instance been discovered in Old English literature. In *Beowulf* there are thirty-seven words for 'hero' or 'prince' and at least a dozen for 'battle' and 'fight'. The same epic contains seventeen expressions for 'sea', to which thirteen more may be added from other Old English poems.[2] An analysis of the vocabulary of the twelfth-century French poet Benoît de Sainte-Maure tells a very similar story: thirteen verbs for 'vanquish', seventeen for 'attack', thirty-six nouns for 'battle' and 'fight', etc.[3] In French slang there are characteristic clusters of synonyms, many of them jocular or euphemistic, for the ideas of 'stealing', 'drunkenness' and 'death', whereas in French dialects there is a profusion of terms for 'horse', 'rich' and 'poor', and especially for 'mean, avaricious'; the latter vice is described by nearly 200 different expressions, nine of which are found within a single dialect.[4]

A similar process, which is fundamentally a case of analogical extension, is the so-called '*radiation of synonyms*'. Students of French slang have found that when a particular word was given a transferred sense its synonyms tended to develop on parallel lines. Thus the verb *chiquer* 'beat' came to be used in the meaning of 'deceive', whereupon other verbs for 'beat'—*torcher, taper, estamper, toquer*—received the same secondary sense.[5] Such developments are sometimes confined to two words: when the English verb *overlook* acquired the transferred meaning of 'deceive', its synonym *oversee* underwent a parallel change.[6] It would be interesting to find out how widespread these processes are in different languages.

4. *Polysemy.*—This, as we have seen (p. 23), is the name given to the use of the same word in two or more distinct meanings. Polysemy

---

[1] See my *Précis de sémantique française*, p. 145.
[2] O. Jespersen, *Growth and Structure of the English Language*, 6th ed., Leipzig, 1930, p. 48.
[3] See Wartburg, *Problèmes et méthodes de la linguistique*, pp. 206 f.
[4] Ibid., pp. 161 f.
[5] See M. Schwob-G. Guieysse, 'Etudes sur l'argot français', *Mémoires de la Société de Linguistique de Paris*, vii (1892), pp. 33–56, and more recently B. Migliorini, 'Calco e irradiazione sinonimica', *Boletín del Instituto Caro y Cuervo*, iv (1948), pp. 3–17, reprinted in *Saggi linguistici*, Florence, 1957.
[6] See S. Kroesch, 'Analogy as a Factor in Semantic Change', *Language*, ii (1926), pp. 35–45.

is without any doubt a semantic universal inherent in the fundamental structure of language. The alternative is quite unthinkable: it would mean that we would have to store in our memories a tremendous stock of words, with separate names for any possible subject we might wish to talk about; it would also mean that there would be no metaphors and that language would thus be robbed of much of its expressiveness and flexibility. As a philosopher, W. M. Urban, rightly points out, 'this double reference of verbal signs ... is a basal *differentia* of semantic meaning. The fact that a sign can intend one thing without ceasing to intend another, that, indeed, the very condition of its being an *expressive* sign for the second is that it is also a sign for the first, is precisely what makes language an instrument of knowing'.[1]

The frequency of polysemy in different languages is a variable which will depend on a number of factors. The progress of civilization will make it necessary not only to form new words but to add fresh meanings to old ones; in Bréal's formula, the more senses a term has accumulated, the more diverse aspects of intellectual and social activity it represents.[2] This is probably what Frederick the Great meant when he saw in the multiplicity of meanings a sign of the superior quality of the French language.[3] It would be interesting to explore the relation between polysemy and culture over a wider field. Meanwhile, the frequency of polysemy will also depend on purely linguistic factors. As already noted (p. 68), languages where derivation and composition are sparingly used will tend to fill gaps in vocabulary by adding new meanings to existing terms. Similarly, polysemy will arise more easily in generic words, whose meaning varies according to context, than in specific terms whose sense is less subject to variation. The relative frequency of polysemy in various languages may thus provide a further criterion for semantic typology, though it is hard to see how this feature could be exactly measured.

There is, however, another aspect of polysemy which can be more precisely quantified: its relation to *word-frequency*. As we saw in the first chapter (pp. 6 f.), G. K. Zipf has argued that there is a correlation between the two features: the more frequently a word is used, the more meanings it tends to develop. While it may be unwise to sum up this relationship, as Zipf did, in a mathematical formula, the existence of some kind of correlation is plausible and deserves to be carefully tested

[1] W. M. Urban, *Language and Reality*, London ed., 1939, pp. 112 f.
[2] *Essai de sémantique*, p. 144.
[3] Ibid.

in different languages. In fact it has always been clear that some of the commonest words in a language have a great diversity of meanings: in Littré's dictionary, nearly forty senses are listed under *aller* 'to go', nearly fifty under *mettre* 'to put', and some eighty under *prendre* 'to take' and *faire* 'to do'.[1]

Polysemy is a fertile source of *ambiguity* in language. In a limited number of cases, two major meanings of the same word are differentiated by formal means such as gender (French *le pendule* 'pendulum'—*la pendule* 'clock', German *der Band* 'volume'—*das Band* 'ribbon'), flexion (*brothers*—*brethren, hung*—*hanged*, German *Worte* 'connected speech'—*Wörter* 'words'), word-order (*an ambassador extraordinary*—*an extraordinary ambassador*, French *une assertion vraie* 'a *true* statement'—*un vrai diamant* 'a *real* (genuine) diamond'), or spelling (*discrete*—*discreet, draft*—*draught*, French *dessin* 'drawing'—*dessein* 'design, plan, scheme').[2] In the vast majority of cases, however, the context alone will suffice to exclude all the irrelevant senses. When all these safeguards break down, a conflict between two or more incompatible meanings will ensue, and this may lead to the disappearance of some of these meanings, or even to that of the word itself. Some examples of such conflicts were cited in the last chapter (pp. 56 f.). As we saw there, recent investigations on the polysemy of English adjectives suggest that such ambiguities will seldom result in the total eclipse of a word; usually it will be sufficient to discard one or more of the conflicting meanings. Further research may show whether this is or is not a general tendency. Linguistic geographers have also thrown some light on the conditions under which such conflicts arise. They have found, for example, that 'co-ordinated' meanings belonging to the same sphere are often an embarrassment, whereas meanings from different spheres can coexist more easily; thus it is inconvenient to have the same word for both 'maize' and 'sorghum', but perfectly feasible for the same term to mean 'vine-shoot' and 'end of a skein'. Furthermore, the two meanings will not clash if there is a clearly perceptible connexion between them, as for instance in the use of the same word for 'head' and, figuratively, for the 'nave of a wheel'. The situation may be further complicated by social factors such as the penetration of the Received Standard into dialect areas.[3] When we have more data available from various languages we shall be in a position to say which, if any, of these tendencies are of general validity.

---

[1] Nyrop, *Sémantique*, p. 26.
[2] See Rudskoger, op. cit., pp. 473 ff. Cf above, p. 33.
[3] See K. Jaberg, *Aspects géographiques du langage*, Paris, 1936, p. 64.

5. *Homonymy.*—Unlike polysemy, homonymy is not necessarily a linguistic universal. Polysemy, as we have seen, is inherent in the very structure of language, whereas one could easily imagine an idiom without homonyms; it would be, in fact, a more efficient medium. Whether such an idiom actually exists could be revealed only by empirical investigations. Even if it does, homonymy is bound to be a statistical universal with a high degree of probability.

As noted in a previous chapter (pp. 31 ff.), some homonyms are due to diverging sense-development, and it is sometimes difficult to determine the precise point where polysemy ends and where homonymy begins. The great majority of homonyms arise, however, in a different way: by *converging sound-development.* This leads to the coincidence of two or more words which were phonetically distinct at an earlier date; thus Old English *męte* and *mētan* have converged and become homonymous in Modern English *meat* and *to meet*, and Latin *laudare* and *locare* have coalesced in the form *louer* which can mean 'to praise' or 'to hire, to let'. Now the chances of such coincidence will mainly depend on two factors: word-length and word-structure. Languages rich in short words will obviously have more homonyms than those where longer words are prevalent. Hence the relative frequency of homonymy in English and French, as compared, for example, to German or Italian. Even more important than length is the productivity of the various types of *word-structure* in a particular language. For English we have some interesting statistics compiled by B. Trnka;[1] these are based on an analysis of words included in the *Pocket Oxford Dictionary of Current English*. Trnka distinguishes fourteen types of monosyllables, ranging from words with one phoneme to those with six. His tables show that the commonest type is the consonant-vowel-consonant sequence which, with 1343 monosyllables out of 3178, represents 42 per cent of the total figure. The same category also contains the largest number of homonyms, namely 333. In some of the smaller classes, however, the proportion of homonyms is relatively higher: in the consonant-vowel combination, there are ninety-one examples out of a total of 174 monosyllables. In French, the general pattern of word-structure is very different; there are, in particular, numerous monosyllables—fifty-two, according to a recent count[2]—

[1] *A Phonological Analysis of Present-Day Standard English*, Prague, 1935, pp. 57–93. It should be noted that the results would be somewhat different if the material were subjected to current techniques of phonemic analysis. See also O. Jespersen, 'Monosyllabism in English', in *Linguistica*, 1933, pp. 384–408.

[2] A. Ewert, *Of the Precellence of the French Tongue* (Zaharoff Lecture), Oxford, 1958, p. 11. See also Bally, *Linguistique générale et linguistique française*, pp. 269 f.; L. C. Harmer, *The French Language Today*, London, 1954, ch. IV; A. Schönhage, *Zur Struktur des französischen*

consisting of a single vowel, and many more where a vowel is preceded by one consonant. Needless to say, the extreme simplicity of this type of word-structure produces a great profusion of homonyms; there are sometimes as many as half a dozen words (not to speak of homonymous inflexions of the same word) consisting of the same vowel or consonant plus vowel: *au* 'to the', *aulx* 'garlics', *eau* 'water', *haut* 'high', *oh* (interjection), *os* 'bones'; *ceint* 'he girds', *cinq* 'five',[1] *sain* 'healthy', *saint* 'holy', *sein* 'breast, bosom', *(blanc-)seing* 'signature to a blank document'. If comparable data could be collected for a great many languages, we could find out whether there are any universal, or at least widespread, tendencies in this field; we would also gain a precise typological criterion for determining the relative frequency of homonymy in general, and that of its various types.

Homonyms, like several meanings of the same word, are sometimes differentiated by formal means such as gender (French *le livre* 'book'— *la livre* 'pound', *le poste* 'station, place, appointment'—*la poste* 'post') or flexion (English *ring, rang—ring, ringed*, German *die Kiefer* 'jaws'— *die Kiefern* 'firs'). In languages like English and French, *spelling* is employed on a massive scale to differentiate between homonyms, and this is often used as an argument against spelling-reform. Bloomfield was sceptical of the value of spelling as a safeguard against homonymy. 'It is wrong to suppose', he claimed, 'that writing would be unintelligible if homonyms (e.g. *pear, pair, pare* or *piece, peace*) were spelled alike; writing which reproduces the phonemes of speech is as intelligible as speech.'[2] This is doubtless true, but the point is that writing is in this respect *more* intelligible than speech. The example of English and French suggests that languages rich in short words, and therefore in homonyms, tend to retain a non-phonetic mode of spelling, and it would not be difficult to establish whether this is a general tendency.

The most important safeguard against homonymic ambiguity is, however, the influence of context. Many homonyms belong to different word-classes; others are so diverse in meaning that they could never occur in the same utterance. Even so, '*homonymic clashes*' happen fairly frequently, and can be reconstructed with great precision from linguistic

Wortschatzes. Der französische Einsilber, Bonn, 1948 (unpublished thesis reviewed by G. Gougenheim in *Le Français Moderne*, xx, 1952, pp. 66–8); P. Miron, 'Recherches sur la typologie des langues romanes', *Atti dell'VIII Congresso di Studi Romanzi*, vol. II, Florence, 1960, pp. 693–7; H. Seiler, 'Laut und Sinn. Zur Struktur der deutschen Einsilber', *Lingua*, xi (1962), pp. 375–87.
   [1] The final consonant of this word is often pronounced; cf. P. Fouché, *Traité de prononciation française*, Paris, 1956, p. 479.
   [2] *Language*, p. 502.

atlases. These clashes, and the various ways in which they are resolved, have been studied so thoroughly by Gilliéron and other linguistic geographers[1] that there is no need to discuss them here; a few examples were quoted in the last chapter (pp. 55 f. and 58). In some cases it is sufficient slightly to alter the form of one of the homonyms: by giving French *héros* a so-called 'aspirate *h*', any possible confusion between *les héros* and *les ẓéros*, 'heroes' and 'zeroes', is effectively obviated.[2] Elsewhere a substitute will have to be found; this may be a derivative, a synonym, a term from the same sphere or from a neighbouring sphere, a borrowing from another language, or even a jocular metaphor: when, in part of south-west France, the words for 'cock' and 'cat' fell together, the cock was renamed 'pheasant' or, more facetiously, 'provost'.[3] When we have more geographical and historical facts about such conflicts in a number of languages, we shall be able to say how common these various solutions are.

    6. *Semantic typology.*—It will have been noticed that four of the five features examined in this section—transparent *versus* opaque words, generic *versus* specific terms, polysemy, and homonymy—may, if studied on a suitable scale, yield criteria for linguistic typology. All four criteria are statistical: they are concerned with relative frequencies. The precision with which these frequencies can be determined will vary with the phenomena themselves: it will be highest in homonymy and lowest in the distinction between specific and generic terms; in the sphere of motivation and polysemy, at least certain aspects of the problem may be amenable to numerical formulation. Two further points are also worth noting. Firstly, some of the above features are interrelated: as we have seen, polysemy is closely connected with motivation on the one hand and with the use of generic terms on the other.[4] Secondly, all our typological criteria, except, perhaps, motivation, have a direct bearing on the *semantic autonomy* of the word, the degree to which the hearer or reader will depend on the context for understanding it. Obviously, a generic term like French *aller* means less in itself, conveys less information and is therefore more 'context-bound', than the more specific German verbs *gehen, reiten, fahren*. Similarly, a word with many meanings will be highly ambiguous if encountered in isolation, without any contextual

---

  1 For detailed references see my *Semantics*, pp. 180–8. See now also W. Rothwell's critical remarks in 'Homonymics and Medieval French', *Archivum Linguisticum*, xiv (1962), pp. 35–48.
  2 This was already recognized by the grammarian Vaugelas in the seventeenth century; cf. J. Orr, *Words and Sounds in English and French*, p. 138.
  3 For a detailed discussion of this change, see Wartburg, *Problèmes et méthodes de la linguistique*, pp. 148 ff.
  4 See above, p. 76.

support, as for example in a newspaper headline or the title of a book or a play, whereas homonyms found in the same isolated position will have no meaning at all. It follows that languages where generic terms, poly-semy and homonymy are prevalent will be relatively context-bound; French is a classic example of this type of semantic structure, as I have tried to show in my *Précis de sémantique française*. Naturally, the extent to which we have to rely on context in a given language cannot be stated with any degree of precision; yet it may emerge fairly clearly from close scrutiny of the various factors involved.

B. Universal Processes in Historical Semantics

1. *Metaphor.*—Since metaphor is based on the perception of simi-larities, it is only natural that, when an analogy is obvious, it should give rise to the same metaphor in various languages; hence the wide currency of expressions like the '*foot* of a hill' or the '*leg* of a table'. There are, however, less obvious associations which are also remarkably widespread. A well-known example is the figurative use of verbs for 'catching' and 'grasping' in the sense of 'understanding': English *catch, grasp*; French *comprendre* (cf. *prendre* 'take'), *saisir*; Italian *capire* (from Latin *capere* 'catch'); German *begreifen* (cf. *greifen* 'seize'), etc.[1] The great difficulty about such correspondences is that they may not be genuine cases of parallel development: the various languages may simply have copied each other or some common model. Thus, to take a very recent example, the close similarity between English *sky-scraper*, French *gratte-ciel*, Italian *grattacielo*, German *Wolkenkratzer*, Hungarian *felhökarcoló*, etc., is not due to a fundamental identity of vision; the only spontaneous metaphor among them is *sky-scraper* which arose in America in the 1890s and was then translated into other languages.[2] When dealing with earlier periods it will often be impossible to distinguish systemati-cally between foreign influence and genuine parallelism.

The names of the constellation known as *Charles's Wain* and the *Greater Bear* (French *le Grand Chariot* or *la Grande Ourse*) show that parallel metaphors are sometimes inextricably interwoven with loan-translation and even with popular etymology. 'The Greek term used for the Greater Bear', writes an eminent comparatist,[3] 'is usually ἄρκτος "bear", although ἅμαξα "wagon" is also used. Now the latter name is

---

[1] See Gombocz, op. cit., pp. 6 f. On parallel metaphors see recently A. Sauvageot, 'A propos des changements sémantiques', *Journal de Psychologie*, xlvi (1953), pp. 465–72.
[2] B. Migliorini, 'Grattacielo', in *Lingua e Cultura*, Rome, 1948, pp. 283 f.
[3] O. J. L. Szemerényi, *Trends and Tasks in Comparative Philology* (Inaugural Lecture), London, 1962, pp. 19 f.

quite clear: it is based on the shape of the constellation and is so natural
for anyone who looks up at the night sky that it is found in the whole
of Europe and Hither Asia, beginning with the English *Charles's Wain,*
continuing with Hungarian *Göncöl-szekér* "the wagon of Göncöl", and
ending up with the Sumerian name ᴹᵁᴸMAR.GÍD.DA "the wagon-star".
But the other term, the "Bear", is not so easy to understand. Our sensi-
tivity may have been blunted by the existence of the term Greater and
Lesser Bears, but these are not indigenous expressions. Bear in this sense
is ultimately, through a series of loan-translations, borrowed from the
Greek term. Now there can be no doubt that the Greeks themselves did
interpret the name *Arktos* as "bear"; the myth of Kallisto, the maiden
turned into a bear and planted in the firmament, is enough to prove it.
But it is also beyond doubt that this is a secondary development. The
name is also found without the *t* (Aeschylus: ἄρκειος "northern")
and thus differs from the inherited Indo-European word for "bear".
The solution lies in the Near East. I have mentioned already that the
Sumerian term for the constellation means "wagon". The same is true of
Akkadian. But here the word is *eriqqu.* It is clear that it is this word, or
its Phoenician equivalent, that was borrowed into the Aegean area in the
form *ṛku,* or *ṛko-* and became the Greek ἄρκος/ἄρκτος.'

The only way of avoiding these pitfalls is to collect instances of the
same metaphor from widely different languages which cannot possibly
have influenced one another. Thus it is interesting to find that the
connexion between physical and mental 'grasping' occurs also in Old
Hungarian and in Turkish, though in a slightly different form: in the
former, *érteni* 'understand' is an old derivative of *érni* 'reach, touch',
while in the latter *akyl ermek* literally means 'to reach with one's mind'.[1]
An impressive example of an interlinguistic survey of parallel metaphors
is Professor C. Tagliavini's article on the names of the 'pupil of the eye'
in various languages.[2] Amongst other things, he has examined the image
underlying Latin *pupilla* and its modern descendants, where the pupil is
compared to a small girl, or sometimes to a small boy, because of the
vague resemblance between a child and the minute figure reflected in the
eye. This analogy, which may at first sight seem far-fetched, is embodied
in the words for 'pupil' in various Indo-European languages: Greek κόρη,
Spanish *niña (del ojo),* Portuguese *menina (do olho),* etc. But it is equally
common in other linguistic groups: Tagliavini has found examples in

[1] See Gombocz, op. cit., p. 7, and G. Bárczi, *Magyar Szófejtő Szótár* (Hungarian Etymological Dictionary), Budapest, 1941, *s.v. ért.*
[2] 'Die alcune denominazioni della "pupilla" ', *Annali dell'Istituto Universitario Orientale
di Napoli,* N.S. iii (1949), pp. 341–78: pp. 363 ff.

some twenty non-Indo-European languages as remote from each other as Swahili, Lapp, Chinese and Samoan.

Such parallel developments are not confined to metaphor: certain 'metonymic' associations, based on relations other than similarity, can be equally widespread. Thus the use of the word for 'tongue', the organ of speech, in the sense of 'language', is common to many Indo-European idioms: English *tongue*, Latin *lingua* and its progeny, Greek γλῶσσα, Russian *jaɀýk*, etc.; it is also found in a number of Finno-Ugrian languages, including not only Finnish and Hungarian but even Zyrian, Cheremiss and others. The same metonymy occurs also in Turkish, in some African idioms and elsewhere.[1] A collection of such parallel metaphors and metonymies would be of outstanding value since the associations on which they are based seem to be deeply rooted in human experience and largely independent of culture and environment. Hence the importance of a project announced at the London congress of linguists in 1952: the compilation of a 'dictionary of semantic parallels'.[2]

Over and above these specific developments, the general movement of metaphors seems to be governed by some broad tendencies which are of great potential interest not only to the linguist but also to the psychologist, the student of literature and others. Four such tendencies may be briefly mentioned here.

(i) Nearly forty years ago, Hans Sperber put forward a 'semantic law' inspired by Freudian ideas. He started from the assumption that if we are intensely interested in a subject, it will provide us with analogies for the description of other experiences; in Sperber's terminology, it will become a centre of metaphorical *'expansion'*. Thus the terrifying weapons of the First World War suggested to French soldiers various jocular metaphors: beans were described as *shrapnels*, and a woman with many children was facetiously referred to as a 'machine-gun' (*mitrailleuse à gosses*). Sperber summed up his 'law' in the following terms: 'If at a certain time a complex of ideas is so strongly charged with feeling that it causes *one* word to extend its sphere and change its meaning, we may confidently expect that other words belonging to the same emotional complex will also shift their meaning.'[3]

---

[1] See Gombocz, op. cit., p. 94; B. Collinder, *Fenno-Ugric Vocabulary*, Stockholm, 1955, pp. 25 (*s.v.* Finnish *kieli*) and 43 (*s.v.* Hungarian *nyelv*); G. Révész, *The Origin and Prehistory of Language*, London, etc., 1956, pp. 56 f.

[2] See J. Schröpfer, 'Wozu ein vergleichendes Wörterbuch des Sinnwandels? (Ein Wörterbuch semasiologischer Parallelen)', *Proceedings of the Seventh International Congress of Linguists*, pp. 366–71.

[3] *Einführung in die Bedeutungslehre*, Bonn—Leipzig, 1923, p. 67; the English translation is the one given by Professor W. E. Collinson in *Modern Language Review*, xx (1925), p. 106.

Stated in these terms, Sperber's law is no more than a bold generalization which would have to be extensively tested in different languages and periods. There are certainly cases where the principle seems to work. In sixteenth-century France, torn by religious strife, there were numerous metaphors and similes derived from the sphere of religion.[1] During the French Revolution, analogies inspired by recent progress in physics and chemistry were remarkably popular;[2] subsequently, the introduction of railways, the spread of electricity and other inventions enriched the metaphorical resources of the language.[3] It would seem, however, that Sperber's law is too categorical; to take but one example, if there were an automatic connexion between emotion and metaphor, then one would expect our air-minded age to have far more images from aviation than are in current use today. The same may be said of the application of this principle to the imagery of a particular writer, which will be considered in a later chapter. Be that as it may, there is obviously an element of truth in the theory, and its implications are so interesting that it deserves to be carefully investigated.

(ii) A very common form of metaphor in the most diverse languages is the *anthropomorphic* type. This was already clearly recognized by the eighteenth-century Italian philosopher Giambattista Vico. 'In all languages,' he wrote, 'the majority of expressions referring to inanimate objects are formed by transfers from the human body and its parts, from human senses and human passions . . . Ignorant man makes himself the yardstick of the universe.'[4] Thus Vico did not hesitate to regard anthropomorphic metaphor as a semantic universal. Modern linguists will be more cautious, but there can be no doubt that such expressions are extremely frequent and widespread. They can describe both concrete and abstract experiences: we talk of the *neck* of a bottle, the *mouth* of a river, the *eye* of a needle, the *brow* of a hill, and also of the *heart* of the matter, the *lungs* of a town, the *sinews* of war; Zola even entitled one of his novels *Le Ventre de Paris*, the 'belly' of Paris. Side by side with these metaphors from the human sphere, there are many others working the other way round, where parts of the human body are named after animals, plants or inanimate objects: *muscle* (from Latin *musculus*,

---

[1] Cf. E. Huguet, *Le Langage figuré au seizième siècle*, Paris, 1933, pp. 1–18.
[2] See F. Brunot, *Histoire de la langue française*, vol. X, pt. 1, pp. 64 ff.
[3] On railway images, see P. J. Wexler, *La Formation du vocabulaire des chemins de fer en France, 1778–1842*, Geneva—Lille, 1955, pp. 130 f., and my *Style in the French Novel*, p. 32, and *The Image in the Modern French Novel*, Cambridge, 1960, pp. 144 f.; on images from electricity, see ibid., pp. 145 f., and F. Brunot, *Histoire de la langue française*, vol. XIII, pt. 1, pp. 103 f. and 185 (by Ch. Bruneau).
[4] Quoted by Gombocz, op. cit., p. 73.

literally 'little rat'), *apple* of the eye, Adam's *apple*, *spine*, spinal *column*, *pelvis*, etc. If wider investigations were to show that both types are universal, a further question would arise: which of the two is the more frequent? A monograph published in 1948 by a Dutch linguist on the semantics of the body[1] suggests that transfers *from* the human sphere are more common than those directed *towards* it; in Sperber's terminology, our body is a centre of metaphorical expansion as well as attraction, but it acts more powerfully in the former than in the latter capacity.

(iii) *From concrete to abstract.*—The fact that, as Bloomfield put it, 'refined and abstract meanings largely grow out of more concrete meanings',[2] is perhaps too well known and too obvious to require detailed study; it would be most surprising to find a language where metaphors from abstract to concrete are more common than those in the opposite direction. It might be more profitable to examine the extension of certain specific forms of metaphor in this category. One such form is the use of images drawn from *light* to describe intellectual and moral phenomena: 'to throw *light* on', 'to put in a favourable *light*', 'leading *lights*', *enlighten, illuminating, brilliant, beaming, coruscating, dazzling, sparkling, scintillating, radiant*, etc. Another common pattern is the use of words denoting sense-impressions to describe abstract experiences: '*bitter* feelings', '*sweet* disposition', '*warm* reception', '*cold* disdain', '*smooth* temper', and others. To us these associations seem obvious and banal; yet only empirical investigations could show how general they actually are.

The fact that transfers from concrete to abstract are more common than the opposite type has an important stylistic corollary; it means that metaphors and similes working in this direction will sound more natural and more convincing than those where a concrete experience is compared to an abstract one, as for example when Sartre writes: 'Sous les mains, l'*herbe* était tentante *comme un suicide*.'[3] The implications of this tendency will be discussed in Chapter IX.

(iv) *Synaesthesia.*—Somewhat akin to this last type are the so-called 'synaesthetic' metaphors where words are transferred from one sense to another: from touch to sound, from sound to sight, etc. Since the advent of Symbolism, such transpositions have been set up as an aesthetic doctrine; Baudelaire proclaimed that 'les parfums, les couleurs et les sons

---

[1] J. J. De Witte, *De Betekeniswereld van het lichaam*, Nijmegen, 1948.

[2] *Language*, p. 429.

[3] 'Under one's hands, the grass was tempting like suicide' (*La Mort dans l'âme*, Paris, 1949, p. 131).

se répondent',[1] and Rimbaud actually wrote a sonnet on the colour of vowels (*Voyelles*). But the modern vogue of synaesthesia should not obscure the fact that this is an ancient and widespread, and quite possibly a universal, form of metaphor. It is found already in Homer and Aeschylus, and also in some ordinary expressions in Greek, such as *barytone* (from βαρύς 'heavy') and *oxytone* (from ὀξύς 'sharp'); similarly in Latin *gravis* and *acutus*, which gave our *grave* and *acute* accent. Commenting on such expressions, Aristotle wrote in *De Anima*: '*Acute* and *grave* are here metaphors transferred from their proper sphere, namely, that of touch … there seems to be a sort of parallelism between what is acute and grave to hearing and what is *sharp* or *blunt* to touch.'[2] Synaesthetic metaphors have been found in China and Japan, India, Persia, Arabia, Egypt, Babylonia and Palestine,[3] and from the language of the Kwakiutl Indians Franz Boas quotes the following powerful image: 'the words of speech strike the guests, as a spear strikes the game or the rays of the sun strike the earth'.[4] Our own modern languages abound in such metaphors, some of them hardened into clichés: '*cold* voice', '*piercing* sound', '*loud* colour' (French *couleur criarde*, Italian *colore stridente*), and many more.[5] There is a rich literature on various aspects of synaesthesia,[6] and by casting the net even wider it would not be too difficult to find out how general the phenomenon is, and whether it is in fact a semantic universal.

Further investigations might also reveal that the movement of synaesthetic metaphors is not haphazard but conforms to a basic pattern. I have collected data for the sources and destinations of such images in a dozen nineteenth-century poets, French, English and American, and have found three tendencies which stood out very clearly: (1) transfers from the lower to the more differentiated senses were more frequent than those in the opposite direction: over 80 per cent of a total of 2000 examples showed this 'upward' trend; (2) touch was in each case the largest single source, and (3) sound the largest single recipient.[7] The same tendencies have been noted in some twentieth-century Hungarian

---

[1] 'Perfumes, sounds, and colours answer each to each' (*Correspondances*—Francis Scarfe's translation in *Baudelaire*, Penguin Books, 1961, p. 37).

[2] Quoted by W. B. Stanford, *Greek Metaphor*, Oxford, 1936, p. 49.

[3] See A. Wellek, 'Das Doppelempfinden im abendländischen Altertum und Mittelalter', *Archiv für die gesamte Psychologie*, lxxx (1931), pp. 122–66.

[4] 'Metaphorical Expressions in the Language of the Kwakiutl Indians', *Donum Natalicium Schrijnen*, Nijmegen—Utrecht, 1929, pp. 147–53: p. 148.

[5] See Gombocz, op. cit., p. 7.

[6] See my *Principles of Semantics*, pp. 266 ff. Cf. now also J. G. O'Malley, 'Literary Synesthesia', *The Journal of Aesthetics*, xv (1957), pp. 391–411.

[7] For details see *The Principles of Semantics*, pp. 277 ff.

poets,[1] and it is interesting to learn that the first and most important among them, the 'hierarchical' principle, agrees with the findings of experimental psychology.[2] Naturally, the inquiry will have to be considerably broadened, and extended from literature to ordinary language, before we can begin to generalize; it should also be borne in mind that the above tendencies are purely statistical, and there are bound to be deviations from them in particular instances. I myself have found such deviations in the poetry of Victor Hugo where there are so many synaesthetic metaphors derived from the visual sphere that only the third of the three tendencies is valid: sound is still the main recipient, but sight takes the place of touch as the chief source of transpositions, and there is no significant difference between 'upward' and 'downward' transfers.[3]

As in the case of (i) and (iii), the general tendencies underlying synaesthetic metaphors have important implications for the student of style. They explain, for example, why images which run counter to the 'hierarchical' principle and transcribe data from a lower sense in terms of a higher one—images in which sounds are made visible, smells visible or audible, etc.—are apt to strike one as bold and unusual. If such images come off, they can have great expressive force. Some synaesthetic transfers in classical and medieval poets have a surprisingly modern air. In Aeschylus, the trumpet sets the shores ablaze with its sound;[4] in Euripides, the trumpet-call flashes out like a beacon.[5] Virgil speaks of the sky 'kindled with shouts',[6] and in an Old English poem the air is said to be darkened with the voices of the dying.[7] There are some remarkable transpositions in seventeenth-century English poetry, such as Donne's 'loud perfume' (*Elegy*, IV: 'The Perfume'), Milton's 'blind mouths' (*Lycidas*, l. 119), or Herbert's line: 'Till ev'n his beams sing, and my musick shine' (*Christmas*).[8] Modern writers are, of course, entirely uninhibited in their intermingling of the various senses. To Oscar Wilde,

[1] Cf. A. H. Whitney, 'Synaesthesia in Twentieth-Century Hungarian Poetry', *The Slavonic and East European Review*, xxx (1951–52), pp. 444–64. See now also M. Mancaş, 'La Synesthésie dans la création artistique de M. Eminescu, T. Arghezi et M. Sadoveanu', *Cahiers de Linguistique Théorique et Appliquée*, i (1962), pp. 55–87; L. Rosiello, 'Le Sinestesie nell'opera poetica di Montale', *Rendiconti*, Bologna, 1963, fasc. 7, pp. 1–19.
[2] Cf. H. Werner, *Language*, xxviii (1952), p. 256.
[3] See my article, 'La Transposition dans la poésie lyrique de Hugo', *Le Français Moderne*, xix (1951), pp. 277–95: pp. 287 ff.
[4] *Persae*, 395 (quoted by W. B. Stanford, *Aeschylus in his Style*, Dublin, 1942, pp. 106 ff.).
[5] *Phoenissae*, 1377 (quoted by Stanford, *Greek Metaphor*, p. 57).
[6] 'Clamore incendunt caelum' (*Aeneid*, X, 895; quoted by E. Struck, *Bedeutungslehre. Grundzüge einer lateinischen und griechischen Semasiologie*, Leipzig—Berlin, 1940, p. 98).
[7] 'Lyft up geswearc fægum stefun' (*Exodus*, XIV, 462; quoted by Yamaguchi, op. cit., p. 103).
[8] See W. B. Stanford, 'Synaesthetic Metaphor', *Comparative Literature Studies*, vi–vii (1942), pp. 26–30, and A. Wellek, 'Renaissance- und Barocksynästhesie', *Deutsche Vierteljahrsschrift für Literaturwissenschaft*, ix (1931), pp. 534–84: p. 569.

G

music may appear as scarlet or as mauve;[1] to Proust it seems decked out in all the colours of the rainbow.[2] Even silence can have a colour—white, black or blue, as the case may be.[3] Smells too may be visualized: Paul Eluard conjures up the image of a 'shining black scent';[4] Proust has a vision of smells standing erect, side by side, in separate blocks;[5] Sartre speaks of green and yellow smells and even of the 'young yellow taste of soft wood'[6] and the 'pink taste' of a cake.[7]

2. *Extension and restriction of meaning.*—Ever since the early days of modern semantics it has been known that two opposite tendencies are at work in the development of words: some terms tend to widen their meaning, others to narrow it. The English word *bird*, for example, has extended its range since Old English times when it was used only in the sense of 'young bird'. As the logicians would say, its 'extension' has been increased and its 'intension' has been reduced: it is now applicable to more things but tells us less about them. On the other hand, an old synonym of *bird*, *fowl*, has developed in the opposite direction: originally it meant 'bird' in general (cf. German *Vogel*), as it still does in the Bible: 'Behold the *fowls* of the air'; subsequently its range was narrowed down to its present meaning which is more distinctive and less comprehensive than the older sense.[8]

Both extension and restriction can result from a variety of causes, some purely linguistic, others psychological or social. Nevertheless several linguists have suggested that restriction of meaning is on the whole more common than extension.[9] This has recently been confirmed by some psychological experiments conducted by Heinz Werner, according to whom there are two main reasons for the disparity: 'One is that the predominant developmental trend is in the direction of differentiation rather than of synthesis. A second reason, related to the first, is that the formation of general concepts from specific terms is of lesser importance

[1] 'The scarlet music of Dvořák' (quoted, after E. F. Benson, by W. B. Stanford, 'Synaesthetic Metaphor', loc. cit., p. 27, n. 1.); 'mauve Hungarian music' (*An Ideal Husband*).
[2] *Du Côté de chez Swann*, vol. II, p. 174.
[3] Cf. the poem 'White Silence' by the Hungarian Symbolist Endre Ady; 'black silence' (Oscar Wilde, *Salome*); 'la surface azurée du silence—the azure surface of silence' (Proust, *Du Côté de chez Swann*, vol. I, p. 119).
[4] 'Le parfum noir rayonne' (*L'Amour la poésie*, 1929).
[5] 'Verticales et debout, elles (les odeurs) se tenaient en tranches juxtaposées et distinctes' (*La Prisonnière*, Paris, NRF, 1949, vol. II, p. 258).
[6] *La Mort dans l'âme*, pp. 45, 233, 251.
[7] Quoted by R. de Champigny, 'L'Expression élémentaire dans *L'Être et le néant*', *Publications of the Modern Language Association of America*, lxviii (1953), pp. 56–64: p. 62.
[8] See recently H. Schreuder, 'On Some Cases of Restriction of Meaning', *English Studies*, xxxvii (1956), pp. 117–24.
[9] Bloomfield, *Language*, p. 151; Bréal, *Essai de sémantique*, p. 107; J. Vendryes, *Le Langage*, Paris, 1950 ed., p. 237.

in non-scientific communication though it is rather a characteristic of scientific endeavour. In other words, language in everyday life is directed toward the concrete and specific rather than toward the abstract and general.'[1] The problem is of great interest, but we shall need many more facts from different languages before we can set up the predominance of restriction as a universal tendency.

3. *Taboo.*—The term *taboo* is of Polynesian origin, and the very fact that we use such an exotic word to denote a phenomenon which is very common in our own culture is symptomatic of the universality of taboo. Here we are concerned only with the linguistic side of the problem. There is a voluminous literature on the subject, and, as in the case of onomato-poeia, any future research project could best be started by compiling a critical inventory of what is already known. Language taboos seem to spring from three main causes. Firstly, there are those inspired by *fear*, or 'holy dread', as Freud preferred to call it:[2] religious restrictions on the use of the name of God, and also superstitious avoidance of any direct reference to the dead, to the devil and to evil spirits, and the widespread and varied taboos on animals. A second type of taboo is dictated by a sense of *delicacy*: when we talk of such unpleasant topics as illness and death, physical or mental deficiencies, and such criminal acts as cheating, stealing or killing, we often have recourse to euphemisms, and this can permanently affect the meaning of the latter: instead of veiling the tabooed subject, the euphemism will become indissolubly linked with it, as has happened with *undertaker, disease, imbecile* (from Latin *imbecillus* or *imbecillis,* 'weak, feeble') and other similar terms. Thirdly, taboo bans may result from a sense of *decency* and propriety: references to sex, names of certain parts and functions of the body, and swear-words are particularly subject to this form of taboo. While all three types are of wide currency, none of them is an absolute universal since they are governed by social and cultural factors and will arise only in certain environments. The first type is bound to become rarer with the progress of civilization, though it will not disappear altogether; the second and especially the third type, on the other hand, will be encouraged by certain modes and standards of social behaviour such as those imposed by the *Précieuses* in seventeenth-century France. Some of these more sophisti-cated taboos may be subsequently rejected as prudish and hypocritical: we no longer say *limbs* or *benders* instead of *legs*, or *waist* instead of *body*,

---

[1] 'Change of Meaning: a Study of Semantic Processes through Experimental Data', *The Journal of General Psychology*, l (1954), pp. 181–208: p. 203.
[2] *Totem and Taboo*, London, Pelican Books, repr. 1940, p. 37.

as did some Boston ladies a hundred years ago.[1] The growth and decay of the various forms of taboo, in relation to social and cultural changes, could be systematically studied in various languages; many data are already scattered in linguistic, anthropological and psychological treatises, but they would have to be broadened, classified and reinterpreted before definitive conclusions could be reached.

Apart from these general tendencies, some specific patterns of taboo and euphemism would also be worth looking into. Perhaps the most striking feature is the frequency and diversity of taboos on names of *animals*. A recent monograph on the subject by a Brazilian linguist[2] cites no less than twenty-four animals whose names have been struck by such bans in various languages: they range from ants, bees and worms to bears,[3] tigers and lions; even butterflies and squirrels appear in the list. One of the most remarkable cases is that of the weasel; the fear inspired by this animal has given rise to a multiplicity of propitiatory euphemisms which are very similar in different languages: in some of them it is described as a 'little woman' (Italian *donnola*, Portuguese *doninha*) or as a 'pretty little woman' (French *belette*, diminutive of *belle*, Swedish *lilla snälla*), while elsewhere a pretence is made of including it within the family by turning it into a 'bride', a 'daughter-in-law', a 'sister-in-law' or a 'gossip'.[4] In other forms of taboo there are also some interesting parallel developments; thus the same mixture of euphemism and irony which gave *imbecile* its present sense lies at the root of a number of similar changes in the same sphere: French *crétin* is a Swiss dialectal form of *chrétien* 'Christian'; French *benêt* 'silly' comes from Latin *benedictus* 'blessed'; English *silly* once meant 'happy, blessed' (cf. German *selig* 'blessed; deceased'), whereas *idiot* goes back to a Greek word meaning 'private person, layman'.

As some of these examples show, euphemism, or ironical 'pseudo-euphemism', will often lead to a permanent depreciation of meaning. The frequency of so-called '*pejorative*' sense-development was noticed by many early semanticists;[5] some saw in it a symptom of a fundamental streak of pessimism or cynicism in the human mind. Yet, as Bréal rightly

---

[1] Jespersen, *Growth and Structure*, p. 226.
[2] R. F. Mansur Guérios, *Tabus lingüísticos*, Rio de Janeiro, 1956, ch. XVIII.
[3] See A. Meillet, *Linguistique historique et linguistique générale*, vol. I, pp. 282 ff., and M. B. Emeneau, 'Taboos on Animal Names', *Language*, xxiv (1948), pp. 56–63.
[4] See Mansur Guérios, op. cit., pp. 152 ff., with further references; cf. also Nyrop, *Sémantique*, pp. 275 f.
[5] On these processes see esp. H. Schreuder, *Pejorative Sense-Development in English*, I, Groningen, 1929, and K. Jaberg, 'Pejorative Bedeutungsentwicklung im Französischen', *Zeitschrift für Romanische Philologie*, xxv (1901), xxvii (1903) and xxix (1905).

pointed out, 'this alleged pejorative tendency is the result of a very human attitude which leads us to veil and disguise awkward, offensive or repulsive ideas'.[1] Thus the notorious deterioration which has affected various words for 'girl' or 'woman', such as English *hussy, quean,* French *fille, garce,* or German *Dirne,* was no doubt due to genuine or pseudo-euphemism rather than to any anti-feminine bias. These and other types of pejorative sense-change—those which arise from national or social prejudice or from a simple association of ideas—are sufficiently widespread to be worth investigating on a broad interlinguistic basis. Side by side with these pejorative changes there are also '*ameliorative*' ones[2] where an unpleasant meaning is either weakened or even becomes positively favourable. An example of weakening is the verb *blame* which is historically the same word as *blaspheme*; a case of positive improvement is English *nice* from Latin *nescius* 'ignorant'. One has the impression that such ameliorative changes are less common than pejorative ones, perhaps because the ranks of the latter are swelled by euphemisms and pseudo-euphemisms; but this would have to be confirmed by further investigations. Another problem which it would be interesting to explore is the development of neutral terms, '*voces mediae*', which often tend to specialize either in a favourable or in an unfavourable meaning. Thus both *luck* and *fate* are in themselves neutral, ambivalent words, but the adjectives *lucky* and *fatal* have become polarized, the former in a positive, the latter in a negative sense. One wonders whether there is any predominant trend of development in one direction or another.

4. *Implications for linguistic reconstruction.*—The processes discussed in this section, to which several others could be added, are of direct relevance to etymology and comparative linguistics. Commenting on the traditional study of semantic changes, Bloomfield stated that, 'aside from its extra-linguistic interest, it gives us some measure of probability by which we can judge of etymologic comparisons'.[3] Such probability would be very considerably increased if some of the tendencies involved turned out to be semantic universals. This would help the etymologist and the comparatist in two ways. Firstly, it would tell him what kinds of changes to expect, and whether a change suggested by his data would

---

[1] *Essai de sémantique*, p. 100.

[2] See G. A. van Dongen, *Amelioratives in English*, I, Rotterdam, 1933.

[3] *Language*, p. 430. On these problems see esp. E. Benveniste, 'Problèmes sémantiques de la reconstruction', *Word*, x (1954), pp. 251–64; G. Bonfante, 'On Reconstruction and Linguistic Method', *Word*, i (1945), pp. 132–61; H. M. Hoenigswald, *Language Change and Linguistic Reconstruction*, Chicago, 1960; O. Szemerényi, 'Principles of Etymological Research in the Indo-European Languages', *II. Fachtagung für Indogermanische und Allgemeine Sprachwissenschaft*, pp. 175–212.

be common or infrequent, normal or exceptional. Secondly, it would enable him to choose between alternative explanations. Let us assume, for instance, that the preponderance of synaesthetic metaphors from the lower to the higher senses (cf. above, pp. 87 ff.) were to be shown by further research to be a universal tendency. Let us also assume that an etymologist were faced with two early meanings of a given word, one related to touch, the other to sound. When deciding as to which of the two meanings came first, it would be logical to surmise that the tactile sense preceded the acoustic one, since transfers from touch to sound are far more common than those from sound to touch. It is true, of course, that these tendencies are purely statistical, and it is perfectly possible that in a particular case the process worked the other way round. Nevertheless, a hypothesis which was in harmony with the general tendency would have a better chance of being correct than the alternative explanation; it might even be possible to calculate the margin of error, which might be large in some cases and negligible in others.

A few years ago, a leading authority on historical semantics uttered the following warning: 'In semantic development, so many different and at times contradictory tendencies are involved that it is impossible to speak of any laws. Semantics resolves itself into a wealth of particular problems. It shows only what *may* happen, not what *must* happen, in the field of semantic change.'[1] This view is perhaps unduly pessimistic. It is true that semantics will never tell us that a given change is *bound* to happen; it may, however, tell us what changes are *likely* to happen; it may even enable us to estimate in precise terms the likelihood of their happening, the 'measure of probability' envisaged by Bloomfield in the statement quoted above.

C. Universal Tendencies in the Structure of the Vocabulary

As we have seen in the preceding chapters, during the last three decades structuralist methods have been introduced into semantics, and there has been a shift of interest from single words to higher lexical units. These studies are still in their infancy, but they have already thrown up several problems with universal implications, three of which may be briefly mentioned here. They arise at three different levels of linguistic analysis: at the level of single words, that of conceptual spheres, and that of the vocabulary as a whole.[2]

---

[1] E. Gamillscheg, 'Streifzüge auf dem Gebiet der Bedeutungslehre', *Akademie der Wissenschaften und der Literatur in Mainz, Abhandlungen der Geistes- und Sozialwissenschaftlichen Klasse*, 1958, no. 5, pp. 273–92: p. 291.
[2] Cf. above, pp. 10 ff.

1. *Lexical constants.*—A comparison of a wide variety of languages would quickly show whether there is such a thing as a 'lexical constant': an object, event or other feature of such fundamental importance that it must somehow be expressed in any language;[1] whether it is expressed by a non-independent root, a simple word, a compound word, or even a phrase, is of secondary significance. Even if the evidence for such constants were so overwhelming that we could set them up as unrestricted universals, we would still have to allow for differences between various languages. Assuming, for example, that the idea of fatherhood is a lexical constant, we find that in Latin there were two words for 'father': *genitor* for the physiological relationship, and *pater* which carried social connotations (cf. *paterfamilias*).[2] But this does not really affect the status of a lexical constant; it merely means that its various aspects may be expressed by separate words in some languages.

If a list of lexical constants could be established—whether as unrestricted universals or as statistical ones with a high degree of probability—this would be of great interest to comparative linguistics. When studying the vocabulary of the Indo-European parent tongue or any other extinct language, we could safely assume that it had some word or other element for the expression of such constants. In some cases these basic words have survived in the idioms descended from the parent tongue, as in English *mother*, Latin *māter*, Greek μήτηρ, Sanskrit *mātár-*, etc. Elsewhere they have been replaced by other terms for a variety of reasons. Taboo in particular has often disturbed the pattern of correspondences. Thus the 'left hand' is quite possibly a lexical constant, yet there are different words for it in various Indo-European languages; some have in fact been borrowed from a foreign source: French *gauche* from Germanic, Spanish *izquierdo* from Basque. This diversity is obviously connected with the superstitions and taboos which have developed around the left hand in many countries. Another possible lexical constant, the 'moon', has also been the object of many superstitions which are still faintly noticeable in our terms *lunatic* and *lunacy*. As Bloomfield points out, 'the Indo-European languages use the most varied words for "moon"; it is notable that Russian has borrowed Latin |'lu:na| as |lu'na|, though otherwise it makes scarcely any but highly learned borrowings from Latin'.[3] When the name of a lexical constant is struck by a taboo ban, a replacement has to be found, and this may lead to the borrowing of

---

[1] Cf. H. J. Pos, 'The Foundation of Word-Meanings: Different Approaches', *Lingua*, i (1948), pp. 281–92: pp. 289 ff.
[2] Cf. Meillet, *Linguistique historique et linguistique générale*, vol. I, p. 241.
[3] *Language*, p. 400.

words which would not normally pass from one language into another.

The problem of lexical constants is directly relevant to a technique which has been elaborated in recent years by comparative philologists. This technique, known as '*glottochronology*', aims at estimating the period which has elapsed since two cognate languages were separated from one another by comparing the 'basic vocabularies' of the two languages. Glottochronology rests on two fundamental assumptions: (1) that there is such a thing as a basic vocabulary, in other words that there are lexical constants which must be expressed somehow in all languages; (2) that, over long periods, the rate of replacement of these basic terms remains unchanged. The second point does not concern us here; as for the first, the author of a well-known textbook, who is on the whole sympathetic to glottochronology, rightly points out that 'only extended trial-and-error, comparing languages and cultures, can assemble the proper reference-list of meanings; this trial-and-error work continues, and the reliable list seems to get smaller and smaller as more languages and cultures are taken into account'. And the same linguist adds, as a sobering afterthought: 'The number of meanings for which a human language *must* have words seems amazingly small.'[1] In spite of these and other reservations, however, he considers that 'no development in historical linguistics in many decades has showed such great promise'.[2] Other linguists are more critical;[3] nevertheless, the very emergence of glottochronology should encourage systematic studies of alleged lexical constants over a wide range of languages and periods.

2. *Lexical fields.*—As we have repeatedly noted,[4] one of the most fruitful concepts evolved so far in structural semantics is that of the 'lexical field' or closely integrated conceptual sphere. The numerous articles and monographs which have recently been published on these problems have all tended to emphasize the differences between these fields in various languages; they have concentrated on what is distinctive and idiosyncratic in them rather than on what they have in common. Yet, beneath all the diversity, there is likely to be an underlying unity which a systematic comparison of these fields would no doubt reveal. Thus we are told of striking differences between the number and nature of colour distinctions (cf. pp. 12 f.), and these discrepancies are certainly

---

[1] Hockett, op. cit., p. 530.

[2] Ibid., p. 535.

[3] See e.g. E. Coseriu, 'Critique de la glottochronologie appliquée aux langues romanes', *Xe Congrès International de Linguistique et Philologie Romanes, Résumés des Communications*, Strasbourg, 1962, p. 9.

[4] See above, pp. 12 ff. and 58 ff.

significant and illuminating; but it would be equally interesting to know whether there are any elements common to all classifications of colours, any distinctions which have to be formulated everywhere and which could therefore rank as lexical constants. The same may be said of kinship terms (cf. p. 13) and other lexical fields on which we possess extensive data for many languages. By collating information from a wide variety of periods and idioms we should be able to establish (a) the number of possible solutions, (b) their relative frequencies, and (c) the common element, if any, which can be found in all of them or at least in most of them.

3. *The classification of concepts.*—It will be recalled (cf. pp. 14f.) that the idea of constructing a general classification of concepts for all languages— the same idea which had inspired Roget's *Thesaurus*—was recently revived by Hallig and von Wartburg in their *Begriffssystem als Grundlage für die Lexikographie*. The aims of the project were practical: if a series of monographs on the vocabulary of different languages, or different periods of the same language, could all conform, within reason, to the same pattern, the results could be easily compared and any differences quickly noticed. Before and since the publication of the Hallig–Wartburg scheme, a number of studies on the vocabulary of French writers from various periods have been based on this system; it has also been applied to several non-French dialects.[1] Professor Wartburg is confident that the same framework could be used, with the necessary modifications, in the description of other Indo-European languages and their dialects; it might even be extended to non-Indo-European idioms.[2] Whatever one may think of the merits or otherwise of this particular scheme, it would be an important step forward if a system of concepts could be generally accepted as a uniform yet flexible framework for lexical studies.

The list of topics discussed above is not meant to be exhaustive in any way; the aim was merely to suggest some directions in which we may look for universals or, more modestly, for general tendencies in semantics. If a co-ordinated research programme could be organized to explore some of these problems, then we would have to establish a rough *order of priorities*, starting with relatively simple questions and gradually working our way towards more complex ones. From this purely practical point of view, the subjects listed above fall into four broad categories:

　　1. It would be best to begin with some clearly defined problems which

---

[1] See Wartburg, *Problèmes et méthodes de la linguistique,* p. 190, n. 2.
[2] Ibid., p. 179 of the German edition.

could be formulated in precise numerical terms. Such problems are, for instance, the relations between polysemy and word-frequency; connexions between homonymy, word-length and word-structure; the sources and destinations of synaesthetic metaphors; the number and nature of lexical constants.

2. In the next phase of the programme we could proceed to the study of certain phenomena which are more complicated in themselves, but about which extensive data are already available from many languages. Onomatopoeia, taboo and parallel metaphors would belong to this category.

3. At a later stage we might be ready to tackle such intricate matters as the ratio of transparent and opaque words; the preponderance of specific or generic terms; the relative frequency of pejorative and ameliorative sense-change and of extension and restriction; the structure of the same lexical field in various languages.

4. Finally, some important research projects will have to wait until we have the means of collecting the necessary data. Thus, if there are any general tendencies behind the conflicts caused by polysemy and homonymy, we shall be in a better position to discover them when linguistic atlases are available for many more languages than at present.

If, in the course of such a programme, some semantic universals could be precisely identified, this would be of great significance not only for linguistics but also for other branches of study. While some of the problems discussed above are of purely linguistic interest, others clearly have wider implications. To mention but a few, the distinction between transparent and opaque words raises important educational issues; onomatopoeic and metaphorical patterns are of direct relevance to stylistics; synaesthesia is basically a psychological phenomenon, with wide ramifications in language and literature. Such problems as taboo and lexical fields could best be attacked by a concerted effort of linguists, anthropologists, ethnologists, psychologists and sociologists. The study of lexical fields, and of the structure of the vocabulary in general, would also throw light on the impact of language upon thinking, which is one of the main themes of contemporary philosophy. Among all branches of linguistics, semantics undoubtedly has the most varied and most intimate contacts with other disciplines, and the discovery of universal tendencies in this field would have far-reaching repercussions in neighbouring spheres.

PART II

PROBLEMS OF STYLE

CHAPTER VI

NEW BEARINGS IN STYLISTICS

In a lecture at Oxford in 1956, Jean Cocteau made the interesting claim that the 'decipherment' and 'exegesis' of the language of poetry is an art in its own right:

'La poésie trouve d'abord et cherche après. Elle est la proie de l'exégèse qui est sans conteste une muse puisqu'il lui arrive de traduire en clair nos codes, d'éclairer nos propres ténèbres et de nous renseigner sur ce que nous ne savions pas avoir dit.'[1]

Some twenty years earlier, Paul Valéry had expressed somewhat similar ideas in less metaphorical language:

'En somme, l'étude dont nous parlions aurait pour objet de préciser et de développer la recherche des effets proprement littéraires du langage, l'examen des inventions expressives et suggestives qui ont été faites pour accroître le pouvoir et la pénétration de la parole.'[2]

It is interesting to set these ambitious statements against the modest and almost humble words of a leading linguist of an earlier generation. As far back as 1899, W. Meyer-Lübke had written, in the preface to the last volume of his monumental comparative grammar of the Romance languages:

'Quant à la stylistique, je l'abandonne à d'autres . . . La stylistique est l'étude de la langue comme art; pour la traiter, il faut posséder le sens artistique, le talent de se pénétrer des sentiments des autres à un degré où il ne m'est pas donné d'atteindre.'[3]

---

[1] 'Poetry finds first and seeks afterwards. It is the quarry of exegesis which is unquestionably a Muse because it is apt to decipher our codes, to illuminate our inner darkness, and to tell us about what we were unaware of having said' (quoted by G. Antoine, 'La Stylistique française. Sa définition, ses buts, ses méthodes', *Revue de l'Enseignement Supérieur*, 1959, no. 1, pp. 42–60: p. 50).

[2] 'In short, the study we have been discussing would aim at specifying and developing research into the strictly literary effects of language; it would seek to examine the expressive and suggestive devices which have been invented in order to enhance the power and penetration of speech' (*Introduction à la poétique*, pp. 12 f., quoted by R. A. Sayce, *Style in French Prose*, Oxford, 1953, p. 7).

[3] 'As for stylistics, I leave it to others . . . Stylistics is the study of language as art; in order to practise it, one needs artistic sensibility, the gift of becoming imbued with the feelings of others to a degree which I am unable to reach' (quoted by L. Spitzer, 'Les Etudes de style et les différents pays', *Langue et littérature. Actes du VIIIᵉ Congrès de la Fédération Internationale des Langues et Littératures Modernes*, Bibliothèque de la Faculté de Philosophie et Lettres de l'Université de Liège, fasc. CLXI; Paris, 1961, pp. 23–38: p. 23).

It is clear from these statements that the study of style is a border-line discipline which faces the student with a double challenge: not only does it lie astride the boundary between linguistics and literary criticism, but it requires a combination of artistic gifts and scholarly qualities; as one of its most brilliant exponents put it, it is the result of 'talent, experience, and faith'.[1] In spite of these difficulties, stylistics has become remarkably popular of late: a recent bibliography of style studies in the Romance field during the period 1955–60 lists nearly 1800 titles.[2] The prominence given to these problems at international congresses and conferences is another indication that stylistics has come of age.[3]

Although the term *stylistics* goes back to the Romantic period,[4] the discipline itself did not become established in its modern form until the early years of the present century. From the very outset, the new science developed along two different lines. One school of thought was interested in the stylistic resources of particular languages, in the expressive devices which they place at the disposal of the speaker and the writer. The other school was more concerned with the use to which these resources are put in the hands of creative authors. We shall therefore have to distinguish between two main types of stylistic study: those which explore the style of a language and those which are focused on the style of a writer.[5]

A. Stylistic Resources of a Language

I. Expressive Devices

To describe the stylistic resources of a language means, as we have just seen, to establish, classify and evaluate its expressive elements. The concept of '*expressiveness*' is clearly fundamental to this approach, and we shall have to define it more precisely before we can go any further. First, however, it might be helpful to see what some of the practitioners of style have to say on the problem. Two of the best known definitions

---

[1] L. Spitzer, *Linguistics and Literary History. Essays in Stylistics*, Princeton, 1948, p. 27.

[2] H. Hatzfeld–Y. Le Hir, *Essai de bibliographie critique de stylistique française et romane* (*1955–1960*), Paris, 1961.

[3] For example at the congress mentioned in p. 99 n. 3, or at the Ninth International Congress of Linguistics (Cambridge, Mass., 1962). For the proceedings of an important conference on style, attended by representatives of various disciplines, see T. A. Sebeok (ed.), *Style in Language*, New York—London, 1960.

[4] The German term *Stilistik* has been in current use since the first half of the nineteenth century; Grimm's dictionary quotes the first example from an undated passage in Novalis. In English, the noun *stylistic*, in the singular, is attested in 1846 (*NED*); French *stylistique* is recorded by Littré's dictionary in 1872, but without indication of source. Cf. A. Sempoux, 'Notes sur l'histoire des mots *style* et *stylistique*', *Revue Belge de Philologie et d'Histoire*, xxxix (1961), pp. 736–46.

[5] Cf. P. Guiraud, *La Stylistique*, Paris, 1954, pp. 41 ff.

of style single out expressiveness as its distinctive quality. According to Stendhal, the essence of style is: 'ajouter à une pensée donnée toutes les circonstances propres à produire tout l'effet que doit produire cette pensée'.[1] The same idea was expressed by Flaubert in a striking simile: 'Je conçois un style qui nous entrerait dans l'idée comme un coup de stylet.'[2] Some modern writers are even more explicit. In a passage already quoted, Valéry has spoken of *expressive and suggestive devices* which increase the power and impact of our words, and Gide declared, towards the end of his life:

'L'emploi des mots *les mieux expressifs*, leur meilleure place dans la phrase, l'allure de celle-ci, son nombre, son rythme, son harmonie—oui, tout cela fait partie du "bien écrire" (et rien ne vaut si tout cela n'est pas naturel).'[3]

For the student of style, 'expressiveness' covers a wide range of linguistic features which have one thing in common: they do not directly affect the meaning of the utterance, the actual information which it conveys. Everything that transcends the purely referential and communicative side of language belongs to the province of expressiveness:[4] emotive overtones, emphasis, rhythm, symmetry, euphony, and also the so-called *evocative* elements which place our style in a particular register (literary, colloquial, slangy, etc.) or associate it with a particular milieu (historical, foreign, provincial, professional, etc.).

It may be noted that there has been a certain shift of emphasis in this branch of stylistics since it was founded by Charles Bally more than half a century ago.[5] Bally had originally limited the scope of the new science to the study of 'emotive' elements; subsequently 'emotive' was found to be too narrow and was replaced by 'expressive'. Even more important, Bally had tried to exclude literary style from the purview of stylistics

[1] 'To add to a given thought all the circumstances calculated to produce the entire effect which that thought ought to produce' (*Racine et Shakespeare*). This formula was taken up and developed by J. Middleton Murry in his treatise, *The Problem of Style* (1922), ch. I.
[2] 'I can imagine a style which would enter like a stiletto into the idea expressed' (quoted by W. v. Wartburg, *Évolution et structure de la langue française*, 5th ed., Berne, 1958, p. 225).
[3] 'The use of the *most expressive* words, their best place in the sentence, the movement of the latter, its balance, rhythm and harmony—yes, all this is part of "good writing" (and none of it is of any value unless it is all natural)' (*Feuillets d'automne*, Paris, 1949, p. 236). In this quotation and those which follow, the italics are always mine.
[4] 'La estilística es el estudio de lo que haya de extralógico en el lenguaje' ('Stylistics is the study of what is "extra-logical" in language') (R. Fernández Retamar, *Idea de la estilística*, Havana, 1958, p. 11). There are obvious similarities between this doctrine and I. A. Richards's famous distinction between 'sense', 'tone', 'feeling' and 'intention'.
[5] See esp. his *Traité de stylistique française*, 2 vols., 3rd ed., Geneva—Paris, 1951. Cf. also *Le Langage et la vie*, 3rd ed., revised, Geneva—Lille, 1952.

and to confine the latter to the study of ordinary speech, whereas his disciples[1] are interested in all forms of language, whether literary or otherwise.

Intimately connected with expressiveness is another key-concept of stylistics, the idea of *choice*: the possibility of choosing between two or more alternatives—'stylistic variants', as they have been called[2]—which mean the same thing but do not put it in the same way. In the words of a recent textbook, 'two utterances in the same language which convey approximately the same information, but which are different in their linguistic structure, can be said to differ in style: *He came too soon* and *He arrived prematurely*'.[3] The choice between two or more 'synonymous' forms will be dictated by considerations of expressiveness: we shall choose the one which carries the right degree of emotion and emphasis, the one whose tone, rhythm, phonetic structure and stylistic register are best suited to the purpose of the utterance and to the situation in which it takes place. As one of the Bally's followers has expressed it, 'notre tâche est d'interpréter le choix fait par l'usager dans tous les compartiments de la langue en vue d'assurer à sa communication le maximum d'efficacité'.[4]

A simple example from Modern French syntax will serve to elucidate this intricate mechanism of choice and expressiveness. It is a well-known fact that both in English and in French the vast majority of sentences are built on the same pattern: the verb is preceded by its subject and followed by its object: 'the dog sees the cat—le chien voit le chat'. In both languages there exist, however, certain well-defined positions where the subject can or must be *inverted*. Compulsory inversion, for example in certain interrogative sentences, is of no interest to the student of style, but optional inversion is a happy hunting-ground for all kinds of stylistic effects. Naturally, the positions in which inversion is permissible will depend on grammatical factors: it will be used only in constructions where it can cause no ambiguity. Thus one may choose in French between 'le scandale que provoqua sa réaction' and 'le scandale que sa réaction provoqua', whereas in English, 'the scandal which caused his reaction' is not the same thing as 'the scandal which his reaction caused'. The

[1] See in particular M. Cressot, *Le Style et ses techniques*, 4th ed., Paris, 1959; G. Devoto, *Studi di stilistica*, Florence, 1950; J. Marouzeau, *Traité de stylistique latine*, 2nd ed., Paris, 1946; Id., *Précis de stylistique française*, 3rd ed., Paris, 1950; R. G. Piotrovskij, *Ocherki po stilistike frantsuzskovo jazyka*, 2nd ed., Leningrad, 1960; H. Seidler, *Allgemeine Stilistik*, Göttingen, 1953.
[2] Guiraud, op. cit., p. 47.
[3] Hockett, *A Course in Modern Linguistics*, p. 556.
[4] 'It is our task to interpret the choice made by the speaker in all the various compartments of language in order to formulate his utterance with the maximum of effectiveness' (Cressot, op. cit., 1st ed., p. 2).

reason obviously lies in the fact that the English pronoun *which* combines the functions of the French nominative *qui* and accusative *que*.[1] Let us consider first of all some of the commonest uses to which inversion is put in Modern French. The best way of appreciating the advantages of the inverted order is to rewrite the sentence in the customary subject-verb sequence and compare the two versions. Take, for example, the following two sentences, the first one as Proust wrote it, the second rewritten by me:

Au fur et à mesure que la saison s'avança, *changea le tableau* que j'y trouvais dans la fenêtre.'[2]

'Au fur et à mesure que la saison s'avança, *le tableau* que j'y trouvais dans la fenêtre *changea*.'

Both sentences mean the same thing; both are grammatically correct. Nevertheless, Proust's version has several solid advantages:

(*a*) The *sound and rhythm* of Proust's sentence is far more satisfying. Not only does it avoid the internal rhyme *s'avança—changea* in two prominent and symmetrical positions, but it ensures a smoother and more balanced rhythm. In the alternative version, the short verb *changea* is preceded by a longer subordinate clause, and this produces an impression of anticlimax and runs counter to the French fondness for 'la cadence majeure', the arrangement of the sentence in groups of increasing volume.[3]

(*b*) *Syntactically*, too, Proust's phrasing is more successful than the alternative. In *changea le tableau*, the verb and its subject are in immediate contact, whereas in the other version they are separated by a subordinate clause.[4] Moreover, the two halves of the sentence are con-

---

[1] On inversion in Modern French, see esp. R. Le Bidois's monumental monograph, *L'Inversion du sujet dans la prose contemporaine (1900–1950) étudiée plus spécialement dans l'œuvre de Marcel Proust*, Paris, 1952. See also ch. IV of my *Style in the French Novel*, where further references will be found. Cf. also K. Rogger, 'Zur Inversion des Subjekts im heutigen Französisch', *Zeitschrift für Romanische Philologie*, lxxii (1956), pp. 219–82.

[2] 'As the season gradually advanced, the scene which I saw from the window changed' (*A l'ombre des jeunes filles en fleurs*, vol. III, Paris, 1949 impr., p. 49).

[3] 'Mettre un mot court après une masse d'une certaine importance, c'est l'exposer à passer inaperçu, ce qui peut nuire à la clarté; c'est bouleverser désagréablement la continuité de la phrase, à moins qu'on n'attende un effet de cette place inattendue' ('To place a short word after a mass of a certain volume means to risk that it might pass unnoticed, which might affect the clarity of the utterance; it also means an unpleasant disturbance in the continuity of the sentence, unless one hopes to obtain a special effect from this unexpected position') (Cressot, op. cit., p. 168).

[4] Another example from Proust will show that some sentences would become impossibly unwieldy and cacophonous were they not saved by inversion: '. . . retrouvé telle de mes terreurs enfantines comme celle que mon grand-oncle me tirât mes boucles et qu'avait dissipée le jour—date pour moi d'une ère nouvelle—où on les avait coupées' ('rediscovered some of my childhood terrors such as that my great-uncle would pull my curls; a terror dispelled by the day—the beginning of a new era for me—when they were cut') (*Du Côté de chez Swann*,

H

structed in Proust in two opposite ways: subject—verb‖verb—subject (*la saison s'avança—changea le tableau*). This contrast effect, known as '*chiasmus*' after the shape of the Greek letter *chi* (χ), gives the sentence an elegance, symmetry and variety which are lacking in the alternative construction.

(*c*) While the two versions have the same *meaning*, Proust's sentence conveys it more forcefully and effectively. The parallel course of the two processes, the progress of the season and the change of scenery, is underlined by the dynamic juxtaposition of the two verbs, *s'avança—changea*, whereas the other version is somewhat ineffectual and invertebrate in comparison.

In the example just discussed, the effects of inversion, though potent enough, were comparatively simple. In the hands of a skilful writer, the same device can produce more subtle and complex results, some of which can be fully appreciated only in the light of the context and within the framework of the whole work of art. Only a few of these special values can be briefly mentioned here:

1. *Emphasis.*—By relegating the subject to the very end of the sentence and thus placing it in a peak position, one may effectively throw it into relief. The following sentence from Proust, severely dislocated and unbalanced, sacrifices elegance to expressiveness by laying particularly heavy stress upon the subject:

'ces acteurs dont l'art, bien qu'il me fût encore inconnu, était la première forme, entre toutes celles qu'il revêt, sous laquelle se laissait pressentir par moi, *l'Art*'.[1]

If one remembers the supreme importance of art in Proust's philosophy of life, the emphasis, and the consequences it entails, will not appear excessive.

Rather more complicated is another case of emphasis by anticlimax in the same writer:

'Legrandin se rapprochait de la duchesse, s'estimant de céder à cet attrait de l'esprit et de la vertu qu'ignorent les infâmes *snobs*.'[2]

vol. I, pp. 14 f.). Without inversion the end of the sentence would have become intolerably clumsy: '. . . et que le jour—date pour moi d'une ère nouvelle—où on les avait coupées avait dissipée'.

[1] '. . . these actors whose art, although I did not know it yet, was the first form, among all those it assumes, which gave me a foretaste of *Art*' (ibid., p. 102).

[2] 'Legrandin drew nearer to the duchess, in the belief that he was yielding to that attraction of wit and virtue which is unknown to infamous *snobs*' (ibid., p. 171).

Once again we have to do with one of the key-terms of Proust's novel. The Anglicism *snob*,[1] un-French and explosive in sound and derogatory in meaning (cf. the adjective *infâmes*), is thrown into prominence by being placed at the end of the sentence, in defiance of the 'cadence majeure'. At the same time Legrandin himself, whose thoughts are transcribed here in a kind of free indirect style, is by no means immune from the vice of snobbery which he is stigmatizing in others, and this gives the construction an ironical twist.

The verb, too, may be strongly stressed by being placed before the subject, as in an often-quoted sentence by the seventeenth-century preacher Fléchier: 'Déjà *frémissait* dans son camp l'ennemi confus et déconcerté.'[2] An impression of dramatic suddenness is conveyed by the inversion in this sentence from Giraudoux: 'Quand dans la rue de Lima *résonnait* le clairon qui annonçait les listes des morts.'[3] The verb may even find itself in so-called 'absolute' inversion at the very beginning of the sentence: '*Arrivait* l'exposition de cette année 1853.'[4] Some modern writers tend to abuse this construction; thus the following sentence by Saint-Exupéry has an unnatural air: '*Pesa* sur mon cœur le poids du monde comme si j'en avais la charge.'[5]

2. *Delay and suspense.*—As far back as 1730, a French critic had pointed out that a poetical sentence differs from a prosaic one by the suspense effect created by inversion.[6] The complicated syntax favoured by Proust can lend itself particularly well to this device: the identity of the subject may be withheld from the reader until the very end of a long sentence. The suspense may be further increased by a number of adjectives, participles and pronouns which, in Professor Spitzer's phrase, 'herald' the subject delayed by inversion:

'*Intercalé* dans la haie, mais aussi *différent* d'elle qu'une jeune fille en robe de fête au milieu de personnes en négligé qui resteront à la maison, tout *prêt* pour le mois de Marie, dont *il* semblait faire partie

---

[1] First used in French in 1857, in the translation of Thackeray's *Book of Snobs* (Bloch-Wartburg).

[2] 'The enemy, confused and abashed, was already trembling in his camp' (*Oraison funèbre de Turenne*).

[3] 'When, in the rue de Lima, the bugle rang out, announcing the casualty lists' (*Suzanne et le Pacifique*, Paris, Grasset, p. 143).

[4] 'Then came the exhibition of the year 1853' (Edmond and Jules de Goncourt, *Manette Salomon*, Paris, Charpentier, p. 215).

[5] 'The weight of the world lay heavy on my heart as though I were responsible for it' (*Citadelle*, p. 148, quoted by Le Bidois, op. cit., pp. 429 f.).

[6] Father du Cerceau, *Divers traités sur l'éloquence et sur la poésie*, Amsterdam, 1730, quoted by Ch. Bruneau in F. Brunot, *Histoire de la langue française*, vol. XII, p. 30.

déjà, *tel* brillait en souriant dans *sa* fraîche toilette rose, *l'arbuste catholique et délicieux.*'[1]

In this passage, as in the preceding ones, the 'build up' is by no means gratuitous, for the *arbuste* referred to is no ordinary plant: it is *l'aubépine*, the hawthorn, which plays a significant part in the structure of Proust's cycle.[2]

A rather different form of suspense effect arises in another sentence by the same author, which has been often discussed. The context is of vital importance here: the young narrator's aunt Léonie, a chronic invalid unable to leave her rooms, suspects every action of her honest maid Françoise, and the twisted and tormented construction faithfully portrays the latter's stealthy movements as they appear to the diseased mind of her employer:

'Peu à peu son esprit n'eut plus d'autre occupation que de chercher à deviner ce qu'à chaque moment pouvait faire, et chercher à lui cacher, *Françoise.*'[3]

3. *Pathos.*—Most forms of inversion are alien to the spoken language and have strong stylistic overtones: archaic, scientific or literary, as the case may be. In suitable contexts, these overtones will give rise to an impression of solemnity and pathos, as in this passage from Proust where the narrator hears Gilberte's name for the first time:

'*Ainsi passa* près de moi *ce nom de Gilberte*, donné comme un talisman ... *Ainsi passa-t-il*, proféré au-dessus des jasmins et des giroflées, aigre et frais comme les gouttes de l'arrosoir vert.'[4]

When such effects are combined with the delay and suspense noted under 2, the result will be even more impressive; to a sophisticated twentieth-century reader it may even appear as inflated and artificial.

---

[1] '*Intercalated* in the hedge, yet as *different* from it as a girl in party dress among people in undress who will stay at home, *ready* for the Month of Mary of which *it* already seemed to form part, thus shone, smiling in *its* fresh pink costume, *the catholic and delightful bush*' (*Du Côté de chez Swann*, vol. I, p. 185).

[2] Cf. my book, *The Image in the Modern French Novel*, Cambridge, 1960, pp. 196 ff.

[3] *Du Côté de chez Swann*, vol. I, p. 157. In Scott Moncrieff's translation, this often-quoted sentence is rendered as follows: 'And so on by degrees, until her mind had no other occupation than to attempt, at every hour of the day, to discover what was being done, what was being concealed from her by *Françoise.*' It will be noted that, in order to preserve the suspense effect and the twisted sentence-structure, the translator has had to put the whole construction in the passive voice, which weakens its impact; at the same time the English version is rather diffuse: thirty-five words against twenty-six in Proust.

[4] '*Thus passed* by me *this name of Gilberte*, presented like a talisman ... *Thus it passed*, uttered over the jasmines and the gillyflowers, sharp and fresh like the drops from the green watering-can' (ibid., p. 187).

A good example of this technique is found in Heredia's sonnet *Soir de bataille* where the subject of the sentence, heralded by all kinds of highly coloured details, is not disclosed till the very end of the poem, where the blood-stained general appears silhouetted against the Wagnerian background of the blazing sky:

> C'est alors qu'apparut, tout hérissé de flèches,
> Rouge du flux vermeil de ses blessures fraîches,
> Sous la pourpre flottante et l'airain rutilant,
>
> Au fracas des buccins qui sonnaient leur fanfare,
> Superbe, maîtrisant son cheval qui s'effare,
> Sur le ciel enflammé, *l'Imperator sanglant*.[1]

4. *Finality*.—Akin to the impression of solemnity and pathos produced by certain inversions is the air of finality which the construction can acquire:

'tandis qu'alentour les chemins se sont effacés et que *sont morts ceux qui les foulèrent* et le souvenir de ceux qui les foulèrent';[2]

'et de nouveau *régnera le silence solennel*, comme devant les nuits'.[3]

This air of finality may explain why some writers like to finish an entire book by an inverted sentence, as Flaubert did in *Salammbô*:

'*Ainsi mourut la fille d'Hamilcar* pour avoir touché au manteau de Tanit',[4]

or Romain Rolland in the tenth and last part of *Jean-Christophe*:

'Et l'ont suivi longtemps leurs railleries et leurs rires.'[5]

The same effect, combined with the dramatic quality of some of the inversions mentioned under 1, may account for a curious stylistic device in a recent novel, Michel Butor's *La Modification* (1957). This is the story

---

[1] 'It is then that appeared, riddled with arrows, red with the vermilion flush from his fresh wounds, beneath the flowing purple and the gleaming bronze, amid the din of the trumpets sounding their fanfare, superb, mastering his frightened horse, against the blazing sky, *the blood-stained Imperator*.'

[2] 'while the roads around have worn away, and those who walked on them, and the memory of those who walked on them, are dead' (*Du Côté de chez Swann*, vol. I, p. 240). Cf. L. Spitzer, *Stilstudien*, vol. II, Munich, 1928, pp. 466 f., and my *Style in the French Novel*, pp. 186 f.

[3] 'and once again a solemn silence will reign, as in the presence of the night' (Fr. Mauriac, *Thérèse Desqueyroux*, Paris, Grasset, p. 22).

[4] '*Thus died the daughter of Hamilcar* for having touched the cloak of Tanit.'

[5] 'And for a long time he was followed by their jokes and laughter' (quoted by R. Le Bidois, *Le Français Moderne*, ix (1941), p. 126). Other examples in my *Style in the French Novel*, p. 187.

of a train journey from Paris to Rome, in the course of which the narrator remembers many previous journeys he had made on the same line. From time to time, his reflections are interrupted by the persistent recurrence of a formula: whenever the train passes through a station, he observes: '*Passe* la gare de . . . *Passe* la gare de . . .' Placed at the beginning of the sentence, the verb *passe*, short and sharp in sound, undoubtedly has a strong dramatic quality evoking the suddenness with which the successive stations loom up and disappear. At the same time, the recurrence of the same formula has an air of finality as inexorable as the progression of the train and that of the traveller's thoughts, which will inescapably lead to a modification of his original plan—hence the title of the novel.[1]

5. *Irony and parody.*—The effects listed under 1–4—emphasis, suspense, pathos, finality—will inevitably give rise to irony and parody wherever there is a contrast between the nature of the context and the stylistic overtones of the construction. In Hugo's *Notre-Dame de Paris*, there is such a contrast between an impressive syntactical 'build up' and the anticlimax on which the sentence ends: the ridiculous and misshapen figure of the hunchback Quasimodo:

'Et sur ce brancard resplendissait, crossé, chapé et mitré, le nouveau pape des fous, le sonneur des cloches de Notre-Dame, *Quasimodo le Bossu.*'[2]

The construction *ainsi* plus a verb in the Past Definite (a tense confined to the written language), of which we saw some specimens under 3 and 4—'*ainsi passa* près de moi ce nom de Gilberte', '*ainsi mourut* la fille d'Hamilcar'—has a particularly solemn air which can be exploited for ironical effects if the solemnity does not fit the context:

'*Ainsi arriva* à midi, un paon blanc grattant du bec sa queue, . . . l'académicien Henri de Régnier . . . *Ainsi vint*, le soir même du jour, . . . l'académicien René Boylesve.'[3]

Inversion may also help to draw the linguistic portrait of a character. As the spoken idiom is allergic to most forms of the construction, its use in speech is bound to appear stilted and somewhat pedantic. This effect may be involuntary or deliberately contrived by the speaker. An ex-

[1] Cf. L. Spitzer, *Archivum Linguisticum*, xiv (1962), pp. 51 f.
[2] 'On this stretcher lay in his splendour, crosiered, coped and mitred, the new Abbot of Unreason, the bell-ringer of Notre-Dame, *Quasimodo the hunchback*' (Nelson ed., vol. I, p. 107).
[3] '*Thus arrived* at noon, a white peacock scratching with its beak the train of his robe, Academician Henri de Régnier . . . *Thus came*, that same evening, . . . Academician René Boylesve' (Giraudoux, *Suzanne et le Pacifique*, p. 128).

ample of the latter occurs in one of Balzac's novels where the ex-convict Vautrin masquerades as a Spanish priest and diplomat and uses a style which befits his alleged station:

'La justice a commis des erreurs encore plus fortes que celle à laquelle *donnerait lieu le témoignage* d'une femme qui reconnaît un homme au poil de sa poitrine.'[1]

Even more interesting are those cases where a character unwittingly gives himself away by his affected language. Legrandin, who has already been mentioned (pp. 104 f.), is an example in point. He is a cultivated man, with an elegant and artistic turn of phrase; but, in the words of the narrator's grandmother, he speaks 'un peu trop bien, un peu trop comme un livre',[2] and this is evident in his syntax as well as in his imagery and his choice of words. He even risks in speech a construction which is barely acceptable in the written language: inversion after *que* in a substantival clause:

'Aux cœurs blessés comme l'est le mien, un romancier que vous lirez plus tard prétend *que conviennent* seulement l'ombre et le silence.'[3]

His use of the more orthodox forms of inversion is hardly less literary:

'*Quand ne sont pas encore fondues* les dernières boules de neige des giboulées de Pâques.'[4]

Vocabulary and syntax concur in such passages to give the style an over-refined and precious quality. It is just possible that in the linguistic caricature of Legrandin Proust was also painting a kind of ironical self-portrait, parodying his own mannerisms and idiosyncrasies which become more obvious when transposed from written into spoken language. As will be seen in a later chapter, some features of Legrandin's imagery may be explained in the same way.

6. *Impressionism.*[5]—Inversion may also enable the writer to record experiences in the order in which they were actually perceived. Take the following sentence where the Goncourt brothers describe a section of Paris seen from a vantage point in the Jardin des Plantes:

---

[1] 'Justice has made even greater mistakes than that *to which would give rise the evidence* of a woman who recognizes a man by the hair of his chest' (*Splendeurs et misères des courtisanes*, p. 329).

[2] 'A little too well, a little too much like a book' (*Du Côté de chez Swann*, vol. I, p. 94).

[3] 'A novelist whom you will read later claims that only darkness and silence will suit wounded hearts like mine' (ibid., p. 168).

[4] 'When the last snowballs of the April showers have not yet melted' (ibid., p. 167).

[5] Cf. the volume, *El Impresionismo en el lenguaje*, Buenos Aires, 1936, with articles by Ch. Bally, E. Richter, A. Alonso and R. Lida.

'Sur le quai, les carrés de maisons blanches, avec les petites raies noires de leurs milliers de fenêtres, formaient et développaient comme un front de caserne d'une blancheur effacée et jaunâtre, sur laquelle *reculait*, de loin en loin, dans le rouillé de la pierre, *une construction plus vieille.*'[1]

This description is impressionistic in two ways. The whole scene is dominated by colours, by the contrast of white, black and red; as in an impressionist painting, the colours are more important than the objects to which they belong. Secondly, the old buildings in the distant background are relegated to the end of the sentence, just as they would be picked out only when the observer focused his eyes, or his binoculars, on them after having explored the objects in the foreground.

A different form of impressionism is seen in this sentence from Flaubert's *L'Education sentimentale*, where a young man is described wandering at night amid the barricades in Paris:

'Au milieu de cette ombre, par endroits, *brillaient des blancheurs de baïonnettes.*'[2]

There are two impressionist devices in this short sentence. Instead of *des baïonnettes blanches*, we have *des blancheurs de baïonnettes*: the adjective is detached from the noun, placed before it and set up as a substance, in the form of an abstract quality noun. Once again, quality predominates over the object in which it is vested. At the same time, the sequence of experiences is faithfully preserved by the word-order: the young man sees something gleaming in the dark, then he realizes that the white flashes are bayonets. Try to rewrite the sentence by changing both devices; the result: 'Au milieu de cette ombre, par endroits, *des baïonnettes blanches brillaient*', will have lost most of its expressive force.

This small list of examples will have given an idea, however incomplete, of the subtle and varied effects which a writer can derive from such a simple grammatical device: the possibility of placing the subject after the verb instead of before. The interplay of choice and expressiveness in style raises many other problems, some linguistic, others aesthetic or psychological; some of these will be examined in the next chapter.

---

[1] 'On the quay, the squares of white houses, with the small black stripes of their thousands of windows, formed and developed a kind of barracks front of a faded yellowish white colour, from which *receded*, now and then, amid the rusty stones, *a more ancient building*' (*Manette Salomon*, p. 3).

[2] 'Amid the darkness, there gleamed here and there white flashes of bayonets' (*L'Education sentimentale*, Paris, Pléiade ed., p. 315). On the construction 'une blancheur de baïonnettes', see my *Style in the French Novel*, pp. 122 ff., with further references.

II. Evocative Devices

Stylistics is usually regarded as a special division of linguistics; since, however, it has a point of view which is peculiar to it and distinguishes it from all other branches of linguistic study, it would perhaps be more logical to regard it as a sister science concerned not with the elements of language as such, but with their expressive potential.[1] On this reading, stylistics will have the same subdivisions as linguistics. If one accepts the view that there are three distinct levels of linguistic analysis: phonological, lexical and syntactical,[2] then stylistic analysis will have to distinguish between the same three levels. 'Stylistics of the sound', or *'phonostylistics'*,[3] will deal, among other things, with the utilization of onomatopoeia for expressive purposes; some aspects of this problem have already been touched upon in earlier chapters.[4] 'Stylistics of the word' will explore the expressive resources available in the vocabulary of a language; it will investigate the stylistic implications of such phenomena as word-formation (Lewis Carroll's and James Joyce's portmanteau words), synonymy, ambiguity, or the contrast between vague and precise, abstract and concrete, rare and common terms. The study of imagery, which will be discussed in Chapter IX, will occupy a prominent place at this level of style analysis. Finally, 'stylistics of the sentence' will examine the expressive values of syntax at three superimposed planes: components of the sentence (individual grammatical forms, passages from one word-class to another), sentence-structure (word-order, negation, etc.), and the higher units into which single sentences combine (direct, indirect and free indirect speech, etc.).

At all these various levels, attention will have to be paid to a fundamental distinction: that between expressive and *'evocative'* devices. The latter, as already noted (p. 101), derive their stylistic effect not from any inherent quality but from being associated with a particular milieu or register of style. A few examples will show how these evocative values work:

1. At the *phonological* level, such devices are a perennial source of comedy and satire. The faulty pronunciation of foreigners has been parodied in countless plays and novels; all readers of Balzac will remember Nucingen, the financier with the inimitable Alsatian brogue, who says 'Hânimâl édaid azez' for 'Animal était assez'.[5] More serious problems

---

[1] G. Devoto, *Studi di stilistica*, pp. 23 and 45.
[2] See my *Semantics*, pp. 23 ff., and *Style in the French Novel*, pp. 10 ff.
[3] N. S. Troubetzkoy, *Principes de phonologie*, French transl., Paris, 1949, pp. 16–29.
[4] Cf. pp. 41 ff., 52 f., 68 ff.
[5] 'Beast would have been quite enough' (*Splendeurs et misères des courtisanes*, p. 190).

are raised when native speakers have an accent which differs from the Received Standard—a situation whose psychological and social implications form the central theme of Shaw's *Pygmalion*. Such speakers will sometimes overcompensate their sense of linguistic insecurity by using 'hypercorrect' forms; the Cockney who, for fear of 'dropping his aitches', inserts an |h| where there is no need for one, has a close parallel in the Roman Arrius, ridiculed by the poet Catullus because he would pronounce *insidias* as *hinsidias* and *Ionios* as *Hionios*, in order to impress people with his superior education.[1]

The minute care with which Proust records, and comments upon, the linguistic peculiarities of his characters extends also to their pronunciation. He notes that the maid Françoise pronounces *lion* as *li-on*[2] and says *estoppeuse* for *stoppeuse*,[3] and he sees in these mistakes 'le génie linguistique à l'état vivant, l'avenir et le passé du français'.[4] He is also interested in discovering the geographical and social origins of people from their accent. In a group of young girls from different parts of France, the narrator admires 'la savoureuse matière imposée par la province originale d'où elles tiraient leur voix et à même laquelle mordaient leurs intonations',[5] whereas in the voice of a hotel manager he detects 'des cicatrices qu'avait laissées l'extirpation … des divers accents dus à des origines lointaines et à une enfance cosmopolite'.[6] He also records a delightful hypercorrect form: English *lift* pronounced as *laift*.

2. At the *lexical* level, there is a wide range of evocative effects: archaisms, neologisms, fashionable slogans, slang, dialect, technical terms, foreign words. One or two of these have already been referred to (pp. 53 f. and 104 f.); here I shall try to illustrate the technique by briefly examining some of the stylistic uses of *Anglicisms* in French. The prime function of foreign words as a device of style is to produce local colour.[7] This may be purely objective, as in Verlaine's lines:

> Même alors que l'aurore allume
> Les *cottages* jaunes et noirs.[8]

---

[1] *Carmina*, 84; cf. Professor C. J. Fordyce's comments in his recent edition of *Catullus* (Oxford, 1961), pp. 373 ff.

[2] *Du Côté de chez Swann*, vol. I, p. 121.

[3] *Sodome et Gomorrhe*, vol. I, Paris, 1949 impr., p. 176. On this and the next example cf. J. Mouton, *Le Style de Marcel Proust*, Paris, 1948, p. 185.

[4] 'The genius of the language in a live state, the future and the past of French' (*Sodome et Gomorrhe*, loc. cit.).

[5] 'The savoury material imposed by their province of origin, from which they drew their voice and into which bit their intonations' (*A l'ombre des jeunes filles en fleurs*, vol. III, p. 176).

[6] 'Scars left behind by the extirpation of the various accents due to his remote origins and to a cosmopolitan childhood' (ibid., vol. II, p. 79).

[7] See on this question ch. I of my *Style in the French Novel*.

[8] 'Even when dawn lights up the yellow and black *cottages*' (*Aquarelles: Streets*).

Elsewhere the evocation will carry emotive overtones, as in Vigny's terse comment on an English character in his play *Chatterton*: 'John Bell, gonflé d'*ale*, de *porter* et de *roastbeef*'.[1] The effect is particularly powerful in another poem by Verlaine where words overheard in a London fog are described:

> Tout l'affreux passé saute, piaule, miaule et glapit
> Dans le brouillard rose et jaune et sale des *sohos*
> Avec des *indeed* et des *all rights* et des *haôs*.[2]

In certain social circles, foreign words are often used because of their snob value, and these affectations are ridiculed by many writers. Musset was particularly adept at parodying the Anglicized speech of the dandies of his time:

> Dans le *bol* où le *punch* rit sur son trépied d'or,
> Le *grog* est *fashionable*.[3]

Among Proust's characters, Odette, the *demi-mondaine* who becomes a leading society hostess, is particularly given to the snobbish use of Anglicisms. She greets people in English,[4] puts *to meet* on her invitation cards, and persuades her husband to call himself *Mr.* Charles Swann on his visiting cards.[5] Here are some specimens of her conversation: 'Vous savez que je ne suis pas *fishing for compliments*';[6] 'prendre un *cup of tea*, comme disent nos voisins les Anglais';[7] 'J'ai obtenu qu'il fasse désormais le *leader article* dans le *Figaro*. Ce sera tout à fait *the right man in the right place*'.[8] Nor is Odette the only character in Proust who indulges in this habit. A university professor, anxious to discuss history in modern terms, describes a seventeenth-century politician as 'ce *struggle for lifer* de Gondi',[9] and the narrator himself says in conversation:

---

[1] 'John Bell, puffed up with *ale*, *porter* and *roast beef*.'

[2] 'The whole hideous past jumps, whines, mews and yelps in the pink and yellow and dirty fog of the *sohos*, with *indeeds* and *all rights* and "*haos*" ' (*Sonnet boiteux*, quoted by C. Cuénot, *Le Français Moderne*, xxix, 1961, p. 187).

[3] 'In the *bowl* where *punch* is smiling on its golden tripod, *grog* is *fashionable*' (*Les secrètes pensées de Rafael*). Other examples will be found in my article, 'Les Anglicismes dans la poésie de Musset', *Le Français Moderne*, xvii (1949), pp. 25-32.

[4] 'elle m'arrêtait et me disait: "*Good morning*" en souriant' ('she stopped me and said "*Good morning*", smiling'; *A l'ombre des jeunes filles en fleurs*, vol. II, p. 49).

[5] Ibid., vol. I, p. 148.

[6] 'You know that I am not *fishing for compliments*' (*Du Côté de chez Swann*, vol. I, p. 251). On Odette's Anglicisms cf. J. Mouton, op. cit., pp. 201 f.

[7] 'to have a *cup of tea*, as our English neighbours say' (*Du Côté de chez Swann*, vol. I, p. 108).

[8] 'I have obtained that from now on he should do the *leader article* (sic) in *Le Figaro*. It will be entirely *the right man in the right place*' (*A l'ombre des jeunes filles en fleurs*, vol. I, p. 191).

[9] *Sodome et Gomorrhe*, vol. II, p. 20.

'Cette odeur de roses ... est si forte, dans la partition, que, comme j'ai le *hay-fever* et la *rose-fever*, elle me faisait éternuer chaque fois que j'entendais cette scène.'[1]

Occasionally, a writer may use an English word because of its exotic quality, without any specific reference to things English. The term *steamer*, borrowed into French in 1829 (Bloch-Wartburg), found its way into poetry, probably because it provided a good rhyme for *mer* 'sea':

> Les wagons ébranlaient les plaines, le *steamer*
> Secouait son panache au-dessus de la mer.[2]
> Hugo, *Chose vue un jour de printemps* (*Les Contemplations*).

The word occurs, however, inside the line, though still in a similar context, in Mallarmé's poem *Brise marine*, where it helps to evoke the 'exotique nature' towards which the ship is setting sail:

> Je partirai! *Steamer* balançant ta mâture,
> Lève l'ancre vers une exotique nature![3]

3. Some examples of the manifold and intricate evocative effects in *syntax* have already been given in our discussion of inversion (pp. 106 ff.); we saw there how this construction, which is rare in the spoken language but frequently used in scientific and literary contexts, acquires from this very fact certain overtones which can be exploited for stylistic ends: to create an impression of solemnity, pathos or finality, and also as a vehicle of irony and parody. A few examples from a different part of syntax, the use of the Imperfect Subjunctive, may be cited here.[4] It is common knowledge that this form is felt to be too pedantic to be used in speech, and people often hesitate to employ it even in writing; Gide actually devised a formula of his own for dealing with this troublesome question.[5] The use of the Imperfect Subjunctive will therefore have strong, at times even explosive, evocatory effects. It will fit into the speech-habits of an affected pedant:

---

[1] 'This scent of roses ... is so strong, in the score, that, as I suffer from *hay-fever* and *rose-fever*, it made me sneeze whenever I heard that scene' (ibid., vol. I, p. 272). I am indebted to my colleague Dr. A. Noach for drawing my attention to this example.

[2] 'The carriages shook the plains, the *steamer* tossed its trail of smoke over the sea.' On this and the following example, cf. Y. Le Hir, *Commentaires stylistiques de textes français modernes*, Paris, 1959, p. 91.

[3] 'I shall leave! *Steamer* trimming your masts, weigh anchor for an exotic land!'

[4] See my article, 'Le Passé défini et l'imparfait du subjonctif dans le théâtre contemporain', *Le Français Moderne*, vi (1938), pp. 347–58. Cf. also *Style in the French Novel*, pp. 19 f.

[5] *Incidences*, Paris, 1924 ed., p. 76; cf. L. C. Harmer, *The French Language Today*, pp. 283 f.

'Je ne me serais jamais pardonné que vous l'*apprissiez* par un autre que moi'[1] (R. de Flers-G.-A. Caillavet, *Le Bois sacré*, Act I, scene 9), or those of a university professor:

'Vous seriez fort aise que je ne *continuasse* point'[2] (J. Romains, *M. le Trouhadec*, Act III, scene 6).

A foreigner over-anxious to speak correctly is also apt to use this form. In Michel Butor's novel, *L'Emploi du temps*, an English girl who is studying French in a British university says: 'Vous êtes notre meilleur ami; nous avons voulu que vous *fussiez* prévenu le premier', and the narrator comments: 'ces phrases mêmes, en français, avec cette grammaire presque trop correcte'.[3] The effect becomes even stronger when the form occurs in an otherwise incorrect sentence: 'Je voudrais je *fusse* bientôt mariée avec toi',[4] says another English girl in Tristan Bernard's farce, *L'anglais tel qu'on le parle*. A different contrast effect arises when a colloquial or slangy verb is put into the strait jacket of the Imperfect Subjunctive, as in this sentence in Edmond Rostand's *Les Romanesques*: 'S'il se pouvait que je *rabibochasse* ensemble ces mignons.'[5]

The Imperfect Subjunctive can also serve to evoke the social background of people who once belonged to the professions but have moved to another career or have become *déclassé*. An example of the former is Pagnol's Topaze, the schoolmaster turned businessman, who still winces when he hears someone offend against the sequence of tenses:

SUZY: Vous méritiez qu'on vous le *cache*.
TOPAZE: *Cachât!*
SUZY: Comment, *cachât?*
TOPAZE: Qu'on vous le *cachât*.[6]

In Albert Camus's novel, *La Chute*, the Imperfect Subjunctive provides one of the earliest clues to the identity of the mysterious Frenchman who accosts people in a bar in Amsterdam and whose shabby appearance is strangely at variance with his witty and polished language:

---

[1] 'I would never have forgiven myself had you learnt it from someone else.'
[2] 'You would be very pleased if I did not pursue the matter.'
[3] ' "You are our best friend; we wanted you to be the first person to be told"—these very sentences, in French, with a grammar which is almost too correct' (p. 189).
[4] 'I wish I were soon married to you' (ed. *Librairie théâtrale*, p. 8).
[5] 'If only I could make it up between the two darlings' (Act II, scene 8).
[6] Suzy: 'It would serve you right if it *was hidden* from you.'—Topaze: '*Were hidden!*'—Suzy: 'What do you mean, *were hidden?*'—Topaze: 'If it *were hidden*.' (Act III, scene 2). I have changed the tenses slightly so as to preserve the stylistic effect.

'Quand je vivais en France, je ne pouvais rencontrer un homme d'esprit sans qu'aussitôt j'en *fisse* ma société. Ah! je vois que vous bronchez sur cet imparfait du subjonctif. J'avoue ma faiblesse pour ce mode, et pour le beau langage, en général.'[1]

To make quite sure that the point will be remembered, it is taken up again a few pages later:

'Broncher sur les imparfaits du subjonctif, en effet, prouve deux fois votre culture puisque vous les reconnaissez d'abord et qu'ils vous agacent ensuite.'[2]

We gradually learn that the speaker is an ex-lawyer who gave up a brilliant career in Paris to lead a shady existence in Amsterdam. In this way, the Imperfect Subjunctive becomes a 'status symbol', and this simple and seemingly trivial device has its part to play in the structure of the book.

The air of pretentiousness which clings to this verbal form is so well known that it is commented on even in an English novel:

'They met in a narrow doorway of the church and the lady said, "Voulez-vous que je *passasse?*" So my mother said, *"Passassassez,* Madame".* She told everyone this joke and for many years would sometimes laugh and say in a whisper, *"Passassassez".*'[3]

It has often been suggested, and is implied in this passage, that the forms of the Imperfect Subjunctive, especially those of the first and second person plural of the first conjugation, are cacophonous and comical. Yet one wonders whether this is not largely an illusion: the same people who object to *que nous cessassions, cassassions, associassions,* find nothing wrong with the homonymous nouns *cessation, cassation, association.*[4] It is conceivable that the written form, and its similarity to the pejorative suffixes *-asser, -assier,* may have been a contributory factor in the decay of this mood and thus indirectly a source of stylistic effects.[5]

Before turning to the other main stream of style studies, there are two brief remarks on research methods which ought to be made:

1. In stylistics, as in certain branches of linguistics proper, there are

---

[1] 'When I was living in France, I never met a man of intelligence without immediately striking up a friendship with him (j'en *fisse* ma société). Oh! I can see that this Imperfect Subjunctive makes you wince. I admit my weakness for this mood, and for flowery language in general' (207th ed., Paris, 1956, p. 10).

[2] 'Indeed, to wince when you hear an Imperfect Subjunctive proves your culture twice over, firstly because you recognize it and secondly because it irritates you' (ibid., p. 13).

[3] Saul Bellow, *Henderson the Rain King* (1959), p. 14. I am indebted to Professor Randolph Quirk for this example.

[4] Cf. Harmer, op. cit., p. 286.

[5] Cf. Bally, *Linguistique générale et linguistique française*, p. 260.

two alternative approaches. In the words of Jespersen, 'any linguistic phenomenon may be regarded either from without or from within, either from the outward form or from the inner meaning. In the first case we take the sound (of a word or of some other part of a linguistic expression) and then inquire into the meaning attached to it; in the second case we start from the signification and ask ourselves what formal expression it has found in the particular language we are dealing with. If we denote the outward form by the letter O, and the inner meaning by the letter I, we may represent the two ways as O → I and I → O respectively'.[1] Contemporary linguistic theory would put the position in somewhat different terms, but there can be no doubt that two alternative methods exist in certain parts of linguistics, such as lexicology and syntax.[2] In stylistics, most studies are based on the O → I procedure: they take a particular device and examine the effects it can produce. This is what we have just done in our discussion of inversion, Anglicisms and the Imperfect Subjunctive in French. In theory, the opposite route, I → O, is equally legitimate; one would then start from a specific effect of style and investigate the devices available for producing it. The reason why this procedure is less popular than the alternative is easy to see: devices are on the whole more definite, more precise and easier to handle than effects and will therefore provide a more suitable starting-point. On the other hand, there are certain clearly defined stylistic effects in whose case the I → O method is feasible and even rewarding; some scholars have examined, for example, the various devices which help to produce emphasis in French or to ensure the symmetry of the sentence.[3]

2. The study of stylistic resources is essentially a *descriptive* discipline since these resources, and the uses to which they are put, are synchronic phenomena which normally have nothing to do with historical antecedents.[4] By comparing the usage of different periods, one could trace the development of these resources, and in this way stylistics could acquire a historical dimension. This would presuppose, however, that one could recapture the stylistic overtones which linguistic elements possessed for successive generations, and this is often a difficult and hazardous task. The problem of stylistic reconstruction will be looked at more closely in Chapter VIII.

[1] *The Philosophy of Grammar*, London—New York, 1929 impr., p. 33.
[2] Cf. my *Semantics*, pp. 63 f.
[3] M. L. Müller-Hauser, *La Mise en relief d'une idée en français moderne*, Geneva, 1943; M. Mangold, *Etudes sur la mise en relief dans le français de l'époque classique*, Mulhouse, 1950; G. Schlocker, *Equilibre et symétrie dans la phrase française moderne*, Paris, 1957.
[4] Cf. above, pp. 53 f.

B. The Style of an Author

In recent years, general linguistics has evolved a new concept which is of direct interest to the student of style: that of *'idiolect'* or individual language. An idiolect may be defined as 'the totality of speech habits of a single person at a given time'.[1] It thus stands half-way between the two opposite poles of language and speech: language, the code which is common to all members of the community, and speech, the use of that code for the encoding of a particular message.[2] The linguist as such is not primarily interested in idiolects; even when he has to rely on the testimony of a small number of informants, his ultimate target is the common norm on which their usage is based. The concept of idiolect is, however, of some importance to the psychologist and the psychiatrist who may find in it valuable clues to the speaker's personality.[3] Studies of the style of an author will also be concerned with his idiolect, or certain parts of it, in so far as these are manifest in his written works.

Among the numerous methods which have been experimented with in the stylistic study of individual authors, three only will be discussed here: the use of statistical techniques, the psychological approach, and the 'functional' point of view which seeks to interpret the role of style in the total structure of a literary work.

I. The Statistical Approach

We live in a statistical era, and it is not surprising that numerical methods should have penetrated into many parts of linguistics and stylistics. In linguistics, the introduction of such methods is on the whole to be welcomed, though it would be wrong to erect them into a fetish. As we saw in the first part of this book, even[4] semantics, the least systematic of all linguistic disciplines, has many aspects amenable to statistical treatment. In stylistics, the use of numerical methods is more problematical. The precision which they undoubtedly introduce into style studies is sometimes bought at too heavy a cost. The following are some of the considerations which limit the usefulness of statistics in this field:

1. The statistical method is too crude to catch some of the subtle nuances of style: emotive overtones, evocative resonance, complex and delicate rhythmic effects and the like.

---

[1] Hockett, op. cit., p. 321.
[2] Cf. my *Semantics*, pp. 21 ff.
[3] Cf. *Style in the French Novel*, p. 26.
[4] See pp. 6 ff. and ch. V, *passim*.

2. Numerical counts may impose a spurious kind of precision on data too intricate or too fluid to admit of such treatment. An example in point is a recent doctoral thesis on the imagery of Proust, only a summary of which has been published. This thesis, meritorious as it may be in other respects, certainly gives a misleading impression when it states that a total of 4578 images have been counted in Proust.[1] Anyone who has studied the imagery of that writer will know that a great many of his similes and metaphors are so inextricably interlinked with each other and form such a maze of overlapping or interlocking analogies that it is quite impossible to make a precise count.[2] It would have been much wiser to confine oneself to approximate figures.

3. One great weakness of the so-called 'stylostatistical' method is that it makes no provision for the influence of context, which, as we already know from the study of inversion and other devices, is of crucial importance in stylistic analysis.

4. Another danger inherent in this approach is that quality is overshadowed by quantity and very diverse elements are lumped together on the ground of some superficial similarity.

5. It also happens that an imposing array of figures produces a result which one could have noticed with the naked eye or which is so obvious that it needs no demonstration. As Leo Spitzer wittily put it, is it really necessary to have numerical data for the high frequency of the word *love* in poetry—a frequency no more unexpected than that of *car* in a report on motor racing, or *penicillin* in a medical journal?[3]

To these objective arguments may be added a subjective but no less real difficulty. Not only are most students of style unfamiliar with statistical techniques (cf. above, p. 8), but many of them are temperamentally hostile to this kind of approach, and although this attitude is less common now than it used to be, it is still a factor with which one has to reckon.

In spite of all this it would be quite wrong to exclude statistics altogether from the stylistic field. There are at least three aspects of style study which can derive very real benefit from numerical criteria:

1. The statistical analysis of style may sometimes help towards the solution of purely literary problems. Three of these '*ancillary*' uses are particularly important. Firstly, such methods may enable us, in conjunction with other evidence, to establish the authorship of anonymous works

[1] V. E. Graham, *The Imagery of Proust*, Columbia University, 1953, summarized in *Dissertation Abstracts*, vol. xiv, p. 1409.
[2] Cf. my *Image in the Modern French Novel*, ch. III, esp. pp. 226 ff.
[3] *Actes du VIIIᵉ Congrès de la Fédération Internationale des Langues et Littératures Modernes*, p. 36.

I

such as the *Imitation of Christ* attributed to Thomas à Kempis.[1] Secondly, they may throw light on the unity or otherwise of such poems as the *Chanson de Roland* or Béroul's *Tristan*.[2] Thirdly, they may serve to determine the chronology of writings by the same author, such as for example the dialogues of Plato or the various parts of Rimbaud's *Illuminations*.[3] Needless to say, one will have to proceed with great circumspection before reaching any definitive conclusions in such matters. It has been found, for example, that the proportion of adjectives in Racine's plays rises steadily from *Andromaque* to *Esther*, with one exception: *Iphigénie* has fewer adjectives than the pattern would require. This has led to the suggestion, in a recent article,[4] that *Iphigénie* may have been written earlier than commonly believed—a possibility which, it is claimed, can be supported by historical and graphological arguments. But surely the drop in the ratio of adjectives need have no bearing on the chronology of Racine's plays; it may be due to the dramatic structure of *Iphigénie*, to a temporary change in Racine's technique, or to other factors. On the other hand, one must fully agree with the wise warning uttered in the same article: 'Analyse historique, analyse stylistique, analyse statistique, ces trois démarches doivent aller de pair. On combinera ces trois méthodes dans un mouvement dialectique qui, sans les confondre, ira de l'une à l'autre en ne demandant à chacune que ce qu'elle peut donner.'[5]

2. Statistics may also be helpful in giving a rough indication of the frequency of a particular device, its *density* in a given work. It is not a matter of indifference whether a certain element occurs once, ten times or a hundred times in a book, and many works on style give tantalizingly little information on this point. One is reminded of one of the golden rules of the Cartesian method: 'Faire partout des dénombrements si entiers et des revues si générales, que je fusse assuré de ne rien omettre.'[6]

3. Numerical data may in some cases reveal a striking anomaly in the

---

[1] See G. U. Yule, *The Statistical Study of Literary Vocabulary*, London, 1944; G. Herdan, *Language as Choice and Chance*, Groningen, 1956; Id., *The Calculus of Linguistic Observations*, The Hague, 1962. Cf. *Style in the French Novel*, pp. 29 ff.

[2] See esp. R.-L. Wagner-P. Guiraud, 'La Méthode statistique en lexicologie', *Revue de l'Enseignement Supérieur*, 1959, no. 1, pp. 154–9.

[3] Cf. P. Guiraud, *Mercure de France*, cccxxii (1954), pp. 201–34.

[4] Wagner-Guiraud, loc. cit., p. 157.

[5] 'Historical analysis, stylistic analysis, statistical analysis, these three operations must proceed *pari passu*. The three methods will be combined in a dialectical movement which, without confusing them, will pass from one to the other, expecting from each no more than it can give' (ibid., p. 159). See on these problems R. Posner, 'The Use and Abuse of Stylistic Statistics', to appear in vol. xv (1963) of *Archivum Linguisticum*.

[6] 'Make everywhere such complete counts and such general surveys that I should be certain not to have omitted anything' (Descartes, *Discours de la méthode*, Cambridge Plain Texts, 1942, p. 17).

distribution of stylistic elements, and may thus raise important problems of aesthetic interpretation. An acute critic has noticed, for example, that the imagery in Camus's novel, *L'Etranger*, is unevenly distributed: twenty-five metaphors are packed into the six paragraphs which relate the murder of the Arab on the beach outside Algiers, whereas there are only fifteen metaphors in the preceding eighty-three pages.[1] Naturally, a purely numerical approach can do no more than draw attention to this discrepancy: the explanation will lie in the psychological and aesthetic structure of the novel, as will be seen in Chapter IX.

II. The Psychological Approach

At a recent symposium on 'Style in Language' it was suggested that the style of an individual is as unique as his fingerprints.[2] The analogy is not entirely convincing since one's fingerprints do not change whereas one's style does. Nevertheless, the idea that style is an integral and fundamental feature of one's personality is widely held and has been voiced, since Buffon's frequently misquoted 'Le style, c'est l'homme même', by a great many writers. According to Schopenhauer, 'style is the physiognomy of the mind'; according to Flaubert, it is 'à lui tout seul une manière absolue de voir les choses'.[3] The same idea recurs, in a more explicit form, in Gide and in Proust. In the view of the former, 'une personnalité neuve ne s'exprime sincèrement que dans une forme neuve. La phrase qui nous est personnelle doit rester aussi particulièrement difficile à bander que l'arc d'Ulysse'.[4] Proust had an interesting theory of style which found its most famous expression in the last volume of his cycle: 'Le style, pour l'écrivain aussi bien que pour le peintre, est une question non de technique, mais de vision.'[5] In an earlier volume, he had made some significant comments on the style of Bergotte, a writer who has various points in common with Anatole France:

'Cette différence dans le style venait de ce que "le Bergotte" était avant tout quelque élément précieux et vrai, caché au cœur de chaque chose, puis extrait d'elle par ce grand écrivain grâce à son génie ... en ce sens

---

[1] W. M. Frohock, 'Camus: Image, Influence and Sensibility', *Yale French Studies*, ii, no. 2 (1949), pp. 91–9, esp. pp. 93 ff.

[2] Roger Brown in the volume *Style in Language*, pp. 378 ff.

[3] 'In itself alone an absolute way of looking at things' (quoted by Wartburg, *Evolution et structure de la langue française*, p. 226).

[4] 'A new personality needs a new form to express itself sincerely. The sentence which is peculiar to us must be as difficult to bend as Ulysses's bow' (*Nouveaux Prétextes*, Paris, 1947 ed., p. 169).

[5] 'Style, for the writer as well as for the painter, is a question not of technique but of vision' (*Le Temps retrouvé*, vol. II, Paris, 1949 impr., p. 43).

chaque nouvelle beauté de son œuvre était la petite quantité de Bergotte enfouie dans une chose et qu'il en avait tirée . . . le génie consistant dans le pouvoir réfléchissant et non dans la qualité intrinsèque du spectacle reflété.'[1]

Among the many critics who have tried to establish a link between an author's psyche and his style, the late Professor Leo Spitzer has obtained the most spectacular results. Spitzer, who was brought up in Vienna, came at an early date under the influence of Freud's teaching; subsequently he was also stimulated by Benedetto Croce's and Karl Vossler's conception of language as a form of creative and artistic self-expression.[2] In a long series of brilliant style studies on authors both living and dead, he gradually evolved his own method, the so-called *philological circle*. In 1948, he summed up this procedure in the following terms:

'What we must be asked to do is, I believe, to work from the surface to the "inward life-centre" of the work of art: first observing details about the superficial appearance of the particular work . . .; then, grouping these details and seeking to integrate them into a creative principle which may have been present in the soul of the artist; and finally, making the return trip to all the other groups of observations in order to find whether the "inward form" one has tentatively constructed gives an account of the whole.'[3]

There are thus three successive phases in the philological circle. In the first phase, the critic will 'read and re-read, patiently and confidently, in an endeavour to become, as it were, soaked through and through with the atmosphere of the work',[4] until he is struck by the persistent recurrence of some stylistic peculiarity. In the second phase, he will look for a psychological explanation of this feature, whereas in the third phase he will try to find further evidence pointing to the same factor in the author's mind.

One of the neatest demonstrations of the philological circle is Spitzer's essay on the style of Diderot. This writer had once declared: 'Les pré-

---

[1] 'This difference in style was due to the fact that the "Bergotte manner" was, above all, some valuable and true element hidden in the heart of every object and extracted from it by this great writer thanks to his genius . . . in this sense each new beauty in his writings was a small quantity of Bergotte buried in an object, which he had brought to light . . . for genius consists in the capacity to reflect and not in any intrinsic quality of the thing reflected' (*A l'ombre des jeunes filles en fleurs*, vol. I, pp. 153 f. and 159).

[2] For an autobiographical sketch of his own development, see ch. I of his *Linguistics and Literary History*; cf. also the article 'Les Etudes de style et les différents pays', referred to in p. 99, n. 3 above.

[3] *Linguistics and Literary History*, p. 19.

[4] Ibid., p. 27.

tendus connoisseurs en fait de style chercheront vainement à me dé-
chiffrer.'[1] Spitzer took up the challenge, and as the starting-point of his
'decipherment' he chose a feature which had struck him in the most
diverse writings by Diderot: a rhythmic pattern in which he 'seemed to
hear the echo of Diderot's speaking voice: a self-accentuating rhythm,
suggesting that the "speaker" is swept away by a wave of passion which
tends to flood all limits'.[2] Here is a typical passage, from *Le Neveu de
Rameau*, which Spitzer does not quote but which fully illustrates his
point:

'C'est le neveu de ce musicien célèbre qui nous a délivrés du plain-
chant de Lulli que nous psalmodiions depuis plus de cent ans; qui a tant
écrit de visions inintelligibles et de vérités apocalyptiques sur la théorie
de la musique, où ni lui ni personne n'entendit jamais rien, *et de qui nous
avons un certain nombre d'opéras où il y a de l'harmonie, des bouts de chants,
des idées décousues, du fracas, des vols, des triomphes, des lances, des
gloires, des murmures, des victoires à perte d'haleine*; des airs de danse qui
dureront éternellement, et qui, après avoir enterré le Florentin, sera
enterré par les virtuoses italiens, ce qu'il pressentait et le rendait
sombre, triste, hargneux ...'[3]

The passage which I have italicized, and which ends characteristically
with the words 'à perte d'haleine', is a clear example of the 'dynamic
accelerating' rhythm which, in Spitzer's view, is fundamental to the style
of Diderot. Having once noticed this rhythmic pattern, Spitzer had no
difficulty in connecting it with Diderot's nervous temperament which,
'instead of being tempered by style, was allowed to energize style'.[4]
Finally, he found further manifestations of the same temperament in
Diderot's philosophy of mobility, his 'perpetual desire to transcend the
rationally graspable', and concluded: 'It would then appear that, in this
writer, nervous system, philosophical system, and "stylistic system" are
exceptionally well attuned.'[5]

[1] 'The alleged connoisseurs of style will try in vain to decipher me' (quoted ibid., p. 136).
[2] Ibid., p. 135.
[3] 'He is the nephew of the famous musician who has liberated us from the plainsong of
Lulli which we had been chanting for over a hundred years; who has written so many unintelligible visions and apocalyptic truths on the theory of music, of which neither he nor
anybody ever understood anything, *and by whom we have a certain number of operas in which
there is harmony, snatches of song, disjointed ideas, din, flights, triumphs, spears, glory, murmurs,
victories, to take your breath away*; dance tunes which will last for ever; and who, having buried
the Florentine, will himself be buried by the Italian virtuosos, a fate which he foresaw and
which made him gloomy, sad and peevish' (*Le Neveu de Rameau*, ed. J. Fabre, Geneva-
Lille, 1950, p. 6). (I have modernized the spelling).
[4] *Linguistics and Literary History*, p. 135.
[5] Ibid.

As was only to be expected, Spitzer's method, and the assumptions on which it was based, have been challenged by a number of scholars.[1] The following are the chief criticisms directed against the theory:

1. Several critics have emphasized the essentially subjective and intuitive nature of the 'philological circle'. Spitzer himself would have accepted this as fair comment, though he would not have regarded it as a criticism. As we have seen (p. 100), he believed that the success of all stylistic analysis depends on 'talent, experience, and faith', and he was at pains to point out that his method provided no guarantee for the initial 'click' to occur; 'the first step, on which all may hinge', he warned, 'can never be planned: it must already have taken place'.[2]

2. Some scholars have also questioned the assumption that stylistic peculiarities must of necessity correspond to some deep-seated feature in the author's mind; very often they are no more than a mere mannerism or a tic. As Cocteau once wrote, 'le goût du tic est tellement développé, pris pour le style, pour l'expression dans les milieux littéraires, qu'on n'y estime que l'écrivain qui accuse ses tics jusqu'à la grimace. Une longue grimace donne vite des rides'.[3]

3. It has been suggested that Spitzer's interpretations are often based on inadequate linguistic evidence, on samples rather than on complete collections of data (cf. above, p. 120). To this Spitzer retorted, in a lecture given a few days before his death: 'Si l'on s'adresse aux dénombrements par peur du subjectivisme et de l'*a priori*, on commet, en fait, un plus grand *a priori* encore en superposant à une œuvre poétique, par esprit de méthode, les casiers de la grammaire au grand complet; et l'attitude méthodique a des chances de détruire, ainsi, chez le critique, le sens du particulier et de l'original.'[4]

4. Some observers have argued that the sequence of the first two

---

[1] See for example J. Hytier, 'La Méthode de M. L. Spitzer', *Romanic Review*, xli (1950), pp. 42–59; M. Riffaterre, 'Réponse à M. Leo Spitzer sur la méthode stylistique', *Modern Language Notes*, lxxiii (1958), pp. 474–80; R. Wellek-A. Warren, *Theory of Literature*, London, 1954 impr., pp. 187 f. Cf. also Antoine, loc. cit., p. 58; Ch. Bruneau, *Romance Philology*, v (1951), pp. 11 ff., and my *Style in the French Novel*, pp. 28 f.

[2] *Linguistics and Literary History*, p. 26.

[3] 'The taste for tics is so greatly developed, and so much identified with style and expression in literary circles, that only those writers are appreciated who exaggerate their tics until they become a grimace. A long-standing grimace will quickly give you wrinkles' (*Le Rappel à l'ordre*, quoted by F. Jones, *La Langue et le style dans la poésie de Jean Cocteau*) (unpubl. Ph.D. thesis, University of Leeds, 1961), p. 49.

[4] 'If, for fear of subjectivity and *a priori* assumptions, one has recourse to frequency counts, one is in fact guilty of an even more serious form of *a priori* reasoning: that of superimposing, for the sake of scholarly method, the whole set of grammatical categories on a poetical work; and there is a danger that this methodical attitude will destroy in the critic the sense of what is peculiar and original' ('Les Etudes de style et les différents pays', loc. cit., p. 37).

phases in the philological circle is sometimes reversed: 'many relationships professing to be thus established are not conclusions really drawn from the linguistic material, but rather start with a psychological and ideological analysis and seek for confirmation in the language'.[1] This was vigorously disputed by Spitzer himself;[2] but even if it were true, it would hardly matter. The great merit of the method is that it has succeeded in establishing an organic connexion between an author's style, his mental make-up, and other manifestations of the latter; in what order these observations were actually made is of secondary importance.

Two further points ought to be borne in mind in any final evaluation of Spitzer's method. Firstly, his starting-point, the initial step in the circle, is not always a linguistic observation: the feature recognized as significant may relate to other aspects of the work of art, such as its composition, the ideas it expresses, etc.[3] Secondly, as his technique matured he gradually moved away from the psychological bias which had dominated his earlier studies. Looking back on his long career, spanning exactly half a century, he gave two reasons for this shift of emphasis. On the one hand he felt that the psychological approach, well suited as it is to the study of modern authors, is not really applicable to earlier periods which favoured a more impersonal way of writing. He also came to the conclusion that 'psychoanalytical stylistics' was no more than a special form of what is known as the 'biographical fallacy'. His words on the subject deserve to be pondered by all students of style:

'Même dans les cas où le critique a réussi à rattacher un aspect de l'œuvre d'un auteur à une expérience vécue, à une *Erlebnis*, il n'est pas dit, il est même fallacieux d'admettre que cette correspondance entre vie et œuvre contribue toujours à la beauté artistique de cette dernière. L'*Erlebnis* n'est en somme que la matière brute de l'œuvre d'art, sur le même plan que, par exemple, ses sources littéraires.'[4]

In this way, Spitzer eventually abandoned the psychological method for what he called a 'structural' approach where 'stylistic analysis is subordinated to an interpretation of the work of art as a poetic organism

---

[1] Wellek and Warren, op. cit., pp. 187 f.
[2] *Archivum Linguisticum*, iii (1951), pp. 1 f., note.
[3] Ibid.
[4] 'Even where the critic has succeeded in connecting one aspect of an author's work with some personal experience, some *Erlebnis*, it does not follow, it would even be wrong to assume, that such correspondence between life and work will always contribute to the artistic beauty of the latter. After all, the *Erlebnis* is no more than the raw material of the work of art, in the same way as are, for example, its literary sources' ('Les Etudes de style et les différents pays', p. 27).

in its own right, without any recourse to psychology'.[1] This brought his conception very close to the functional point of view which will be discussed in the next section.

More ambitious but less profound than Spitzer's microscopic studies of individual style are certain attempts to devise a *stylistic typology* on psychological grounds. A well-known Spanish critic has suggested that there are six cardinal types of style, according to the relative importance of three basic ingredients: reason, feeling and imagination.[2] Much more detailed is the system put forward by Henri Morier in his book, *La Psychologie des styles* (Geneva, 1959), which has been hailed by an authoritative bibliography as 'à cette date, la plus fine et la plus spirituelle des études de stylistique générale malgré tout ce qu'elle peut avoir de systématique et de parti-pris'.[3] The author distinguishes between eight fundamental types of style, each corresponding to a certain form of character and temperament: weak, delicate, balanced, positive, strong, hybrid, subtle and defective. Each of these is further subdivided so that in the end we have a total of seventy subtypes, all duly exemplified, and some of them endowed with picturesque or facetious names. Under the heading 'defective characters' there are, for example, six subdivisions: 'style hirsute, code civil, lâché, pachyderme, tarabiscoté, plat'.[4] These elaborate constructions are certainly interesting and thought-provoking, but their ultimate value seems somewhat doubtful. In the study of literary style, progress has always come through close scrutiny of specific texts from which conclusions were then drawn concerning wider aspects of theory and method. In this field, Pascal's 'esprit de finesse' is of far greater importance than the 'esprit de géométrie'.

A more specialized method of psychological stylistics, the study of an author's psyche through his imagery, will be discussed in Chapter IX.

III. The Functional Approach

According to a recent article, a 'stylistic fact' may be defined as a 'linguistic element considered in its utilization for literary purposes in a given work'.[5] Looked at in this way, style appears not as a psychological document but as one of the essential components of any literary work,

[1] Ibid., pp. 27 f.
[2] Dámaso Alonso, *Poesía española; ensayo de métodos y límites estilísticos*, Madrid, 1950.
[3] 'The subtlest and wittiest study of general stylistics to date, systematic and biased as it may be' (Hatzfeld-Le Hir, op. cit., p. 24).
[4] 'Shaggy, statute-book, slovenly, thick-skinned, finicky, flat style.'
[5] 'Le fait de style, c'est l'élément de langage considéré pour son utilisation à des fins littéraires dans une œuvre donnée' (P. Delbouille, 'Définition du fait de style', *Cahiers d'Analyse Textuelle*, ii (1960), pp. 94–104: p. 103).

which has its own distinctive part to play in the structure of the latter. This functional view immediately raises two questions: (1) what is the optimum context for such studies, and (2) on what aspects of style should they be based?

1. The problem of context in style studies has been considerably clarified by the introduction of two concepts: the immediate or *'micro-context'* and the wider or *'macro-context'*.[1] Either of these can provide a workable basis for stylistic inquiries; each has its advantages and its disadvantages. If one chooses a 'micro-context', for example a short poem or an extract of limited length, one can study the ways in which words interact, set off and influence each other. A popular form of this method is the stylistically oriented *explication de texte* in which Spitzer obtained some of his most striking successes.[2] Another form is the technique applied by Dr. R. A. Sayce in his valuable *Style in French Prose* (Oxford, 1953), where the stylistic resources of French are elucidated in the light of ten brief passages ranging from Rabelais to Proust. Naturally, these 'micro-contexts' are too narrow to reveal any significant preferences, recurrences, aversions and the like, nor can one draw from them any conclusions about the role of a given element in the structure of a major work. If, on the other hand, one chooses a wider context, one has a good chance of detecting dominant trends and of evaluating the part played by each device in the total effect of a book; at the same time one is apt to lose sight of the actual setting in which the words are used and of the ways in which they influence their neighbours or are influenced by them.

If one opts for the use of 'macro-contexts', a further question arises: where should one draw the line? In a passage already quoted (p. 25, n. 2), a leading linguist has spoken of the 'serial contextualization of our facts, context within context, each one being a function, an organ of the bigger context and all contexts finding a place in what may be called the context of culture'.[3] Which of these ever widening circles will provide the best framework for style studies? The answer will depend on the nature of the text and also on the aims of the inquiry. In my two books, *Style in the French Novel* and *The Image in the Modern French Novel*, I confined myself, with one exception,[4] to the context set by the authors themselves:

---

[1] M. Riffaterre, 'Stylistic Context', *Word*, xvi (1960), pp. 207–18. I am using these terms in rather a different sense than M. Riffaterre.

[2] Cf. *Archivum Linguisticum*, iii (1951), pp. 1 f. See also a list of recent works in this field in Hatzfeld-Le Hir, op. cit., pp. 39 ff.

[3] J. R. Firth, *Papers in Linguistics*, p. 32.

[4] The chapters on Proust do not cover the whole cycle of *A la recherche du temps perdu* but only certain parts of it.

each study examined the role of one stylistic element in the structure of an entire novel. This may be suitable when one deals with fiction, but it would obviously be inappropriate to other *genres*; a single poem, a short story or even a play would not usually provide an adequate context for this kind of analysis. Even in fiction there may be difficulties. Ideally, the student of Proust's style ought to cover the cycle of fifteen volumes in its entirety, since it represents one coherent whole; in practice, however, this cannot be done in any detail, given the richness, density and complexity of those stylistic features which really matter in that author.

On the other hand, the student may wish to transcend the limits of single works even where these form a suitable 'macro-context'. Many scholars prefer to examine the style, or some aspect of the style, of a writer in all his works and to trace the development of his manner. Others aim even higher and try to describe the style of a literary school, an epoch or an entire *genre*. All these different types of studies are equally legitimate in themselves, as long as it is remembered that as one widens the circle one is bound to lose in depth what one gains in breadth, and to move farther away from that close vision of stylistic realities which only a 'micro-context' can afford.

2. Functional stylistics has also to make another choice, especially in studies involving wider contexts. Such inquiries can be conducted on two different planes: they may concentrate on a particular element or group of elements, or they may seek to embrace the entire style of a work or a writer. The latter formula is very popular with postgraduate students working on the language of an author. No one would dispute the value of this method or the usefulness of some of its products; at the same time it suffers from certain inherent weaknesses. In spite of the skill of some of its practitioners, there is inevitably something monotonous and mechanical in the application of the same general categories to one writer after another; there is also sometimes a tendency to treat these monographs as mere inventories or collections of data which will find their place in some future synthesis.[1] Some scholars prefer, therefore, to confine their attention to a single device and to explore its function in one work or one author. In such studies there is room for more originality and if the point of penetration is rightly chosen, the inquiry can take one right to

---

[1] Cf. Ch. Bruneau, *Romance Philology*, v (1951), pp. 8 ff. Among the most important products of this approach the following may be mentioned here: F. Gray, *Le Style de Montaigne*, Paris, 1958; Y. Le Hir, *Lamennais écrivain*, Paris, 1948; M. Cressot, *La Phrase et le vocabulaire de J.-K. Huysmans*, Paris, 1938; M. Riffaterre, *Le Style des 'Pléiades' de Gobineau*, Paris, 1957; J. Schérer, *L'Expression littéraire dans l'œuvre de Mallarmé*, Paris, 1947; P. Nardin, *La Langue et le style de Jules Renard*, Paris, 1942; J. Mouton, *Le Style de Marcel Proust*, Paris, 1948.

the heart of the author's aesthetics.[1] A *sine qua non* of success in this kind of analysis is that the device examined should emerge from the text itself instead of being superimposed on it from outside. Leo Spitzer's warning, uttered fifteen years ago, has lost nothing of its timeliness:

'I should like to set down as a rule for all the generations of dissertation-writers to come: *never start writing on a subject of literary history unless you have made a particular observation of your own on this subject!* If you have been struck by a certain quality of Diderot's imagery, then write on this imagery—but not if you have only thought coldly, in the abstract: "Diderot is missing from the list of those whose imagery has been covered; why not fill the gap?"'[2]

Yet another method of style analysis may be mentioned here: the study of an author through his *key-words*. This procedure cuts across the three approaches just discussed since key-words can be studied both statistically[3] and by direct observation, and can be interpreted either psychologically or functionally: they can provide clues to the author's mind and also to the inner structure of his works. In this way Corneille has been re-examined in the light of such key-terms as *mérite, estime, devoir, vertu, générosité* and *gloire*.[4] More recently, a series of studies on the idea of the abyss, 'le gouffre', in Baudelaire have made a valuable contribution to our understanding of that poet.[5] On reading these works one is reminded of what Baudelaire himself wrote in *L'Art romantique*:

'Je lis dans une critique: "Pour deviner l'âme d'un poëte, ou du moins sa principale préoccupation, cherchons dans ses œuvres quel est le mot ou quels sont les mots qui s'y représentent avec le plus de fréquence. Le mot traduira l'obsession."'[6]

---

[1] Cf. J. Marouzeau, *Précis de stylistique française*, p. 16, and esp. G. Antoine, loc. cit., p. 44. In his little book, *Les Cinq Grandes Odes de Claudel ou la poésie de la répétition*, Paris, 1959, M. Antoine has given an admirable demonstration of this method.

[2] *Linguistics and Literary History*, p. 170, n. 1.

[3] For the statistician, a 'key-word' is a term whose frequency in a particular work or author is significantly higher than its frequency in ordinary language; cf. P. Guiraud, *Les Caractères statistiques du vocabulaire*, pp. 64 ff. and 100 ff. For the concept of key-word in lexicology, see above, p. 14.

[4] O. Nadal, *De quelques mots de la langue cornélienne*, Paris, 1948. Cf. also the studies of key-terms in W. Empson's *The Structure of Complex Words* (London, 1951).

[5] For a survey of the whole problem see recently G. Antoine, 'Pour une nouvelle exploration "stylistique" du gouffre baudelairien', *Le Français Moderne*, xxx (1962), pp. 81–98.

[6] 'I read in a review: "To discover the mind of a poet, or at least his main preoccupation, let us find out in his works which is the word or which are the words which occur most frequently. The word will express the obsession"' (*L'Art romantique*, XXII, 7; p. 1111 of the Pléiade ed.). I am indebted to my colleague Dr. P. M. Wetherill for this information.

In his inaugural lecture at the Collège de France, Valéry gave a memorable expression to the same idea:

'Le seul timbre du violoncelle exerce chez bien des personnes une véritable domination viscérale. Il y a des mots dont la fréquence, chez un auteur, nous révèle qu'ils sont en lui tout autrement doués de résonance, et, par conséquent, de puissance positivement créatrice, qu'ils ne le sont en général. C'est là un exemple de ces évaluations personnelles, de ces *grandes valeurs-pour-un-seul*, qui jouent certainement un très beau rôle dans une production de l'esprit où la singularité est un élément de première importance.'[1]

The general impression which emerges from this rapid survey of current trends in stylistics is that of an active and vigorous young science which is still somewhat inchoate and unorganized. There are many experiments, many ideas in ferment; at the same time there exists as yet no accepted terminology nor is there any general agreement on aims and methods. Under the circumstances it would be difficult to draw up anything in the nature of an interim balance-sheet. Nevertheless, several points already stand out very clearly. Quite apart from the intrinsic importance of the problems which it poses and of the results which it achieves, this new border-line science, neatly poised astride the frontier between linguistic and literary studies, has already begun to make its influence felt in the following ways:

1. The disappearance of traditional rhetoric has created a gap in the humanities, and stylistics has already gone a long way to fill this gap. In fact it would not be altogether wrong to describe stylistics as a 'new rhetoric' adapted to the standards and requirements of contemporary scholarship in the linguistic as well as the literary field.[2]

2. For the student of literature, stylistics provides a precise yet sensitive instrument which can play its full part only if it is closely coordinated with other aspects of literary criticism.

---

[1] 'The mere tone of the 'cello has a truly visceral fascination for many people. There are words whose frequency in a writer shows that they possess for him a resonance and, therefore, a positively creative power far stronger than in ordinary usage. This is an example of those personal evaluations, those *great private values*, which certainly play a significant part in a product of the mind where singularity is an element of prime importance' (*Variété V*, Paris, 1944 ed., p. 318). I am grateful to Dr. R. Posner, of Girton College, Cambridge, for drawing my attention to this passage.

[2] On rhetoric see H. Lausberg's fundamental *Handbuch der literarischen Rhetorik*, 2 vols., Munich, 1960; for a short account cf. P. Guiraud, *La Stylistique*, ch. I. Recent works on the subject are listed in Hatzfeld-Le Hir, op. cit., pp. 206 ff.; cf. also the latter author's *Rhétorique et stylistique de la Pléiade au Parnasse*, Paris, 1960. A special aspect of the rhetorical tradition, the survival of stock metaphors and similes, has been fully explored in E. R. Curtius's invaluable *European Literature and the Latin Middle Ages*, English transl., London, 1953. See also H. Morier, *Dictionnaire de poétique et de rhétorique*, Paris, 1961.

3. Its effect on linguistics is equally beneficial since it strengthens the humane and artistic side of the subject at a time when powerful influences are at work in the opposite direction (cf. pp. 15 f.).

4. More than any other development, the advent of stylistics may help to heal the rift which exists at present, both in teaching and in research, between linguistic and literary studies. It may be noted that this situation is peculiar to the modern humanities; the classics have remained happily immune from it. Thanks to stylistics, the fundamental unity of the subject may be restored on the plane of a higher synthesis, that of 'total criticism', which aims at a comprehensive and integrated study, in all its aspects, of the structure and impact of a literary work.[1]

[1] Some helpful suggestions for the combination of linguistic and literary methods will be found in R. A. Sayce's article, 'Literature and Language', *Essays in Criticism*, vii (1957), pp. 119–33. See also a recent symposium on 'Stylistics, Linguistics and Literary Criticism', published in 1961 by the Hispanic Institute in the United States, New York (S. Saporta, E. de Chasca, H. Contreras, R. Martínez-López); the volume *Style et littérature*, The Hague, 1962 (articles by P. Guiraud, P. Zumthor, A. Kibédi Varga, J. A. G. Tans); P. Valesio, 'Problemi di metodo nella critica stilistica', *Saggi linguistici dell'Istituto di Glottologia*, III, Bologna, 1962, pp. 9–69, and two articles in the *Preprints of Papers for the Ninth International Congress of Linguists*: M. A. K. Halliday, 'The Linguistic Study of Literary Texts' (pp. 197–202), and M. Riffaterre, 'The Stylistic Function' (pp. 209–13).

CHAPTER VII

CHOICE AND EXPRESSIVENESS IN STYLE

WE saw in the last chapter that there is an intimate connexion between choice and expressiveness, and that the interaction of the two factors plays a vital part in the production of style. In this chapter, certain important aspects of the problem will be examined more closely: the difference between conscious and unconscious choice; the aesthetic significance of the choices we make; their implications; finally, the limits within which they operate.

A. Conscious and Unconscious Choice

The question is often asked as to how far a writer is aware of the choices which he makes or, in a more general way, of the stylistic devices which he employs. Among students of style, Professor Guiraud has paid particular attention to this problem. He distinguishes between two kinds of stylistic values: 'expressive' and 'impressive'. The former are more or less unconscious; they constitute 'une socio-psycho-physiologie de l'expression'. 'Impressive' values, on the other hand, are conscious and intentional: they represent 'une esthétique, une éthique, une didactique, etc., de l'expression' and fall into two groups, according to whether the intention is 'direct and natural' or 'secondary and imitative'.[1]

There can be no doubt that the distinction between conscious and unconscious choice is both valid and important. We all know from personal experience that there are unconscious choices which we make either spontaneously, instinctively and at the first attempt, or even quite mechanically and automatically, whereas in other cases our choice is quite conscious and deliberate: we hesitate, correct ourselves, cast round for the right word or construction, until eventually we opt for one or the other of the alternatives which are open to us. Usually, all traces of this process are removed from the final version, but some writers like to preserve them so as to give a faithful picture of their effort at self-expression. Péguy, for example, was fond of accumulating synonyms rather than choosing between them. Here is a typical specimen of such a string of collocations:

'Je sens déjà l'*incurvation*, l'*incurvaison* générale ... Il faut aussi dire

[1] *La Stylistique,* p. 47.

que c'est le *courbement*, la *courbure*, la *courbature*, l'*inclinaison* de l'écrivain sur sa table de travail.'[1]

But if the distinction between conscious and unconscious choice is valid in theory, it is only too often inapplicable in practice. There are, to be sure, some cases where we have clear indications that a choice was made quite deliberately. Occasionally, the writer himself will comment on what he has just written. Elsewhere, the study of manuscripts, variants or proofs may be illuminating; one has to think only of the innumerable alterations with which Balzac riddled the proofs of his novels. There may also be internal evidence of a certain degree of consciousness and deliberateness. The persistent recurrence of certain important stylistic devices and *leit-motivs*, such as we shall encounter in the chapter on imagery, is an unmistakable sign of conscious and purposeful artistry. The same may be said of what has been called 'stylistic convergence': the use of several devices which all concur to express the same idea or to produce the same effect.[2] But even when full allowance has been made for these and other indications that a particular choice was taken consciously and deliberately, there will always remain a vast number of cases where there are no such indications, where we just do not know whether the choice was fully conscious, semi-conscious, unconscious, or even subconscious. This is a limitation inherent in the subject-matter of stylistics, and there is no need to exaggerate its seriousness, for, after all, the artistic value of a device of style does not in any way depend on whether the author was fully aware of the choice he was making.

B. The Aesthetic Significance of the Choice

In the previous chapter we saw on a concrete example, inversion of the subject in Modern French, the wide variety of effects which a sensitive writer can obtain from even such a simple device. Some of these effects—euphony, balance and cohesion of the sentence, etc.—are common and even banal; others are more recondite and can be fully grasped only if we replace them in their immediate and wider context. In order to understand the painfully dislocated structure of the sentence where Proust describes aunt Léonie's suspicions about Françoise (p. 106), the critic has to bear in mind the invalid mentality of the former and the

---

[1] 'I am already feeling the *incurvation*, the general *incurving* ... One should also say that it is the *bowing*, the *curving*, the *backache*, the *bending* of the writer over his desk' (*Cahiers de la Quinzaine*, October 23rd, 1910).
[2] On 'convergence' see Riffaterre, *Word*, xv (1959), pp. 172 ff., and Y. Louria, *La Convergence stylistique chez Proust*, Geneva—Paris, 1957.

whole nature of the relationship between the two women. There are stylistic choices which raise even wider issues: the whole aesthetics of an author may be involved in his preference or aversion for an important mode of expression. A good example of this is the well-known predilection of Flaubert for the so-called 'free indirect style'.[1] This is a compromise between the two orthodox forms of reported speech, which foreshadows such modern experiments as internal monologue and the 'stream of consciousness technique'. As in indirect speech proper, pronouns and tenses are shifted; at the same time there is no introductory verb and no subordinating conjunction, and all the expressive and evocative elements which give direct speech its flavour—questions, exclamations, interjections and the like—are faithfully preserved. A short extract from Thackeray will show how the construction works:

'I don't envy Pen's feelings as he thought of what he had done. *He had slept, and the tortoise had won the race . . . Oh! it was a coward hand that could strike and rob a creature so tender . . . how could he bear to look any of them in the face now?*'[2]

The sentences I have italicized are really Pendennis's thoughts, though it is nowhere explicitly stated that we have passed from the narrative plane to that of his inner speech. Naturally, the words actually spoken by the various characters can be transcribed in the same way.

In French literature, something like free indirect style had existed for many centuries; there are some highly interesting examples of it in the *Chanson de Roland*, and La Fontaine in particular showed great skill and virtuosity in handling it. Yet the construction was comparatively rare even in the first half of the nineteenth century. It was in the novels of Flaubert, especially from *Madame Bovary* onwards, that it became an invaluable and virtually omnipresent stylistic device. This sudden rise of the construction faces the critic with an intriguing problem: what was there in Flaubert's aesthetic doctrine, in his attitude to his craft, which predisposed him so strongly in favour of a hitherto neglected possibility? Over and above the general advantages of free indirect style—variety, flexibility, a certain surprise effect, an undercurrent of irony, and others— there were several specific reasons which explain Flaubert's fondness for this construction. Some of these reasons were purely linguistic. The

---

[1] The problem is fully discussed in ch. II of my *Style in the French Novel*. See now also J. A. Verschoor, *Etude de grammaire historique et de style sur le style direct et les styles indirects en français*, Groningen, 1959.
[2] Quoted by Jespersen, *The Philosophy of Grammar*, pp. 290 f. Cf. recently R. Quirk, *The Use of English*, London, 1962, pp. 246 ff. See also B. Blackstone, *Indirect Speech. Its Principles and Practice*, London, 1962.

monotonous repetition of the conjunction *que*, which seemed perfectly harmless to writers in the Classical period, was repugnant to the hypersensitive ear of Flaubert; as he wrote in his correspondence: 'Jusqu'à nous, jusqu'aux très modernes, on n'avait pas l'idée de l'harmonie soutenue du style, les *qui*, les *que* enchevêtrés les uns dans les autres reviennent incessamment dans ces grands écrivains.'[1] Free indirect style, with its avoidance of explicit subordination, provided an easy way out of this difficulty. It also commended itself to Flaubert because it transposed the present tense of direct speech into the Imperfect, a form of which he was particularly fond.

At a deeper level, free indirect style, a self-effacing mode of presentation in which the author disappears behind his characters, fitted admirably into Flaubert's doctrine of impassivity, the withdrawal of the writer from his work. In a famous passage of his correspondence, he wrote:

'L'auteur, dans son œuvre, doit être comme Dieu dans l'univers, présent partout et visible nulle part. L'Art étant une seconde nature, le créateur de cette nature-là doit agir par des procédés analogues. Que l'on sente dans tous les atomes, à tous les aspects, une impassibilité cachée et infinie. L'effet, pour le spectateur, doit être une espèce d'ébahissement. Comment tout cela s'est-il fait? doit-on dire, et qu'on se sente écrasé sans savoir pourquoi.'[2]

At the same time, free indirect style, enabling as it does the author to slide imperceptibly from the plane of the narrative on to that of inner speech, provided an ideal vehicle for another fundamental attitude of Flaubert, for what he himself called his 'pantheistic faculty': his complete self-identification with his characters. This sympathetic self-identification went so far that, when relating the story of Emma Bovary's suicide, he felt the taste of arsenic in his mouth and actually had two attacks of indigestion. In a letter to Louise Colet he wrote: 'C'est une délicieuse chose que d'écrire, que de n'être plus soi, mais de circuler dans toute la création dont on parle.'[3] Free indirect style is the exact linguistic equivalent of this attitude.

---

[1] 'Before us, before the very modern writers, people had no idea of the sustained harmony of style; *qui*-s and *que*-s entangled with one another constantly recur in these great authors.'
[2] 'The author in his work should be like God in the universe, present everywhere and visible nowhere. Since Art is a second nature, the creator of this nature must work by similar processes. In every atom, in every aspect one should feel a hidden and infinite impassivity. The effect on the spectator should be a kind of astonishment. How has all this come about? one should ask, and one should feel crushed without knowing why.'
[3] 'It is a delightful thing to write, not to be oneself any more, but to circulate in the whole creation one is talking about.'

K

It will be seen that the critic has to cast his net very wide in order to appreciate the full significance of certain choices. From a purely grammatical point of view, the difference between traditional and free indirect speech may seem slight; from a stylistic and aesthetic point of view, the extensive use which Flaubert made of the latter was fraught with far-reaching consequences. Indeed Proust did not exaggerate when he wrote about the 'new Imperfect': 'Cet imparfait, si nouveau dans la littérature, change entièrement l'aspect des choses, comme font une lampe qu'on a déplacée, l'arrivée dans une maison nouvelle, l'ancienne si elle est presque vide et qu'on est en plein déménagement.'[1]

C. THE IMPLICATIONS OF THE CHOICE

Many of the choices we make are confined to a particular occasion and have no further implications. One may, in French, invert the subject in one sentence and place it before the verb in the next; put one adjective before its noun and another after it; use free indirect style in one utterance and then switch over to direct speech or to ordinary indirect discourse. Other choices, without being binding in themselves, commit us in a general way to a certain tone or level of style. If a French writer hazards a highly literary form such as an Imperfect Subjunctive (see above, pp. 114 ff.), this does not necessarily mean that he will have to employ that mood throughout the text; it does mean, though, that he has opted for a cultured and meticulously correct style from which he will not depart unless he has some special reason to do so.

There are, however, other situations where a writer may have to make a choice which will 'commit' him in the Existentialist sense of that term: a choice which will determine once and for all one of the fundamental features of his style and which will thus affect the whole texture of his work. Two examples from the art of the novelist will help to elucidate this point.

When Albert Camus wrote his experimental novel, *L'Etranger,* he was faced with an unusual stylistic problem. He had to give the narrator, Meursault—the incarnation of the author's theory of 'absurdity'—a language of his own, and then use this unpromising material in telling a coherent and carefully thought-out narrative. There was one choice in particular which he had to make from the very outset: he had to decide whether to tell the story in the Past Definite or the Past Indefinite.

---

1 'This Imperfect, so new in literature, entirely changes the appearance of things, like a lamp which has been moved, like arriving in a new house, like the old one when it is almost empty and the removal is in progress' ('A propos du "style" de Flaubert', *Nouvelle Revue Française*, xiv, 1 (1920), pp. 72–90).

Normally he would no doubt have opted for the former, as he did in his two subsequent novels, *La Peste* and *La Chute*, both of which are told in the first person singular. Here, however, he chose the Past Indefinite, and once the choice had been made it had to be adhered to till the very end. An example taken at random will show how different the novel would be if he had chosen the other alternative:

'Masson *a fait* un bond en avant. Mais l'autre Arabe s'était relevé et il *s'est placé* derrière celui qui était armé. Nous *n'avons pas osé* bouger. Ils *ont reculé* lentement... Quand ils *ont vu* qu'ils avaient assez de champ, ils *se sont enfuis* très vite.'[1]

'Masson *fit* un bond en avant. Mais l'autre Arabe s'était relevé et il *se plaça* derrière celui qui était armé. Nous *n'osâmes pas* bouger. Ils *reculèrent* lentement ... Quand ils *virent* qu'ils avaient assez de champ, ils *s'enfuirent* très vite.'

The choice of the Past Indefinite had a number of important consequences. As Sartre has pointed out in his masterly analysis of Camus's novel,[2] this form weakens the verb by 'breaking it in two', and thus produces an impression of feebleness, inertia and inconclusiveness which fits in perfectly with the narrator's personality. It also gives the narrative an air of disjointedness and discontinuity, as opposed to the orderly sequence of events expressed by a succession of Past Definites. This again is characteristic of the psychology of the 'absurd' man who is unable, or unwilling, to relate his experiences to one another and to arrange them into a meaningful pattern. To quote again Sartre, 'une phrase de *L'Etranger*, c'est une île ... Au lieu de se jeter comme un pont entre le passé et l'avenir, elle n'est plus qu'une petite substance isolée qui se suffit'.[3] There is also a further point. The Past Definite is a 'preterite', a pure past, whereas the Past Indefinite is a 'perfect', a hybrid form in which the past impinges on the present: *j'ai écrit* 'I have written' (as opposed to *j'écrivis* 'I wrote') means that the writing was done in the past, but that its consequences are still relevant. As an English critic of Camus puts it, 'the preterite is the tense of *lived* experience whereas the perfect

---

[1] 'Masson leapt forward. But the other Arab had risen and stood behind the one who was armed. We did not dare to move. They withdrew slowly ... When they saw that they had enough room, they fled very fast' (1957 ed., Paris, p. 81).
There are, however, one or two cases where the Past Definite is used in the novel; cf. H. Yvon, 'Le Passé simple est-il sorti d'usage?', *Le Français moderne*, xxxi (1963), pp. 161–76: pp. 168 ff.
[2] 'Explication de *L'Etranger*', reprinted in *Situations I*, 4th ed., Paris, 1947, pp. 99–121: pp. 117 f.
[3] 'Each sentence in *L'Etranger* is an island ... Instead of throwing a bridge between past and future, it is merely a small, isolated, self-contained substance.'

is the tense of *living* experience'.[1] This makes it a congenial mode of expression for a man like Meursault who lives entirely in the here and now, who is capable of recording his sensations but is not given to analysing his experiences. In the words of the same critic, 'the tense used renders very strong the impression that one is experiencing these events directly, before they have been analysed, classified—and misrepresented—by rational scrutiny'.[2] To all this must be added the all-important difference in 'stylistic climate' between the two tenses. The Past Definite is peculiar to the written language, and some of its forms have a stilted and highly literary air, whereas the Past Indefinite is the tense commonly used in the spoken idiom both for the preterite and for the perfect;[3] a form like *nous osâmes*, which occurs in the rewritten version of the extract quoted above, would sound utterly incongruous in *L'Etranger*, though it would be perfectly acceptable in the totally different stylistic register of *La Peste* and *La Chute*.

The time-perspective adopted in a novel has a profound influence on its whole structure and impact; yet there are some choices which have even more decisive implications. Such a choice is that of the *point of view* from which the story is told—a problem which has greatly exercised writers since Flaubert and Henry James as it is bound up with the vexed question of the author's 'omniscience' and of artistic verisimilitude.[4] Until quite recently it was thought that the novelist could choose between two alternatives: he could either tell the story himself or could have it told by a narrator. There were of course certain variations and refinements: instead of one narrator one could have two, as in André Maurois's *Climats*, or even three, as in Gide's trilogy, *L'Ecole des Femmes*, *Robert* and *Geneviève*;[5] one could even alternate between the first and the third person, as Simone de Beauvoir did in *Le Sang des autres*. In these various ways one could achieve valuable contrast effects[6] whilst still remaining confined to a choice between two alternatives.

[1] J. Cruickshank, *Albert Camus and the Literature of Revolt*, London, 1959, p. 160.
[2] Ibid.
[3] On this contrast, see recently E. Benveniste, 'Les Relations de temps dans le verbe français', *Bulletin de la Société de Linguistique de Paris*, liv (1959), pp. 69–82, and P. Imbs, *L'Emploi des temps verbaux en français moderne*, Paris, 1960, Pt. I, ch. IV. Cf. R. Queneau, *Exercices de style*, 5th ed., Paris, 1947, where the same story is told in four different tenses.
[4] Cf. N. Friedman, 'Point of View in Fiction: the Development of a Critical Concept', *Publications of the Modern Language Association of America*, lxx (1955), pp. 1160–84.
[5] See my *Image in the Modern French Novel*, pp. 81–8.
[6] Cf. the end of the first and the beginning of the second chapter in Simone de Beauvoir's *Le Sang des autres* (9th ed., Paris, 1945, p. 33): 'Il n'y a aucun salut. Pas même l'ivresse du désespoir et la résolution aveugle, puisque tu es là, sur ce lit, dans la lumière sauvage de ta mort.
La bicyclette était toujours là, neuve, flambante. avec son cadre bleu pâle et son guidon

An interesting experiment was made by Michel Butor in his novel, *La Modification* (1957), which has already been mentioned (pp. 107 f.). As the author himself has explained on another occasion,[1] the main character of a novel can play *three* different roles in the presentation of the story: he can be 'celui dont on raconte l'histoire', 'celui qui raconte son histoire', or 'celui à qui l'on raconte sa propre histoire'.[2] In *La Modification*, M. Butor chose this third method: the story is told in the second person plural addressed to the principal character, Léon Delmont. This formula is applied with the utmost consistency throughout the novel, from the first sentence where we see Delmont getting into the Paris–Rome train:

'*Vous avez mis* le pied gauche sur la rainure de cuivre, et de *votre* épaule droite *vous essayez* en vain de pousser un peu plus le panneau coulissant',[3]

right to the last sentence which marks the end of his journey:

'Le couloir est vide. *Vous regardez* la foule sur le quai. *Vous quittez* le compartiment.'[4]

This unusual form of presentation adds to the story a curious undertone which will affect various readers in different ways. According to M. Butor himself, the second person plural gives the narrative a 'didactic' air.[5] Some readers may detect in it the voice of the judge rather than the teacher; others may agree with Spitzer that the *vous* gives the whole novel an ironical colouring.[6] Another leading *avant-garde* novelist, Alain Robbe-Grillet, once told me that in his view it was God who was speaking to Delmont. Be that as it may, this original and intriguing mode of narration

---

nickelé qui étincelait contre la pierre morne du mur. Elle était si svelte, si élancée: immobile, elle semblait encore fendre l'air; jamais Hélène n'avait vu une bicyclette si raffinée.'
    'There is no salvation. Not even the intoxication of despair and blind determination, for you are there, on this bed, in the savage light of your death.
    The bicycle was still there, brand-new, with its pale blue frame and its nickelled handle-bar, gleaming against the dull stone wall. It was so tall and slim; although it stood still, it seemed as if it were still cleaving the air; Helen had never seen such a refined bicycle.'
    On the narrative technique applied in this book, see also Simone de Beauvoir's own remarks in *La Force de l'âge*, Paris, 1960, pp. 557 f. For a rather more complex experiment on similar lines, see the novel, *Mutmassungen über Jakob*, by a young German writer, Uwe Johnson.
    [1] *Colloque sur les problèmes de la personne* (Royaumont, 1960), 'Programme; résumés des exposés', no. xxii (summary of a paper on 'Usage des pronoms personnels dans le roman').
    [2] 'He whose story is told—he who tells his own story—he who is told his own story.'
    [3] '*You have put* your left foot in the copper groove and with *your* right shoulder *you are trying* in vain to push the sliding panel a little further.'
    [4] 'The corridor is empty. *You are looking* at the crowd on the platform. *You are leaving* the compartment.'
    [5] Cf. the paper referred to in n. 1 above.
    [6] *Archivum Linguisticum*, xiv (1962), p. 62.

puts an entirely new complexion on a story which in itself is somewhat meagre and commonplace.

It would seem, then, that a novel can be told, in theory, in either of the three persons distinguished in the pronominal and conjugational system. One could even think of further refinements resulting from a choice between singular and plural, especially in the second person. The tone of *La Modification* would be entirely different if Butor had opted for *tu* instead of *vous*. But perhaps we may go one step further. In addition to the three persons of traditional grammar, there is yet another possibility: what one might call a 'zero' narrator. An example of this 'negative' technique is Robbe-Grillet's novel, or 'anti-novel', *La Jalousie* (1957), where the story is obviously told by a narrator, the jealous husband, but where there is never any direct reference to this person. We are told, for example, that the table is laid for three people, two of whom, the wife and her lover, are mentioned whereas the third one is not:

'Les trois couverts occupent trois des côtés, la lampe le quatrième. A . . . est à sa place habituelle; Franck est assis à sa droite—donc devant le buffet.'[1]

This trick is not merely a challenge to the author's ingenuity: it surrounds the story with an aura of mystery and elusiveness; there is a kind of vacuum in the centre of the narrative, which exercises a powerful fascination on the reader. It may be doubted, of course, whether such experiments, however interesting in the first instance, can be repeated and can lead anywhere; one may even wonder whether this excessive preoccupation with technique, started by Gide and similar writers, is really a good thing for the future of the novel. From our point of view, on the other hand, these extreme cases are significant in that they provide examples of difficult and fundamental choices which predetermine the whole shape of a work of art.

D. THE LIMITS OF THE CHOICE

The choices that a writer can make are limited by the expressive resources of the language, by the number and nature of the alternatives open to him in a given situation. In many cases he will be faced with a simple '*binary*' choice: he will have to choose between two synonyms

---

[1] 'The table is laid for three, on three sides; the lamp stands on the fourth side. A . . . is at her usual place; Franck is sitting on her right—that is, in front of the sideboard' (*La Jalousie*, Paris, 1957, p. 21).

(*help—aid*, *grateful—thankful*, French *gratitude—reconnaissance*), two
morphological variants (*I do not—I don't*, French *je peux—je puis*
'I can', *je sais—je sache* 'I know'), or two constructions (inversion or
non-inversion of the subject, anteposition or postposition of the adjective
in French). The simplicity of these minimum choices does not mean in
any way that the effects obtained from them are also simple. We saw in
the last chapter what an invaluable device inversion can be in the hands
of a skilful artist, and the subtle shades and overtones of meaning which
can be produced in French by placing the adjective before the noun are
well known. When the newspaper *Le Monde* spoke in 1948, during one of
the Government crises which were chronic under the Fourth Republic,
of 'les *rituelles consultations* de M. Vincent Auriol', instead of the more
normal '*consultations rituelles*', it passed judgment on a whole regime by
the ironic anteposition of the adjective.[1] The more unusual the construction, the more expressive force it will have. Even such purely classificatory
adjectives as *républicain* and *français* can be anteposed in special contexts.
Roger Martin du Gard writes: 'ils abdiqueront peut-être jusqu'à leur
républicaine prétention à la souveraineté',[2] and Cocteau: 'cette *française*,
lourde et légère torpeur.'[3] In English, where the place of the adjective
is fixed, these delicate nuances will have to be conveyed by different
means.

Some binary choices can raise even wider issues and can play a distinctive part in the structure of a literary work. A good example of this is a
possibility which exists in French but not in English: that of choosing
between two pronouns of address, *tu* and *vous*.[4] One or two illustrations
from literature will give an idea of some of the uses to which this resource
can be put:

1. In ordinary language, the choice between the two pronouns depends,
amongst other things, on the degree of *intimacy* between speaker and
hearer, and the passage from *vous* to *tu* usually marks an important stage
in the development of relations between two people; in some societies

[1] Cf. my *Style in the French Novel*, pp. 7 ff. See now on the whole problem K. Wydler, *Zur Stellung des attributiven Adjektivs vom Latein bis zum Neufranzösischen* (Romanica Helvetica LIII), Berne, 1956.
[2] 'They will perhaps renounce even their *very republican* claim to sovereignty' (*Les Thibault*, Pt. VIII, p. 195).
[3] 'This *very French*, heavy and light torpor' (quoted from F. Jones's unpublished thesis referred to on p. 124, n. 3).
[4] On the stylistic aspects of pronouns of address, see R. Brown-A. Gilman, 'The Pronouns of Power and Solidarity', *Style in Language*, pp. 253–76, and F. Berry, *Poets' Grammar. Person, Time and Mood in Poetry*, London, 1958, chs. III–IV. Cf. also A. Niculescu, 'Notes sur la structure de l'expression pronominale de la politesse', *Cahiers de Linguistique Théorique et Appliquée*, i (1962), pp. 179–83.

there is a whole ritual attached to the change, and a toast is drunk to celebrate it. These conventional values can be exploited by a writer in unexpected ways, as an example from Racine's *Phèdre* will show. It is an interesting feature of the composition of this play that, although it hinges on Phèdre's love for her stepson Hippolyte, there is only one scene (Act II, scene 5) where the two protagonists come face to face; in a later scene (Act III, scene 4) their paths cross for a moment, but they do not talk to each other. In the crucial scene, Phèdre addresses Hippolyte in a formal way:

> On dit qu'un prompt départ *vous* éloigne de nous,
> Seigneur.[1]

At first she controls herself, but gradually she is carried away by her passion and betrays her closely guarded secret. Yet she keeps up the pretence of formal address; she clings to the *vous,* as her last defence, even when Hippolyte begins to guess the truth about her feelings for him:

> Et sur quoi jugez-*vous* que j'en perds la mémoire,
> Prince? Aurois-je perdu tout le soin de ma gloire?[2]

But when Hippolyte, confused and bewildered, apologizes, the barrier suddenly breaks down; she interrupts him, switching over, abruptly and brutally, to the pronoun of guilty intimacy:

> Ah, cruel! *tu* m'as trop entendue![3]

Now that her defences have collapsed, her repressed passion gushes forth in a torrent of confessions and self-accusations, expressed throughout in this illicitly intimate form of address, right down to the end when she implores Hippolyte to kill her or at least to give her his sword so that she may take her own life:

> Ou si d'un sang trop vil *ta* main seroit trempée,
> Au défaut de *ton* bras prête-moi *ton* épée;
> Donne.[4]

If one re-reads the scene from this point of view, one cannot help feeling that the change in the form of address is one of the most potent

[1] 'It is said that an early departure is taking you (*vous*) away from us, my Lord.'

[2] 'And what makes you (*vous*) think, Prince, that I am oblivious of it? Would I have ceased to care about my reputation?'

[3] 'Oh cruel man, you (*tu*) have understood me only too well!'

[4] 'Or if you feel that your hand would be imbrued in too vile blood, instead of your arm, lend me your sword; give it to me.'

means by which Racine conveys the critical transformation in Phèdre's attitude.

2. In ordinary speech, one usually employs *tu*, not *vous*, when talking to a *child*. In one of his plays, *Les Chaises*, Eugène Ionesco uses this convention to produce a pathetic effect when a Peter Pan-like character comforts himself with the thought that people address him as *vous*, which is clear proof of his adult status:

> Le Vieux.— . . . On me répondit: Il est minuit, un gosse ne se couche pas si tard. Si *vous* ne faites pas encore dodo c'est que *vous* n'êtes plus un marmot. Je ne les aurais quand même pas crus s'ils ne m'avaient pas dit *vous* . . .
> La Vieille (écho).—'*Vous*.'
> Le Vieux.—Au lieu de *tu* . . .
> La Vieille (écho).—*Tu* . . .[1]

3. In some societies, one of the most important functions of pronouns of address is, or was at one time, to serve as *status symbols* expressing social differences between speakers. This was the situation in France 'until the Revolution when the Committee for Public Safety condemned the use of *vous* as a feudal remnant and ordered a universal reciprocal *tu*. On October 31, 1793, Malbec made a Parliamentary speech against *vous*: "Nous distinguons trois personnes pour le singulier et trois pour le pluriel, et, au mépris de cette règle, l'esprit de fanatisme, d'orgueil et de féodalité, nous a fait contracter l'habitude de nous servir de la seconde personne du pluriel lorsque nous parlons à un seul."[2] For a time revolutionary "fraternité" transformed all address into the mutual *Citoyen* and the mutual *tu*. Robespierre even addressed the president of the Assembly as *tu*. In later years solidarity declined and the differences of power which always exist everywhere were expressed once more'.[3]

How acutely conscious pre-revolutionary French society was of this distinction can be seen from one of Voltaire's poems, *Epître XXXIII*, which bears the characteristic sub-title: 'Les *Vous* et les *Tu*.' The poem

---

[1] THE OLD MAN: 'They answered: "It's midnight, a kid doesn't go to bed so late. If you (*vous*) haven't yet gone to bye-bye, it's because you aren't a child any more." I still wouldn't have believed them if they hadn't said *vous* . . .'
THE OLD WOMAN (echoing): '*Vous*.'
THE OLD MAN: 'Instead of *tu* . . .'
THE OLD WOMAN (echoing): '*Tu* . . .'
                           (E. Ionesco, *Théâtre*, I, Paris, 1954, p. 166).
[2] 'We distinguish between three persons in the singular and three in the plural, and, in defiance of this rule, the spirit of fanaticism, arrogance and feudalism has given us the habit of using the second person plural when talking to a single individual.'
[3] R. Brown-A. Gilman, loc. cit., p. 264.

is addressed to a certain 'Philis' whom the author used to know as a poor and flighty young woman of loose morals and who subsequently became rich and respectable. The form of address alternates skilfully between *tu* and *vous*, *Philis* and *Madame*; sometimes there are variations within the same stanza or even within the same sentence:

> Ces deux lustres de diamants
> Qui pendent à *vos* deux oreilles;
> Ces riches carcans, ces colliers,
> Et cette pompe enchanteresse,
> Ne valent pas un des baisers
> Que *tu* donnais dans *ta* jeunesse.[1]

As Spitzer has pointed out in his masterly analysis of this text,[2] the linguistic game, the sudden changes in register give the poem a light and playful air and divert the reader's attention from the main theme. Yet there is a deeper significance: 'as the poet shifts from *tu* to *vous*, he passes easily from pleasant memories of Philis's frivolous past to an indictment of her present setting of chilly respectability: from idealization of the healthy and amoral life of the senses he once knew with her, to a pitiless exposure of her vain, ostentatious luxury'.[3]

4. Certain traditionally minded speakers prefer the *formality* of *vous* to the intimacy of *tu* even when talking to members of their own family. In Camus's *La Peste*, there is a terse thumb-nail sketch of a pretentious judge of the old school who, we are told, 'dit *vous* à sa femme et à ses enfants, débite des méchancetés polies à la première et des paroles définitives aux héritiers'.[4] The judge and his family will play an important role in the development of the story, and this linguistic habit helps the reader to size up his character and to place him at the exact social level where he belongs. 'Le vouvoiement', writes Professor Bruneau, 'caractérise une bourgeoisie traditionaliste et prétentieuse, qui s'essaie à imiter la noblesse de jadis.'[5]

---

[1] 'These two diamond pendants which hang on your (*vos*) ears; these costly chokers, these necklaces and all this entrancing luxury are not worth one of the kisses you (*tu*) used to give when you (*tu*) were young.'
[2] *A Method of Interpreting Literature*, Northampton, Mass., 1949, ch. II: '*Explication de Texte* Applied to Voltaire.'
[3] Ibid., p. 68.
[4] 'He addresses his wife and children as *vous*, says politely unkind things to the former and peremptory words to the heirs' (*La Peste*, Paris, 1958 impr., p. 39).
[5] 'The use of *vous* is characteristic of a traditionalist and pretentious bourgeoisie which tries to imitate the nobility of bygone days' (*La Prose littéraire de Proust à Camus*, Oxford, 1953, p. 21).

In all these examples, a seemingly trivial linguistic detail has enabled a writer to sum up a human attitude or relationship more incisively than any explicit comment could have done. Such cases constitute a real challenge to the translator whose own language does not possess this facility.

Somewhat more complicated than these binary choices are '*ternary*' ones where we can choose from among three synonyms (*end—finish—conclude, kingly—royal—regal*), three morphological variants (French *j'assiérai—j'assoirai—j'asseyerai* 'I shall set'), or three alternative constructions (direct—indirect—free indirect speech,[1] French *parler de la politique—parler de politique—parler politique* 'to talk about politics'). Elsewhere there are '*quaternary*' or more complex choices. In Italian, for example, one has to choose between four pronouns of address (*tu, voi, lei, ella*), which complicates the pattern just outlined for French. In *La Chartreuse de Parme*, Stendhal has exploited the possibilities offered by this finer system of distinctions; speaking of the arrogant way in which the governor of Parma gaol treats his aristocratic prisoner, Fabrice del Dongo, he specifies: 'il fut d'une insolence plus qu'ordinaire envers le prisonnier; il lui adressait la parole en l'appelant *voi*, ce qui est en Italie la façon de parler aux domestiques'.[2]

In the grammatical system of a language, the number of alternatives from among which one may choose is, as a rule, strictly limited. In the lexical system, the position is more flexible; as we have seen (p. 75), there exist certain privileged spheres of vocabulary which command a formidable battery of synonyms. An Old English poet could choose between three dozen words for 'hero' and 'prince', and a French writer of the twelfth century had a comparable wealth of synonyms available for the idea of 'fight' and 'battle'. But even here, our choices are confined within a limited range, while in the vast majority of cases we have only a very small number of alternatives to play with. There is, however, one field where our possibilities of choice are infinitely wider and may indeed seem at first sight unlimited: the realm of *figurative expressions*, simile and metaphor. In theory, the speaker or writer may compare anything to any other thing provided that there is any kind of similarity, analogy or correspondence between them—and, as will be seen in the chapter

[1] According to Professor Harmer (op. cit., pp. 300 f.) there is even a fourth alternative which he calls 'free direct style': the interpolation of direct speech into the narrative, without any explicit sign of the change.
[2] 'He was more insolent than usual towards the prisoner; he addressed him as *voi* which, in Italy, is the way one speaks to a servant' (Paris, Pléiade ed., 1933, p. 262). On a somewhat similar situation in Swedish cf. Françoise Sagan's play, *Château en Suède*, Act III.

on imagery, modern writers, always on the look-out for novelty and surprise effects, tend to treat this condition in a very liberal way.

Yet, even though the choice of analogies gives free scope to the author's imagination, he will have to observe certain limits inherent in the nature of the work of art. One or two of these limitations may be briefly mentioned here:

1. One factor which limits freedom of choice in the matter of images is the need to *conform* them to the personality of the people who use them. Legrandin in Proust is an example in point. As we already know (pp. 104f. and 109), this character talks in an elegant and poetic, but stilted and affected manner. In this peculiar stylistic climate, only certain types of images will be acceptable, and those which arise in it with disarming spontaneity —'la musique que joue le clair de lune sur la flûte du silence'[1]—would be completely out of place in the speech of other characters.

The necessity to adapt images to the personality of the speaker or writer may impose serious limitations on the author of a play or of a novel told by a narrator. If the adaptation is successful, it may give rise to valuable evocative effects. In his novel *L'Immoraliste*, Gide hit on an image, or rather a symbol, which sums up the narrator's metamorphosis in a concise and striking way and which is at the same time in perfect harmony with the personality of this young historian, a product of the Ecole des Chartes:

'Et je me comparais aux palimpsestes; je goûtais la joie du savant qui, sous les écritures plus récentes, découvre sur un même papier un texte ancien infiniment plus précieux. Quel était-il, ce texte occulté? Pour le lire, ne fallait-il pas tout d'abord effacer les textes récents?'[2]

But there are also cases where the author's own style shines through that of the narrator. As already noted (pp. 136 ff.), Camus succeeded, in *L'Etranger*, in giving his strange and absurd 'hero' a language of his own. He did, however, have to pay a heavy price, and sometimes one has the impression that he is ill at ease within his self-imposed limitations and that he makes the narrator talk in a way which does not sound quite right. This is what Sartre had in mind when he wrote: 'A travers le récit essoufflé de Meursault, j'aperçois en transparence une prose poétique plus

---

[1] 'The music which the moonlight plays on the flute of silence' (*Du Côté de chez Swann*, vol. I, p. 168).

[2] 'And I compared myself to a palimpsest; I experienced the joy of the scholar who, underneath more recent writing, discovers on the same paper an old and infinitely more valuable text. What was it, this hidden text? In order to read it, would one not have first to erase the recent texts?' (*L'Immoraliste*, Paris, 1926 ed., p. 83).

large qui le soustend et qui doit être le mode d'expression personnel de M. Camus.'[1] When Meursault says: 'Du fond de mon avenir, pendant toute cette vie absurde que j'avais menée, un souffle obscur remontait vers moi à travers des années qui n'étaient pas encore venues',[2] one seems to hear the author's own voice behind the narrator's monotonous soliloquy. It is also significant that two poetic and therefore unconvincing images, which occurred in the 1942 edition of the novel, were subsequently deleted: 'Au cœur de cette maison pleine de sommeil, la plainte est montée lentement, comme une fleur née du silence';[3] '(la lumière) a coulé sur tous les visages comme un jus neuf'.[4]

2. Another limiting factor is the general *atmosphere* of the work in question. A study of imagery in Jean Giono's novel *Regain* has shown that the analogies, though numerous and highly original, are drawn from a very limited area and form a kind of closed circle: they describe natural phenomena, animals, plants and peasant life in the Basses-Alpes by comparing them to plants, animals, objects and activities peculiar to that same environment. Analogies derived from other spheres such as fine art, science, technology or urban life, would be completely out of place in this stylistic milieu. Such a technique has several advantages: the images are homogeneous and perfectly attuned to the subject; they have the authentic ring of personal experience; even more important, they overlie the boundaries which separate human beings, animals, plants and inanimate objects: they posit a dense network of analogies and correspondences which cut across these various spheres and thus help to emphasize the author's pantheistic philosophy. At the same time, the virtuosity with which Giono manipulates his meagre metaphorical resources succeeds in averting the danger of narrowness and monotony which was inherent in his material.[5]

3. Yet another limiting factor is the *tone* of the passage and, in a more general way, the author's attitude to his subject. If he wishes to produce a comical or pejorative effect, then certain types of images will be automatically excluded while others will arise almost inevitably. Parallels between human beings and animals will often appear in such contexts

---

[1] 'Behind Meursault's breathless narrative I perceive a more ample poetic prose which subtends it and shines through it and which must be M. Camus's personal mode of expression' (loc. cit., pp. 113 f.).

[2] 'From the depth of my future, throughout this absurd life which I had led, a dark breath rose towards me across the years which had not yet come' (p. 169).

[3] 'In the heart of this house full of slumber, the groan rose slowly, like a flower born of silence' (Paris, 1942 ed., p. 48).

[4] 'The light flowed on all the faces like a fresh juice' (ibid., p. 100).

[5] See my *Style in the French Novel*, pp. 217–31, esp. pp. 224 ff.

since such images are apt to debase man, to reduce him to the level of beasts and to expose the animal side of his nature. Every reader of Proust will remember caricatures like that of M. de Palancy 'qui, avec sa grosse tête de carpe aux yeux ronds, se déplaçait lentement au milieu des fêtes en desserrant d'instant en instant ses mandibules comme pour chercher son orientation',[1] or that of Robert de Saint-Loup: 'Devant la curiosité moitié mondaine, moitié zoologique qu'il vous inspirait, on se demandait si c'était dans le faubourg Saint-Germain qu'on se trouvait ou au Jardin des Plantes et si on regardait un grand seigneur traverser un salon, ou se promener dans sa cage un merveilleux oiseau.'[2]

Elsewhere the pejorative overtones become more strident. In Sartre's *La Mort dans l'âme*, the account of the great exodus of 1940 is punctuated with repellent images where the people and vehicles on the crowded roads are likened to painfully crawling insects:

'. . . les longues *fourmis* sombres tenaient toute la route . . . Les *insectes* rampaient devant eux, énormes, lents, mystérieux . . . les autos grinçaient comme des *homards*, chantaient comme des *grillons*. Les hommes ont été changés en *insectes* . . . nous ne sommes plus que des pattes de cette interminable *vermine*.'[3]

The wider implications of this disturbing concentration of insect images will be considered in a later chapter.[4]

4. In addition to these limiting factors, the choice of analogies will also be conditioned by the author's *personality* and experience. As will be seen in the chapter on imagery, an exaggeration of this principle can lead the critic to strange conclusions; nevertheless there are some cases where the choice of a particular image or type of image was clearly dictated by special circumstances. A famous example is Rimbaud's synaesthetic sonnet *Voyelles*, where he attributes colours to the different vowels and compares them to a wide variety of objects:

---

[1] 'Who, with his large carp's head and round eyes, moved about slowly in the midst of the party, opening and closing his mandibles as if to find his bearings' (*Du Côté de chez Swann*, vol. II, p. 143).

[2] 'In view of the curiosity, half fashionable, half zoological, which he aroused in one, one wondered whether one was in the Faubourg Saint-Germain or in the Botanical Gardens and whether one was watching an aristocrat crossing a drawing-room or a wonderful bird walking in its cage' (*Le Temps retrouvé*, vol. I, p. 15).

[3] 'The long dark *ants* covered the whole road . . . *Insects* were crawling in front of them, huge, slow, mysterious . . . the cars creaked like *lobsters*, chirped like *crickets*. Men have been turned into *insects* . . . now we are merely the legs of this endless *vermin*' (pp. 20 f. and 24).

[4] See below, pp. 186 ff.

A noir, E blanc, I rouge, U vert, O bleu, voyelles,
Je dirai quelque jour vos naissances latentes.
A, noir corset velu des mouches éclatantes
Qui bombillent autour des puanteurs cruelles . . .[1]

It has been suggested—though one can never be quite certain in such matters—that these colours, and the images which illustrate them, were derived from a spelling-book used in Rimbaud's childhood or from other early memories.[2] In a more general way, the range and quality of an author's imagery will be inevitably influenced by his experiences, his environment, his habits, his reading, his human contacts and similar factors. A writer who did not possess the curiosity and the encyclopaedic culture of a Proust would never have been able to think of the precise and detailed images which the latter drew from the various sciences, from fine art, music, the theatre and similar spheres.[3]

There are thus a number of factors which impose certain limits on the choice of analogies. These limits are, however, incomparably wider and more flexible than those with which a writer is faced in other parts of the linguistic system. This discrepancy goes a long way to explain why students of style and literary critics give so much prominence to the problem of imagery. All this does not mean that one should necessarily agree with Proust who claimed that metaphor alone can give eternity to style;[4] it is quite clear, on the contrary, that if one succeeds in discovering, in a given writer, persistent preferences or aversions for a particular word or word-group, rhythmic pattern, morphological category, part of speech or syntactical construction, one will have identified an idiosyncrasy just as significant as the tendencies which govern the dynamics of his imagery. At the same time there can be no doubt that it is in the realm of figurative language that an author's creative imagination can assert itself with the maximum of freedom, and the choices he makes among the inexhaustible possibilities of simile and metaphor will be particularly revealing.

Enough has been said to show that the concept of choice, if carefully handled, provides a useful approach to style. It can be helpful in both types of stylistic study discussed in the last chapter: those which are

[1] 'Black *A*, white *E*, red *I*, green *U*, blue *O*, vowels, one day I shall tell your secret birth. *A*, hairy black corset of bright flies buzzing around foul stenches . . .'
[2] Cf. H. Héraut, 'Du nouveau sur Rimbaud', *Nouvelle Revue Française*, xliii (1934), pp. 602–8, and J.-F. Barrère, 'Rimbaud, l'apprenti sorcier', *Revue d'Histoire Littéraire de la France*, lvi (1956), pp. 50–64.
[3] Cf. my *Image in the Modern French Novel*, ch. III, esp. pp. 130–76. See now also J. Seznec, *Marcel Proust et les dieux* (Zaharoff Lecture), Oxford, 1962.
[4] See below, p. 175.

concerned with the expressive resources of a language, and those which explore the usage of a particular writer. As Spitzer once put it, the former deal with the choices which are *possible* in a given idiom, whereas the latter are more interested in those choices which have *actually* been made by certain outstanding practitioners of literary style.[1] Both approaches are legitimate, and though the emphasis is different, it is by no means impossible to combine the two, as I have tried to do in some of the examples discussed in this chapter.

But while no one would doubt the importance of choice as a factor in style, it would be a dangerous fallacy to exaggerate its significance and to regard it as the be-all and end-all of stylistic study. It will be sufficient to mention one or two considerations which recommend caution in this field. There is, first of all, something slightly mechanical and unrealistic in the picture of a writer choosing all the time between two or more alternatives, even if we constantly remind ourselves that the choice may have been unconscious and that the alternatives may not even have crossed the author's mind. A passage in *La Peste* almost reads like a caricature of this conception. An amateur novelist, who cannot get beyond the first sentence of his book, complains:

'A la rigueur, c'est assez facile de choisir entre *mais* et *et*. C'est déjà plus difficile d'opter entre *et* et *puis*. La difficulté grandit avec *puis* et *ensuite*. Mais, assurément, ce qu'il y a de plus difficile c'est de savoir s'il faut mettre *et* ou s'il ne faut pas.'[2]

Secondly, there are a number of important features of style to which the whole idea of choice seems inapplicable. How could one explain the presence of a certain onomatopoeic pattern or rhythmic scheme in such terms? What were the choices, conscious or unconscious, which Racine had to make before he wrote his haunting line about Oreste's hallucinations: 'Pour qui *s*ont *c*es *s*erpents qui *s*ifflent *s*ur vos têtes'?[3] The same may be said of certain forms of ambiguity. By what other means could Shakespeare have achieved the effect he obtained from the homonymy of *grave*, noun, and *grave*, adjective, in Mercutio's famous pun: 'Ask for me tomorrow, and you shall find me a *grave* man'[4]? It would

---

[1] *Actes du VIIIe Congrès de la Fédération Internationale des Langues et Littératures Modernes*, p. 23.

[2] 'At a pinch, it is fairly easy to choose between *but* and *and*. It is already more difficult to opt between *and* and *then*. The difficulty increases with *then* and *afterwards*. But, surely, what is most difficult is to know whether or not to put an *and*' (p. 118).

[3] 'For whom are these snakes that hiss on your heads?' (*Andromaque*, Act V, scene 5).

[4] *Romeo and Juliet*, Act III, scene 1. Cf. my *Semantics*, pp. 190 f.

seem that the criterion of choice is germane to certain aspects of style but scarcely relevant to others.

Indiscriminate use of this criterion lays itself open to a third and even more serious objection. It can only too easily lead to the notion that language and thought are independent entities, that thought in the abstract exists in our minds before we have chosen a suitable linguistic expression for it. This may be true of scientific or purely factual statements but is obviously not the case with many other uses of language. It is an oversimplified and antiquated conception which was current in the eighteenth century and found its classic expression in Dr. Johnson's dictum: 'Language is the dress of thought.'[1] In closely similar terms, Lord Chesterfield defined style as the 'dress of thoughts' (*NED*). The nineteenth century reacted violently against these ideas. Instead of regarding language as something external to thought, it proclaimed that the two are 'consubstantial' and inseparable. 'Language is called the garment of thought,' Carlyle wrote in *Sartor Resartus*; 'however, it should rather be, language is the flesh-garment, the body of thought'.[2] In his correspondence, Flaubert inveighed against the old cliché in a similar vein: 'Ces gaillards-là s'en tiennent à la vieille comparaison: La forme est un manteau. Mais non! la forme est la chair même de la pensée, comme la pensée est l'âme de la vie.'[3] By giving undue prominence to the concept of choice, stylistics may unwittingly revert to out-of-date ideas about language and thinking.

The organic unity and 'consubstantiality' of thought and expression is particularly important in the field of imagery. There are no doubt many similes and metaphors which are the result of deliberate choice; it even happens that an author corrects himself, dismisses an analogy as inadequate and replaces it by a more appropriate one. Thus Proust's narrator, discussing the surprise his aunt would have felt had she known of the aristocratic connexions of their friend Swann, launches forth on a mythological simile, but abandons it for one from the Arabian Nights, which is more likely to have occurred to the old lady:

'ou, pour s'en tenir à une image qui avait plus de chance de lui venir à l'esprit, car elle l'avait vue peinte sur nos assiettes à petits

---

[1] Cf. R. Quirk's comments in *The Use of English*, pp. 33 ff.

[2] Quoted by *The Oxford Dictionary of Quotations*, p. 81.

[3] 'These fellows stick to the old comparison: form is a cloak. No indeed! form is the very flesh of thought, just as thought is the soul of life' (quoted by W. v. Wartburg, *Evolution et structure de la langue française*, p. 226).

L

fours de Combray, d'avoir eu à dîner Ali-Baba, lequel, quand il se saura seul, pénétrera dans la caverne éblouissante de trésors insoupçonnés.'[1]

On the other hand, many of the most convincing images in poetry and even in prose are inseparable from the idea they express, and the latter could never have arisen without the metaphor in which it is embodied. Imagery of this kind has an air of inevitability and of spontaneous authenticity, a compulsive—at times even an obsessive—force which seems to negate any real possibility of choice. The position is thus somewhat paradoxical: in one sense, images give the writer the widest possible scope for choice, while in another sense the best among them admit of no real choice at all.

Perhaps one should go even further. Language and thought are not only indissolubly intertwined, but they may actually stimulate each other, and there are cases, especially in poetry, where language precedes and to some extent predetermines the idea which it is supposed to express. Here one might almost say that the sequence is reversed: instead of choosing an adequate expression for a pre-existent idea, we rather adjust the idea to some vaguely pre-existent linguistic pattern. There is a highly significant statement by Valéry on this process of 'linguistic inspiration':

'Je me suis trouvé un jour obsédé par un rythme, qui se fit tout à coup très sensible à mon esprit, après un temps pendant lequel je n'avais qu'une demi-conscience de cette activité latérale. Ce rythme s'imposait à moi, avec une sorte d'exigence. Il me semblait qu'il voulût prendre un corps, arriver à la perfection de l'être. Même il ne pouvait devenir plus net à ma conscience qu'en empruntant ou assimilant en quelque sorte des éléments *dicibles,* des syllabes, des mots, et ces syllabes et ces mots étaient sans doute, à ce point de la formation, déterminés par leur valeur et leurs attractions musicales.'[2]

Without probing any deeper into the role of language in poetry, it is clear that too rigid adherence to the principle of choice may distort our ideas about creative self-expression.

---

[1] 'Or, to keep to an image which was more likely to occur to her, for she had seen it depicted on our biscuit plates at Combray, the idea of having had for dinner Ali Baba who, once he knew he was alone, would penetrate into the dazzling cave of unsuspected treasures' (*Du Côté de chez Swann,* vol. I, pp. 31 f.).

[2] 'One day I felt obsessed by a rhythm which suddenly became very perceptible to my mind, after a period during which I was only semi-conscious of this marginal activity. This rhythm forced itself upon me with a kind of imperiousness. It seemed to me as if it were trying to take shape, to arrive at the perfection of being. It could only become clearer to my consciousness by borrowing or assimilating *expressible* elements, syllables, words, in some way, and these syllables and words were no doubt determined, at this stage of the

These and other reservations[1] should warn the student of style not to place undue reliance on the concept of choice. Needless to say, this concept, if properly handled, remains none the less a valuable tool of analysis which will throw light in many cases on the expressive resources of a language and on the way an author exploits these resources, and which may even grant illuminating insights into the psychology of a writer and into his aesthetic theory and practice.

process, by their musical value and attraction' (quoted by G. W. Ireland, 'A Note on Language and Inspiration in *La jeune Parque*', *Studies in Romance Philology and French Literature Presented to John Orr*, pp. 112–17: p. 112). Cf. T. S. Eliot's statement: 'I know that a poem, or a passage of a poem, may tend to realize itself first as a particular rhythm before it reaches expression in words, and that this rhythm may bring to birth the idea and the image; and I do not believe that this is an experience peculiar to myself' (*On Poetry and Poets*, New York, 1957, p. 32, quoted by W. Babilas, *Tradition und Interpretation*, Munich, 1961, p. 10).

[1] See recently R. A. Sayce, 'The Definition of the Term "Style" ', *Proceedings of the Third Congress of the International Comparative Literature Association*, The Hague, 1962, pp. 156–66: pp. 158 f.

CHAPTER VIII

THE RECONSTRUCTION OF STYLISTIC VALUES

According to Paul Valéry, style is essentially a *deviation* from a norm.[1] This view, which is shared by many critics,[2] implies that the student of style must become thoroughly familiar with the norm before he can detect any deviations from it. But even if one hesitates to equate style with deviation and to regard stylistics as 'la science des "écarts" ',[3] it is clear that one cannot evaluate the linguistic skill and originality of an author unless one can set them against the wider background of contemporary usage. When dealing with a modern writer, this task is comparatively simple: we can, up to a point, rely on our own knowledge of the language even though we may often have to seek confirmation in more objective evidence. When, however, we study the literature of the past, we are immediately faced with difficulties. Even for the nineteenth century our information is incomplete and often uncertain. The author of a recent monograph on the style of Gobineau had to take a great deal of trouble to piece together the main features of usage prevalent at the time;[4] another critic, working on the language of Théophile Gautier, has spoken of 'cette langue si mal connue qu'est le français de la première moitié du XIXe siècle'.[5] As we probe deeper into the past, the gap will inevitably widen and stylistic reconstruction become more hazardous. As Professors Wellek and Warren pertinently ask: 'If we admit the necessity of historical reconstruction . . . , can we stipulate its possibility in all cases? Can we ever learn Anglo-Saxon or Middle English, not to speak of ancient Greek, well enough to forget our own current language?'[6] The same authors even wonder whether such reconstruction is always desirable. They quote as an example these lines from Andrew Marvell's poem, *To his Coy Mistress*:

[1] Cf. Guiraud, *La Stylistique*, p. 105.

[2] For a discussion and critique of this view, see M. Riffaterre, *Word*, xv (1959), pp. 167 ff. Cf. also R. A. Sayce, 'The Definition of the Term "Style" ', pp. 159 f.

[3] 'The science of "deviations" ' (Ch. Bruneau, *Romance Philology*, v, 1951, p. 6).

[4] See M. Riffaterre's book referred to on p. 128, n. 1.

[5] 'This idiom which is so little known, the French language of the first half of the nineteenth century' (G. Matoré, *Le Vocabulaire et la société sous Louis-Philippe*, p. 11).

[6] Op. cit., pp. 180 f. On this problem see recently J. Fox, *The Poetry of Villon*, London etc., 1962, chapter II.

> My *vegetable* love would grow
> Vaster than empires and more slow,

where *vegetable* meant 'vegetative' and there was obviously no suggestion, for any contemporary reader, of an 'erotic cabbage outlasting the pyramids and overshadowing them'. The authors are not sure whether the associations which the word calls forth in a twentieth-century reader should not be retained as an enrichment of meaning, 'whether it is desirable to get rid of the modern connotation and whether, at least, in extreme cases, it is possible'. From a purely scholarly point of view, there can be no two answers to this question: the student of style must scrupulously try to avoid any anachronistic associations even though the latter may add piquancy to his private enjoyment of the text.

The problem of stylistic reconstruction involves all aspects of language: sounds, vocabulary, morphology and syntax. In this chapter I shall confine myself to grammatical and lexical questions since the reconstruction of sound values is, on the whole, a more simple and straightforward matter. Yet even here there are some pitfalls. A critic trying to estimate onomatopoeic effects should constantly bear in mind what the passage sounded like at the time of writing. In Corneille's *Horace*, Act IV, scene 5, the famous 'curses of Camille', from the powerful anaphoric repetition of *Rome* at the beginning of the first four verses:

> *Rome*, l'unique objet de mon ressentiment!
> *Rome*, à qui vient ton bras d'immoler mon amant!
> *Rome*, . . .[1]

to the hysterical climax of the last two lines:

> Voir le dernier Romain à son dernier soupir,
> Moi seule en être cause, et mourir de plaisir,[2]

will have an appreciably different onomatopoeic orchestration if one remembers certain features of contemporary pronunciation: the fact that |r| was still an apical and not a velar consonant, with the tip of the tongue rolled in the way described by Molière in the elocution lesson of *Le Bourgeois Gentilhomme*;[3] that final |r| tended to be dropped in certain positions where it is sounded today; that *oi* was pronounced as |wɛ|, not |wa|, etc. The same may be said of rhyme and other elements of

---

[1] '*Rome*, sole object of my resentment; *Rome*, to whom your arm has just sacrificed the man who loved me; *Rome*, . . .'
[2] 'To see the last Roman at his last gasp, to be solely responsible for it, and to die of delight.'
[3] Act II, scene 6.

versification. When, in *Andromaque*, Act IV, scene 1, Racine rhymes *croître* with *maître*:

> Quel plaisir d'élever un enfant qu'on voit *croître*,
> Non plus comme un esclave élevé pour son *maître* . . .[1]

this is not a poetic licence but a perfectly good rhyme since *oi* was still pronounced |wɛ|, not |wa|, as we have just seen.

The modern critic may also miss a pun if he forgets about contemporary pronunciation. In the seventeenth century, the words *grammaire* and *grand-mère* were still homonymous and could give rise to ambiguity in the spoken language; yet one would hardly have noticed this if Molière had not used it in an amusing *quid pro quo*:

> BÉLISE: Veux-tu toute ta vie offenser la *grammaire?*
> MARTINE: Qui parle d'offenser *grand-mère* ni grand-père?
>
> > *Les Femmes savantes*, Act II, scene 6.[2]

In the reconstruction of stylistic values, the critic has to steer clear of two kinds of errors. He has to avoid '*errors of addition*': the fallacy of projecting our own modern reactions into the text and of discovering in it stylistic effects which did not yet exist at the time. But he has also to beware of '*errors of omission*': failure to recognize stylistic values which did exist in the past but which have subsequently disappeared.[3] I shall try to illustrate both types of error by a few examples from vocabulary and grammar, and shall also discuss a special problem connected with reconstruction: the recognition of *archaisms* in earlier texts.

A. ERRORS OF ADDITION
I. Vocabulary

One common error of perspective in dealing with earlier authors is to see an expressive image in something which, to the contemporaries, was no more than a cliché or a fashionable slogan. Take the following lines from Victor Hugo's poem, *Réponse à un acte d'accusation*:

> J'ai dit à la narine: Eh mais! tu n'es qu'un nez!
> J'ai dit au long fruit d'or: Mais tu n'es qu'une poire!
> J'ai dit à Vaugelas: Tu n'es qu'une *mâchoire*.[4]

---

[1] 'What a pleasure to bring up a child whom one sees growing up, no longer as a slave brought up to serve his master . . .'

[2] BÉLISE: Do you want to offend against *grammar* throughout your life?
    MARTINE: Who speaks of offending *grandmother* or grandfather?

[3] On these terms see Riffaterre, *Word*, xv, pp. 166 f.

[4] 'I said to the nostril: Why, you are but a nose! I said to the long golden fruit: Why, you are but a pear! I said to Vaugelas: You are but a *jawbone!*'

To call the venerable seventeenth-century grammarian a 'jawbone' strikes the modern reader as an irreverent image which fits perfectly into the context and into the spiritual climate of the period. One may even sense in it a vague reminiscence of the grave-digger scene in *Hamlet*; 'That skull had a tongue in it, and could sing once. How the knave jowls it to the ground, as if 'twere Cain's *jawbone*.' All this, though eminently plausible, is completely off the point. *Mâchoire* was not an expressive metaphor but a fashionable witticism: one of a series of facetious designations which the young Romantics used for their elders. Gautier mentions *ci-devant, faux-toupet, aile de pigeon, perruque, étrusque, mâchoire, ganache,* and there were several others.[1] To Hugo and his readers, *mâchoire* was no more than a jocular colloquialism; it could be rendered in Modern English by *old fogey* or some similar expression.

Another factor making for misunderstandings of this type is pejorative sense-development (cf. above, pp. 90 f.). Words which have at present strongly unfavourable connotations may have been perfectly harmless when our text was written. Thus when Alceste says to Célimène, in Molière's *Misanthrope*, Act II, scene 1: 'Vous avez trop d'*amants* qu'on voit vous obséder',[2] he is not nearly as offensive as a twentieth-century reader might think; *amant* meant at the time 'someone in love with a woman, admirer', not 'lover'. In extreme cases such as this, the context will usually preclude any gross misinterpretation; yet the history of another pejorative word, French *imbécile*, should warn us that even an acute critic may fall into the trap. As we have seen (p. 89), *imbécile* comes from a Latin adjective meaning 'weak, feeble', and it still had that sense in the seventeenth century: Pascal spoke of 'l'homme *imbécile*—ver de terre',[3] and Corneille wrote in *Œdipe*: 'Le sang a peu de droits dans le sexe *imbécille*.'[4] By the next century, this meaning had become so obsolete that Voltaire completely misunderstood Corneille's phrase and indignantly described it as 'une injure très déplacée et très grossière, fort mal exprimée'.[5]

The same Voltaire showed more historical sense in his comments on another word with a similar background. French *pédant*, borrowed from Italian in the sixteenth century, originally meant 'pedagogue, schoolmaster', but from the very beginning it tended to carry pejorative

---

[1] See Matoré, *Le Vocabulaire et la société sous Louis-Philippe,* p. 234; cf. also p. 76.
[2] 'You have too many *admirers* whom one sees besieging you.' Cf. Nyrop, *Sémantique,* p. 299.
[3] '*Weak* man—earthworm.' For this and the next two examples see ibid., pp. 22 and 285.
[4] 'Blood has few rights among the *gentle* sex.'
[5] 'A very rude and unwarranted insult, very badly expressed.'

connotations which eventually ousted its neutral meaning.[1] Voltaire writes in this connexion: 'Que de termes éloignés de leur origine! *Pédant* qui signifiait instructeur de la jeunesse est devenu une injure.'[2] Yet even in Voltaire's lifetime the novelist Lesage had written, in a passage which sounds odd to modern ears: 'Le docteur Godinez, qui passait pour le plus habile *pédant* d'Oviédo.'[3] The English word had a similar development; when, in *Twelfth Night*, Act III, scene 2, Malvolio is compared to 'a *pedant* that keeps a school i' th' church' (*NED*), this is still the old sense of the noun, which fell into disuse after the beginning of the eighteenth century.

Even where the meaning of a word has not actually deteriorated, it may have changed in such a way that some earlier uses will strike us as comical or ironical whereas they were perfectly neutral at the time. The adjective *admirable*, introduced into English in the late sixteenth century, could mean 'to be wondered at' until the end of the eighteenth; this explains the following sentence, written in 1639: 'It may justly seem *admirable* how that senseless religion should gain so much ground on Christianity.'[4] In the same century, *vivacious* had some meanings which are now rare or obsolete: 'long-lived', 'difficult to kill', etc.; a sentence like: 'hitherto the English Bishops had been *vivacious* almost to wonder' (*NED*), would therefore carry different overtones from those it has today.

II. Grammar

In the grammatical field, errors of interpretation may be caused by changes in the meaning or the stylistic value of certain specific forms and constructions. Take, for instance, La Fontaine's well-known lines in *Le Loup et l'agneau*:

> Mais plutôt qu'elle considère
> Que je me *vas* désaltérant
> Dans le courant,
> Plus de vingt pas au-dessous d'Elle.[5]

---

[1] Bloch-Wartburg quote the sixteenth-century grammarian Henri Estienne: 'J'enten *pedant* en sa propre signification et non comme ils en usent par dérision' ('I mean *pedant* in its proper sense and not as people use it derisively').

[2] 'How many terms which have moved away from their origins! *Pedant*, which used to mean a teacher of youth, has become an affront' (quoted by Nyrop, op. cit., p. 126).

[3] 'Dr. Godinez, who was considered to be the best *teacher* in Oviedo' (quoted by K. Jaberg, *Zeitschrift für Romanische Philologie*, xxvii, 1903, p. 51, n. 1).

[4] On these and other examples see A. Rudskoger, *'Fair, Foul, Nice, Proper': a Contribution to the Study of Polysemy*, pp. 463–73.

[5] 'A moment's thought will clearly show you I'm drinking twenty yards below you.' This and the following examples from La Fontaine are quoted from Sir Edward Marsh's translation.

The modern critic, accustomed to regarding *je vas*, for *je vais*, as a vulgar or dialectal form, may be tempted to read a similar effect into this passage, whereas in actual fact *je vas* was perfectly respectable in the seventeenth century; though some grammarians frowned upon it, Vaugelas declared that the whole court said *je vas* and looked down on *je vais* as provincial or popular.[1]

A similar example from syntax is the shift in the meaning of the adjective *sacré* according to whether it precedes or follows the noun. In the modern language, *sacré* in postposition means 'holy, sacred, consecrated', whereas in anteposition it is charged with pejorative overtones and corresponds to English 'confounded, cursed, damned'; we say, as in the *Marseillaise*, 'amour *sacré* de la patrie', '*sacred* love of the fatherland', but 'ce *sacré* chien', 'this *confounded* dog'. We are therefore mildly amused to find Du Bellay advising French poets to enrich their vocabulary with words from Latin and Greek and to ransack 'les *sacreẓ* thresors de ce temple Delphique'.[2] Yet to the sixteenth-century reader this passage was anything but comical; such petrified phrases as *le Sacré-Cœur* and *le Sacré Collège* 'the College of Cardinals' show that for a long time the adjective meant 'sacred' even when it stood before the noun.

Far more difficult and elusive are those cases where we have to recapture the exact value of an entire grammatical category. We saw in an earlier chapter (pp. 114 ff.) that the Imperfect Subjunctive, a cumbersome and pedantic tense, can produce a variety of stylistic effects in Modern French: it can provide a vehicle for comedy, irony and parody and can also play its part in psychological and social portrayal. Modern speakers have been so thoroughly conditioned to recognize these effects that they are prone to look for them even in older texts. Much has been made in this respect of the sonnet scene in *Le Misanthrope* where Oronte, a pompous and affected fop, tries to crush his opponent with a particularly heavy and pedantic Imperfect Subjunctive:

Je voudrois bien, pour voir, que, de votre manière,
Vous en *composassieẓ* sur la même matière.[3]

Yet one may wonder whether this form made the same impression on a seventeenth-century audience as it does on a modern one. Only a detailed study of the Imperfect Subjunctive in the classical period could

---

[1] See Nyrop, *Grammaire historique de la langue française*, vol. II, 2nd ed., p. 90.

[2] 'The *sacred* treasures of this Delphic temple' (*La Deffence et illustration de la langue françoyse*, quoted ibid., vol. I, 4th ed., p. 51).

[3] 'I should like, just to see, that you *should compose* some, in your own manner, on the same subject' (Act I, scene 2).

settle the question; meanwhile it is easy to find some pointers in Molière himself and other contemporary authors. That our form did in fact have an affected and pretentious air at the time is clear from a passage in *Les Précieuses ridicules*, scene 8, where the valet Mascarille, posing as a marquis, says:

'Voudriez-vous, faquins, que j'*exposasse* l'embonpoint de mes plumes aux inclémences de la saison pluvieuse, et que j'*allasse* imprimer mes souliers en boue?'[1]

Here the situation, the style of the passage and the repetition of the form make it more than likely that Molière was using the Imperfect Subjunctive in the same way as a modern writer would. But would the same be necessarily true of the more stylized language of verse plays? It is not difficult to collect examples from poetic drama where our tense is used without any comical or ironical intent. Even its more cumbrous forms are found in such contexts:

> Pour bien faire il faudroit que vous le *prévinssiez*.
> *Andromaque*, Act II, scene 1.[2]

> Et qu'il n'est point de rois, s'ils sont dignes de l'être,
> Qui, sur le trône assis, n'*enviassent* peut-être
> Au-dessus de leur gloire un naufrage élevé,
> Que Rome et quarante ans ont à peine achevé.
> *Mithridate*, Act II, scene 4.[3]

The very same form as the one used by Oronte, the objectionable second person plural of the first conjugation, occurs in a perfectly neutral context in the part of *Psyché* written by Corneille:

> Vous dis-je plus que je ne dois,
> Moi, de qui la pudeur devroit du moins attendre
> Que vous m'*expliquassiez* le trouble où je vous vois?
> *Psyché*, Act III, scene 3.[4]

[1] 'Do you wish me to *expose* the excellency of my plumes to the inclemency of the rainy season, you rascals, and *let* the mud receive the impression of my shoes?' (A. R. Waller's translation).
[2] 'The right thing for you to do would be to *forestall* him.'
[3] 'And that there are no kings worthy of their rank who, seated on their throne, *do not* perhaps *envy* a shipwreck which rises above their fame, and which Rome and forty years could hardly conquer.'
[4] 'Am I telling you more than I should, I whose modesty should at least wait till you *have explained* to me the agitation in which I see you?'

In view of this background it would seem that, in the peculiar atmosphere of seventeenth-century poetic drama, the Imperfect Subjunctive had in itself little expressive force, but that its stylistic potential could be activated when placed in a suitable context.

B. ERRORS OF OMISSION

This kind of mistake is more difficult to avoid than the previous type. Errors of addition are, with certain exceptions, a crude and naive form of misinterpretation. Even a sophisticated critic may be caught unawares, as the example of the Imperfect Subjunctive has shown; on the whole, however, he can train himself to distrust his own modern reactions until they have been checked against the usage of the period. But how is one to guard against errors of omission? How can one make sure that a word, grammatical form or construction which is perfectly normal and neutral today did not carry potent connotations at the time of writing? A few examples from French literature will show some of the difficulties involved and some of the ways in which they can be overcome.

I. Vocabulary

Words move up and down the social scale, and it often happens that a term which is today part of our ordinary vocabulary was regarded not so long ago as slangy or vulgar. English *joke,* which appears in the second half of the seventeenth century and was apparently derived from Latin *jocus,* was originally a slang term,[1] and we have seen (pp. 53 f.) that the French verb *blaguer,* which is now colloquial but quite harmless, was branded in Balzac's days with an intense social stigma. The same writer, who was passionately interested in words, has noted several similar cases for posterity. Thus he included the verb *cambrioler* 'burgle' in a list of expressions pertaining to thieves' cant, and described *chantage* 'blackmail' as an 'invention de la presse anglaise, récemment importée en France'.[2] It may be added that both terms were recorded as argotic by Vidocq, the ex-convict who had become head of the Sûreté and who was one of Balzac's chief authorities on the language of the underworld. Without this information, the modern reader would hardly have noticed the social status and evocative value of these words.

[1] See the *Shorter OED.* Cf. on such words G. E. van Dongen, *Amelioratives in English,* pp. 15 ff.

[2] 'An invention of the English press, recently imported into France.' See on these words R. Dagneaud, *Les Eléments populaires dans le lexique de la Comédie Humaine,* pp. 179 and 235; cf. also Matoré, *Le Vocabulaire et la société sous Louis-Philippe,* pp. 105 and 184.

Errors of omission may also creep in through failure to appreciate a neologism.[1] It is difficult for us to realize that words which we use every day and which seem quite indispensable to us may have appeared at one time as doubtful or even shocking innovations. In some cases, we have explicit remarks by a contemporary writer, or even by the person who launched the new term. Thus *exactitude*, recorded in 1634, incurred the wrath of Vaugelas: 'C'est un mot que j'ai vu naître comme un monstre et auquel on s'est accoutumé.'[2] It is interesting to note that two alternatives, *exacteté* and *exactesse*, were experimented with at about the same time (Bloch-Wartburg). In 1780, Jeremy Bentham coined the adjective *international*, adding half apologetically: 'The word *international*, it must be acknowledged, is a new one, though, it is hoped, sufficiently analogous and intelligible.'[3] Balzac was similarly apologetic for coining the noun *exclusivité* which had actually been used before him as a technical term.[4] As this last example shows, it is not even sufficient for the critic to look up in the dictionaries the date at which a given word was first used. Quite apart from the fact that dictionary dates are seldom definitive, a new word may remain rare for decades after its first appearance and may continue to be regarded as a neologism; witness the term *individualité*, which is found as far back as 1760 (Bloch-Wartburg), and about which Hugo wrote three-quarters of a century later: 'son *individualité*, comme on dit aujourd'hui en assez mauvais style'.[5] One wonders how many of these nuances pass unnoticed because we happen to have no information about them.

Words taken over from foreign languages undergo a similar process of acclimatization, and it is often difficult to estimate the precise value they had at a given moment. English *sport*, introduced—or rather re-introduced—into French in 1828 (Bloch-Wartburg), is now an integral and indispensable part of the French vocabulary; yet not so long ago it aroused the protests of purists; in 1855, Viennet fulminated against it and against a number of other Anglicisms some of which have since been completely assimilated into the language whereas others have been less successful:

[1] See esp. M. Riffaterre, 'La Durée et la valeur stylistique du néologisme', *Romanic Review*, xliv (1953), pp. 282–9. Cf. also G. Matoré, 'Le Néologisme: naissance et diffusion', *Le Français Moderne*, xx (1952), pp. 87–92.
[2] 'It is a word which I saw being born like a monster and to which people have become accustomed' (Bloch-Wartburg).
[3] See B. Migliorini, *The Contribution of the Individual to Language*, Oxford, 1952, p. 9.
[4] See F. Brunot, *Histoire de la langue française*, vol. XII (by Ch. Bruneau), pp. 378 f.; cf. Bloch-Wartburg, *s.v. exclure*.
[5] 'His *individuality*, as people say nowadays in rather bad style' (*Les Chants du crépuscule*, Preface; cf. Matoré, *Le Vocabulaire et la société sous Louis-Philippe*, p. 41).

Faut-il, pour cimenter un merveilleux accord,
Changer l'arène en *turf* et le plaisir en *sport?*
Demander à des *clubs* l'aimable causerie?
Flétrir du nom de *grooms* nos valets d'écurie,
Traiter nos cavaliers de *gentlemen-riders?*
Et de Racine enfin parodiant les vers,
Montrer, au lieu de Phèdre, une *lionne* anglaise
Qui, dans un *handicap* ou dans un *steeple-chase*,
Suit de l'œil un *wagon* de *sportsmen* escorté
Et fuyant sur le *turf* par un *truck* emporté.[1]

II. Grammar

As in the previous type, we have to distinguish here between two kinds of error: failure to recognize the stylistic value of particular elements and that of an entire grammatical category. An interesting example of the former, which has recently come to light,[2] is the singular *cheveu* in the collective sense of 'hair'. In ordinary French, *cheveu* means a single hair and the plural is used for the collective meaning. Yet Gide writes in *Les Caves du Vatican*: 'longtemps, sous l'abondant *cheveu* qu'il ramenait en boucle par-dessus, il put dissimuler l'excroissance'.[3] The same form recurs elsewhere in the novel, which should warn us that it is a little more than a momentary and whimsical freak; yet its real significance might well have eluded us for ever had not Proust, interested as always in even the minutest details of language, recorded the exact circumstances of its rise and vogue. In *Sodome et Gomorrhe*, he makes Madame de Cambremer say: 'Agé? Mais il n'a pas l'air âgé, le *cheveu* est resté jeune',[4] whereupon the narrator remarks:

'Car depuis trois ou quatre ans le mot "cheveu" avait été employé au singulier par un de ces inconnus qui sont les lanceurs des modes littéraires, et toutes les personnes ayant la longueur de rayon de Mme de

---

[1] 'Must we, to cement a wonderful agreement, change arena to *turf* and pleasure to *sport?* Must we turn to *clubs* for pleasant conversation? Must we brand our stable-boys with the name *groom*, and dub our horsemen *gentlemen riders?* And lastly, must we, parodying Racine's lines, show, in the place of Phèdre, an English *lioness* who, in a *handicap* or a *steeple-chase*, watches a *waggon* escorted by *sportsmen*, which is racing down the *turf*, carried along by a *truck?*' (*Epître à Boileau*, quoted by Nyrop, *Grammaire historique de la langue française*, vol. I, p. 102).

[2] See M. Riffaterre, 'Sur un singulier d'André Gide. Contribution à l'étude des clichés', *Le Français Moderne*, xxiii (1955), pp. 39–43. Cf. also my remarks, ibid., xxv (1957), pp. 199 f.

[3] 'For a long time he was able to hide the excrescence under his thick *hair* which he combed over it in a curl' (201st ed., Paris, 1922, p. 18).

[4] 'Aged? But he does not look aged, his *hair* has remained young.'

Cambremer disaient "le cheveu", non sans un sourire affecté. A l'heure actuelle on dit encore "le cheveu", mais de l'excès du singulier renaîtra le pluriel.'[1]

Far more significant than such details are the stylistic connotations of a whole grammatical category, and here the modern critic runs a very real risk of missing nuances of great psychological importance and aesthetic value. The position of the Past Definite in French classical drama will illustrate the point.[2] We saw in the last chapter (pp. 136 ff.) some of the differences between this tense and its rival, the Past Indefinite, in Modern French. In the classical period, the situation was very different. The distribution of the two tenses was regulated by a formula which Henri Estienne had enunciated in the sixteenth century: the so-called 'rule of twenty-four hours'. According to this, the Past Definite had to be used for events which had occurred before the preceding night and the Indefinite for those which had happened since; thus one would say: 'il *écrivit* hier', 'he *wrote* yesterday', but 'il *a écrit* ce matin', 'he *has written* this morning'. This rule was strictly insisted on by the grammarians and was, in most cases, scrupulously observed in literature;[3] when Corneille departed from it in *Le Cid*, the Academy did not hesitate to rebuke him. In Racine, however, there are one or two obvious infringements of the law of twenty-four hours. Racine's meticulous observance of grammatical rules is well known; he must therefore have had very good reasons for violating this law. A study of the relevant passages, replaced in their wider context, will show what these reasons were.

Our first example is found in *Andromaque*, Act IV, scene 3, one of the crucial scenes of that play. Hermione, distracted with jealousy, asks Oreste to assassinate Pyrrhus and promises to marry him if he does. Oreste protests, but Hermione brushes aside his scruples:

> Ne vous suffit-il pas que je l'ai condamné?
> Ne vous suffit-il pas que ma gloire offensée

---

[1] 'For during the last three or four years the word "*cheveu*" had been used in the singular by one of those unknown people who launch literary fashions, and all those who lived within the radius of Mme. de Cambremer said "*le cheveu*", not without an affected smile. At the present time people still say "*le cheveu*", but the plural will be reborn from the excessive use of the singular' (*Sodome et Gomorrhe*, vol. II, pp. 85 f.).

[2] See my article, 'The Vitality of the Past Definite in Racine', *French Studies*, ii (1948), pp. 35–53, and H. Saunders, 'Obsolescence of the Past Definite and the Time-Perspective of French Classical Drama', *Archivum Linguisticum*, vii (1955), pp. 96–122.

[3] Saunders, loc. cit., p. 110.

Demande une victime à moi seule adressée;
Qu'Hermione est le prix d'un tyran opprimé;
Que je le hais; enfin, seigneur, que je l'*aimai*?[1]

From a strictly and pedantically grammatical point of view, *je l'aimai* is incorrect since until quite recently Hermione was overtly in love with Pyrrhus; in fact she has never ceased to love him, and never will. The unusual Past Definite is part of Hermione's pretence; it is meant to suggest that her love is dead, that it is definitely a thing of the past, with no possible relevance to the present. The sudden and complete break with the past is conveyed, with the utmost economy, by the use of the form *aimai*. At the same time, the finality of the break is immediately cancelled out when Hermione goes on to warn Oreste not to rely too much on the death of her love which may flare up again as long as Pyrrhus is alive: 'S'il ne meurt aujourd'hui, je puis l'aimer demain.'[2]

Another example of what one might call the 'pregnant' use of the Past Definite occurs in *Mithridate*, Act IV, scene 4. The context, though very different in tone, is similar in two respects: in both cases the use of our tense implies a sudden and definitive break with the recent past, and in both cases it is part of a deception. In the previous act (scene 5), the aged king, infatuated with a young princess, Monime, had laid a trap to the latter: in order to make her reveal her love for his son, Xipharès, he had pretended to renounce her hand and had actually asked her to marry the prince. When they next meet, he drops the pretence with the brutality of an oriental despot:

MITHRIDATE: Venez, et qu'à l'autel ma promesse accomplie
Par des nœuds éternels l'un à l'autre nous lie.
MONIME: Nous, seigneur?
MITHRIDATE: Quoi, madame! osez-vous balancer?
MONIME: Et ne m'avez-vous pas défendu d'y penser?
MITHRIDATE: J'*eus* mes raisons alors: oublions-les, madame.
Ne songez maintenant qu'à répondre à ma flamme.[3]

---

[1] 'Is it not enough for you that I have condemned him? Is it not enough for you that my injured reputation demands a victim destined for me alone; that Hermione is the prize for the overthrow of a tyrant; that I hate him; in short, my Lord, that I *loved* him?' Cf. Saunders, loc. cit., pp. 111 f.
[2] 'If he does not die today, I might love him tomorrow.'
[3] MITHRIDATE: Come, let my promise made at the altar bind us together by eternal bonds.
MONIME: Us, my Lord?
MITHRIDATE: What, Madam! You dare hesitate?

Once again we have a Past Definite referring to an event which had just taken place. By saying *j'eus* instead of *j'ai eu* or *j'avais*, Mithridate relegates his previous decision to the irrevocable past: the king has changed his mind, and all that happened before is utterly irrelevant and ought to be forgotten. There is a subtle contrast between Mithridate's and Monime's language; for the princess, the king's last order is still valid and is therefore expressed in the Past Indefinite: 'Et ne m'*avez-vous pas défendu* d'y penser?'

Racine also violated the law of twenty-four hours in a well-known purple passage in *Phèdre*, Act V, scene 6, the 'récit de Théramène': the story of how Hippolyte was killed when his horses were frightened by a sea-monster. In the description of the monster's sudden arrival there occurs the line: 'Le flot qui l'*apporta* recule épouvanté.'[1] Much has been written on this line ever since the famous controversy about its 'verisimilitude', in which Boileau came to Racine's defence;[2] some critics have explored the deeper significance of the metaphor while others have concentrated on the 'faulty' syntax, although the two aspects are ultimately inseparable. From the point of view of contemporary grammar, the syntax is indeed faulty: the Past Definite *apporta* is obviously inappropriate when referring to an event which had just taken place. A few years ago, Dr. H. Saunders published a detailed study on the time-perspective of French classical drama and, by replacing Théramène's line in the wider context of the play, of Racine's practice, and of the traditions and conventions on which this practice was based, he succeeded in giving a satisfactory explanation of the anomaly.[3] He began by pointing out that the juxtaposition of the Past Definite and the Present Indicative in order to obtain a strong contrast effect was part of the stylistic tradition of the classical theatre; there are numerous examples of this device, including one in another famous 'récit', the Cid's story of his victory over the Moors: 'Le flux les *apporta*, le reflux les remporte',[4] which may be regarded as the prototype of Théramène's line. Dr. Saunders goes on:

'Racine's task in the story of Théramène is to make the appearance of the monster convincing at second hand and to heighten the curve of tragic emotion by showing the Gods accomplice and the elements partial. In this

MONIME: And have you not forbidden me to think of it?
MITHRIDATE: I *had* my reasons then; let us forget them, Madam. Think now only of responding to my passion.
[1] 'The wave that *brought* it recoils, horrified.'
[2] Cf. Spitzer, *Linguistics and Literary History*, p. 115.
[3] Loc. cit., pp. 113 f.
[4] 'The tide *brought* them, the ebb takes them back' (*Le Cid*, Act IV, scene 3).

pattern the sentient wave finds its place. We see it roll forward throwing up its fateful cargo; we see, and the wave sees, the monster in all its horror in the bare light of day. There is the pause between ebb and flow, the slow gathering of the wave's strength, the leap of its broken crest and then, the fateful pause, its drawing back—it is only given to the poetic mind to see this natural phenomenon as Nature's nearest approach to human recoil from crime and horror!'

As these three examples show, a critic unfamiliar with the intricacies of the syntax of tenses in the seventeenth century could easily have missed the powerful stylistic implications of Racine's departures from the norm.

C. THE RECOGNITION OF ARCHAISMS

As already noted (p. 54 f.), archaism is an important source of stylistic effects. The device has many forms: it can involve pronunciation and spelling, grammar and idiom, words and their meanings. When such archaisms occur in older texts it is sometimes difficult to identify them. We must always bear in mind the possibility that an element which strikes us as archaic may already have been so hundreds of years ago and may have been employed by the author as a stylistic device. There are scores of examples in La Fontaine;[1] at a time when old-fashioned words were carefully avoided by most writers,[2] he did not hesitate to use them in order to give his fables and *contes* an old-world flavour which the casual reader may not always notice. A few examples from the fables may be quoted here:

> Il avait dans la terre une somme enfouie,
> Son cœur avec, n'ayant d'autre *déduit*
> Que d'y ruminer jour et nuit,
> Et rendre sa *chevance* à lui-même sacrée.[3]

> Genre de mort qui ne *duit* pas
> A gens peu curieux de goûter le trépas.[4]

---

[1] A list will be found in the preface to vol. X of Henri Régnier's edition of La Fontaine in the *Grands Ecrivains de la France* series.

[2] See F. Brunot, *Histoire de la langue française*, vol. IV, part 1, book IV, ch. 2: 'Les mots vieux.'

[3] 'Deep underground his treasure was enholed, His heart as well; for 'twas his one delight, To brood upon it day and night: Ev'n from himself he kept it sacrosanct' (*L'Avare qui a perdu son trésor*).

[4] 'A form of death which could appeal Only to a sensation-monger' (*Le Trésor et les deux hommes*).

M

On l'emporte, on la sale, on en fait maint repas
Dont maint voisin s'*éjouit* d'être.[1]

Un Loup donc étant de *frairie*
Se pressa, dit-on, tellement
Qu'il en pensa perdre la vie.[2]

Tous renonçaient au *lôs* des belles actions.[3]

... on vit presque détruit
L'*ost* des Grecs; et ce fut l'ouvrage d'une nuit.[4]

Many of La Fontaine's archaisms will be recognized at a glance; in other cases one may hesitate; some one may miss altogether, in the erroneous belief that they were still current at the time of writing. British readers will also note that a number of French words which had fallen into disuse by the latter half of the seventeenth century have survived in English, though not always in the same meaning (*host, purchase*,[5] *remembrance*,[6] *solace*,[7] etc.).

The identification of archaisms will depend on three main factors: the length of time which has elapsed since the text was written; the amount of information we have about the linguistic background; lastly, the kind of context in which the archaism occurs. There are three types of context in which archaisms arise. Firstly, there is the concentrated and systematic use of antiquated language for purposes of pastiche. This art is older than one might think: Villon already wrote a ballade in what he described as 'vieil françois', and even in the classical period La Bruyère, a writer greatly concerned about the disappearance of ancient words,[8] included in his *Caractères* a pastiche of Montaigne and also a passage from an unnamed 'vieil auteur', which is now believed to have been written by La Bruyère himself.[9] Secondly, archaisms are apt to be

---

[1] 'Salted and cured, he next appeared as venison For the Good-man to feast his friends on' (*L'Œil du maître*).

[2] 'And one (viz. wolf), upon a festive night, Bolted his meat so greedily, They say he nearly breathed his last' (*Le Loup et la cigogne*).

[3] 'The meeds of Fame and Honour left them cold' (*Les Compagnons d'Ulysse*).

[4] 'Phoebus in a night Laid half his army low in death' (*Le Fermier, le chien et le renard*).

[5] *Contes*, I, 3, 36.

[6] Ibid., II, 15, 266.

[7] Ibid., I, 1, 523.

[8] See a famous passage on the subject in *Les Caractères*, ed. R. Garapon, Paris, Garnier, 1962, pp. 440 ff. Cf. also F. Brunot's comments in *Histoire de la langue française*, vol. IV, part 1, pp. 232 ff.

[9] Op. cit., pp. 162 f. and 237. Cf. J. Damourette's article, 'Archaïsmes et pastiches', referred to on p. 54, n. 4.

used whenever one is writing about an earlier period; since the Romantic Movement in particular, this form of local colour has been prominent in historical novels.[1] In neither of these cases does the recognition of archaisms present any major difficulty, though one may occasionally have to check the accuracy or the implications of some of them against the usage of the period portrayed. Finally, archaisms may occur in contexts which have nothing to do with the past, such as some of the passages just quoted from La Fontaine, and it is in these cases that one can most easily overlook them.

Sometimes the author himself will warn the reader that he is using an archaic word, phrase or saying. La Fontaine opens his fable, *La Grenouille et le rat*, with these words:

> Tel, comme dit Merlin, *cuide engeigner* autrui,
> Qui souvent s'*engeigne* soi-même.
> J'ai regret que ce mot soit trop vieux aujourd'hui:
> Il m'a toujours semblé d'une énergie extrême.[2]

Other archaisms can be recognized as such by their form and also by the situation in which they appear. In seventeenth-century French literature there are some examples of the longer demonstrative pronouns *icelui, icelle* instead of the modern *celui, celle*:

> Témoin trois procureurs, dont *icelui* Citron
> A déchiré la robe.[3]
>
> Racine, *Les Plaideurs*, Act III, scene 3.

> Il peut l'avantager ...
> Et cela par douaire, ou préfix qu'on appelle,
> Qui demeure perdu par le trépas d'*icelle*.[4]
>
> Molière, *L'Ecole des femmes*, Act IV, scene 2.

Whoever has even a smattering of seventeenth-century French will immediately know that these forms were already antiquated at the time;

---

[1] Cf. my *Style in the French Novel*, pp. 64 ff.

[2] 'A cony-catcher, Merlin taught, Will sometimes prove a cony caught. (Pity that forcible old word On modern lips is never heard!)' In his translation of La Fontaine's fables, Sir Edward Marsh notes that 'The Life and Sayings of the Wizard Merlin were published in Paris in 1528' and quotes a parallel from Chaucer's *The Reeves Tale*: 'the gylour shal himself bigyled be' (p. 77, n. 1).

[3] 'Witness three attorneys who had their gowns torn by the *aforesaid* Citron.'

[4] 'He can make an arrangement in her (viz. his future wife's) favour ... by making a marriage settlement, or stipulated jointure, as it is called, which lapses on the decease of the *aforesaid*.'

it will also be noted that they are used in legal, or mock-legal, contexts which are notorious for their archaizing style.[1]

In more doubtful cases, the evidence of contemporary grammarians, lexicographers or others may come to our aid. It is common knowledge that the particle *ès*, which is historically a contracted form of *en les* 'in the', has been obsolete for a long time, except in one or two set phrases like *docteur ès lettres* 'doctor of literature'. Some writers who use it as a deliberate archaism are even unaware that it is a plural: Baudelaire originally dedicated *Les Fleurs du mal* to Théophile Gautier, 'parfait magicien *ès langue française*'; subsequently he changed it to '*ès lettres françaises*'.[2] One may wonder, however, whether *ès* was already archaic in the seventeenth century when Bossuet wrote '*ès* siècles', 'in the centuries', and Pascal '*ès* choses temporelles', 'in things temporal', and '*ès* choses spirituelles', 'in things spiritual'.[3] The evidence of two contemporary grammarians, Vaugelas and Ménage, enables us to settle the point; according to the former, *ès* 'est bannie du beau langage',[4] whereas Ménage stigmatizes the legal expressions *ès mains*, 'in the hands of', and *ès prisons*, 'in prison', in the following terms: 'Cette façon de parler qui estoit si élégante autrefois, est devenue barbare: & il faut bien prendre garde de s'en servir, mesme dans le Palais'.[5] By similar arguments one can prove that La Fontaine was archaizing, or at least using an obsolescent construction, when he wrote in *Le Loup et le renard*: 'Je le veux, dit le Loup; il m'est mort *un mien frère.*'[6]

If we have no clear indication one way or another, then the only thing we can do is to compare the usage of a writer with that of his contemporaries to find out whether it is or is not archaic. Thus the negative particle *mie*, common in Old French, has been obsolete for many centuries though it still exists as an archaism in literature: 'd'autres que

[1] See F. Brunot, *Histoire de la langue française*, vol. IV, part 1, book IV, chs. 12–13.

[2] 'Perfect magician *in the French language* (*in French letters*).' Cf. E. Lerch, *Hauptprobleme der französischen Sprache*, vol. I, Braunschweig, 1930, pp. 254 ff.; Ch. Bally, 'En été: au printemps; croire en Dieu: croire au diable', *Festschrift für E. Tappolet*, Basel, 1935; C. Fahlin, *Étude sur l'emploi des prépositions 'en', 'à', 'dans' au sens local*, Uppsala, 1942; G. Gougenheim, *Journal de Psychologie*, xliii (1950), pp. 180–92; A. Dauzat, *Mélanges Ch. Bruneau*, Paris, 1954, pp. 1–9.

[3] The example from Bossuet is quoted by E. Gamillscheg, *Historische Syntax der französischen Sprache*, Tübingen, 1957 ff., p. 269; those from Pascal are quoted by Nyrop, *Grammaire historique de la langue française*, vol. II, p. 374.

[4] 'Banished from the language of educated people' (quoted by F. Brunot-Ch. Bruneau, *Précis de grammaire historique de la langue française*, p. 216).

[5] 'This way of speaking, which was formerly so elegant, has become barbarous, and one should be careful not to use it, even in the law-courts' (quoted by Nyrop, loc. cit.).

[6] 'I will,' replied the Wolf, 'One of my race Is newly dead.' See on this construction F. Brunot, *Histoire de la langue française*, vol. III, part 2, pp. 490 f., and Brunot-Bruneau, op. cit., pp. 240 f.

je ne nommerai *mie*', writes M. Georges Duhamel.[1] The modern reader will therefore be struck by phrases like 'il ne le faisoit *mie*', 'he did *not* do it', which occur repeatedly in Rabelais. We cannot be sure, however, that *mie* was already archaic in Rabelais's time. No contemporary pronouncement will throw light on the matter, and we have to examine sixteenth-century usage in order to see *mie* in its proper perspective. A recent study on the history of negative particles in French[2] has shown that 'there are good grounds for considering that, as a feature of normal literary usage, *mie* did not outlast the fifteenth century'; it has also revealed that Rabelais used *mie* more frequently than any of his contemporaries or any author during the previous century and a quarter whose language was examined. It is clear therefore that *mie* was a deliberate archaism in this writer, one of the innumerable eccentricities with which his style is interspersed.

The recognition of archaisms may be complicated by a further factor. It sometimes happens that a word which had fallen into disuse is revived and readmitted into literary language or even into ordinary speech. A number of obsolete terms, Shakespearian, Spenserian and others, were rejuvenated in this way by English writers during the Pre-Romantic and Romantic period. The history of the word *glee* may serve as a warning that what may be an archaism in the usage of one generation may cease to be archaic for the next. In Dr. Johnson's *A Dictionary of the English Language* (1755), we read under *glee*: 'It is not now used, except in ludicrous writing, or with some mixture of irony and contempt.' This is how the *NED* sums up the vicissitudes of this term: 'In Old English and Middle English the word is chiefly poetic. After the fifteenth century it seems to have been rarely used, and in the seventeenth century is almost entirely absent from literature. Phillips (1706) marks it as obsolete, and Johnson considered it a merely comic word. It again became common towards the end of the eighteenth century, but the cause of its revival is not apparent.' These data enable us to estimate the stylistic value of the term before and after the crucial period. It ought no doubt to be regarded as an archaism in a line quoted by Dr. Johnson from John Gay's *The Shepherd's Week* (1714): 'Is Blouzelinda dead? farewel my *Glee*!' One may hesitate about its interpretation in the description of the schoolmaster in Goldsmith's *Deserted Village* (1770):

[1] 'Others, whom I shall *not* name' (quoted by M. Grevisse, *Le bon Usage*, 7th ed., Gembloux —Paris, 1959, p. 819).
[2] G. Price, 'The Negative Particles *Pas, Mie* and *Point* in French', *Archivum Linguisticum*, xiv (1962), pp. 14–34: pp. 26 f.

Well had the boding tremblers learn'd to trace
The day's disasters in his morning face;
Full well they laugh'd, with counterfeited *glee*,
At all his jokes, for many a joke had he,[1]

but the context seems to fit in with the comical or ironical connotation which Dr. Johnson had detected in the word. But there is certainly no such connotation in Blake's lines:

Piping down the valleys wild,
Piping songs of pleasant *glee*,
On a cloud I saw a child,
And he laughing said to me . . .
Songs of Innocence, Introduction,[2]

or in Wordsworth's:

Not far we travelled ere a shout of *glee*,
Startling us all, dispersed my reverie.
Epistle to Sir George Howland Beaumont, Bart.

Other English words, such as *blithe, lay, strand, wreak*, etc., were also archaic at one time and were revived by the Romantics in the same way.[3]

In spite of all these difficulties, there is no need whatever to take a defeatist view of the prospects of stylistic reconstruction. The success of the operation will ultimately depend on two factors, one subjective, the other objective. It will depend in the first place on the attitude of the critic himself, on whether his mind has been thoroughly sensitized to these problems and whether he is fully aware of the difficulties involved and of the ways in which they can be tackled. The other condition of success is that we should have sufficient information about the linguistic background at the time when the text was written. Even under the most favourable circumstances we can never hope, of course, to have a complete picture of a past state of a language and of all the expressive, suggestive and evocatory nuances which enriched its words, its forms and its constructions for a contemporary reader. We may, however, reach precise conclusions on a number of important points, and as more

[1] *NED*; cf. F. Mossé, *Esquisse d'une histoire de la langue anglaise*, Lyons, 1947, p. 178, n. 1.
[2] See the *Oxford Dictionary of Quotations*, p. 32.
[3] Mossé, op. cit., p. 178.

and more elements regain their pristine colour and lustre, the critic will experience something of the thrill which Proust's narrator felt when the memories of his childhood rose in all their freshness and splendour from a piece of *madeleine* dipped in tea.

CHAPTER IX

THE NATURE OF IMAGERY

MALLARMÉ summed up the essence of the poetic image in a terse yet profound formula when he wrote to Vielé-Griffin in 1891: 'Tout le mystère est là: établir les identités secrètes par un deux à deux qui ronge et use les objets, au nom d'une centrale pureté.'[1] Since the Symbolist Movement, poets and prose-writers have vied with each other in exalting the image and its role in literature. The most diverse analogies have been used to describe its nature and impact. For Supervielle, the image is the poet's magic lantern;[2] for Saint-Exupéry, it is a spell cast upon the reader;[3] others have likened it to a narcotic,[4] an equestrian leap,[5] an explosive,[6] and even an earthquake.[7] The most extravagant statements, however, are those expressed in direct, non-metaphorical language. Baudelaire saw in the cult of imagery his 'great, only and primitive passion'.[8] Mallarmé has spoken of the 'absolute power' of metaphor,[9] and the Surrealist poet André Breton has declared: 'To compare two objects, as remote from one another in character as possible, or by any other method put them together in a sudden and striking fashion, this remains the highest task to which poetry can aspire.'[10] Proust, as we already

[1] 'This is the whole mystery: to establish secret identities by a "two by two" which eats and wears away objects, in the name of some central purity' (quoted by G. Davies, 'The Demon of Analogy', *French Studies*, ix (1955), pp. 195–211 and 326–47: p. 201).

[2] 'L'image est la lanterne magique qui éclaire les poètes dans l'obscurité' (*Naissances; En songeant à un art poétique*, Paris, 1951, p. 61; cf. Ch. Bruneau, *Petite Histoire de la langue française*, vol. II, Paris, 1958, p. 310).

[3] 'Un acte qui, à son insu, noue le lecteur. On ne touche pas le lecteur: on l'envoûte' (preface to *Le Vent se lève*, by Anna Morrow Lindbergh; reprinted in *Confluences*, Nouvelle Série, no. 12–14 (1947), p. 192).

[4] 'Le stupéfiant image' (Aragon). This and the next five examples are quoted after G. Antoine, 'Pour un eméthode d'analyse stylistique des images', in *Langue et littérature. Actes du VIIIe Congrès de la Fédération Internationale des Langues et Littératures Modernes*, pp. 151–62.

[5] 'La métaphore unit deux mondes antagonistes dans le saut équestre de l'imagination' (F. Garcia Lorca).

[6] 'L'image littéraire est un explosif' (G. Bachelard).

[7] 'En certaines images, il y a l'amorce d'un tremblement de terre' (André Breton).

[8] 'Glorifier le culte des images, ma grande, mon unique, ma primitive passion.'

[9] 'Quelque puissance absolue, comme d'une Métaphore.'

[10] 'Comparer deux objets aussi éloignés que possible l'un de l'autre, ou, par toute autre méthode, les mettre en présence d'une manière brusque et saisissante, demeure la tâche la plus haute à laquelle la poésie puisse prétendre' (*Les Vases communicants*, Paris, 1955 ed., p. 148). The English translation is by I. A. Richards, *The Philosophy of Rhetoric*, New York—London, 1936, p. 123. Dr. Richards adds the pertinent comment: 'As the two things put together are more remote, the tension created is, of course, greater. That tension is the spring

know, believed that 'metaphor alone can give a kind of eternity to style',[1] and Ezra Pound has actually stated that 'it is better to present one Image in a lifetime than to produce voluminous works'.[2]

In the midst of this vogue of imagery, some protests have been uttered against the tendency to overwork and thus to debase the device. In *Micromégas*, Voltaire had already warned his fellow-writers, through the mouth-piece of a visitor from Sirius: 'La nature est comme la nature. Pourquoi lui chercher des comparaisons?'[3] This view was echoed by Gide when, taking up an expression made fashionable by Mallarmé, he wrote in his diary: 'Il n'y a pas pire ennemi de la pensée que le *démon de l'analogie* ... Quoi de plus fatigant que cette manie de certains littérateurs qui ne peuvent voir un objet sans penser aussitôt à un autre.'[4] Proust was too deeply convinced of the paramount importance of imagery to accept in-adequate analogies: 'Tous les à peu près d'images ne comptent pas', he declared in his preface to a book by Paul Morand. 'L'eau (dans des con-ditions données) bout à 100 degrés. A 98, à 99, le phénomène ne se produit pas. Alors mieux vaut pas d'images.'[5] In recent years, a reaction has begun, in French fiction, against the whole tradition of artistry in style, which some writers want to replace by a bare, simple and colourless idiom described as the 'zero degree of writing'.[6] It should be noted, however, that these criticisms are directed solely against idle, artificial or ornamental imagery; they do not concern 'functional' images which are part of the fabric of a literary work. As will be seen later, such images play a vital part in the structure of the very novel which started the vogue of the new style: Albert Camus's *L'Etranger*.

The high esteem in which the image is held by most writers is matched by the prominent place it occupies in stylistic research. Not only is it the theme of countless special studies, but it also has the lion's share in many monographs on the style of particular works or authors. When reading such monographs one often has the impression that the most

---

of the bow, the source of the energy of the shot, but we ought not to mistake the strength of the bow for the excellence of the shooting; or the strain for the aim' (ibid., p. 125). Cf. below, pp. 178 f.

[1] 'Je crois que la métaphore seule peut donner une sorte d'éternité au style' (in the article on the style of Flaubert, referred to on p. 136 n. 1). See also above, p. 149.

[2] Quoted by C. Day Lewis, *The Poetic Image*, London, 1947, p. 25.

[3] 'Nature is like nature. Why try to find comparisons for it?'

[4] 'There is no worse enemy of thought than the *demon of analogy* ... What could be more tiresome than the mania of certain literary men who cannot see an object without immediately thinking of another' (*Journal*, August 20th, 1926).

[5] 'Approximate images do not count. Water, under given conditions, boils at 100 degrees. At 98, at 99, the phenomenon does not occur. In that case it is better to have no images at all' (preface to *Tendres Stocks*, by Paul Morand, 7th ed., Paris, 1923, p. 35).

[6] See R. Barthes, *Le Degré zéro de l'écriture*, Paris, 1953.

original and most successful section is precisely the one dealing with imagery. Attempts have also been made to construct a *typology* of images. Some of these schemes were based on psychological criteria and were influenced by Freudian or Jungian ideas; thus it has been suggested that there is a fundamental distinction between 'animizing' and 'de-animizing' images;[1] that metaphors should be classified according to the four elements—earth, water, air, and fire—on which they are based,[2] etc. Other typologies aim at a classification of images on aesthetic grounds. Nearly forty years ago, Henry Wells distinguished seven types of imagery which he called the Decorative, the Sunken, the Violent, the Radical, the Intensive, the Expansive, and the Exuberant.[3] More recently, Charles Bruneau has divided writers into two types according to the nature of their images: 'les chimistes' and 'les inspirés'.[4] The former—poets like Mallarmé and Valéry—are given to intellectual and analytical imagery, whereas the latter—Rimbaud, Apollinaire, Paul Eluard—tend to express themselves in irrational, visionary and even primitive images. The same may be said of these experiments as of the even more ambitious typologies of style discussed in Chapter VI (p. 126); they are interesting and stimulating, but altogether too abstract and oversimplified to be of real help in ordinary research. In this chapter I shall therefore confine myself to more immediate problems facing the critic in the analysis and interpretation of imagery. There are three questions in particular which have important implications for the aims and methods of research in this field: the form of the image; its inner structure; lastly, its function within the wider context of an entire literary work. Each of these problems will be discussed in the light of my own researches on the style of the modern French novel.[5] First, however, it will be necessary to clarify our terms and to define more closely the concept of image itself.

A. What is an Image?

The term 'image' has several meanings which must be carefully distinguished from each other. There is in particular a certain danger of confusion between 'image' in the sense of 'mental representation' and 'image' in the sense of 'figure of speech expressing some similarity or analogy'. When Alain-Fournier wrote to a friend: 'Quand j'aurai assez

---

[1] For a summary of this theory, put forward by H. Pongs, see Wellek and Warren, op. cit., pp. 210 ff.

[2] On this theory, expounded by G. Bachelard, see recently C. G. Christofides, 'Gaston Bachelard's Phenomenology of the Imagination', *Romanic Review*, lii (1961), pp. 36–47.

[3] See Wellek and Warren, op. cit., pp. 205 ff.

[4] 'L'Image dans notre langue littéraire', *Mélanges A. Dauzat*, Paris, 1951, pp. 55–67.

[5] See my two books, *Style in the French Novel* and *The Image in the Modern French Novel*.

d'*images*, c'est-à-dire quand j'aurai le loisir et la force de ne plus regarder que ces *images*, où je vois et je sens le monde mort et vivant mêlé à l'ardeur de mon cœur, alors peut-être j'arriverai à exprimer l'inexprimable',[1] he was no doubt thinking of mental representations and not of metaphors. Sometimes it is rather difficult to establish the exact meaning of the term in passages which could be of the highest importance for the aesthetics of an author; only close scrutiny of the context, and of the general attitude of the writer, will enable us to resolve the ambiguity.

As we have just seen, an 'image' in the sense which concerns us here may be defined as 'a figure of speech expressing some similarity or analogy'. 'Every poetic image . . .', writes Mr. C. Day Lewis, 'is to some degree metaphorical. It looks out from a mirror in which life perceives not so much its face as some truth about its face'.[2] One may wonder, however, whether this view, which is held by many critics, is not too narrow, whether we are justified in limiting the field of imagery to the expression of similarities and analogies. Two objects or ideas may be associated with one another in two ways: by similarity or by 'contiguity', the fact that they coexist in the same mental context. Simile and metaphor arise from the former type whereas *metonymy* and allied figures spring from the latter.[3] It is true that metonymy lacks the originality and the expressive power of metaphor; as a French linguist pertinently points out, 'la métonymie n'ouvre pas de chemins comme l'intuition métaphorique, mais brûlant les étapes de chemins trop connus, elle raccourcit des distances pour faciliter la rapide intuition de choses déjà connues'.[4] But this does not mean that metonymy has no expressive force at all and that it cannot give rise to genuine images.

Let us look at one or two examples. In *Du Côté de chez Swann*, the narrator speaks of 'la couleur vive, empourprée et charmante' of the name *Champi* in George Sand's novel *François le Champi*.[5] Proust's ideas on the magic of proper names are well known (cf. pp. 45 and 49); one might therefore be inclined to regard the 'crimson colour' of the name *Champi* as

---

[1] 'When I have enough *images*, that is to say when I have the leisure and the strength to look at nothing but these *images*, where I see and feel the world, dead and live, mingled with the ardour of my heart, then perhaps I shall succeed in expressing the inexpressible' (*Lettres d'Alain-Fournier au petit B.*, Paris, 1940 ed., p. 26 (September 20th, 1906)).

[2] Op. cit., p. 18.

[3] Cf. my *Semantics*, pp. 212–20. See also R. Jakobson-M. Halle, *Fundamentals of Language*, The Hague, 1956, pp. 76 ff.

[4] 'Metonymy does not open new paths like metaphorical intuition, but, taking too familiar paths in its stride, it shortens distances so as to facilitate the swift intuition of things already known' (G. Esnault, *Imagination populaire, métaphores occidentales*, Paris, 1925, p. 31).

[5] 'The vivid, crimson and charming colour' of the name *Champi* (*Du Côté de chez Swann*, vol. I, p. 62).

a synaesthetic metaphor in the tradition of Baudelaire's *Correspondances* and Rimbaud's *Voyelles*.[1] Yet if we look more closely at the context we notice that the connexion between the colour and the name is metonymic, not metaphorical; it is based, not on some hidden resemblance or analogy, but on a purely external relation: the accidental fact that the book had a red binding.[2] Nevertheless, this fortuitous association has resulted in an expressive image in which, according to André Breton's formula, 'two objects remote from one another are put together in a sudden and striking fashion'. The same is true of a curious expression found in the same novel: 'la surface azurée du silence'.[3] Here again we have a bold and graphic image based on a metonymic association: the coexistence, in the same mental context, of two simultaneous impressions, one visual, the blue sky, the other acoustic, the quiet and stillness of a Sunday afternoon. Or, to take a very different example, in the title of Stendhal's novel *Le Rouge et le noir*, the two colours are, as everyone knows, metonymic: 'red' stands for the army and 'black' for the cloth. At the same time their bald juxtaposition produces a violent clash which has the effect of an authentic image.[4]

It should, however, be added at once that the vast majority of images are metaphorical; the remarks which follow will therefore be confined to this type. Even in this limited sense, the term 'image' remains somewhat ambiguous; there are many metaphors and comparisons which cannot be regarded as images. We possess several criteria which enable us, in a very rough way, to distinguish between imagery and other expressions of similarity or analogy. In the first place, there can be no question of an image unless the resemblance it expresses has a concrete and sensuous quality. A comparison between two abstract phenomena, however acute and illuminating it may be, will not constitute a real image. Secondly, there must be something striking and unexpected in every image: it must produce a surprise effect due to the discovery of some common element in two seemingly disparate experiences. If the two terms are too close to each other—or, as Dr. Sayce would say, if the 'angle' of the metaphor is not wide enough[5]—no image proper will result. As Wordsworth put it:

---

[1] See above, pp. 85 ff. and 148 f.   [2] *Du Côté de chez Swann*, vol. I, p. 61.
[3] 'The azure surface of silence' (ibid., p. 119); cf. above, p. 88.
[4] Cf. M. Wandruszka, 'Zum Stil Stendhals', *Zeitschrift für Französische Sprache und Literatur*, lii (1939), pp. 429–36: p. 435. For further examples of metonymic imagery, see R. A. Sayce, 'La Métonymie dans l'œuvre de Racine', *Actes du premier congrès international racinien*, Uzès, 1961, pp. 37–41.
[5] *Style in French Prose*, pp. 62 f.; cf. above, p. 174. For a critique of this principle, see recently H. Weinrich, *Romanische Forschungen*, lxxiii (1961), pp. 201 f.

>The song would speak
>Of that interminable building reared
>By observation of affinities
>In objects where no brotherhood exists
>To passive minds.[1]

To give a concrete example, in a highly coloured passage describing the water-lilies of the Vivonne, which may have been influenced by Monet's famous *Nymphéas*,[2] Proust brings into play all kinds of analogies to evoke the experience with the maximum of precision. Amongst other things, he compares the water-lilies to moss-roses, rocket-flowers and pansies.[3] These comparisons are apposite and useful in so far as they help to specify the various aspects of the object; but they do not yield an image since the analogy they enunciate, the similarity of one flower to another, does not produce that impression of 'double vision' which is a *sine qua non* in imagery.

Another distinctive trait of the genuine image is a certain freshness and novelty. Needless to say, it is not essential for every image to be absolutely original; but if its expressive force has been weakened by repetition, if it has hardened into a set phrase or a cliché, then the writer will have to rejuvenate it and infuse new life into it. Thus Proust ridicules Dr. Cottard who, in his naive delight in stock phrases and idioms, does not hesitate to inquire: 'Sarah Bernhardt, c'est bien la *Voix d'Or*, n'est-ce pas?';[4] yet, in a later volume of the cycle, the narrator restores to life the same cliché when he tries to imagine how a famous actress would recite some well-known lines from *Phèdre*: 'je les verrais enfin baigner effectivement dans l'atmosphère et l'ensoleillement de la *voix dorée*'.[5] Here the nature of the context, and in particular the proximity of the luminous word *ensoleillement*, suffice to revive the faded synaesthetic metaphor which underlies the cliché.[6]

B. The Form of the Image

The form of the image immediately raises a problem of fundamental importance: the distinction between *simile* and *metaphor*. The difference

---

[1] Quoted by C. Day Lewis, op. cit., p. 36.

[2] J. Mouton, *Le Style de Marcel Proust*, p. 84. Cf. also J. Monnin-Hornung, *Proust et la peinture*, Geneva–Lille, 1951, pp. 181 ff.

[3] *Du Côté de chez Swann*, vol. I, p. 222.

[4] 'Sarah Bernhardt, that's the *Golden Voice*, isn't it?' (ibid., p. 263).

[5] 'I would at last see them bathed, in actual fact, in the atmosphere and sunshine of the golden voice' (*A l'ombre des jeunes filles en fleurs*, vol. I, p. 19).

[6] Cf. above, pp. 45 ff. See also V. Väänänen, 'Métaphores rajeunies et métaphores ressuscitées' ,*Atti dell 'VIII. Congresso Internazionale di Studi Romanzi*, vol. II, pp. 471–6.

is essentially one between explicit and implicit imagery, or, as Paul Eluard once put it, between 'image by analogy' (A is *like* B) and 'image by identification' (A *is* B).[1] Apart from certain border-line cases, it is easy to distinguish between the two types; what is more delicate is to decide how, and to what extent, the critic should take the distinction into account.

A leading authority on metaphor has defined the latter as 'a condensed comparison by which we assert an intuitive and concrete identity'.[2] This formula brings out very well the difference in density and concentration between the two figures, and this difference has important consequences for their expressive force. Professor Antoine gave recently an interesting illustration of this contrast.[3] The paradoxical image of the 'black sun', which was introduced by the Romantics into French literature, is used by some poets as a terse and cryptic metaphor:

> Ma seule étoile est morte—et mon luth constellé
> Porte le *soleil noir* de la mélancolie.[4]
>
> Gérard de Nerval, El Desdichado.

> Et l'on voit maintenant tout chargés de désastres,
>   Rouler, éteints, désespérés,
> L'un semant dans l'espace une effroyable graine,
> L'autre traînant sa lèpre et l'autre sa gangrène,
>   Ces *noirs soleils* pestiférés.[5]
>
> Victor Hugo, La Légende des Siècles, 'Inferi'.

The same image recurs in Baudelaire in the attenuated form of a hesitant comparison: 'Je la *comparerais à un soleil noir*, si l'on pouvait concevoir un astre noir versant la lumière et le bonheur.'[6] Proust had no such qualms about the incompatibility of the two terms, but he too put the image in the form of a simile when he wrote about the steeple at Combray:

---

[1] 'L'image par analogie (ceci est *comme* cela) et l'image par identification (ceci *est* cela)' (quoted from *Donner à voir* by G. Antoine, loc. cit., p. 155).

[2] 'La métaphore est une comparaison condensée par laquelle l'esprit affirme une identité intuitive et concrète' (G. Esnault, op. cit., p. 30).

[3] Loc. cit., p. 161, from where the next three examples are taken. Cf. H. Tuzet, *Revue des Sciences Humaines*, fasc. 88 (1957), pp. 479–502.

[4] 'My only star is dead—and my star-spangled lute bears the *black sun* of melancholy.'

[5] 'And one can now see, all charged with disasters, rolling, extinct, desperate, one sowing hideous seeds in space, another dragging about its leprosy and a third its gangrene, these pestilential *black suns*.'

[6] 'I would *compare it to a black sun*, if one could imagine a black star shedding light and happiness' (*Petits poèmes en prose*: 'Le désir de peindre').

'De ma chambre je ne pouvais apercevoir que sa base qui avait été recouverte d'ardoises; mais quand, le dimanche, je les voyais, par une chaude matinée d'été, flamboyer *comme un soleil noir* . . .'[1]

It should, of course, be noted that the first two passages are in verse and the last two in prose, which is one of the reasons why Nerval and Hugo preferred a concise metaphorical formulation where Baudelaire and Proust chose to be more explicit and thus to weaken the paradox.

This difference in density and impact goes a long way to explain why certain authors have a marked preference for one or the other of the two figures. An epic writer like Jean Giono, imbued with the Homeric tradition, will often favour the explicit type;[2] others, given to shock-tactics and surprise effects, will agree with Mallarmé's principle: 'Je raye le mot *comme* du dictionnaire.'[3] An extreme form of condensed and elliptical imagery is the so-called 'maximum metaphor' practised by Victor Hugo: the abrupt juxtaposition of two nouns the first of which is a metaphorical equivalent of the second: 'le pâtre promontoire', 'le vautour fatalité', 'l'océan pensée', 'le fossoyeur oubli'.[4]

But if it is part of the critic's business to discover and interpret these preferences, it would be quite wrong to keep simile and metaphor in watertight compartments. Whether an image is explicitly or implicitly formulated, it springs ultimately from the same intuition, the same 'observation of affinities'. One and the same analogy may be expressed, in the same text, by both similes and metaphors; a systematic separation of the two figures, as practised by certain scholars, would therefore distort the whole perspective and would prevent the critic from seeing the general pattern of the imagery and from identifying the broad tendencies underlying it. Even more serious are those cases where the similes of a writer are studied in detail while his metaphors are completely disregarded,[5] or vice versa. Such methods will never lead to a comprehensive picture of imagery in an entire work, which is the ultimate objective of research in this field.

---

[1] 'From my room I could see only its base which had been covered with slates; but when, on Sunday, I saw them, on a warm summer morning, blazing *like a black sun* . . .' (*Du Côté de chez Swann*, vol. I, p. 90).

[2] Cf. my *Style in the French Novel*, pp. 218 f.

[3] 'I have struck out the word *like* from the dictionary' (quoted by G. Davies, loc. cit, p. 326).

[4] 'The shepherd promontory', 'the vulture fate', 'the ocean thought', 'the grave-digger oblivion'. Cf. Ch. Bruneau in F. Brunot's *Histoire de la langue française*, vol. XII, pp. 239 f., and vol. XIII, part I, pp. 37 f.; see also H. Temple Patterson, 'The Origin of Hugo's Condensed Metaphors', *French Studies*, v (1951), pp. 343-8.

[5] As, for example, in W. Bal's otherwise useful study, *La Comparaison. Son emploi dans 'Gaspard des Montagnes' d'H. Pourrat*, Leopoldville, 1958.

The formal analysis of imagery involves two distinct sets of operations. We can focus our attention on the form of particular figures; alternatively, we can try to identify the larger units into which these figures combine. Single images may be described in purely grammatical terms, specifying whether the comparison is expressed by a conjunction, a verb or some other element, whether the metaphor is located in an adjective, a noun, a verb, a subordinate clause, etc. These grammatical details may seem trivial; yet a recent book, Christine Brooke-Rose's *A Grammar of Metaphor*,[1] has shown that they can lead to interesting observations. More complicated are those cases where two images arise simultaneously and develop on parallel lines so that the reader has to follow them concurrently. There is a curious example of this device in Proust when he compares Swann's infatuation for Odette with the plight of a drug addict and a consumptive. Once the double analogy has been formulated the two images progress side by side until they reach their inevitable conclusion:

'l'amour de Swann en était arrivé à ce degré où le médecin et, dans certaines affections, le chirurgien le plus audacieux, se demandent si *priver un malade de son vice* ou *lui ôter son mal,* est encore raisonnable ou même possible.'[2]

There is also another form of double image: the device which Spitzer described as 'the fitting of one image into another'.[3] We have already seen that, in the passage on the water-lilies of the Vivonne, Proust compares these flowers to pansies, but that the angle of this analogy is too narrow to produce an expressive image. Proust, however, reinforces it by adding a subsidiary simile in which the pansies themselves are personified and likened to butterflies: 'on eût dit des *pensées* de jardins qui étaient venues poser *comme des papillons* leurs ailes bleuâtres et glacées sur l'obliquité transparente de ce parterre d'eau'.[4]

The formal analysis of imagery will also distinguish between simple images and those which are *developed* in various ways. The development may be either static or dynamic. It is static when the writer lingers over

---

[1] London, 1958. Cf. also T. Pavel, 'Notes pour une description structurale de la métaphore poétique', *Cahiers de linguistique théorique et appliquée,* i (1962), pp. 185–207.
[2] 'Swann's love had reached the stage where the physician and, in certain diseases, the most daring surgeon, wonder whether it is still reasonable or even possible to *wean the patient from his vice* or to *rid him of his illness*' (*Du Côté de chez Swann,* vol. II, pp. 118 f.).
[3] *Stilstudien,* vol. II, pp. 459 f.
[4] 'One might have taken them for garden *pansies* which had come to place, *like butterflies,* their bluish and glossy wings on the transparent obliqueness of this watery flower-bed' (*Du Côté de chez Swann,* vol. I, p. 222).

an analogy, embroidering and elaborating its various aspects whilst remaining all the time within the limits of a single image; it is dynamic when he transcends the original analogy by adding all kinds of variations on the same theme. Both processes can be illustrated with examples from Proust. A case of static development occurs in the passage where the young narrator sends a note to his mother, which the maid Françoise is to deliver to her during dinner, and which, he fondly hopes, will persuade her to come and see him in his room. The situation reminds the author of that of a man waiting desperately, in front of an hotel or a theatre, for the woman he loves, and eventually asking a friend to call her. At this point Proust seems to forget that the imaginary scene is no more than a comparison; he enlarges on it and adds all kinds of poignant details obviously derived from personal experience, until he arrives at the brief and melancholy conclusion: 'Souvent, l'ami redescend seul.'[1]

The process of dynamic development is clearly seen in the famous passage where the narrator describes the smells permeating the rooms of his aunt Léonie at Combray. The author's imagination is set in motion by a queer analogy: the idea that the fire is baking the smells like a cake. From this point onwards, the analogy gathers like a snowball, generating a long series of metaphors, all from the same sphere and elaborating the same idea:

'le feu cuisant comme une pâte les appétissantes odeurs dont l'air de la chambre était tout *grumeleux* et qu'avait déjà fait *travailler* et *"lever"* la fraîcheur humide et ensoleillée du matin, il les *feuilletait,* les *dorait,* les *godait,* les *boursouflait,* en faisant un invisible et *palpable gâteau* provincial, un immense *"chausson".* '[2]

It may also happen that a series of totally different images arise, by a kind of chain-reaction, around the same theme. Some of Victor Hugo's poems consist almost entirely of a sequence of metaphors illuminating various facets of one central experience. In the words of another poet, 'une image peut se composer d'une multitude de termes, être tout un poème et même un long poème'.[3] Hugo's *Réponse à un acte d'accusation:*

---

[1] 'Often, the friend returns alone' (ibid., pp. 48–9).

[2] 'The fire, baking like dough the appetizing smells which made the air in the room feel as if it had been *curdled* and which the damp and sunny freshness of the morning had already *kneaded* and '*raised*', *puffed* them, *glazed* them, *puckered* them, *swelled* them, making them into an invisible and *tangible* provincial *cake*, a huge *turn-over*' (ibid., p. 72). Cf. on this passage Ch. Bruneau, *La Prose littéraire de Proust à Camus*, p. 5, and G. Matoré, 'Les Images gustatives dans *Du Côté de chez Swann*', *Mélanges de linguistique et de littérature romanes à la mémoire d'István Frank*, Universität des Saarlandes, 1957, pp. 685–92.

[3] 'An image may consist of a multiplicity of terms, it may be an entire poem and even a long poem' (Paul Éluard, *Donner à voir*, quoted by G. Antoine, loc. cit., p. 156).

N

Suite, where he expounds his theory of the word, is a good example of this technique. The images follow each other at such speed that one scarcely has time to visualize them. Carried away by his own momentum, the poet accelerates the rhythm still further: at the climactic point, six short and powerful metaphors explode in a single line, leading up to an apotheosis of the Word reminiscent of the opening verse of St. John's Gospel:

Il est vie, esprit, germe, ouragan, vertu, feu;
Car le mot, c'est le Verbe, et le Verbe, c'est Dieu.[1]

In a less concentrated form, the same process is found in many passages by Proust and other prose-writers.

With these dynamic developments we have already moved from the plane of single images on to that of the *patterns* into which they combine. The most significant of these patterns are those where the same images, or variations on them, reappear like a Wagnerian *leit-motiv* whenever the author mentions the experience which had originally called them forth. Proust likes to present in this way some of the great metaphorical themes of his cycle: hawthorns, the 'petite phrase' of Vinteuil's sonata, the geological structure of our memories, the workings of time. At this point, the formal analysis of imagery merges into the study of its functions, which is largely based, as will be seen, on the persistent recurrence of certain metaphorical motifs.

C. THE STRUCTURE OF THE IMAGE

'As to metaphorical expression, that is a great excellence in style, when it is used with propriety, for it gives you two ideas for one.' This statement by Dr. Johnson[2] sums up very neatly one of the essential features of both simile and metaphor. Both figures are based on a binary relation: an association between two terms which have some element or elements in common. It was an important step forward in the study of imagery when Dr. I. A. Richards suggested that we need special names for the two terms involved, and proposed 'tenor' for the thing we are talking about, and 'vehicle' for that to which the tenor is compared, whereas the common feature or features would be called the 'ground' of the image.[3] The existence of these three factors, tenor, vehicle and ground, means that images can be classified from three different points

[1] 'It is life, spirit, germ, hurricane, virtue, fire; for the name is the Word, and the Word is God.'
[2] Quoted by I. A. Richards, *The Philosophy of Rhetoric*, p. 93.
[3] Ibid., pp. 96 ff. and 117. French linguists have an even simpler terminology: they call the tenor 'le comparé' and the vehicle 'le comparant',

of view, to which a fourth criterion may be added: the relation between tenor and vehicle.

1. By far the most popular of the four methods is the classification of imagery according to its *vehicles*: according to the sources from which an author draws his analogies. As we saw on pp. 148 f., these will to some extent depend on the writer's personality, his environment, his reading and similar factors. Some critics have gone even further and have tried to interpret the frequent recurrence of certain types of imagery as a symptom of the author's interests and tastes, fears and aspirations, likes and dislikes (cf. pp. 83 f.). This theory has been severely criticized,[1] and in this form it is patently untenable. It has been shown, for example, that the most absorbing interests and the most crucial experiences of a writer have sometimes left no trace whatever in his imagery. There is no image from fishing in Izaak Walton's *Life of Donne*, nor is there any image from music in the poetry of the great fourteenth-century composer Guillaume de Machaut.[2] In the imagery of Camus's novels there is only one reference to tuberculosis, an illness which played an important part in his life.[3] Conversely, the fact that an author uses images from a certain sphere does not necessarily indicate any interest in that sphere. As Proust has shrewdly observed, Sainte-Beuve was anything but attracted to army life, sport or the sea; yet he did derive some of his metaphors from these fields.[4]

Carried to unreasonable lengths—as for instance in Professor C. F. E. Spurgeon's well-known book, *Shakespeare's Imagery and what it tells us*—this approach reminds one of what Dr. Johnson said in a more general way about attempts to discover an author's tastes from his writings. Speaking of an admirer of the poet Thomson, Dr. Johnson wrote:

'She could gather from his works three parts of his character: that he was a great lover, a great swimmer, and rigorously abstinent; but, said [his intimate] Savage, he knows not any love but that of the sex; he was perhaps never in cold water in his life; and he indulges himself in all the luxury that comes within his reach.'[5]

---

[1] See esp. L. H. Hornstein, 'Analysis of Imagery: a Critique of Literary Method', *Publications of the Modern Language Association of America*, lvii (1942), pp. 638–53. Cf. also Wellek and Warren, op. cit., pp. 214 ff., and my *Style in the French Novel*, pp. 31 ff. For a new approach to the problem, see now Ch. Mauron, *Des Métaphores obsédantes au mythe personnel*, Paris, 1963.

[2] Wellek and Warren, op. cit., p. 214.

[3] In *La Chute*, pp. 123 f.

[4] In the preface to Paul Morand's *Tendres Stocks*; cf. F. Gray, *Le Style de Montaigne*, pp. 151 f.

[5] Quoted by Wellek and Warren, op. cit., p. 214.

Nevertheless it would be quite wrong to dismiss the theory altogether. There may be circumstances where an early shock, a traumatic experience, an obsession, a deeply rooted preoccupation or anxiety will influence the choice of imagery. Miss Spurgeon herself has made out a plausible case for connecting the large number of flood images in Shakespeare with floods of the river Avon which he saw as a child.[1] In cases of this kind one can never be quite sure; occasionally, however, we have direct evidence about the psychological motivation of certain images. A remarkable example is the use of insect imagery in Sartre. We have already seen (p. 148) some passages from his novel *La Mort dans l'âme* (1949), where the people and vehicles cluttering the roads of France in the summer of 1940 are assimilated to ants, lobsters, crickets and vermin, and human beings are actually transformed into insects. These visionary images can assume Surrealist proportions:

'nous sommes le rêve d'une vermine, nos pensées s'épaississent, deviennent de moins en moins humaines; des pensées velues, pattues courent partout, sautent d'une tête à l'autre: la vermine va se réveiller.'[2]

This form of imagery is extraordinarily persistent in the works of Sartre. Apart from its prominent role in the mythological play *Les Mouches* where, as the title itself indicates, it is closely bound up with the central theme,[3] it is already conspicuous in his first novel, *La Nausée*, published eleven years before *La Mort dans l'âme*. The narrator, looking at himself in a mirror, sees something not merely sub-human but below the animal level: something reminiscent of a polyp or even of a plant.[4] His own hand reminds him of a crab, with the fingers moving like the animal's legs: 'Elle a l'air d'une bête à la renverse. Les doigts, ce sont les pattes. Je m'amuse à les faire remuer, très vite, comme les pattes d'un crabe qui est tombé sur le dos. Le crabe est mort: les pattes se recroquevillent, se ramènent sur le ventre de ma main.'[5] Even more disturbing is the transformation of a human tongue into a centipede:

---

[1] Op. cit., pp. 98 ff.

[2] 'We are the dream of vermin, our thoughts thicken, they become less and less human; hairy thoughts, with legs, are running about everywhere, jumping from one head to another: the vermin is about to wake up' (p. 89).

[3] See esp. the chorus of the Erinnyes in Act III, scene 1. Cf. P. Thody, *Jean-Paul Sartre. A Literary and Political Study*, London, 1960, p. 74.

[4] 81st ed., Paris, Gallimard, pp. 30 f.

[5] 'It looks like an animal on its back. The fingers are legs. I amuse myself by moving them, very fast, like the legs of a crab which has fallen on its back. The crab is dead: the legs curl in, are pulled back against the belly of my hand' (p. 128). On the use of the same image in *Le Mur*, see Thody, op. cit., p. 26.

'Et un autre trouvera qu'il y a quelque chose qui le gratte dans la bouche. Et il s'approchera d'une glace, ouvrira la bouche: et sa langue sera devenue un énorme mille-pattes tout vif, qui tricotera des pattes et lui raclera le palais. Il voudra le cracher, mais le mille-pattes, ce sera une partie de lui-même et il faudra qu'il l'arrache avec ses mains.'[1]

It is significant that some of the same motifs reappear, twenty-two years after *La Nausée*, in the play *Les Séquestrés d'Altona* (1960), where a German war criminal, 'sequestered', that is shut away from the outside world in an upstairs room of his father's house, pleads on behalf of his contemporaries before an imaginary tribunal of crabs in the thirtieth century—the crabs being the descendants of the human species;[2] at times he imagines, or pretends, that he himself has changed into a crab and speaks of men turned into vermin.[3] This last motif, which, on Sartre's own admission, was inspired by Kafka,[4] recurs even in one of his critical essays where members of the Resistance are said to have felt under torture 'qu'ils n'étaient que des insectes, que l'homme est le rêve impossible des cafards et des cloportes et qu'ils se réveilleraient vermine comme tout le monde.'[5]

The aesthetic and philosophical significance of this sinister imagery has been well summed up by a recent critic: 'It is, of course, perfectly true that insect imagery has been widely used in fiction in order to express vividly man's physical and mental abasement, but what we meet in Sartre's work is the fusion of imaginative detail and philosophical theme. The two elements coalesce, and the image ceases to be a general one about human abasement and embodies instead a particular and recurring metaphysical notion, that of man being merged with the brute contingency of Nature.'[6] In other words, such images are not merely

---

[1] 'Someone else will feel that there is something scratching in his mouth. And he will go to a mirror, open his mouth: and his tongue will have become a huge live centipede kicking about with its legs and scraping his palate. He would like to spit it out, but the centipede will be part of himself, and he will have to pull it out with his hands' (p. 199). Cf. also this image from *L'Age de raison*: 'Sa bouche se pinça sur les derniers mots: une bouche vernie avec des reflets mauves, un insecte écarlate, occupé à dévorer ce visage cendreux' ('Her mouth pinched together on the last words: a varnished mouth with mauve glints, a scarlet insect busy devouring this ashen face'; quoted by F. Jameson, *Sartre. The Origins of a Style*, Yale University Press, 1961, pp. 161 and 222, whose translation I have reproduced).

[2] See esp. Act II, scene 1, p. 86. I am grateful to my colleague Dr. J. A. Hiddleston for drawing my attention to this imagery.

[3] Act IV, scene 2, p. 170; Act IV, scene 9, p. 196; Act V, scene 1, p. 207.

[4] S. John, 'Sacrilege and Metamorphosis: Two Aspects of Sartre's Imagery', *Modern Language Quarterly*, xx (1959), pp. 57–66: p. 64.

[5] 'That they were mere insects, that man is the impossible dream of cockroaches and wood-lice, and that they would wake up as vermin, like everybody else' (quoted ibid., p. 65, from the essay 'Qu'est-ce que la littérature?', in *Situations II*).

[6] S. John, loc. cit., pp. 63 f.

repellent, frightening or hallucinatory; they are part of Existentialist philosophy, of that 'hantise d'une métamorphose' of which Sartre spoke in *L'Etre et le néant*.[1]

Quite apart from their aesthetic and philosophical interest, these images also have a psychological, or psychiatrical, significance which became apparent when Simone de Beauvoir published in 1960 the second volume of her memoirs, under the title *La Force de l'âge*. Here she relates that, a few years before he wrote *La Nausée*, Sartre asked a doctor friend to give him an injection of mescaline so that he could watch the hallucinations induced by the drug. Though he declared that he had no hallucinations proper, 'les objets qu'il percevait se déformaient d'une manière affreuse: il avait vu des parapluies-vautours, des souliers-squelettes, de monstrueux visages; et sur ses côtés, par derrière, grouillaient des *crabes*, des *poulpes*, des choses grimaçantes'.[2] On the way home, he imagined that the ends of shoe-laces had changed into huge beetles. It took him some time to get rid of these obsessions: we hear, in particular, that on several occasions he had the impression of being followed by a lobster.[3]

It is impossible not to connect these experiences with the vision of a hand as a crab in *La Nausée*, with the lobsters crawling on the roads of France in *La Mort dans l'âme*, and with the tribunal of the crabs in *Les Séquestrés d'Altona*. Sartre's metamorphosis images had several roots and were closely entwined with his philosophy and his aesthetics; at the same time, some of the specific forms which this imagery took were without any doubt determined by the pathological states recorded by Simone de Beauvoir. It should, however, be emphasized that this psychological motivation, interesting as it is, has no bearing whatever on the artistic merits of the imagery or on its usefulness in conveying Sartre's philosophical ideas. What was said above (p. 125) of the 'biographical' approach to style in general may be repeated here: the intimate background of an author's images has nothing to do with their intrinsic qualities, their appropriateness or their role in the structure of his works, and the critic is primarily concerned with the latter aspects of imagery rather than with its psychological interpretation.

2. Images can also be classified according to their *tenor*: according to

---

[1] 'Obsession of metamorphosis' (ibid., p. 62; cf. F. Jameson, op. cit., ch. V).

[2] 'The objects he perceived were deformed in a frightful way: he saw umbrellas turned into vultures, shoes which looked like skeletons, monstrous faces; and by his side, from behind, *crabs*, *octopuses*, grimacing creatures were crawling' (*La Force de l'âge*, p. 216). I am indebted for these references to Madame Escoffier, of Lyons University.

[3] Ibid., pp. 217, 228, 282.

the subjects which call for metaphorical expression. As Sperber showed
some forty years ago (cf. pp. 75 and 83 ff.), there are two kinds of centres
governing the general movement of analogies: centres of 'expansion',
which supply terms of comparison, and centres of 'attraction', which are
in need of such terms. Both kinds of foci will have to be identified before
we can obtain a complete picture of the pattern of imagery in a literary
work. It may then be found that some spheres can act in both capacities:
in Proust, for example, music is not only a fertile source of images but
also a powerful centre of attraction for analogies from various directions.
A study of the main themes round which images cluster in a given work
will help the critic in establishing the functions and the structural role of
the imagery, as will be seen in the next section of this chapter.[1]

3. One can also classify images according to their *'ground'*, the nature
of the similarity on which they are based. Some semanticists find it
sufficient to distinguish between two kinds of similarity: objective and
emotive. Others prefer a finer mesh of distinctions; one linguist, for
example, has suggested that there are four types of metaphor: perceptual,
synaesthetic, affective and pragmatic.[2] This criterion, though useful in
semantics, does not appear to be particularly helpful in stylistic studies.

4. The student of images will not be content with resolving them into
their components. This analytical phase will have to be followed by a
synthesis which will explore the *relation between tenor and vehicle*.[3] In
examining this relationship, attention will have to be paid first of all to
the distinction between *concrete* and *abstract* terms. In theory there are
four possible combinations since both the tenor and the vehicle may be
either abstract or concrete. In practice one of the four combinations can
be disregarded: the one where both terms are abstract ideas. As we
already know (p. 178), such combinations cannot yield a genuine image
since they lack that element of concreteness, that appeal to the senses,
which is an essential feature of all imagery. Of the other three combinations, two are so common that they need no comment: those where both
tenor and vehicle are concrete, and those where an abstract idea is compared to a concrete experience. The third type, where a concrete tenor

---

[1] Cf. H. Hatzfeld, *Actes du VIIIᵉ Congrès de la Fédération Internationale des Langues et
Littératures Modernes*, pp. 162 f.

[2] A. Carnoy, *La Science du mot. Traité de sémantique*, Louvain, 1927, ch. XX.

[3] In his interesting review of my *Image in the Modern French Novel* (*Romanische Forschungen*, lxxiii, 1961, pp. 197–203), Professor H. Weinrich has strongly argued against the
practice of splitting metaphors into their components. 'Metaphor', he writes, 'is by definition
the combination of a vehicle with a tenor; what will remain of it if we methodically isolate
the vehicles on the one hand and the tenors on the other?' (p. 201). There is some truth in
this argument; yet this 'methodical isolation' and decomposition may enable the critic to
discover certain significant tendencies which could not have been noticed in any other way.

is described by means of an abstract vehicle, is relatively rare; as already noted (p. 85), transfers from concrete to abstract are one of the basic forms of metaphor and simile, whereas transfers in the opposite direction are exceptional and tend to have an artificial air. Nevertheless, there are some examples both in poetry and in prose:

> La lune, froide et claire *comme un doute,*
> Sourit et passe.[1]
>
> Vielé-Griffin, Minuit.

> Et nous, jaillis de plus loin *comme un aveu plus hardi* ...[2]
>
> Jules Romains, Europe.

'. . . et quand rien plus ne les (*viz.* des îles) a retenues profondément au roc natal, alors, *comme des actions non sincères,* elles ont été au hasard des dérives, emportées par tous les courants' (Gide, *Le Voyage d'Urien*).[3]

These figures owe their expressiveness to the very fact that they are unusual and run counter to our ingrained habits of thought: rather than putting an abstract experience in concrete terms, as we are accustomed to do, they work the other way round and 'dematerialize' concrete objects by assimilating them to abstract phenomena.

If one considers the imagery of a work as a whole one can sometimes discover special relations between certain tenors and vehicles. It may happen, for instance, that an entire sphere of experience is consistently and systematically transcribed in terms of another sphere. An example of such '*correlative*' spheres, as they may be called,[4] is the use of numerous medical images to describe Swann's love for Odette in the second part of *Du Côté de chez Swann*. The parallel between illness and love is by no means new; it was already used by Ovid and became a stock metaphor in the Middle Ages. Proust, however, has rejuvenated and modernized the cliché by the accumulation of technical details and specific symptoms; a typical example is the double image, already quoted (p. 182), where Swann's condition is compared to that of a consumptive and a drug addict. A critic given to the biographical interpretation of imagery would no doubt point out that Proust, who was not only the son and brother of distinguished medical men but was himself a chronic invalid spending

---

[1] 'The moon, cold and clear *like a doubt,* smiles and passes.'
[2] 'And we, sprung from more afar *like a bolder confession.*'
[3] 'And when they (viz. the islands) were no longer deeply attached to their native rock, then, *like insincere actions,* they were at the mercy of the waves, swept away by all the currents' (Paris, 1929 ed., p. 24).
[4] Cf. my *Image in the Modern French Novel*, p. 229.

much of his life in the midst of medicine bottles, was very familiar with these matters and greatly preoccupied by them. This is perfectly true, but it does not explain why medical imagery should be more concentrated and more insistent in this part of the cycle than elsewhere;[1] besides, it is difficult to imagine that such a sustained and systematic device should be no more than an unconscious reflex. The real reason for the efflorescence of medical images in *Un Amour de Swann* is twofold. By assimilating Swann's passion for Odette to illness and disease in general, and even to such specific forms of it as cholera, tuberculosis, morphinomania or eczema, Proust was making an implicit diagnosis: he was deliberately emphasizing, by the oblique but all the more effective method of metaphorical formulation, the pathological nature of Swann's love. Furthermore, he adopted the detached, objective and scientific tone of a physician in order to step back and dissociate himself from experiences which the narrator, and the author himself, knew only too well; he was sheltering, as André Maurois once put it, behind a façade of 'heroic technicalness'.[2]

Such correspondences between tenor and vehicle are even more striking when the relation between the two spheres is reversible. We then have what linguists call '*reciprocal*' metaphors.[3] Proust, for instance, is fond of personifying hawthorns and other flowers and comparing them to young girls; conversely, he also likes to picture girls as flowers and has even enshrined this image in the title of the second part of his cycle: *A l'ombre des jeunes filles en fleurs*. There is also in Proust a perpetual to-and-fro movement between nature and art: he sees nature—a landscape, a flower, a human face, etc.—in terms of painting or sculpture whereas works of art are compared to plants and inanimate objects; a village church, for example, is likened, somewhat elliptically, to a haystack,[4] and, in a more detailed simile, its two steeples are pictured as two ears of corn: 'effilés, écailleux, imbriqués d'alvéoles, guillochés, jaunissants et grumeleux, *comme deux épis*'.[5] The deeper meaning of this interchange between the two spheres has been well summed up by Ernst Robert Curtius:

'Life can be transformed into art, and art into life. It is a peculiarity of Proust's mind that this reciprocal transposition forms one of its basic rhythms ... The two spheres of existence which we are accustomed to

[1] See R. Virtanen, 'Proust's Metaphors from the Natural and the Exact Sciences', *Publications of the Modern Language Association of America*, lxix (1954), pp. 1038–59: p. 1039.
[2] 'Attitude scientifique de Proust', *Nouvelle Revue Française*, xx (1923), pp. 162–5.
[3] See B. Migliorini, 'La Metafora reciproca', *Saggi linguistici*, pp. 23–30; M. Sala, 'Sur les métaphores réciproques', *Revue de Linguistique* (Bucharest), v (1960), pp. 311–17.
[4] *Du Côté de chez Swann*, vol. I, p. 241.
[5] 'Slender, scaly, honeycombed, chequered, yellowing and gritty, *like two ears of corn*' (ibid., p. 192).

separate, and to set against each other, as art and life, have become fluid and have merged into one another. Art has lost some of its isolation, and life some of its reality.'[1]

A similar interpenetration of two spheres has been noticed in the imagery of Donne. 'In *Songs and Sonnets*, his poems of profane love, the metaphoric gloss is constantly drawn from the Catholic world of sacred love: to sexual love he applies the Catholic concepts of ecstasy, canonization, martyrdom, relics, while in some of his *Holy Sonnets* he addresses God in violent erotic figures ... The interchange between the spheres of sex and religion recognizes that sex is a religion and religion is a love.'[2]

A peculiar pattern of reciprocal imagery is the 'closed circle' of analogies which we have already noted (p. 147) in Giono's novel *Regain*. In most cases, both the tenor and the vehicle are drawn from the scenery and activities of the region where the story takes place. Only rarely does the author step outside this closed and narrow circle, as for example when he speaks of the 'squadron of clouds casting off their moorings' and of the evening sky 'foaming under the stern of the last cloud'.[3]

The study of relations between tenor and vehicle will also take the *tone* of the two elements into account. In many cases, the two do not belong to the same register, and the author will use the discrepancy for stylistic purposes. There are images which ennoble their tenor, and others which give it a homely air, ridicule it, or even degrade it. If, on the other hand, the disparity is not motivated by the context, the result will be a disproportionate—or, as Spitzer once called it, an 'excessive'—image.[4] This device is one of the characteristic forms of irony in Proust's style. Thus a casual remark by Eulalie, the old maid who amuses aunt Léonie with her gossip, is inordinately magnified by an imposing comparison: 'une révélation d'Eulalie—comme ces découvertes qui ouvrent tout d'un coup un champ insoupçonné à une science naissante et qui se traînait dans l'ornière—prouvait à ma tante qu'elle était, dans ses suppositions, bien au-dessous de la vérité'.[5] In the same way, Françoise chooses the ingredients for her meat jelly with the same meticulous care as Michelangelo did when he spent eight months in the mountains of Carrara in

---

[1] *Französischer Geist im zwanzigsten Jahrhundert*, Berne, 1951 ed., p. 294.
[2] Wellek and Warren, op. cit., pp. 213 f.
[3] 'L'escadre des nuages a largué les amarres ... on a vu bouillonner le ciel libre sous la poupe du dernier nuage' (p. 233).
[4] *Stilstudien*, vol. II, pp. 454 ff.
[5] 'A revelation by Eulalie—like those discoveries which suddenly open up an unsuspected field to a nascent science which had been moving in a rut—proved to my aunt that her assumptions were far under the mark' (*Du Côté de chez Swann*, vol. I, p. 157).

order to find the most perfect blocks of marble for the tomb of Pope Julius II.[1] It may be noted that this image is taken up once more towards the end of the cycle, but this time the terms are reversed: it is a work of art, the book which the narrator intends to write, that is compared to Françoise's culinary masterpiece 'whose jelly was enriched by adding to it so many choice pieces of meat'.[2]

D. The Functions of the Image

According to I. A. Richards, there are two basic types of imagery: 'functional' and 'ornamental'.[3] Another critic distinguishes between four uses of metaphor: 'illustrative', 'decorative', 'evocative', and 'emotive'.[4] In addition to these general categories, one can sometimes discover more specific functions by examining the imagery of a work as a whole and relating it to its wider context. I shall confine myself to discussing half a dozen such functions which play a prominent part in the craft of the modern novelist.

1. A particularly important class of images are those which develop into *symbols*. The term 'symbol' is notoriously ambiguous; here it simply means an image which expresses, in a memorable form, one of the main themes of a literary work. In most cases such images will recur time and again in the book; they may even, as we already know (p. 184), play the role of a kind of Wagnerian *leitmotiv*. In the words of a modern textbook, a metaphor will become a symbol (*a*) when its vehicle is 'concrete-sensuous', and (*b*) when it is recurrent and central.[5] Such is the importance of these symbolic images that they will sometimes be embodied in the title of the work, as for instance in several of Gide's books: *Les Nourritures terrestres*, *Paludes*, *La Porte étroite*, *La Symphonie pastorale*, *Les Faux-Monnayeurs*. In the last two novels there is a further complication: the titles, though clearly symbolic, may also be taken in the literal sense. In the former, Gertrude and the pastor actually attend a performance of Beethoven's *Pastoral Symphony* at Neuchâtel,[6] whereas in the latter there really are some counterfeit coins in circulation. Even more complicated is the symbolism of the plague in Camus's *La*

---

[1] *A l'ombre des jeunes filles en fleurs*, vol. I, p. 24.
[2] *Le Temps retrouvé*, vol. II, p. 213. Cf. J.-Y. Tadié, 'Invention d'un langage', *Nouvelle Revue Française*, lxxxi (1959), pp. 500–13: p. 511.
[3] *Speculative Instruments*, London, 1955, p. 46.
[4] F. W. Leakey, 'Intention in Metaphor', *Essays in Criticism*, iv (1954), pp. 191–8.
[5] Wellek and Warren, op. cit., pp. 330 f.
[6] In addition to the literal and symbolic significance of the title, there is also a pun on the adjective *pastoral* which may be taken to refer to the narrator who is a Protestant pastor. Cf. my *Image in the Modern French Novel*, p. 59.

Peste. The title itself is symbolic or, more precisely, allegorical, and the reader is warned of its implications in the epigraph which is taken from Defoe: '. . . it is as reasonable to represent one kind of imprisonment by another, as it is to represent anything that really exists by that which exists not'. In the literal sense, the plague means an epidemic which devastated the town of Oran in the 1940s; at the same time it is also the symbol of Nazi occupation and, at a far more general level, of evil in all its forms, human and non-human, moral and metaphysical, of the whole 'absurd' universe in which we live.[1] Furthermore, the idea of the plague itself gives rise to a variety of images which elaborate both its literal meaning and its symbolic aspects. Among these figures of the plague, the most gripping is that developed by Father Paneloux in his first sermon. This is a composite metaphor in which the double meaning of the word *fléau*, 'threshing-flail' and 'scourge, plague', is fused with the traditional image of the angel of the plague designating his victims by striking their houses with his hunting-spear. Carried away by his eloquence, the priest evokes 'l'immense pièce de bois tournoyant au-dessus de la ville, frappant au hasard et se relevant ensanglantée, éparpillant enfin le sang et la douleur humaine pour des semailles qui préparent les moissons de la vérité'.[2] Once this lurid image has been crystallized, it goes on haunting the narrator, Dr. Rieux, like an obsession; from time to time he seems to hear the hissing noise of the 'invisible flail ceaselessly stirring the warm air' over the town.[3] The symbol recurs for the last time towards the end of the epidemic when Rieux's friend Tarrou succumbs to the disease:

'Le fléau ne brassait plus le ciel de la ville. Mais il sifflait doucement dans l'air lourd de la chambre. C'était lui que Rieux entendait depuis des heures. Il fallait attendre que là aussi il s'arrêtât, que là aussi la peste se déclarât vaincue.'[4]

2. While Rieux's hallucinations have no practical consequences, those of Meursault in *L'Etranger* provide the only explanation, the psychological *motivation* of his crime. Dazed by the heat and glare of the sun, which

[1] See on this point J. Cruickshank, 'The Art of Allegory in *La Peste*', *Symposium*, xi (1957), pp. 61–74, and ch. VIII of his book, *Albert Camus and the Literature of Revolt*. Cf. also my *Image in the Modern French Novel*, pp. 256 ff.
[2] 'The immense piece of wood turning round and round over the town, striking at random and rising again, covered with blood, scattering human blood and suffering like seeds sown for the harvest of truth' (p. 112).
[3] 'L'invisible fléau qui brassait inlassablement l'air chaud' (p. 116).
[4] 'The plague no longer stirred the sky over the town. But it was hissing softly in the heavy air of the room. This is what Rieux had been hearing for hours. One had to wait until it stopped here too, until here too the plague admitted defeat' (p. 308).

pours down 'like a blinding rain' on the Algerian beach, Meursault is assailed by hallucinatory sensations which he expresses in the only way open to him—by a series of violent images:

'L'Arabe a tiré son couteau qu'il m'a présenté dans le soleil. La lumière a giclé sur l'acier et c'était *comme une longue lame étincelante* qui m'atteignait au front . . . Je ne sentais plus que *les cymbales* du soleil sur mon front et, indistinctement, *le glaive éclatant* jailli du couteau toujours en face de moi. *Cette épée brûlante rongeait* mes cils et *fouillait* mes yeux douloureux.'[1]

Unable to distinguish any longer between illusion and reality, Meursault seems to have identified the 'long flashing blade' of light reflected from the knife with the knife itself; and when the light hit his forehead and penetrated into his aching eyes 'like a burning sword', he pulled the trigger in a kind of muddled self-defence. Without the implicit motivation furnished by the imagery, his crime would be completely unexplained and incomprehensible; it would be a gratuitous act. This is the reason for the curiously uneven distribution of images in the novel, which was noted on p. 121: in a narrative which sedulously avoids idle or ornamental similes and metaphors, functional imagery comes to the fore at a crucial point in the story, to play a vital role in the inner structure of the work.

3. Some images and image-patterns carry strong emotional overtones and convey implicit *value-judgments*. These sometimes take the form of animal imagery which, as already noted (pp. 147 f.), tends to have pejorative connotations and to suggest that human beings look or behave like beasts. In a particularly repellent scene in Proust, the vividness and cruelty of the image helps to impress on the reader's mind an episode which will play an important part much later in the cycle:

'elles se poursuivirent en sautant, faisant voleter leurs larges manches comme des ailes et gloussant et piaillant comme des oiseaux amoureux.'[2]

In a different key, the parallels which Proust constantly draws between Swann's love for Odette and various forms of illness and disease bring out,

[1] 'The Arab drew his knife which he held out towards me in the sun. The light splashed up from the steel and it was *like a long flashing blade* which hit me on the forehead. . . . All I could now feel were *the cymbals* of the sun on my forehead and, indistinctly, the *dazzling sword* which had flashed up from the knife still facing me. *This burning sword was scorching* my eyelashes and *thrusting* into my aching eyes' (pp. 87 f.). For a detailed analysis of the passage, see my *Image in the Modern French Novel*, pp. 248 ff.

[2] 'They pursued each other leaping, their wide sleeves fluttering like wings, clucking and squealing like birds in love' (*Du Côté de chez Swann*, vol. I, p. 212).

as we have seen, the morbid nature of the infatuation more forcefully than any direct statement could have done.

4. The general movement of imagery can also express the *philosophical* ideas or personal aspirations of a writer. We have seen how Sartre conveys an important aspect of his doctrine through the unpleasant medium of insect images, and how Giono's pantheism shines through the dense network of analogies which interknit the various spheres of nature: human, animal, vegetal and inanimate. 'All the errors of man', this writer has proclaimed, 'spring from imagining that he is treading a dead earth, while his footsteps are imprinted in a flesh of good will',[1] and this philosophical attitude finds its congenial expression in the imagery.

In a less articulate way, the deepest *aspirations* of Alain-Fournier are revealed in the poetic images he derives from the sea which was for him the symbol of infinity, of purity, of an unattainable ideal, and also a symbol of mystery and adventure. In a story which takes place miles away from the sea, these images transport us into a kind of 'other landscape', to use the author's own phrase;[2] thanks to them, ordinary everyday objects and experiences 'suffer a sea-change into something rich and strange': houses and rooms are transmuted into ships sailing in mid-ocean or lying at anchor for the night, or again into lonely rocks on the sea-shore: 'demeure d'où partirent et où revinrent se briser, comme des vagues sur un rocher désert, mes aventures'.[3]

5. Imagery will also enable a writer to talk about experiences which could not have been expressed, or even conceived of, in any other way. How could Proust have formulated his inner vision of memory and of time without the numerous and delicate images which help to fix and clarify their elusive aspects? This process of metaphorical expression begins quite early in the cycle, in the analysis of sleep and awakening on the opening pages, in the episode of the piece of *madeleine* dipped in tea, with its powerful imagery of light and weight, and in the 'Einsteinian' picture of a four-dimensional space-time continuum, inspired by the village church at Combray:

'un édifice occupant, si l'on peut dire, un espace à quatre dimensions —la quatrième étant celle du Temps—déployant à travers les siècles son vaisseau qui, de travée en travée, de chapelle en chapelle, semblait

---

[1] Quoted by H. Peyre, *The Contemporary French Novel*, New York, 1955, p. 147.
[2] See H. March, 'The "Other Landscape" of Fournier', *Publications of the Modern Language Association of America*, lvi (1941), pp. 266–79; cf. also my *Image in the Modern French Novel*, pp. 110 f.
[3] 'The house from which my adventures set out and where they came back, to break like waves against a lonely rock' (*Le Grand Meaulnes*, Paris, 1933 ed., p. 2).

vaincre et franchir, non pas seulement quelques mètres, mais des époques successives d'où il sortait victorieux.'[1]

And the process continues throughout the cycle, right down to the nightmarish vision which concludes the last volume:

'comme si les hommes étaient juchés sur de vivantes échasses, grandissant sans cesse, parfois plus hautes que des clochers, finissant par leur rendre la marche difficile et périlleuse, et d'où tout d'un coup ils tombent . . . ils touchent simultanément, comme des géants, plongés dans les années, à des époques vécues par eux, si distantes—entre lesquelles tant de jours sont venus se placer—dans le Temps.'[2]

6. Images may also have an indirect or oblique function: they may be part of the linguistic *portrait*, or caricature, of a person. The writer may try to adapt the imagery used by his characters to their occupation, interests and experiences. In Victor Hugo's *Booz endormi*, which is based on the Book of Ruth, we see Ruth herself gazing up at the night sky after a day spent working on the land, her mind still full of the people and objects she saw during the day:

> Le croissant fin et clair parmi ces fleurs de l'ombre
> Brillait à l'occident, et Ruth se demandait,
> Immobile, ouvrant l'œil à moitié sous ses voiles,
> Quel dieu, quel *moissonneur* de l'éternel été,
> Avait, en s'en allant, négligemment jeté
> Cette *faucille* d'or dans le *champ* des étoiles.[3]

Even when the imagery is not so closely modelled on the speaker's personality, there must be some general correspondence and harmony between the two (cf. pp. 146 f.). Proust excels in this as in other forms of linguistic portrayal: one need think only of the clichés and stock metaphors of Dr. Cottard (cf. p. 179), of the macaronic style and pseudo-

---

[1] 'A building which occupied, if one may put it that way, a four-dimensional space—the fourth being that of Time—unfolding its nave over the centuries, which, from bay to bay, from chapel to chapel, seemed to conquer and to cross not merely a few yards but successive epochs from which it emerged victorious' (*Du Côté de chez Swann*, vol. I, p. 86). On points of similarity between the ideas of Proust and Einstein, see my *Image in the Modern French Novel*, pp. 140 f.

[2] 'As though men were perched on living stilts, constantly growing, sometimes higher than steeples, which in the end make their progress difficult and perilous, until they suddenly fall down . . . like giants immersed in the years, they touch simultaneously the periods through which they lived, so far away—separated by so many days—in Time.'

[3] 'Amid these flowers of darkness, the fine and clear crescent shone in the West, and Ruth, motionless, half-opening her eyes beneath her veils, wondered what god, what *harvester* of the eternal summer had, when leaving, casually thrown this golden *sickle* on the *field* of the stars.'

Homeric images of Bloch ('par Apollon, tu goûteras, cher maître, les joies nectaréennes de l'Olympos'),[1] or of the modern analogies which Professor Brichot uses when talking about history to fashionable audiences:

'Je crois avoir entendu que le docteur parlait de cette vieille chipie de Blanche de Castille ... Je reconnais d'ailleurs que notre ineffable république athénienne—ô combien!—pourrait honorer en cette capétienne obscurantiste le premier des préfets de police à poigne.'[2]

A more ambiguous case of portrayal through imagery is that of Legrandin whom we have already encountered on several occasions (pp. 104 f., 109, 146). His conversation, as we already know, is a curious mixture of discordant elements: it is refined, cultivated, and not without a certain poetic quality; at the same time it is affected, bookish and at times ridiculously pretentious. Some of his high-flown images would sound outright comical if one did not remember the context in which they occur: he is anxious to avoid awkward questions about his social contacts, and his rhetoric enables him to go off at a tangent:

'la brise de votre jeunesse apporte jusqu'à moi l'odeur des parterres que mes vieilles prunelles ne distinguent plus';[3]

'J'ai des amis partout où il y a des troupes d'arbres blessés, mais non vaincus, qui se sont rapprochés pour implorer ensemble avec une obstination pathétique un ciel inclément qui n'a pas pitié d'eux.'[4]

Not all of Legrandin's images are, however, ridiculous; some are almost indistinguishable from the narrator's own style, as for example when he speaks of 'l'émail polychrome des pensées'[5] or when he describes the poet Paul Desjardins as a 'limpid water-colourist'.[6] Or take this poetic, if somewhat precious, evocation of the evening sky at Balbec, which has some unmistakably Proustian touches:

---

[1] 'By Apollo, you will taste, my dear sir, the nectarine pleasures of Olympus' (*Du Côté de chez Swann*, vol. I, p. 123).

[2] 'I think I heard the doctor mention that old cat, Blanche de Castille ... I admit, incidentally, that our unspeakable Athenian republic—and how!—might honour this obscurantist Capetian as the first prefect of police with a strong hand' (ibid., vol. II, pp. 49–50).

[3] 'The breeze of your youth brings me the scent of flower-beds which my old eyes can no longer discern' (ibid., vol. I, p. 170).

[4] 'I have friends wherever there are groups of wounded but unconquered trees which have drawn together to implore jointly, with pathetic persistence, an unmerciful sky that has no pity for them' (ibid., vol. I, p. 174).

[5] 'The polychrome enamel of pansies' (ibid., vol. I, p. 168).

[6] Ibid., vol. I, p. 160.

'dans cette atmosphère humide et douce s'épanouissent, le soir, en quelques instants, de ces bouquets célestes, bleus et roses, qui sont incomparables et qui mettent souvent des heures à se faner. D'autres s'effeuillent tout de suite, et c'est alors plus beau encore de voir le ciel entier que jonche la dispersion d'innombrables pétales soufrés ou roses.'[1]

Even Proust's synaesthetic vision reappears in another rather precious passage part of which has already been quoted:

'où les yeux las ne tolèrent plus qu'une lumière, celle qu'une belle nuit comme celle-ci prépare et distille avec l'obscurité, où les oreilles ne peuvent plus écouter de musique que celle que joue le clair de lune sur la flûte du silence.'[2]

One has again the impression, as we had in discussing Legrandin's syntax (p. 109), that the author is indulging here in a kind of self-parody, in what one critic has called a 'Proustian pastiche of Proust' himself.[3] An explicit statement on this ambiguous attitude is found in a later volume of the cycle where Albertine surprises the narrator by producing a number of highly sophisticated images from art, which she obviously learnt from him but—and this is the crucial point—which he would never have thought of using in speech:

'ces paroles du genre de celles qu'elle prétendait dues uniquement à mon influence, à la constante cohabitation avec moi, ces paroles que pourtant, je n'aurais jamais dites, comme si quelque défense m'était faite par quelqu'un d'inconnu de jamais user dans la conversation de formes littéraires ... en la voyant se hâter d'employer, en parlant, des images si écrites et qui me semblaient réservées pour un autre usage plus sacré et que j'ignorais encore.'[4]

---

[1] 'In this moist and mild atmosphere, some of those incomparable celestial bouquets, blue and pink, blossom out, in the evening, in a matter of seconds, and often take hours to fade. Others shed their leaves at once, and then it is an even lovelier sight when the whole sky is strewn with countless scattered petals, yellow or pink' (ibid., vol. I, p. 173).

[2] 'When there is only one kind of light your tired eyes can bear, that which a lovely night like this prepares and distils from darkness, when there is only one kind of music your ears can listen to, that which the moonlight plays on the flute of silence' (ibid., vol. I, p. 168; cf. above, p. 146).

[3] F. C. Green, *The Mind of Proust*, Cambridge, 1949, p. 40.

[4] 'Words of the kind which, she claimed, were due solely to my influence, to her permanent cohabitation with me, but which I myself would never have said, as though some unknown person had somehow forbidden me ever to use literary forms in conversation ... seeing her in such a hurry to employ, in speech, images which belong to written language and which seemed to me reserved for another, more sacred use of which I was as yet unaware' (*La Prisonnière*, vol. I, pp. 159 f.; cf. M. Hindus, *The Proustian Vision*, New York, 1954, p. 55).

To talk of the 'sacred' use of imagery may seem surprising; yet if one remembers the central place which metaphor occupied not only in Proust's aesthetics but in his whole doctrine of involuntary memory,[1] one will understand what he had in mind.

The same technique of portrayal through imagery is applied on a much larger scale in novels told by a narrator (cf. pp. 146 f.). A final example, from Gide's *Symphonie pastorale*, will show the subtle effects which can be obtained from this device. In this novel, the pastor unwittingly reveals his nascent love for the blind girl by using some highly poetic images which contrast with the simple, unadorned style of the narrative:

'C'était moins un sourire qu'une transfiguration. Tout à coup ses traits *s'animèrent*; ce fut comme un éclairement subit, pareil à cette lueur purpurine dans les hautes Alpes qui précédant l'aurore, fait vibrer le sommet neigeux qu'elle désigne et sort de la nuit; on eût dit une coloration mystique; et je songeai également à la piscine de Bethesda au moment que l'ange descend et vient réveiller l'eau dormante.'[2]

At the time when he writes this, the pastor is not yet aware of the real nature of his feelings for Gertrude, but his love is betrayed by the lyricism of his style. The delicate irony of the passage is an instance of that quality of 'Racinian' economy for which the *Symphonie* has been rightly praised.[3]

André Breton once made a significant statement about the way he is affected by images. 'Seule l'image,' he wrote, 'en ce qu'elle a d'imprévu et de soudain, me donne la mesure de la libération possible et cette libération est si complète qu'elle m'effraye.'[4] One can well understand the sense of liberation, of unfettered self-expression, that imagery can produce in the poet or indeed in any creative writer. As we saw in another chapter, his grammatical and even his lexical choices are normally restricted to a small number of alternatives whereas his metaphorical resources, though not unlimited, range over an incomparably wider field. To this freedom of choice should be added the infinite plasticity of imagery: the wide variety of forms it can assume, the multiplicity of

[1] See my *Image in the Modern French Novel*, pp. 124 ff.

[2] 'It was not so much a smile as a transfiguration. All at once her features *came to life*; it was like a sudden illumination, similar to that crimson glimmer in the high Alps which, just before dawn, makes a snowy peak vibrate by designating it and lifting it out of the night; it reminded you of a mystical halo; and I also thought of the pool of Bethesda at the moment when the angel descends to wake up the sleeping water' (Paris, 1921 ed., pp. 42–3).

[3] E. Starkie, *André Gide*, Paris, 1953, p. 38.

[4] 'The image alone gives me, by its unexpectedness and suddenness, a full sense of potential liberation, and this liberation is so complete that it frightens me' (quoted by G. Antoine, loc. cit., p. 151).

relations it can posit, the diversity of functions it can fulfil. If we consider, with Flaubert and Proust, that style is primarily a personal and idiosyncratic mode of vision (cf. p. 121), then imagery holds a key-position in style, for human language is made in such a way that it is through images that this vision can be communicated in the most direct, most original and most memorable form. The more deeply one probes into the nature of imagery the more one is struck by the perennial validity of Aristotle's statement: 'The greatest thing by far is to have a command of metaphor. This alone cannot be imparted to another: it is the mark of genius.'[1]

[1] Quoted by C. Day Lewis, op. cit., p. 17.

PART III

LANGUAGE AND THOUGHT

CHAPTER X

WORDS AND CONCEPTS

IT is almost a commonplace for a writer and a thinker to complain about the inadequacy of the words he has to use. This critical attitude to language has a long tradition behind it. Plato already voiced similar ideas when he wrote in his *Seventh Epistle*: 'No intelligent man will ever be so bold as to put in language those things which his reason has contemplated ... if he should be betrayed into so doing, then surely not the gods but mortals have utterly blasted his wits.'[1] In recent centuries, this preoccupation with language has become increasingly persistent. A few voices from the past and the present will show the mood in which the problem was approached by different periods:

'Men imagine that their minds have command of language: but it often happens that language bears rule over their minds' (Francis Bacon).[2]

'I am not yet so lost in lexicography, as to forget that words are the daughters of earth, and that things are the sons of heaven' (Dr. Johnson, *A Dictionary of the English Language*, Preface).[3]

He gave man speech, and speech created thought,
Which is the measure of the universe ...
Language is a perpetual orphic song,
Which rules with Daedal harmony a throng
Of thoughts and forms, which else senseless and shapeless were.
                          Shelley, *Prometheus Unbound*[4].

So here I am, in the middle way, having had twenty years—
Twenty years largely wasted, the years of *l'entre deux guerres*—
Trying to learn to use words, and every attempt
Is a wholly new start, and a different kind of failure
Because one has only learnt to get the better of words
For the thing one no longer has to say, or the way in which

---

[1] Quoted by W. M. Urban, *Language and Reality*, p. 53.
[2] Quoted by S. Potter, *Language in the Modern World*, London, 1960, p. 19.
[3] Quoted by the *Oxford Dictionary of Quotations*, p. 212.
[4] Act II, scene 4, ll. 72–3; Act IV, ll. 415–17. See L. J. Zillman (ed.), *Shelley's 'Prometheus Unbound'. A Variorum Edition*, Seattle, 1959, pp. 212 and 288.

One is no longer disposed to say it. And so each venture
Is a new beginning, a raid on the inarticulate
With shabby equipment always deteriorating
In the general mess of imprecision of feeling,
Undisciplined squads of emotion.

T. S. Eliot, Four Quartets: East Coker[1].

Similar views are expressed by poets and prose writers in other countries. 'Name is but sound and smoke, shrouding heaven's golden glow', says Goethe's Faust,[2] and Schiller exclaims: 'Why cannot the living spirit appear to the spirit? When the mind *speaks*, alas, it is no longer the *mind* that is speaking.'[3] To Flaubert, human speech is like a 'tinny old piano on which we beat out tunes fit to make a bear dance, when we would like to touch the stars'.[4] Valéry likens words to light planks thrown over an abyss: you may walk across, but you must not try to stop.[5] The acme of disillusionment and scepticism about language is reached in Albert Camus's picture of man's isolation in a universe where words are devoid of meaning: 'Il s'agit de savoir si même nos mots les plus justes et nos cris les plus réussis ne sont pas privés de sens, si le langage n'exprime pas, pour finir, la solitude définitive de l'homme dans un monde muet.'[6]

Among the various aspects of human speech singled out in these and other statements, one of the most intriguing and most disturbing is the one referred to by Bacon and, more explicitly, by Shelley: the idea that language is not merely a means for expressing our thoughts, but that it can exercise a decisive influence on the latter. This idea, though not entirely modern, looms large in contemporary linguistics and philosophy. When Shelley published *Prometheus Unbound* in 1820, a reviewer contemptuously remarked: 'Prometheus, according to Mr. Percy Bysshe Shelley, "Gave man speech, and *speech created thought*"—which is

---

[1] Cf. R. Quirk, *The Use of English*, p. 232.

[2] Act III, scene 9 (Sir Theodore Martin's translation). ('Name ist Schall und Rauch, umnebelnd Himmelsglut.')

[3] *Votivtafeln*, 84: 'Die Sprache.' ('Warum kann der lebendige Geist dem Geist nicht erscheinen? Spricht die Seele, so spricht ach! schon die *Seele* nicht mehr.')

[4] 'La parole humaine est comme un chaudron fêlé où nous battons des mélodies à faire danser des ours quand on voudrait attendrir les étoiles' (quoted from *Madame Bovary* by Wartburg, *Evolution et structure de la langue française*, p. 225).

[5] 'J'en suis venu, hélas, à comparer ces paroles par lesquelles on traverse si lestement l'espace d'une pensée, à des planches légères jetées sur un abîme, qui souffrent le passage et point la station' (*Monsieur Teste*, 32nd ed., Paris, Gallimard, p. 74).

[6] 'The question is whether even our most exact words and our most successful cries are not devoid of meaning, whether, in the last analysis, language does not express the final loneliness of man in a silent world' ('Sur une philosophie de l'expression', *Poésie 44*, no. 17, pp. 15–23, quoted by J. Cruickshank, *French Studies*, x, 1956, p. 245).

exactly, in our opinion, the cart creating the horse; the sign creating the inn; the effect creating the cause.'[1] Nowadays we are no longer so sure as to which is the cart and which is the horse; in fact the whole analogy seems to us inappropriate and misleading. But while it is generally agreed that language can influence our thoughts, that it can shape them, fix them, canalize them, limit them, or even distort and sidetrack them, it is not very easy to find concrete examples of such influence. Only close co-operation between a number of disciplines—philosophy, psychology, neurology, anthropology, linguistics and others—can hope to throw light on these difficult and delicate processes. The problem is further complicated by the fact that all elements of language—sounds and spellings, suffixes and prefixes, words and idioms, inflexions, syntactical constructions, etc.—can have a share in influencing our thoughts, and we shall need different techniques to study their impact at these various levels.[2]

The remarks which follow will be confined to one aspect of the process: the part played by *words* in the elaboration of our concepts and in our analysis of the world. We shall approach the problem from three different angles. First we shall consider certain disorders of language which may help to explain the influence of words on thinking under normal conditions. Next we shall discuss one or two methods devised by modern linguistics to deal with these questions. Finally we shall examine some of the shortcomings of our words and the effects of these shortcomings on philosophical as well as on ordinary thought.

A. The Evidence of Aphasia

In a recent article, the eminent neurologist Lord Brain has distinguished between three main schools of thought in aphasia studies.[3] First in the field were the 'psycho-anatomists' who tried to connect specific disorders of speech with localized lesions of the brain. Next came the 'clinical psychologists' whose main concern was to describe and classify the various forms of aphasia as psychological disturbances. A famous example of this method was Henry Head's distinction between four types of disorder: verbal (defective word-formation), syntactical (defective grammar and sentence-structure), nominal (defective naming), and

---

[1] Quoted in Zillman, op. cit., p. 693.
[2] See esp. J. H. Greenberg, 'Concerning Inferences from Linguistic to Nonlinguistic Data', in H. Hoijer (ed.), *Language in Culture*, pp. 3–19.
[3] 'The Neurology of Language', *Speech Pathology and Therapy*, iv (1961), pp. 47–59: pp. 48 ff.

semantic (inability to understand the significance of words and phrases in normal sequence).[1] The third school, which may be described as 'empirical', prefers to avoid any psychological interpretations; it merely states that certain forms of aphasia can be clinically recognized, and emphasizes that these forms are apt to merge into one another. Lord Brain himself has thrown into the debate a new concept which he borrowed from Kant: that of the *schema* or physiological disposition which enables us to recognize a sound, a word or other linguistic element. 'A single word', he writes, 'may be uttered in an unlimited number of ways, which differ from each other in pitch and volume to say nothing of the differences produced by local dialect . . . as we learn to speak we learn to attend physiologically to the pattern of sounds which are characteristic of a particular word however it may be uttered, and in order that we may do this there must exist in the nervous system a physiological disposition for each word which I have called an auditory word-schema. This schema is, as it were, a resonator which reacts to the pattern structure of an individual word, and it is thus an essential link between the word and its meaning.'[2] Lord Brain distinguishes between five kinds of schemas, any one of which, as well as combinations of them, may be disorganized by aphasia: (1) auditory phoneme-schemas, (2) central word-schemas, (3) word-meaning schemas, (4) sentence schemas and (5) motor phoneme-schemas.[3]

Among the various forms of aphasia, those are particularly relevant to our problem where a 'word-meaning schema' is lost or damaged. Our words, except proper names, stand for class-concepts: they denote, not single objects, qualities, events, etc., but whole categories of these. If the word is lost, if the relation between name and sense is disrupted, then the class-concept, our awareness of the category, may perish with it. 'Nomina si nescis, perit et cognitio rerum', said Linnaeus.[4] A classic example of this process is the case, recorded by Gelb and Goldstein nearly forty years ago, of a patient suffering from colour amnesia. In a more recent work, Professor Goldstein himself has given the following account of this case:

---

[1] H. Head, *Aphasia and Kindred Disorders of Speech*, Cambridge, 1926, vol. I, Part II, ch. 4. A detailed account of Head's theory will be found in Stern, *Meaning and Change of Meaning*, pp. 90–102. Cf. R. Jakobson, 'Aphasia as a Linguistic Problem', in H. Werner (ed.), *On Expressive Language*, Worcester, Mass., 1955, pp. 69–81; Id., 'Kindersprache, Aphasie und allgemeine Lautgesetze', reprinted in R. Jakobson, *Selected Writings*, vol. I, The Hague, 1962, pp. 328–401.

[2] 'The Semantic Aspect of Aphasia', *Archivum Linguisticum*, viii (1956), pp. 20–7: pp. 21 f.

[3] 'The Neurology of Language', p. 56.

[4] 'If you do not know the names, the knowledge of things is also lost.'

'If the patient were asked to choose, using a given sample in a heap of many nuances of all colours . . . all similar ones, regardless of brightness or darkness, he proceeded very hesitatingly and slowly; he picked out *seemingly totally wrong ones* and put them aside; sometimes he rejected a (for us) right one, after he had taken it in his hand; he apparently had the greatest difficulty with this task. He compared the sample again and again with the skeins in the heap, till he chose some which were *identical or very similar to the sample.* Thus, of course, he could choose only very few. The task of choosing identical colours he fulfilled quickly and absolutely correctly.

'Apparently the patient *did not make his choices according to the basic colour quality, but to the experience he had with each individual skein.* This became evident in other kinds of behaviour: he might match a given very bright shade of red with a blue or green skein of great brightness, apparently determined in his choice by the identical brightness. His choice might be determined by another attribute of the given skein, by coldness, warmth, etc. But it is an amazing thing that this patient, who seemed to be choosing according to a certain attribute, was not able to follow this procedure if it were demanded of him, e.g. to choose all bright ones. He further did *not seem to be able to hold on to a certain procedure.*'[1]

Professor Goldstein sums up the position by saying that 'the patient's approach was directed *not to the colour categories* to which the skein belonged but to the *individual appearance of the skein* . . . According to which characteristic of the sample impressed him in the moment he proceeded, he *did not sort, but simply matched*'.[2]

Rather similar observations were made by Head on certain cases which he classified as 'nominal aphasia':

'During the tests with colours, No. 2 made such gross mistakes that he might have been thought to be colour-blind; for white was called "green", black "red", and green "blue". Exactly the same kind of error occurred when he chose a colour from its printed name on a card; on this occasion he even chose white for black, and black for green. More or less similar mistakes were made by all the patients of this group, and No. 22 was sent to me as an example of aphasia with colour-blindness. But not one of them had the slightest difficulty in choosing, from amongst the colours on the table, that which matched the one I had shown him. From these observations we might be tempted to think that they had lost this

[1] K. Goldstein, *Language and Language Disturbances*, New York, 1948, p. 255.
[2] Ibid., pp. 255 f.

knowledge of the nature of colour, that they were in fact "mind-blind". But No. 2, in his attempts to explain to me his difficulty in reading the printed cards, began to point to my white coat, to his khaki tie, the blue band on his arm which he wore as a wounded officer, and the green of the trees outside his window. Instead of the names of the colours, he was therefore encouraged to use a set of similitudes; black was "what you do for the dead", red "what the Staff wear", or, pointing to the lapel of his tunic, "where the Staff have it", blue was "my arm" . . .'[1]

The same patient was better than average at chess, but could no longer play bridge. 'The names of the cards bother me', he complained. 'It's just names; I used to play a good game at bridge.'[2]

The loss of class-concepts and of the corresponding ability to generalize, to classify one's experiences and to organize them into categories, restricts the aphasic to a highly concrete form of language which is reminiscent of the speech-habits of children and of primitive races (cf. above, pp. 72 ff.). When a woman patient was shown a knife next to a pencil, she described it as a 'pencil sharpener'; when the knife was next to an apple, it became an 'apple parer'; next to bread, it was a 'bread-knife'; when she saw it together with a fork, she called them 'knife and fork'. Yet she was unable to find the word *knife* by itself, and when she was asked whether one could not simply call the object a *knife* in each case, she disagreed.[3] As Professor K. Goldstein, who recorded this case, puts it, such a patient 'cannot use words in naming because he cannot assume the abstract attitude . . . He cannot even understand what we mean by naming because that presupposes the abstract attitude, which he cannot assume . . . What appear to us as objects in an organized world are for them complex sense experiences of an individual singular character which can be reacted to in a definite way but which are not connected with each other in a systematic unit'.[4]

Observations like these clearly show the profound and lasting effect which speech disturbances can have on the patient's thinking and on his whole outlook. Yet, as Lord Brain has warned us at a recent symposium on semantics,[5] one should handle such evidence with great circumspection

---

[1] Head, op. cit., vol. I, p. 242; cf. Stern, op. cit., p. 97.

[2] Head, op. cit., vol. I, p. 256; cf. Stern, loc. cit.

[3] K. Goldstein, 'The Nature of Language', in R. N. Anshen (ed.), *Language: An Enquiry into its Meaning and Function*, New York, 1957, pp. 18–40: pp. 20 f.

[4] Ibid., pp. 23 f. and 28. Cf. by the same author: *Language and Language Disturbances*, Part I, ch. 4, and *passim*; 'On Naming and Pseudonaming, from Experiences in Psychopathology', *Word*, ii (1946), pp. 1–7. See also R. Brown, *Words and Things*, pp. 287 ff.

[5] 'The Semantic Aspect of Aphasia', pp. 20 f. Cf. also R. Jakobson, 'The Cardinal Dichotomy in Language', in Anshen, op. cit., pp. 155–73: pp. 161 ff.

and avoid jumping to conclusions. For one thing, a word which an aphasic is unable to utter in isolation may not be completely lost; it may merely be 'less generally available'. In the case just mentioned, the patient could not say *knife* by itself, but was able to produce the word in the combinations 'bread-knife' and 'knife and fork'. There is the famous story of the aphasic who seemed to have forgotten the word *no* until, exasperated by the neurologist's attempts to make him say it, he exclaimed: 'But I can't say *no!*' Another patient was unable to say *five* when requested, but he could say it when counting from one to ten. Elsewhere, a word may be totally lost but some general impression of its meaning, or of the word-class to which it belongs, may still survive: the patient may choose another term from the same class or sphere (*lawyer* instead of *doctor*), a vague expression for a specific one ('these ladies' for 'the nurses'), etc.

It may also happen that a patient's processes of thought are less damaged than his speech might suggest. An instructive example, rather different from those mentioned so far, has been reported by Lord Brain:

'An elderly solicitor had had a stroke which had rendered him aphasic, and, it was suggested, had so reduced his mental powers as to make him demented. In order to test this I put to him two questions of law, and, in spite of his gross speech difficulty, he made it clear that he knew the right answers. I asked him to explain the difference between a void and a voidable contract. (The first is invalid from the beginning, the second can be declared invalid.) He said: "Voidable is means that entirely finished. No. Abinit. Abnationally. Voidable is estopped." Then he started again: "Void is ab initio. Voidable is at the decision of the court." '[1]

Examples like the above emphasize the need for caution in speculating about the effects of aphasia on thought. Yet everyone would agree that these effects are both deep and far-reaching, that the aphasic is not simply 'a normal person minus language'.[2] Naturally, there are differences of opinion regarding the consequences of aphasia. Professor Goldstein goes so far as to claim that aphasics 'have no "world" ' and that they 'are deprived of the essential characteristics of men ... The words of the patient have lost their symbolic function and with that the ability to work as a mediating agent between sense experiences and the world in which man alone can be man'.[3] Others would put the

[1] 'The Semantic Aspect of Aphasia', p. 24.
[2] F. Kainz, *Psychologie der Sprache*, vol. II, 2nd ed., Stuttgart, 1960, p. 350.
[3] 'The Nature of Language', pp. 28 f.

effects of aphasia rather lower, without, however, minimizing their importance. Lord Brain's carefully worded conclusions are worth quoting:

'In the highly selective forms of aphasia, which may be said to involve one channel of communication only, thought does not seem to be impaired as a rule ... in expressive aphasia thought may be much more normal than would be supposed, judging from what the patient has power to express. Nevertheless, I believe that all patients who have any substantial degree of expressive aphasia are hampered in thought. The solicitor who remembered much more law than he could easily formulate, would have been incapable of dealing with new problems. This effect of expressive aphasia upon thinking is not surprising if we realize the essential part played by words in the acquisition of all abstract ideas.'[1]

In spite of the complex and somewhat inconclusive nature of the evidence, research on aphasia has already made a valuable contribution to the study of relations between language and thought, and clearly remains one of the most promising avenues of approach to the problem. Further progress will partly depend on effective co-operation between neurologists, psychologists, linguists and others concerned with various aspects of this difficult question.

B. The Evidence of Ordinary Language

In present-day linguistics, two major theories have been evolved to explore the influence of language upon thinking. The two theories apply different methods; they work on different data and, until quite recently, there was no liaison whatever between them. Yet, on closer inspection, there is a fundamental affinity between the two movements, and they turn out to be complementary rather than incompatible.

I. The Sapir-Whorf Hypothesis

As we saw in an earlier chapter (pp. 72 f.), philologists, anthropologists and others have often remarked on the profusion of specific terms and the paucity of generic ones in the languages of 'primitive' races. This impression, if substantiated by solid factual evidence, would be of direct relevance to our theme, for the alleged plethora of concrete, particular terms—'polyonomy', as it has been called[2]—does not merely *reflect* a certain view of the world but *perpetuates* it by passing it on to

---

[1] 'The Semantic Aspect of Aphasia', p. 26.
[2] Kainz, op. cit., vol. II, pp. 214 ff.

oncoming generations. A young savage born into a community which has no general term for 'tree' will be prevented by this very fact from rising to the level of abstraction which the concept of 'tree' represents. In the same way, as we have seen, the idea of 'plant' was non-existent for Roman and medieval speakers until Albertus Magnus crystallized it in the thirteenth century by giving a new and wider meaning to Latin *planta* 'sprout, slip, cutting'.

This theory sounds plausible enough at first sight, and it probably contains an element of truth; it does, however, suffer from some serious weaknesses. As already noted, the evidence supporting it is uneven, haphazard, and in some cases palpably unreliable; it would have to be carefully sifted and greatly extended before any conclusions could be reached. Nor is it easy to collect unimpeachable evidence in this field. It is a well-known fact that, in primitive communities, word-meanings are often fluid, context-bound and difficult to determine; as one authority puts it, 'words are practically unintelligible unless one knows the situation in which they are spoken'.[1] The picture may be further complicated and distorted by such factors as taboo and word-magic. But even if all these difficulties could be overcome, the theory of 'prelogical mentality' would still be vitiated by another, even more serious weakness. When it claims that the vocabulary of exotic languages is 'primitive' and 'over-concrete', that it suffers from a 'plethora' of specific and a 'paucity' of generic terms, it simply means that these languages are *different* from ours, that they analyse and divide up the world on other principles. In other words, the theory is based on a naive fallacy: the assumption that our own linguistic structure, and the general outlook which it embodies, are an ideal yardstick by which everything else should be judged.

There is also another error of perspective inherent in the theory. As already mentioned on p. 73, the alleged superabundance of concrete and particular terms may have nothing to do with faulty powers of generalization: it may be dictated by dire necessity, by the influence of climate and environment. Benjamin Lee Whorf has given an interesting example of the impact of living conditions on language. 'The Hopi (an American Indian tribe),' he writes, 'call insect, airplane, and aviator all by the same word, and feel no difficulty about it . . . This class seems to us too large and inclusive, but so would our class "snow" to an Eskimo. We have the same word for falling snow, snow on the ground, snow packed hard like

[1] A. Sommerfelt, *La Langue et la société. Caractères sociaux d'une langue de type archaïque*, Oslo, 1938, p. 125, quoted by Entwistle, *Aspects of Language*, p. 227. Cf. B. Malinowski, 'The Problem of Meaning in Primitive Languages', Supplement I to Ogden and Richards's *The Meaning of Meaning*, and Kainz, op. cit., vol. II, pp. 220 ff.

ice, slushy snow, wind-driven flying snow—whatever the situation may be. To an Eskimo, this all-inclusive word would be almost unthinkable; he would say that falling snow, slushy snow, and so on, are sensuously and operationally different, different things to contend with; he uses different words for them and for other kinds of snow. The Aztecs go even farther than we in the opposite direction, with "cold", "ice", and "snow" all represented by the same basic word with different terminations; "ice" is the noun form; "cold", the adjectival form; and for "snow", "ice mist" '.[1]

These and other considerations led Whorf to look afresh at the whole problem of language and thought, and to attack it on a far broader basis, free from any preconceptions. In this he had a predecessor in Edward Sapir who, as far back as 1929, had written these prophetic words:

'Human beings . . . are very much at the mercy of the particular language which has become the medium of expression for their society . . . the "real world" is to a large extent unconsciously built up on the language habits of the group . . . Even comparatively simple acts of perception are very much more at the mercy of the social patterns called words than we might suppose. If one draws some dozen lines, for instance, of different shapes, one perceives them as divisible into such categories as "straight", "crooked", "curved", "zigzag" because of the classificatory suggestiveness of the linguistic terms themselves. We see and hear and otherwise experience very largely as we do because the language habits of our community predispose certain choices of interpretation.'[2]

During the last ten years or so of his short life—he died in 1941, at the age of 44[3]—Whorf developed these ideas in a series of articles written with great verve and eloquence, and at times with an almost messianic fervour. In order to rid himself of any preconceptions inspired by 'Standard Average European', he concentrated on languages with a totally different structure, history and cultural background. His work on Hopi in particular convinced him that every language 'conceals a metaphysics'[4] which predetermines the speakers' outlook and view of the world. This led him to the formulation of the principle of 'linguistic

[1] *Language, Thought, and Reality. Selected Writings of Benjamin Lee Whorf*, ed. by J. B. Carroll, Massachusetts Institute of Technology, 1956, p. 216.
[2] Quoted by H. Hoijer in *Language and Culture*, ed. H. Hoijer, p. 92, from E. Sapir, *Selected Writings*, p. 162.
[3] See J. B. Carroll's introduction to Whorf, op. cit., p. 21.
[4] Ibid., p. 58.

relativity'. In an article published a year before his death he wrote:

'The background linguistic system (in other words, the grammar) of each language is not merely a reproducing instrument for voicing ideas but rather is itself the shaper of ideas, the program and guide for the individual's mental activity, for his analysis of impressions, for his synthesis of his mental stock in trade . . . We dissect nature along lines laid down by our native languages. The categories and types that we isolate from the world of phenomena we do not find there because they stare every observer in the face; on the contrary, the world is presented in a kaleidoscopic flux of impressions which has to be organized by our minds—and this means largely by the linguistic systems in our minds. We cut nature up, organize it into concepts, and ascribe significances as we do, largely because we are parties to an agreement to organize it in this way—an agreement that holds throughout our speech community and is codified in the patterns of our language . . . We are thus introduced to a new principle of relativity, which holds that all observers are not led by the same physical evidence to the same picture of the universe, unless their linguistic backgrounds are similar, or can in some way be calibrated.'[1]

One of Whorf's most spectacular achievements is his analysis of the concept of time in Hopi and Standard Average European, and of the linguistic foundations of that concept. Hopi, according to him, is in a sense a 'timeless language', operating not with 'mathematical time', as we do, but with a kind of 'psychological time' reminiscent of Bergson's duration. This psychological time varies with each observer and does not permit of the idea of plurality; instead of saying: 'I stayed five days', the Hopi would say: 'I left on the fifth day.' Our time is conceived in terms of space or motion in space; Hopi time is inconceivable in such terms. Certain ideas suggested by our conception of time, such as the notion of simultaneity, would be meaningless in the Hopi system.[2]

The development of the Whorfian hypothesis was arrested by the premature death of its author. Since then there have been many interesting discussions on the theory and its implications,[3] but the position is still

[1] Ibid., pp. 212 ff.
[2] Ibid., pp. 158 and 216.
[3] See esp. the volume *Language and Culture. Conference on the Interrelations of Language and Other Aspects of Culture*, ed. H. Hoijer, which has already been mentioned, and H. Henle, 'Language, Thought, and Culture', which forms ch. I of the book of the same title. Cf. my reviews of these two volumes in *Romance Philology*, x (1957), pp. 225–32, and xiii (1959), pp. 68–72. For a recent critique of the Whorfian hypothesis, see Antal, op. cit., ch. VII. On the whole problem see now H. Schulte-Herbrüggen, *El Lenguaje y la visión del mundo*, Santiago, 1963.

P

inconclusive. Few scholars would accept Whorf's over-dramatized picture of man trapped within the walls of his native language; most of them would agree, however, that there is some truth in his basic principle. What is more difficult is to find specific instances which would prove or disprove the theory. As a philosopher has recently observed, 'it turns out very hard even to find incontrovertible illustrations of Whorf's thesis, let alone a demonstration of it'.[1] This is due to some extent to the nature of the problem itself. Thought and language are so closely linked, and it is so difficult to conceive of the former without the latter, that it is often impossible to say which influenced the other. Apart from this inherent difficulty, there are also two further limitations which restrict the usefulness of the theory and which could easily be remedied:

1. Whorf's attempt to free himself from any 'Standard Average European' bias was very laudable; one may wonder, however, whether he was right in confining himself almost exclusively to American Indian languages. Both Sapir and Whorf reacted violently against the intrusion of unwarranted value-judgments into linguistics, against the naively arrogant attitude which looked down on exotic languages as 'primitive' and inferior. At times they actually went to the other extreme. Speaking of the Hopi distinction between sense-data and inference ('I see that it is red—I see that it is new'), Whorf declared: 'In this field and in various others, English compared to Hopi is like a bludgeon compared to a rapier.'[2] Many years earlier Sapir had written: 'The lowliest South African Bushman speaks in the forms of a rich symbolic system that is in essence perfectly comparable to the speech of the cultivated Frenchman', and had added as an afterthought: 'It goes without saying that the more abstract concepts are not nearly so plentifully represented in the language of the savage, nor is there the rich terminology and the finer definition of nuances that reflect the higher culture. Yet the sort of linguistic development that parallels the historic growth of culture and which, in its later stages, we associate with literature is, at best, but a superficial thing.'[3] Many people would disagree with the view that the higher forms of linguistic expression, the harnessing of language to scientific, philosophical and legal needs or to artistic purposes, are in any sense superficial; but even if they are, they would provide an ideal testing-ground for the Sapir-Whorf hypothesis.

Let us take a specific example. In an article on punctual and segmen-

---

[1] L. J. Cohen, *The Diversity of Meaning*, p. 64.
[2] Op. cit., p. 85.
[3] *Language. An Introduction to the Study of Speech*, p. 22.

tative aspects of the verb in Hopi, Whorf concludes that this tribe has a language 'better equipped to deal with . . . vibratile phenomena than is our latest scientific terminology . . . According to the conceptions of modern physics, the contrast of particle and field of vibrations is more fundamental in the world of nature than such contrasts as space and time, or past, present, and future, which are the sort of contrasts that our own language imposes upon us. The Hopi aspect-contrast . . . being obligatory upon their verb forms, practically forces the Hopi to notice and observe vibratory phenomena, and furthermore encourages them to find names for and to classify such phenomena'.[1] The suggestion that Hopi is better adapted than 'Standard Average European' to the expression of certain concepts of modern science reminds one of Fritz Mauthner's dictum: if Aristotle had spoken Dacotan he would have had to adopt an entirely different logic or at any rate an entirely different theory of categories.[2] Such speculation, interesting as it may be, is purely gratuitous and unverifiable. It would be much more to the point to investigate the impact of language on scientific or philosophical ideas in communities which did actually evolve a physics or a logic of their own. The study of Chinese language and thought from this point of view would be more illuminating than that of Hopi, and one awaits with interest the discussion of these matters in a forthcoming volume of Dr. Needham's *Science and Civilization in China*.[3]

2. Another limitation of the Whorfian hypothesis is closely connected with the previous point. Although Whorf did occasionally deal with odd aspects of vocabulary,[4] his whole theory was focused on grammatical structure and on the categories which that structure imposes on human thought and behaviour. In an article which was not published till some months after his death, he clearly stated the reason for this preference: 'Because of the systematic, configurative nature of higher mind, the "patternment" aspect of language always overrides and controls the "lexation" or name-giving aspect. Hence the meanings of specific words are less important than we fondly fancy. Sentences, not words, are the essence of speech, just as equations and functions, and not bare numbers, are the real meat of mathematics.'[5] This statement calls for two comments. Firstly, we now know—though few people did at the time when

---

[1] Op. cit., pp. 55 f. Cf. also p. 151, n. 1, and p. 217.
[2] Quoted by A. H. Basson-D. J. O'Connor, 'Language and Philosophy. Some Suggestions for an Empirical Approach', *Philosophy*, xxii, no. 81, April 1947, pp. 49–65.
[3] See vol. I, Cambridge, 1954, p. 36. Cf. Gipper, op. cit., ch. III.
[4] Op. cit., pp. 135 ff., 199 ff., 208 ff., etc.
[5] Ibid., p. 258.

Whorf wrote these lines—that 'patterning' is not restricted to phonology and grammar, but that the vocabulary too has an organization and a structure of its own and that some of its sectors are closely integrated and rigidly hierarchized. Secondly, even though it is perfectly true that grammatical categories are deeper and more fundamental than lexical elements, they are also more general, and it is more difficult to determine the precise influence they exercise on our thinking. Once again we find that the Sapir-Whorf hypothesis has deliberately refrained from exploring the most promising testing-ground for its theses.

In view of these self-imposed limitations, it is clear that the Sapir-Whorf hypothesis can be usefully supplemented by another great movement in contemporary linguistics: the theory of lexical fields. The two schools of thought, based on similar premises which they have developed independently of each other,[1] are indeed complementary on both the points just mentioned: while Whorf concentrates on American Indian idioms, his European colleagues are more interested in the history and structure of their own languages; while he is primarily concerned with grammatical categories, they deal mainly, though by no means exlusively,[2] with lexical problems.

II. The Theory of Lexical Fields

It is often stated that certain words referring to intellectual or moral, psychological or social phenomena are untranslatable, that they have no real equivalent in any foreign language. Such statements are not always objective: in some cases they are obviously dictated by chauvinism or xenophobia. The *NED* quotes the following comment on the German term *Schadenfreude*: 'There is no English word for *Schadenfreude*, because there is no such feeling here.'[3] It is rather piquant to find the same term in a passage in Goethe's *Wilhelm Meister*, where one of the characters holds forth on the connotations of the 'untranslatable' French adjective *perfide*:

'French is an admirable language for reservations, half-truths and lies; it is a perfidious (*perfide*) language! I can find, thank God, no German word which would render *perfide* in its entire range. Our poor "disloyal" (*treulos*) is an innocent child in comparison. *Perfide* is disloyal with

[1] Cf. L. Weisgerber, *Vom Weltbild der deutschen Sprache*, vol. II, pp. 255 ff. See also Gipper, op. cit., ch. V.
[2] Cf. Weisgerber's *Grundzüge der inhaltbezogenen Grammatik*, mentioned on p. 12, n. 2, above.
[3] Quoted by L. Spitzer, 'Schadenfreude', *Essays in Historical Semantics*, New York, 1948, pp. 135–46: p. 135.

delight, arrogance and *Schadenfreude*. How enviable is the culture of a nation which can express such fine shades of meaning in one word!'[1]

Among these allegedly untranslatable terms, none has been more widely debated than French *esprit*. Maupassant has declared: 'Seul au monde, le Français a de l'*esprit*, et seul il le goûte et le comprend.'[2] Various German writers and thinkers, among them Goethe and Hegel, have been intrigued by the word and have probed its implications, and Kant included it in a list of French terms which cannot easily be rendered in any other language:

'The words *esprit* (instead of *bon sens*), *frivolité*, *galanterie*, *petit-maître*, *coquette*, *étourderie*, *point d'honneur*, *bon ton*, *bureau d'esprit*, *bon mot*, *lettre de cachet*, etc., cannot easily be translated into other languages, because they express the peculiar mentality of the nation using them rather than the object which one has in mind when one is thinking.'[3]

Before one can draw any conclusions from such discrepancies between languages, one must first be quite sure of one's facts. Even such a seemingly simple case as German *Schadenfreude* invites several comments:[4]

1. German is by no means the only language which has a name for this vice. Similar compounds exist in Russian (*zloradstvo*: *zlo* 'evil, harm' + *rad* 'glad'),[5] in Swedish (*skadeglädje*: *skada* 'harm, damage' + *glädje* 'joy'), and elsewhere. Even such a totally different idiom as Hungarian has an exact equivalent: *káröröm* (*kár* 'damage' + *öröm* 'joy'), which was coined, no doubt under German influence, during the great language-reform of the late eighteenth century.[6]

2. German *Schadenfreude* is not a native product but a direct or indirect reflex of Greek ἐπιχαιρεκακία 'joy over one's neighbour's

---

[1] 'Zu Reservationen, Halbheiten und Lügen ist es eine treffliche Sprache; sie ist eine perfide Sprache! ich finde, Gott sei Dank, kein deutsches Wort, um *perfid* in seinem ganzen Umfange auszudrücken. Unser armseliges *treulos* ist ein unschuldiges Kind dagegen. *Perfid* ist treulos mit Genuss, mit Übermut und Schadenfreude. O, die Ausbildung einer Nation ist zu beneiden, die so feine Schattierungen in *einem* Worte auszudrücken weiss' (*Wilhelm Meisters Lehrjahre*, Book V, ch. 16; *Goethes Werke*, Berlin, 1908, vol. VI, p. 325). Cf. Spitzer, loc. cit., p. 142, n. 1, and M. Wandruszka, *Der Geist der französischen Sprache*, Hamburg, 1959, pp. 20 f.

[2] 'The French are the only people in the world who have *esprit*, and they alone can appreciate and understand it' (*Sur l'eau*). For this and other quotations, see Wandruszka, op. cit., ch. XII: 'Was ist *Esprit*?'

[3] Quoted from Kant's *Anthropologie* by Wandruszka, op. cit., p. 17. On a similar statement by M. Mendelssohn, cf. F. Schalk, 'Das Ende des Dauerfranzosen', *Neue Jahrbücher für Wissenschaft und Jugendbildung*, viii (1932), pp. 51–69: p. 57.

[4] Most of the data which follow are derived from Spitzer's article on *Schadenfreude* mentioned on p. 218, n. 3 above.

[5] Ibid., p. 140.

[6] See G. Bárczi's *Hungarian Etymological Dictionary*, s.v. *kár*.

misfortune, spite, malignity', which was already used by Aristotle and Plutarch and was taken over by early Christian writers.[1]

3. Although there is no single word corresponding to *Schadenfreude* in English and French, the idea can be rendered without difficulty: Voltaire, for example, speaks of 'une joie maligne' and Macaulay of 'malicious delight'.[2] It should also be noted that while English has no abstract noun denoting the vice, the verb *to gloat* can express exactly the same idea. In a recent German-English dictionary, *Schadenfreude* is actually translated as 'malicious pleasure, gloating'.[3]

4. There is little doubt that the existence of a word, set phrase or idiom for such an abstract concept has a certain influence on the mentality of the ordinary speaker: it directs his attention to the vice and makes him more aware of it. This does not mean, however, that malicious joy is more common in those countries which have a name for it. The reason for the existence of a word may be purely linguistic: as we already know, German is more 'motivated' than English or French and forms compounds more freely than the latter languages (cf. p. 9 f.). It is interesting to find that when, in the fourteenth century, Nicolas Oresme translated Aristotle into French, he did not even attempt to render the Greek compound: 'Et celui qui deffaut en ce a trop sauvage nom, en grec *epykayrekacus*.'[4] But even apart from morphological differences between languages, the mere fact that a vice is given a name does not necessarily mean that it is characteristic of the people in question. As Spitzer rightly points out, 'the coining of an expression for a vice in a given speech-community implies not only the existence of that vice, but also the fact that it has been noticed and criticized. In *Schadenfreude, perfidie, cant,* the reactions and defence mechanisms of the peoples concerned must also have been at work against these allegedly national defects'.[5]

Differences in vocabulary are particularly significant when they involve 'key-words' in which the ideals of a community are crystallized (cf. p. 14). The existence of terms like the Greek καλοκάγαθός,[6] the Italian *cortegiano*, the French *galant* and *honnête homme*, the English *gentleman*,

[1] See Liddell and Scott, *A Greek-English Lexicon*, Oxford, 1940 ed., *s.v.* ἐπιχιρεκακέω, and Spitzer, loc. cit., pp. 136 ff.

[2] Ibid., p. 136.

[3] *Cassell's German and English Dictionary*, revised and re-edited by H. T. Betteridge, 6th ed., London, 1962.

[4] 'And he who is lacking in this has too savage a name, in Greek *epykayrekacus*' (quoted by Spitzer, loc. cit., p. 143, n. 5).

[5] Ibid., pp. 142 f., n. 4.

[6] 'Beautiful and good, noble and good; a perfect man, a man as he should be' (Liddell and Scott).

etc., had a profound influence on the whole attitude and outlook of successive generations. They represented an ideal standard to which the individual had to conform and by which his performance was judged. The normative value of such words is clear from certain well-known definitions. In the middle of the seventeenth century, Vaugelas tried to grasp the quintessence of *galant* by artificially separating its favourable from its unfavourable features: the form *galant* with a *t*, he suggested, should be reserved for the former, and *galand* with a *d* for the latter. The positive term he defined as 'a compound into which entered an indefinable quality or gracefulness, a courtly air, wit, judgment, civility, courtesy and gaiety, all this without constraint, affectation or vice'.[1] Even more profound and more lasting was the influence of *gentleman*. To foreigners, this concept seems so typically British that in most cases no attempt is made to translate the word.[2] The ideal norm of moral qualities and social attitudes which the term represented for generations of Englishmen is well brought out in Izaak Walton's statement: 'I would rather prove my self to be a *Gentleman* by being learned and humble, valiant and inoffensive, vertuous and communicable, then by a fond ostentation of riches',[3] and in Steele's famous formula: 'The Appellation of *Gentleman* is never to be affixed to a Man's Circumstances, but to his Behaviour in them.' In later writers, different undertones begin to creep in:

> He was the mildest manner'd man
> That ever scuttled ship or cut a throat,
> With such true breeding of a *gentleman*,
> You never could divine his real thought.
> Byron, Don Juan, Canto III, stanza 41.

> And thus he bore without abuse
> The grand old name of *gentleman*,
> Defamed by every charlatan,
> And soil'd with all ignoble use.
> Tennyson, In Memoriam, CXI.

---

[1] 'Un composé où il entroit du je ne sçay quoy ou de la bonne grâce, de l'air de la Cour, de l'esprit, du jugement, de la civilité, de la courtoisie et de la gayeté, le tout sans contrainte, sans affectation, et sans vice' (quoted by Brunot, *Histoire de la langue française*, vol. III, Part I, pp. 238 ff.). Cf. Wandruszka, op. cit., pp. 88 ff.

[2] See K. Nyrop, 'Qu'est-ce qu'un gentleman', in *Linguistique et histoire des mœurs*, Paris, 1934, ch. II.

[3] The examples which follow are taken from the *NED*, except for the one from Tennyson which is from the *Oxford Dictionary of Quotations*. For further examples see my *Semantics*, p. 51.

'Now I am so completely a *gentleman*, that I have sometimes a little difficulty to pass the day' (Darwin, in a letter dated October 3rd, 1859).

Here we are witnessing the incipient depreciation of an all-important key-word—a depreciation due partly to loose and indiscriminate usage, partly to a change in the social and spiritual climate.

Lexical discrepancies between languages can thus be very revealing; yet there is a danger of exaggerating their importance. Such discrepancies may sometimes mean no more than that the same sphere is divided up in each idiom in a different way. This was clear to Goethe when he discussed with Eckermann the lack of symmetry between French *esprit* and German *Geist*.[1] According to Goethe, the fundamental difference between the two terms is that *Geist* implies an element of creativeness whereas *esprit* does not. Thus there are two words in German, *Witz* and *Geist*, which correspond to the various aspects of *esprit*, whereas *Geist* has three partial equivalents in French: *esprit*, *âme* and *génie*. This is, of course, no more than a first step towards the solution of a complex problem, but it is a reminder that words should not be studied in isolation, without reference to the associative fields and conceptual spheres to which they belong. In Saussure's words, 'dans l'intérieur d'une même langue, tous les mots qui expriment des idées voisines se limitent réciproquement: des synonymes comme *redouter, craindre, avoir peur* n'ont de valeur propre que par leur opposition; si *redouter* n'existait pas, tout son contenu irait à ses concurrents'.[2]

It is to remedy this error of perspective that the theory of 'lexical fields' was evolved by Trier, Weisgerber and their followers. Several aspects of this theory have already been discussed in earlier chapters (see pp. 12 ff., 58 ff., 94 f.), but it also has a direct bearing on the influence of words upon thought. This will become clear if we consider from this point of view some of the lexical fields which have already been discussed. In the sphere of concrete phenomena, the relativity of colour distinctions has often been remarked upon (cf. pp. 12 f.). As Bloomfield points out, 'physicists view the colour-spectrum as a con-

---

[1] J. P. Eckermann, *Gespräche mit Goethe*, Berlin, Knaur, pp. 338 f. (March 21st, 1831). Cf. Wandruszka, op. cit., pp. 107 f. See on these terms E. Wechssler, *Esprit und Geist*, Bielefeld, 1927. On the semantic ramifications of French *esprit*, cf. Ch. Bruneau, '*Esprit:* Essai d'un classement historique des sens', in *Etudes romanes dédiées à Mario Roques*, Paris, 1946, pp. 169–80.

[2] 'Within one language, all words which express neighbouring ideas delimit each other reciprocally: synonyms like *redouter* ("to dread"), *craindre* ("to fear"), *avoir peur* ("to be frightened" or "afraid") have no real value except through their opposition to one another; if *redouter* did not exist, its whole content would go to its rivals' (*Cours de linguistique générale*, p. 160).

tinuous scale of light-waves of different lengths, ranging from 40 to 72 hundred-thousandths of a millimetre, but languages mark off different parts of this scale quite arbitrarily and without precise limits . . . and the colour-names of different languages do not embrace the same gradations'.[1] One is so accustomed to the classification embodied in one's own mother tongue that one tends to look upon it as the only natural one. We saw how aphasics suffering from colour amnesia have sometimes been 'diagnosed' as colour-blind although their sense of colour was completely unimpaired (pp. 209 f.). There is a curious parallel to this in the famous controversy about Homer's colour-blindness, which was started by Gladstone more than a century ago.[2] The ready-made system of classification which the mother tongue provides for each speaker will inevitably affect, if not his actual colour vision, at least his awareness of colour distinctions. As already noted, the Navaho Indians have single terms for 'grey' and 'brown' and for 'blue' and 'green'; it is therefore probable 'that on many occasions of casual perception they would not bother to notice whether an object were brown or grey, and that they would not merely avoid discussions as to whether a shade of colour in a trying light was blue or green, but they would not even make the distinction'.[3] Naturally, these linguistic preconceptions can be dispelled by contact with other languages where the same sphere is differently organized: a bilingual Welshman's awareness of colour will scarcely be affected by the fact that the same Welsh word, *glas*, can mean 'blue', 'green' and 'grey'.[4]

The influence of lexical fields on our picture of the world is even more evident in the sphere of abstract thought. In this sphere, to quote a well-known psychologist, 'such stability as does occur would appear to derive almost wholly from the fact of concepts being expressed and employed in conventionally accepted language (especially written). They thus become like molten bullion poured into coining moulds, whence—after due rolling, punching, and pressing—they issue as legal tender for general circulation'.[5] The number and nature of abstract terms, and the system of distinctions which they build up, will therefore be of decisive importance for our analysis of experience. As Trier's researches have shown (cf. pp. 14 and 58 f.), a German around 1200 had no single word for 'clever'; the specific combination of qualities which we denote by that term simply

---

[1] *Language*, p. 140.
[2] See S. Skard, *The Use of Colour in Literature. A Survey of Research*, *Proceedings of the American Philosophical Society*, vol. XC, no. 3, Philadelphia, 1946, p. 166.
[3] P. Henle, *Language, Thought, and Culture*, p. 7.
[4] A. Martinet, *A Functional View of Language*, p. 23.
[5] C. Spearman, *The Nature of 'Intelligence' and the Principles of Cognition*, London, 1923, p. 264.

did not exist for him as an independent concept. At the same time he had two separate nouns for courtly and non-courtly skills and would therefore automatically make the distinction, with all the value-judgments it involved. To step outside this closely integrated system would have required an originality and independence of mind which few speakers could command.

This example throws a clear light on the reciprocity of relations between language and thought. It is perfectly true to say that language *expresses* thought, that in this particular case the lexical field merely reflected the scale of values which underlay the feudal system and other aspects of medieval society. At the same time, once such a field has taken shape, it will confer fixity and permanence on the conceptual scheme; it will also perpetuate it and hand it down to future generations (cf. pp. 212 f.). Whorf has given an admirable account of this relationship, and although he was primarily thinking of grammatical categories, his formula is equally applicable to lexical fields:

'Which was first: the language patterns or the cultural norms? In main they have grown up together, constantly influencing each other. But in this partnership the nature of the language is the factor that limits free plasticity and rigidifies channels of development in the more autocratic way. This is so because a language is a system, not just an assemblage of norms. Large systematic outlines can change to something really new only very slowly, while many other cultural innovations are made with comparative quickness.'[1]

It might be useful at this point to show on a concrete example how such a lexical field is constituted, how the semantic space corresponding to a given sphere of experience is gradually filled with a dense network of terms and concepts, and from what sources these new words are drawn. The history of terms for 'person', 'individual' and allied ideas in French affords a good illustration of this process. Only one small corner of this field has been properly investigated so far,[2] but from the dictionaries one can piece together the main facts about the emergence of the present system. I shall confine myself to a few indications about the three key-terms of the field, *personne*, *individu* and *caractère*, and about the numerous derivatives, nouns, adjectives and verbs, which were grafted on them as more and more distinctions became necessary.[3]

[1] Op. cit., p. 156.
[2] H. Rheinfelder, *Das Wort 'Persona'*, *Beihefte zur Zeitschrift für Romanische Philologie*, LXXVII (1928).
[3] The account which follows is based on data collected from Rheinfelder's monograph, mentioned in the preceding note, from the French etymological dictionaries of Wartburg,

1. *Personne* is the regular French descendant of Latin *persona*, a word of Etruscan origin, which meant in the first instance 'a mask, especially that used by players, which covered the whole head, and was varied according to the different characters to be represented' (Lewis and Short). At an early stage the Latin term acquired a wide range of meanings, ecclesiastical, legal, grammatical and more general. With the eclipse of the classical theatre, the original sense of *persona* fell into disuse, though its connexions with the stage reappear in the derivative *personnage* which can mean 'character in a play or novel'. Among the semantic ramifications of *personne* there are some unexpected uses: since the fourteenth century it has become a negative pronoun ('Je ne vois *personne*' 'I can see *nobody*'; 'Qui va là?—*Personne*' 'Who goes there?—*Nobody*'), and once it could also mean 'rector of a parish', a sense which survives in Breton as well as in the English *parson*.[1]

In the course of time, French *personne* gave rise to a series of important derivatives some of which had prototypes in Latin:

(*a*) *Personnel* and *impersonnel*, both attested in the twelfth century, are reflexes of the Latin technical terms *personalis* and *impersonalis*, used in grammatical, religious and legal contexts. Both *personnel* and *impersonnel* were employed, to begin with, only as grammatical terms; *personnel* remained rare till the fifteenth century, whereas *impersonnel* did not acquire its philosophical sense till the nineteenth. The use of *personnel* as a noun is also a nineteenth-century development which may have been due to German influence.

(*b*) *Personnage* first appears in the thirteenth century, in an ecclesiastical meaning corresponding to English *parsonage*; its main modern sense is not found before the fifteenth century.

(*c*) *Personnalité*, based on Latin *personalitas*, a derivative of *personalis*, occurs once at the end of the fifteenth century but does not reappear until two hundred years later.

(*d*) *Personnifier* was formed in the seventeenth century, and *personnification* in the eighteenth.

2. If *personne* came ultimately from the Roman theatre, our second key-word, *individu*, is a learned Latinism taken over from medieval philosophy. It is derived from Latin *individuus* 'not divided, indivisible', an adjective formed from the verb *dividere*; the neuter *individuum*, used as a noun, was employed by Cicero as the equivalent of the 'atom' of

Bloch-Wartburg and Dauzat, from *The Shorter Oxford English Dictionary*, Lewis and Short's *Latin Dictionary*, and G. Matoré's two volumes, *Le Vocabulaire et la société sous Louis-Philippe* and *La Méthode en lexicologie*.

[1] On the semantic development of English *parson*, see the *NED*.

Democritus.[1] In French, *individu* first appears in the middle of the thirteenth century; the adjective *individuel* was formed two and a half centuries later; *individualiser* and *individualité* emerged in the second half of the eighteenth century, *individualisme* and *individualiste* in the 1830s. Some of these neologisms did not fail to arouse misgivings and protests; Victor Hugo, as we have seen (p. 162), was doubtful about *individualité*, Balzac criticized *individualiser* and other verbs in *-iser*,[2] while Philarète Chasles stigmatized 'ce sentiment effroyable que la langue a cru digne d'un mot sauvage, *l'individualisme*'.[3] Whatever the merits or weaknesses of these formations, they have enriched the language with a set of valuable concepts which would otherwise have remained unformulated.

3. The third key-term, *caractère*, again has a different background. It goes back, through Latin, to the Greek χαρακτήρ 'a mark engraved or impressed', which also had various figurative senses. In the Christian Latin of the fourth century, *character* meant the mark imposed on man by the sacrament of baptism: '*characterem* dominicum portatis in sacramento', writes Saint Augustine.[4] The Latin word was taken over into French in the thirteenth century, and in the sixteenth it acquired, under Greek influence, the meaning of 'distinctive feature'. It was not till the seventeenth century that the term developed its full modern sense and was enshrined in the title of La Bruyère's *Les Caractères*. Subsequently the word became one of the principal slogans of the Romantic Movement; Victor Hugo went so far as to contrast the style of the Greeks with the 'character' of 'Gothic' writers.[5] From *caractère*, two derivatives, whose prototypes already existed in Greek, were formed in the sixteenth century: the verb *caractériser* and the adjective *caractéristique*; in the eighteenth century, the latter began also to be used as a feminine noun, possibly under English influence.

If sufficient data were available it would be interesting to compare the development and present structure of this lexical field in different languages. In western Europe, the influence of Greek and Latin and the cross-currents of borrowing and loan-translation have produced substantially similar results; there were, however, certain differences, semantic as well as chronological. Thus there are some discrepancies between English and French: English *character* overlaps with French

---

[1] See several quotations from Cicero in Lewis and Short, *s.v. individuus*.
[2] See Matoré, *Le Vocabulaire et la société sous Louis-Philippe*, p. 108.
[3] 'That frightful feeling which language has thought worthy of a barbarous name, *individualism*' (quoted ibid., p. 23, n. 1).
[4] 'You bear the Lord's mark in the sacrament' (quoted by Wartburg, *Französisches Etymologisches Wörterbuch, s.v. character*).
[5] See Matoré, *Le Vocabulaire et la société sous Louis-Philippe*, p. 70.

personnage; the French noun *individu* and the adjective *individuel* have a single equivalent in English *individual*, etc. It is also worth noting that, while *individualism* and *individualist* appeared in English within a few years of their French counterparts, *individuality* is attested early in the seventeenth century, nearly 150 years before French *individualité* which, as we have seen, had some difficulty in establishing itself.

If we look at more distant languages, the differences become more significant. In Russian, for example, the three key-terms exist in their international forms, but there is also an interesting case of *pars pro toto:* the use of the word for 'face', *litsó*, in the sense of 'person'. In Hungarian, the lexical field of personality was extremely meagre until the beginning of the nineteenth century. Of the three key-terms we have found elsewhere, only one, 'person', has an old equivalent in Hungarian: the noun *személy*, a derivative of *szem* 'eye'. For the concepts of 'individual' and 'character', there were no words in Hungarian until the 1820s and 1830s. During that period, when the vocabulary of the language was extended and modernized on a large scale, a name was found for 'individual' by forming the noun *egyén* from the numeral *egy* 'one', whereas the idea of 'character' was expressed by adding a suffix to the term *jel* 'sign' (*jellem*). How acute the need was can be seen from the fact that, within a few years of the creation of these two words, several derivatives were formed from them: an adjective for 'individual', a noun for 'individuality', a verb for 'to characterize', etc.[1]

Without drawing any general conclusions from a cursory study of a single field, one can see fairly clearly the forces which have shaped this sector of our abstract vocabulary. Three points in particular are worth noting:

1. Our field shows the decisive and enduring role of classical influence. Of the three key-terms in French, only one, *personne*, is a native word; the other two are learned borrowings from Latin or, via Latin, from Greek. Even some of the derivatives (*personnel, impersonnel, personnalité, caractéristique, caractériser*) had Greek or Latin prototypes. At the same time, our modern languages have also influenced one another, by imitation, loan-translation and in other ways. It is hardly a coincidence that *individualism* appears in English a bare two years later than in French, and *individualist* four years after its French counterpart. The great Hungarian language-reform of the late eighteenth and early nineteenth centuries was certainly inspired by modern rather than classical models. Direct borrowing from a living language is not so

[1] See G. Bárczi's *Hungarian Etymological Dictionary*, s.v. *egyén, jellem, személy*.

common in these abstract spheres; yet it is significant that French *personne* was taken over into German in the Middle Ages: German *Person* is still stressed on the second syllable, as in French.[1]

2. Our data show that the constitution of the present system of concepts was a slow and gradual process; they also enable us to discern the main stages of its emergence: the part played by early Christian theology, Scholasticism, the Renaissance and later currents of thought. What is particularly striking is that some concepts which seem indispensable to us did not take shape till a comparatively recent date: *individualism*, that crucial feature of our modern life, did not have a name in England or in France till the third decade of the last century.

3. We can also see from our material that the present network of terms has come into being in three main ways. Firstly, elements which were already in the language were combined to form new words. In this particular field, most of the terms coined in this way were produced by adding suffixes to native or foreign words; elsewhere, prefixes have been used for the same purpose, or two or more terms have been joined together to form a compound, as in the case of *Schadenfreude* which was discussed above (pp. 218 ff.). Other words were borrowed, translated or adapted from foreign material, classical or modern.[2] A third group was obtained by changing the meaning of existing terms: by extending or restricting their range, by using them metaphorically or as *a pars pro toto*, etc. It is in these various ways that a lexical field is gradually built up, and each new word represents a distinct intellectual achievement and provides a tool of analysis for millions of future speakers.

C. The Shortcomings of Words

Modern linguists are anxious to avoid value-judgments about languages or any of their elements; their task, as they see it, is to describe and to interpret, not to praise or to criticize. Such an objective attitude is correct and indeed essential as long as we are dealing with purely linguistic data. When, however, we have to transcend language and explore its impact on thought, certain value-judgments are bound to creep in. It cannot be denied that some features of our vocabulary can have a negative

[1] See R. Priebsch-W. E. Collinson, *The German Language*, 3rd ed., London, repr. 1952, p. 271.
[2] On these processes, see L. Deroy, *L' Emprunt linguistique*, Paris, 1956; cf. also two recent articles by T. E. Hope: 'The Analysis of Semantic Borrowing', in *Essays Presented to C. M. Girdlestone*, Newcastle, 1960, pp. 125–41, and 'Loan-words as Cultural and Lexical Symbols', *Archivum Linguisticum*, xiv (1962) and xv (1963).

effect on our thinking: they can block it, misdirect it, or hamper it in various other ways. Such features fall into two broad groups: general shortcomings, which are inherent in the very nature of language, and specific ones, which are peculiar to a given idiom.

I. General Shortcomings

1. *Vagueness.*—Many of our words are vague, imprecise, without any clear-cut boundaries. Wittgenstein has spoken of concepts with 'blurred edges', adding: 'But is a blurred concept a concept at all?—Is an indistinct photograph a picture of a person at all? Is it even always an advantage to replace an indistinct picture by a sharp one? Isn't the indistinct one often exactly what we need?'[1] This is perfectly true of everyday speech and also of certain forms of literary style; vagueness is, however, a disadvantage in all situations where clarity and precision are required— hence the endless discussions among philosophers, lawyers and politicians on the exact meaning and delimitation of the terms they use.

I have discussed elsewhere the various factors which make for vagueness in language;[2] here it will be sufficient to mention two points. In many cases, it is not our words that are vague, but the objects or experiences to which they refer. The nomenclature of colours, which we have already discussed (pp. 222 f.), is a good example of such 'referential vagueness'. As Bloomfield points out, 'we should have a hard time deciding at what points on the actual scale the domain of each English colour-name begins and ends. If we showed people colours in minute grades of variety, we should find that between the frequencies which were named consistently, say, as *yellow* and as *green*, there would be a border-zone, where the naming wavered'.[3] If this is true of a concrete sphere, it is much more true of abstract ideas which are far more fluid, elusive and difficult to delimit.

Another source of vagueness is the generic nature of our vocabulary. As we saw in the section on aphasia (pp. 208 ff.), most of our words stand for class-concepts, not for individual persons, objects, qualities or events. It is precisely this 'abstract', generic mode of thinking that the aphasic tends to lose; as his control over words is reduced, he finds himself in the proverbial position of the man who cannot see the wood for the trees. An element of generality is a *sine qua non* in any language, though, as we

---

[1] *Philosophical Investigations*, p. 34.
[2] *Semantics*, pp. 116–28. On the philosophical aspects of the problem, see esp. W. V. O. Quine, *Word and Object*, Massachusetts Institute of Technology, 1960, ch. IV.
[3] *Language*, p. 280.

already know, some idioms go further than others in this direction (cf. pp. 71 ff.). The price we have to pay for the generality of our concepts is a certain vagueness, a tendency to ignore finer nuances and to lump together very different items under the same label. The crudeness of this process has often been deplored by writers and thinkers. In *Don Juan*, Canto VI, stanza cix, Byron complained:

> Oh that my words were colours! but their tints
> May serve perhaps as outlines or slight hints.

A contemporary poet's comments on the same theme strike a very different note:

> Were vaguenesses enough and the sweet lies plenty,
> The hollow words could bear all suffering
> And cure me of ills.
> Dylan Thomas, Out of the sighs[1].

Philosophers are more explicit. Voltaire writes: 'Il n'est aucune langue complète, aucune qui puisse exprimer toutes nos idées et toutes nos sensations; leurs nuances sont trop imperceptibles et trop nombreuses . . . On est obligé, par exemple, de désigner sous le nom général d'*amour* et de *haine*, mille amours et mille haines toutes différentes; il en est de même de nos douleurs et de nos plaisirs.'[2] Bergson has spoken of the 'crude word, which stores up that which is stable, common and therefore impersonal in the experiences of mankind, and crushes or at least overlays the delicate and fleeting impressions of our intellectual consciousness'.[3] Elsewhere he comments:

'Le mot, qui ne note de la chose que sa fonction la plus commune et son aspect banal, s'insinue entre elle et nous . . . Nous ne saisissons de nos sentiments que leur aspect impersonnel, celui que le langage a pu noter une fois pour toutes parce qu'il est à peu près le même, dans les mêmes conditions, pour tous les hommes.'[4]

---

[1] Quoted by R. Quirk, *The Use of English*, p. 231.

[2] 'There is no complete language, none which could express all our ideas and all our sensations; their shades are too imperceptible and too numerous. . . . One is forced, for example, to denote by the general terms *love* and *hatred* a thousand entirely different loves and hatreds; and the same happens with our pains and our pleasures' (quoted by Nyrop, *Sémantique*, p. 444).

[3] Quoted ibid., p. 448.

[4] 'The word, which notes only the commonest function and the banal aspect of the object, interposes itself between the object and ourselves . . . We can grasp only the impersonal aspect of our feelings, that which language has noted once and for all because it is approximately the same for all men under the same conditions' (*Le Rire*, 15th ed., Paris, 1916, pp. 156 f.; cf. Nyrop, loc. cit., p. 447).

2. *'Hypostatized' abstractions.*—The ease with which quality-nouns can be formed from adjectives (*whiteness* from *white, freedom* from *free*), and action-nouns from verbs (*movement* from *to move, suffering* from *to suffer*), may suggest that these alleged 'entities' have some kind of existence in their own right, whereas, strictly speaking, there is no 'whiteness' in the abstract, only white objects, there can be no such thing as 'movement' apart from moving bodies, etc. There is a famous pronouncement by J. S. Mill on the subject:

'The tendency has always been strong to believe that whatever receives a name must be an entity or being, having an independent existence of its own: and if no real entity answering to the name could be found, men did not for that reason suppose that none existed, but imagined that it was something peculiarly abstruse and mysterious, too high to be an object of sense.'[1]

This tendency to 'hypostatize' abstractions, to set them up as substances and independent entities, lies at the root of many of our *-isms* and similar 'fictions'. English adjectives like *beautiful, harmful, spiteful*, and even the tautological *plentiful*, are symptomatic of this tendency: their very formation seems to suggest that the persons or objects in question are 'full' of some mysterious essence called Beauty, Harm, Spite, or Plenty. This issue is one of the perennial moot points of philosophy where it is bound up with the existence of universals, with the great debate between nominalism and realism, and ultimately with the whole problem of idealism which, since Plato, has reappeared time and again in various garbs.[2] The fight against loose and uncritical uses of abstractions is one of the main themes of the movement known as 'general semantics'[3] and also of Ogden and Richards's *Meaning of Meaning*. These authors never tire of warning their readers against 'universal "qualities"', phantoms due to the refractive power of the linguistic medium; these must not be treated as part of the furniture of the universe, but are useful as symbolic accessories enabling us to economize our speech material'.[4] They have also spoken of the fallacy known as the 'hypostatic subterfuge', which is 'difficult to discourage because it is a misuse of an indispensable linguistic convenience. We must, if we are ever to finish making any general remark, contract and condense our language, but

---

[1] Quoted by Ogden and Richards, *The Meaning of Meaning*, p. xxiv.
[2] For a recent discussion of these problems, see A. Schaff, *Introduction to Semantics, passim.*
[3] See above, p. 3.
[4] Op. cit., p. 96.

Q

we need not hypostatize our contractions . . . how popular and how influential is this practice may be shown by such a list of terms as the following:—Virtue, Liberty, Democracy, Peace, Germany, Religion, Glory. All invaluable words, indispensable even, but able to confuse the clearest issues'.[1] In their campaign against the misuse of abstractions, these authors had an illustrious predecessor in Jeremy Bentham whose statement on linguistic fallacies they quote in the epigraph of their book: 'Error is never so difficult to be destroyed as when it has its root in Language.'

II. Specific Shortcomings

1. *Gaps in vocabulary.*—In the previous section we saw several cases where a new concept was needed and where a name was found for it by derivation or composition, by borrowing or translating a foreign term, by changing the meaning of an existing word, or in some other way. Such neologisms are acts of creative innovation, and until someone takes the initiative and the new term succeeds in establishing itself, the concept will remain unformulated. In some cases we have direct evidence that the maker of a new word was fully aware of the existence of such a gap. In another chapter we saw Jeremy Bentham apologizing for his temerity in coining the adjective *international* which, he admitted, 'is a new one, though, it is hoped, sufficiently analogous and intelligible' (p. 162). Earlier in the eighteenth century, the Abbé de Saint-Pierre had launched another useful innovation, *bienfaisance* 'beneficence, charity', with rather similar comments: 'J'ai cherché un terme qui nous rappelât précisément l'idée de faire du bien aux autres, et je n'en ai pas trouvé de plus propre pour me faire entendre que le terme de *bienfaisance*.'[2] The abbé was, of course, unaware of the fact that the word had been used once before him, as far back as the fourteenth century. In a very different sphere, a French journal of horse-breeding deplored, in 1828, the lack of a word for 'sport' in French: 'le mot de *sports*, dont l'équivalent n'existe pas dans notre langue'[3] (cf. above, p. 162).

Some neologisms have a more obscure motivation. The adjective *blatant*, invented by Edmund Spenser who used it repeatedly in *The Faerie Queene*:

[1] Ibid., pp. 133 f.
[2] 'I looked for a term which would precisely convey the idea of doing good to others, and I could not think of one more suitable for making my meaning clear than the word *bienfaisance*' (quoted by Bloch-Wartburg, *s.v. faire*). In the same sphere, the term *altruisme* was coined by Comte in 1830 (ibid.).
[3] 'The word *sports*, which has no equivalent in our language' (Bloch-Wartburg). Cf. similar comments on the word *sentimental* (ibid.), first used in French in 1769, in the translation of Sterne's *Sentimental Journey*.

A monster, which the *Blatant* beast men call,
A dreadful fiend of gods and men ydrad
(Book V, canto xii, l. 37),

seems to be connected with Latin *blatire* 'utter foolish things, babble, prate'.[1] The drug *veronal* owes its name to an accident: the fact that the inventor, a German, happened to be in Verona in 1903 when he suggested the name (Bloch-Wartburg). Even more remarkable is the case of *gas*, coined in the seventeenth century by the Flemish scientist Van Helmont. This word looks completely arbitrary, without any roots in any language; yet we have Van Helmont's own statement that he took it from Graeco-Latin *chaos*; since both *ch* and *g* would be pronounced as velar fricatives in Flemish, the phonetic difference between the two forms was not nearly so marked as in English or in French.[2]

How greatly our thinking has benefited by certain neologisms can best be seen if we try to imagine what it would be like to do without them. In his Taylorian lecture on 'The Contribution of the Individual to Language', Professor B. Migliorini made up an artificial sentence to show the immense debt which our abstract vocabulary owes to Cicero. The sentence, which includes five key-terms of our modern culture, is as follows: 'His *indifference* to *Providence* seemed out of *proportion* to his *moral qualities*.' Professor Migliorini comments:

'All the abstract terms, *all* of them, are coinages which go back to a single author. It is Cicero who from the Greek has coined the corresponding Latin words *indifferens* and *indifferentia, providentia, proportio, qualitas, moralis*.'[3]

To take a more modern example, we saw in the last chapter that the study of metaphor was greatly hampered for many centuries by the lack of separate terms for the thing compared and what it is compared to, until I. A. Richards filled the gap by proposing 'tenor' for the former and 'vehicle' for the latter (p. 184).

It has been suggested that such gaps in vocabulary are not a very serious handicap since they can easily be filled when the need arises. 'Clearly people who have a word for lions in their language', writes a philosopher, 'will be able to think about them much more easily than those who have not, and people who have no numerical expressions

---

[1] Cf. the *NED*, the *Oxford Dictionary of Quotations*, and Lewis and Short.
[2] See Bloch-Wartburg, *s.v. gaz*.
[3] Op. cit., p. 4.

except "one", "two" and "many" will be unable to develop a general theory of numbers. But lexical impediments of this kind are comparatively unimportant because they can so easily be remedied by additions to a language's vocabulary when cross-cultural contacts or other historical developments make the need felt.'[1] This may be so in scientific and technical nomenclatures, but the position is rather different in ordinary language. For one thing, it is often difficult, and requires a major intellectual effort, to recognize the need for a concept which has as yet no name. We have seen (pp. 73 and 213) how long it took even for such a seemingly obvious notion as 'plant' to take shape. But even when a genuine need arises, people may hesitate to form a new term. As Ben Jonson wisely noted in his *Discoveries*, 'a man coins not a new word without some peril and less fruit; for if it happen to be received, the praise is but moderate; if refused, the scorn is assured'.[2] Other authors are even more categorical. It is not surprising that the custodian of linguistic purity, Vaugelas, should have baldly declared: 'Il n'est jamais permis de faire des mots';[3] but even the Romantics, who prided themselves on being iconoclasts in linguistic matters, drew the line at neologism. 'Nous ne sachons pas qu'on ait fait des mots nouveaux', Hugo protested. 'Or, ce sont les mots nouveaux, les mots inventés, les mots faits artificiellement, qui détruisent le tissu d'une langue.'[4] Similarly, Théophile Gautier proclaimed: 'S'il est permis de créer des mondes, il ne l'est pas de créer des mots.'[5] It is true, on the other hand, that some writers have no such qualms and that there have been whole periods of intense lexical activity such as the tremendous expansion of the French vocabulary during the Renaissance, which will be discussed in the next chapter.

One must also bear in mind that, as we already know, it is not always merely a question of filling isolated gaps; sometimes a whole conceptual field and hierarchy of values has to be recast. If one also remembers that any innovation has to be accepted by millions of speakers before it becomes an integral part of the language, one realizes that any permanent addition to the central part of our vocabulary, to our basic stock-in-trade, is a more complex process than would appear at first sight.

[1] L. J. Cohen, *The Diversity of Meaning*, p. 64.

[2] Quoted by A. C. Baugh, *A History of the English Language*, 2nd ed., New York—London, 1959, p. 266.

[3] 'It is never permissible to coin words' (quoted by Brunot, *Histoire de la langue française*, vol. III, Part I, p. 196).

[4] 'We are unaware that new words have been formed; and it is new words, invented words, words artificially coined, which destroy the fabric of a language' (quoted ibid., vol. XII, p. 233 (by Ch. Bruneau)).

[5] 'If it is permissible to create worlds, it is not permissible to create words' (quoted ibid., p. 263).

2. *Ambiguity*.—The fact that some words have two or more meanings which can make sense in the same contexts is not only a fertile source of misunderstandings in communication, but can even create confusion in the speaker's or writer's own mind. In the *Critique of Practical Reason*, Kant has given a penetrating analysis of such a situation in Latin, which deserves to be quoted in full:

'The expressions *boni* and *mali* contain an ambiguity due to the poverty of the language. These words are capable of a double meaning and therefore inevitably bring practical laws into a precarious position; and philosophy, in using these expressions, becomes aware of the divergence of concepts associated with the same word even though it can find no special expressions for them, and is forced to subtle distinctions about which later agreement cannot be obtained, since the difference cannot be directly stated by any suitable expression. The German language has the good fortune to possess expressions which do not permit this difference to be overlooked. It has two very different concepts and equally different expressions for what the Latins named with the single word *bonum*. For *bonum*, it has *das Gute* (the good) and *das Wohl* (well-being); for *malum*, *das Böse* (evil, wicked) and *das Übel* (bad, ill) or *das Weh* (woe). Thus there are two very different judgments if in an action we have regard to its goodness or wickedness or to our weal or woe (ill).'[1]

Professor Ryle has recently drawn attention to a somewhat similar case: the ambiguity of the Greek word ὄνομα and, in a more general way, the lack of a clear-cut grammatical terminology, which hampered Plato's ideas on syntax. 'The Greek language', writes Professor Ryle, 'had only the one word ὄνομα where we have the three words "word", "name" and "noun". It was hard in Greek even to say that the Greek counterpart to our verb "is" was a word but not a noun. Greek provided Plato with no label for verbs, or for adverbs, conjunctions, etc. That "is" is a word, but is not a name or even a noun was a tricky thing to say in Greek where ὄνομα did duty both for our word "word", for our word "name" and, eventually, for our word "noun".'[2]

Another ambiguity in the same sphere was less serious in its consequences but left a permanent trace in our grammatical terminology. The *accusative* case owes its name to a misunderstanding: the Greek αἰτιατική πτῶσις, on which it is modelled, is derived from αἰτία which could

[1] I. Kant, *Critique of Practical Reason and Other Writings in Moral Philosophy*, transl. by L. W. Beck, Chicago, 1949, pp. 168 f. Cf. A. Flew, 'Philosophy and Language', in *Essays in Conceptual Analysis*, ed. by A. Flew, London, 1955, ch. I: p. 5.
[2] 'The Theory of Meaning', pp. 243 f.

mean both 'charge, accusation' and 'cause'. The translator obviously took the Greek term in the former sense whereas it actually meant 'causative case'.[1]

The classic example of this type of ambiguity is the problem of Greek λόγος. This term had two main meanings: 'the word or that by which the inward thought is expressed, Latin *oratio*', and 'the inward thought itself, Latin *ratio*'.[2] Since the term occurs in the opening verses of Saint John's Gospel, its interpretation is a matter of great theological importance. The traditional view is that in this context λόγος means 'word'; the Vulgate translates it by *verbum*, and even in the New English Bible we read: 'When all things began, the Word already was. The Word dwelt with God, and what God was, the Word was.' Goethe's Faust, however, disagreed with this interpretation. He decided to translate the Gospel into German by going back to the 'primal text', but as soon as he set pen to paper he was held up by this difficulty:

> 'In the Beginning was the Word!' 'Tis writ.
> Here on the threshold I must pause, perforce;
> And who will help me onwards in my course?
> No, by no possibility is't fit,
> I should the naked Word so highly rate.
> Some other way must I the words translate,
> If by the Spirit rightly I be taught.
> 'In the Beginning was the Sense!' 'Tis writ.
> The first line ponder well. Is it
> The Sense, which is of each created thing
> The primal cause, and regulating spring?
> It should stand thus: 'In the Beginning was
> The Force!' Yet even as I write, I pause.
> A something warns me, this will not content me.
> Lo! help is from the Spirit sent me!
> I see my way; with lightning speed
> The meaning flashes on my sight,
> And with assured conviction thus I write:
> 'In the Beginning was the Deed'.[3]

[1] Migliorini, 'Calco e irradiazione sinonimica', p. 9.
[2] Liddell and Scott. Cf. J. Barr, *The Semantics of Biblical Language*, Oxford, repr. 1962. pp. 221 f., and L. R. Palmer, *The Latin Language*, London, 1954, p. 197.
[3] Act I, scene 3 (Sir Theodore Martin's translation). The original text is as follows:
> Geschrieben steht: Im Anfang war das *Wort*!
> Hier stock' ich schon! Wer hilft mir weiter fort?
> Ich kann das *Wort* so hoch unmöglich schätzen,
> Ich muss es anders übersetzen.

Victor Hugo, as we have seen (p. 184), had no such scruples but proclaimed without hesitation: 'Car le mot, c'est le Verbe, et le Verbe, c'est Dieu.'

In the examples just mentioned, it was a noun or a substantivized adjective which gave rise to ambiguity. But other parts of speech can be no less equivocal. It has been suggested, for example, that Hegel's 'dialectic', the famous passage from thesis to antithesis and then to synthesis, owes much of its persuasiveness to the ambiguity of the German verb *aufheben* which can mean 'to lift up', 'to preserve', and 'to cancel'. Since there is no English word with the same range of meanings, Hegel's expositors have been forced to invent neologisms such as *to sublate*, in order to convey the implications of this crucial term.[1]

Even such a simple ambiguity as that of the French adjective *grand*, which can mean either 'big, large' or 'great', can lay a trap to a naive speaker. In Proust, the maid Françoise believes that the Guermantes are 'une *grande* famille', not only because of their illustriousness but also because they have many members. The narrator comments:

'Car n'ayant que ce seul mot de "grand" pour les deux choses, il lui semblait qu'elles n'en formaient qu'une seule, son vocabulaire, comme certaines pierres, présentant ainsi par endroit un défaut et qui projetait de l'obscurité jusque dans la pensée de Françoise.'[2]

3. *Misleading figures of speech.*—As this last example shows, certain ambiguities arise through confusion between the literal and the figurative meaning of a word. But metaphor can also mislead the unwary in other ways. By unthinkingly and mechanically repeating the same image, we

> Wenn ich vom Geiste recht erleuchtet bin.
> Geschrieben steht: Im Anfang war der *Sinn*.
> Bedenke wohl die erste Zeile,
> Dass deine Feder sich nicht übereile!
> Ist es der *Sinn*, der Alles wirkt und schafft?
> Es sollte stehn: Im Anfang war die *Kraft*!
> Doch, auch indem ich dieses niederschreibe,
> Schon warnt mich was, dass ich dabei nicht bleibe.
> Mir hilft der Geist! Auf einmal seh' ich Rat
> Und schreibe getrost: Im Anfang war die *Tat*!

See on this passage the comments of G. Witkowski (*Goethe's Faust*, 8th ed., Leipzig, 1929, vol. II, p. 214) and A. Gillies (*Goethe's Faust. An Interpretation*, Oxford, 1957, pp. 40 f.). Witkowski notes that Herder too had been exercised by the ambiguity of λόγος.

[1] T. D. Weldon, *The Vocabulary of Politics*, Penguin Books, London, 1953, p. 107; cf. Flew, op. cit., p. 5. On the language of politics, see now J. Dubois, *Le Vocabulaire politique et social en France de 1869 à 1872*, Paris, 1962.

[2] 'For, having this one word *grand* for both things, it seemed to her that they formed one thing only; her vocabulary, like certain stones, thus showed in places a flaw which cast darkness into the very thoughts of Françoise' (*Le Côté de Guermantes*, Paris, 1949 ed., vol. I, p. 26).

may in the end forget that it is metaphorical; moreover, our feelings for the tenor may be affected by those for the vehicle.[1] The figurative element in such expressions as Juggernaut, Moloch, Armageddon, 'cordon sanitaire', 'doodle-bug', Axis, Iron Curtain and others has, in various ways, undoubtedly coloured the emotional attitude of many people to the objects and ideas in question.

There are also examples of scholars being influenced, confused or even mesmerized by the metaphors and similes, metonymies and personifications which they use when talking about their subject. In the appendix to his *Essai de sémantique*, Bréal warned linguists against the danger of picturing languages as living organisms which exist independently of the people who speak them. It was misleading, he argued, to talk of the birth, growth, development, decay and death of a language. 'All these expressions', he wrote, 'are excellent as long as they are taken for what they are: namely, for images . . . But it ought not to be necessary to point out that they are mere figures of speech, and it would seem that people professionally accustomed to metonymies and other tropes should have been the last to fall into this trap.'[2]

Nearly seventy years have passed since the publication of Bréal's book, yet his warning has lost nothing of its timeliness. We still talk glibly of words as if they were living beings which 'carry an overload of meaning', 'clash' or 'collide' with each other, are involved in 'pathological' situations, 'lose their vitality' and may even 'die' unless 'curative' devices are applied in time. One of Gilliéron's books bears the characteristic title: 'Pathologie et thérapeutique verbales.' The following sentence, where I have italicized all the images, is typical of the figurative language used by this scholar and many other linguists: 'L'homonymie n'est pas une *force* qui *va*, *fatale*, *inéluctable*, *détruisant sans merci* tout ce que lui *livre* une phonétique *aveugle*: pour qu'elle ait à *agir*, encore faut-il qu'il y ait *rencontre*, et la *rencontre* ne se produit que pour des mots *engagés* dans les mêmes *chemins* de la pensée.'[3] As Bréal said, there is nothing wrong with such metaphors as long as we remember that they are metaphors. Constant repetition of these dramatic images and personifications may create, like the hypostatizing of abstract ideas, a mythology of its

---

[1] Cf. P. Henle, *Language, Thought, and Culture*, p. 191.
[2] Op. cit., p. 315.
[3] 'Homonymy is not a *force* which *advances inevitably, inescapably, destroying mercilessly* everything that a *blind* phonetics *delivers* to it: it will have to *act* only if there is an *encounter*, and such an *encounter* will arise only in the case of words *engaged* in the same *paths* of thought' (J. Gilliéron-M. Roques, *Etudes de géographie linguistique*, Paris, 1912, pp. 149 f.). On the authorship of this passage, see I. Iordan-J. Orr, *An Introduction to Romance Linguistics*, p. 162, n. 1, and M. Roques, *Romania*, lxxiv (1953), p. 140.

own; it can engender a peculiar vision of language as an active, conscious and purposeful being, as when the same Gilliéron states: 'le rôle destructeur de l'homonymie n'apparaît que lorsque *le parler a pleinement conscience* du caractère intolérable des conflits',[1] where the curious expression I have italicized masks the fact, self-evident but apt to be forgotten, that it is not 'language', but millions of speakers who, on countless occasions, become aware of some embarrassing ambiguity.

One case where a metaphor of this kind has been positively harmful was mentioned on pp. 19 f. above. One of the most frequent objections to analytical theories of meaning is that the distinction between name and sense, 'signifiant' and 'signifié', 'expression' and 'content', etc., implies a kind of 'psycho-physical parallelism' modelled on the metaphysics of body and soul. To compare the form of a word to the human body and its meaning to the soul is no more than a metaphor; it is not even a very satisfactory metaphor, as Saussure had already pointed out. The distinction between form and meaning has nothing to do with metaphysics: it is simply an example of the duality inherent in any kind of sign and symbol. One could argue with just as much cogency that, in traffic lights, the green colour is the 'body' of the signal and the meaning: 'the traffic may proceed' is its 'soul'.

The lengths to which metaphorical language can go was seen at a conference held in 1960 at Royaumont, near Paris, on the concept of personality, where an eminent aesthetician maintained that works of art affect us in the same way as if they had a personality of their own, and that the term 'person' ought to be so defined that it will include such works.[2]

4. *Grammatical factors.*—According to Nietzsche, 'by the grammatical structure of a group of languages everything runs smoothly for one kind of philosophical system, whereas the way is as it were barred for certain other possibilities'.[3] As a British philosopher more concisely put it, 'different languages offer different temptations'.[4] Here we are concerned with one kind of 'temptation' only: the influence which the morphology or the syntax of a language may have on the meaning of words and on the concepts for which they stand. Such influence may take more than one form:

---

[1] 'The destructive role of homonymy appears only when *the language is fully aware* of the intolerable nature of the conflicts' (*Généalogie des mots qui désignent l'abeille*, p. 58).
[2] *Colloque sur les problèmes de la personne*, 'Programme; résumés des exposés', no. XXVI (summary of a paper by E. Souriau on 'L'œuvre d'art comme personne').
[3] Quoted by Ogden and Richards, *The Meaning of Meaning*, p. xxiv.
[4] Flew, loc. cit., p. 5.

(*a*) The ease with which abstract nouns are coined may encourage indiscriminate hypostatization. In Classical Greek, for example, such nouns could be formed by the simple device of prefixing the neuter article τό to the neuter of the adjective: from αἰσχρός 'ugly, shameful, disgraceful, infamous', we have the derivative τὸ αἰσχρόν 'dishonour, disgrace'; from καλός 'beautiful, fair, noble', τὸ καλόν 'physical or moral beauty'; from a combination of the two abstractions, the phrase τὸ καλὸν καὶ τὸ αἰσχρόν, used by Aristotle in the sense of 'virtue and vice' (Liddell and Scott). It has been suggested that this syntactical possibility may have played a certain role in Plato's theory of forms.[1] Such formations are notoriously difficult to render in English where adjectives cannot be so easily substantivized. The richness of certain languages in compounds and derivatives may also facilitate the creation of abstract concepts, as our discussion of *Schadenfreude* has shown (pp. 218 ff.).

(*b*) The morphological structure of certain words may suggest wrong ideas based on their form or on their etymology rather than on their actual use. In an earlier chapter (p. 47) we saw how profoundly the philosophy of Martin Heidegger was influenced by etymological, or pseudo-etymological, arguments: how he posited a gratuitous connexion between *Zeichen* 'sign' and *zeigen* 'to show', and analysed *Entschlossenheit* 'resoluteness' as 'openness, opening up', because it contains the verb *schliessen* 'to close' and the privative prefix *ent-*. Such oddities as Claudel's interpretation of *connaissance* as *co-naissance*, and of *naître* as *n'être* (p. 46), represent the *reductio ad absurdum* of this attitude.

(*c*) Yet another grammatical temptation is false analogy or, as Ogden and Richards rather misleadingly call it, the 'phonetic subterfuge'.[2] Just as the ambiguity of a word may give rise to confusion, one may be misled by the ambiguity of a prefix or suffix. A celebrated example is J. S. Mill's analysis of the adjective *desirable* as if it were on all fours with *knowable, visible* and similar formations, although it means 'worthy of being desired' and not 'capable of being desired'.[3]

We have considered the influence of words upon thought from three different points of view: that of speech-disturbances, of ordinary language, and of the shortcomings of our vocabulary. Needless to say, there are various other possible approaches to the problem; to mention but one,

---

[1] Ibid., pp. 5 f. Cf. G. Ryle, 'Plato's *Parmenides*', *Mind*, xlviii (1939), pp. 129–51, 302–25: pp. 142 f.
[2] Op. cit., p. 133.
[3] Ibid.; cf. Flew, loc. cit., p. 5.

the child's acquisition of language may throw a great deal of light on some of these processes.[1] The whole question is too difficult, and many of its aspects are too little known, for even tentative conclusions to be hazarded at this stage; there are, however, one or two general impressions which emerge from the data we have examined:

1. On the negative side it is probably an exaggeration to say that certain things cannot be expressed at all in a given idiom. A speaker at an American conference on the Sapir-Whorf hypothesis was no doubt nearer the mark when he suggested that 'languages differ not so much as to what *can* be said in them, but rather as to what it is *relatively easy* to say'.[2] Naturally there will be many cases where the difficulty of expressing certain ideas is so great that a major intellectual effort will be needed to overcome it.

2. The positive side of the influence can also be exaggerated. It is probably more correct to say that our words *predispose* us in favour of certain lines of thought than that they actually *predetermine* our thinking. But here again there will be cases where the suggestive power of language is so strong, or so insidious, that few speakers, if any, will be able to resist it.

3. When studying these matters one must always bear in mind the inextricable unity of language and thought, the fact that they are interdependent and constantly stimulate, activate and influence each other.

4. Another point to remember is that language serves an infinite variety of purposes, so that what may be a liability in some situations may prove an asset in others. Ambiguity is a major shortcoming in law, diplomacy, science, and often also in everyday life; yet it can be a valuable source of stylistic effects. Vagueness of meaning is a serious disadvantage wherever precision is needed; many poets, however, will prefer the chiaroscuro of hints and suggestions, of emotive overtones and evocative nuances, to clearly delineated contours which leave no scope to the reader's imagination. As Verlaine wrote in his *Art poétique*:

> Il faut aussi que tu n'ailles point
> Choisir tes mots sans quelque méprise:
> Rien de plus cher que la chanson grise
> Où l'Indécis au Précis se joint.[3]

---

[1] See recently the English translation of L. S. Vygotsky's *Thought and Language*, Massachusetts Institute of Technology, 1962. Cf. also T. Slama-Cazacu, *Relaţiile dintre gândire şi limbaj in ontogeneză* (The Relationships between Thinking and Language in Ontogenesis), Bucharest, 1957.

[2] C. F. Hockett in *Language in Culture*, ed. by H. Hoijer, p. 122.

[3] 'It is also necessary that you should not always choose the right word: there is nothing more precious than the grey song where Vagueness and Precision meet.'

5. Faced with the inadequacies of his mother tongue, the creative writer may adopt two attitudes which have been described as 'constrictive' and 'explosive'.[1] 'Explosive' temperaments—authors like Rabelais, Shakespeare, Gerard Manley Hopkins, Proust, James Joyce—will try to burst the limits imposed on them by language. The 'constrictive' type, of which Racine is the supreme example, will make a virtue of necessity and will accept linguistic limitations as a challenge and as a salutary discipline, believing, in Gide's words, that 'art is born of restraint, lives on struggle, dies of freedom'.[2] Whichever attitude the artist may choose, both his thoughts and his style will be clarified, tempered and enriched in what T. S. Eliot has called the 'intolerable wrestle with words and meanings',[3] the unending battle with a resistant yet infinitely plastic medium.

---

[1] G. Devoto, *Studi di stilistica*, p. 48. The actual terms used are *costrizione* and *evasione*.

[2] 'L'art naît de contrainte, vit de lutte, meurt de liberté' (*Nouveaux Prétextes*, Paris, 1947 ed., p. 17).

[3] That was a way of putting it—not very satisfactory:
    A periphrastic study in a worn-out poetical fashion,
    Leaving one still with the intolerable wrestle
    With words and meanings.
        (*East Coker*; cf. R. Quirk, *The Use of English*, p. 232)

CHAPTER XI

CLASSICAL INFLUENCE ON THE VOCABULARY OF THE FRENCH RENAISSANCE

A FEW years ago, an eminent French linguist published an article on the 're-Latinization' of the French vocabulary during the Renaissance.[1] From a strictly philological point of view, this is indeed an accurate description of what happened. For various reasons—geographical position, Germanic invasions, the internal strains and stresses of the linguistic system— French had moved farther away from the Latin prototype than any other Western Romance language. The introduction of hundreds of Latinisms, or Latinized Hellenisms, during and since the Renaissance has certainly gone a long way to restore the Latin character of the French vocabulary. The process was not, of course, peculiar to France; yet it acquired special significance in the particular context of the history of French. Two other aspects of this lexical influence are, however, even more important. Firstly, this vast expansion of the French vocabulary also meant the creation or crystallization of hosts of new concepts, in the sense discussed in the last chapter. Secondly, the adoption of so many alien elements was bound to have far-reaching repercussions in the structure of the receiving idiom. Saussure, it will be remembered,[2] had likened language to a game of chess whose inner balance will be disturbed even if a single piece is moved; the addition of so many new pieces would therefore inevitably revolutionize the whole situation on the linguistic chess-board.

By the sixteenth century, the process of re-Latinization had assumed such dimensions that even Frenchmen with a humanistic culture were alarmed. There were protests against the excesses of writers described by such picturesque phrases as 'écumeurs de latin', 'jargonneurs', and 'revendeurs de vieux mots tous moisis et incertains'.[3] In 1529, Geofroy Tory, in his *Champ fleury*, made an amusing parody of the current vogue of Latinism:

---

[1] G. Gougenheim, 'La Relatinisation du vocabulaire français', *Annales de l'Université de Paris*, January–March 1959, pp. 5–18.
[2] See above, pp. 4, 26, 60.
[3] 'Pilferers of Latin', 'jargon-mongers', 'dealers in mouldy and obscure old words'. Quoted by Nyrop, *Grammaire historique de la langue française*, vol. I, p. 53.

'Quant Escumeurs de Latin disent: Despumons la verbocination latiale et transfretons la Sequane au dilucule et crepuscule; puis deambulons par les Quadrivies et Platees de Lutece; et comme verisimiles amorabundes, captivons la benivolence de l'omnigene et omniforme sexe feminin, me semble qu'ils ne se moquent seullement de leurs semblables, mais de leur personne.'[1]

This passage was echoed by Rabelais in the chapter entitled: 'Comment Pantagruel rencontra un Limousin qui contrefaisoit le langaige françois.'[2] Even Ronsard joined the chorus. In the second preface to his *Franciade* he declared: 'C'est un crime de leze-majesté d'abandonner le langage de son pays, vivant et fleurissant, pour vouloir deterrer je ne sçay quelle cendre des anciens.'[3] He repeated the same warning in his 'philological testament', recorded by Agrippa d'Aubigné in the preface to *Les Tragiques*:

'Mes enfants, deffendez vostre mère de ceux qui veulent faire servante une Damoyselle de bonne maison . . . Je vous recommande par testament que vous ne laissiez point perdre ces vieux termes, que vous les employiez et deffendiez hardiment contre les maraux qui ne tiennent pas elegant ce qui n'est point escorché du latin et de l'italien et qui aiment mieux dire *collauder, contemner, blasonner* que *louer, mespriser, blasmer*: tout cela est pour l'escholier de Limousin.'[4]

In spite of these protests, the vogue of Latinism and Hellenism continued throughout the sixteenth century. In his linguistic manifesto, *La Deffence et Illustration de la Langue françoyse* (1549), Joachim du Bellay encouraged his fellow-writers to 'amplify the French language by imitating the ancient Greek and Roman authors' and to ransack without any qualms 'the sacred treasures of this Delphic temple',[5] and a genera-

---

[1] 'When the pilferers of Latin say: Let us discontinue our Latin verbiage and let us traverse the Sequana at day-break and nightfall; then let us perambulate along the quadrivia and avenues of Lutetia; and, like verisimilar devotees of love, let us capture the benevolence of the omnigenous and omniform female sex, it seems to me that they are making fun not only of their likes but of themselves' (ibid.).

[2] 'How Pantagruel met a man from the Limousin who deformed the French language' (ibid.).

[3] 'It is a crime of high treason to abandon the language of one's native land, live and flourishing, in order to disinter heaven knows what ashes of the ancients' (ibid., p. 52).

[4] 'My children, protect your mother against those who want to treat a young lady of good family as a servant . . . It is my last will and testament to you that you should not allow these old terms to be lost, that you should use them and protect them fearlessly against the villains who find nothing is elegant unless it has been extracted from Latin or Italian, and who prefer to say *collauder, contemner, blasonner* rather than *louer* ("to praise"), *mespriser* ("to despise"), *blasmer* ("to blame"): all this is fit for the student from the Limousin' (ibid.).

[5] 'Amplifier la langue Françoyse par l'imitation des anciens auteurs Grecs et Romains' . . . 'les sacrez thresors de ce temple Delphique' (ibid., p. 51; cf. above, p. 159).

tion later Montaigne wrote: 'Si vous allez tendu, vous sentez souvent qu'il (nostre langage) languit soubs vous et fleschit, et qu'à son default le latin se presente au secours et le grec à d'autres.'[1]

The invasion of the French vocabulary by countless 'mots savants', learned terms borrowed directly from Classical or medieval Latin, is usually associated with the Renaissance and more particularly with the influence of Humanism. Yet the process had begun many centuries earlier, during another great revival of learning: the 'Carolingian Renaissance'. Charlemagne's efforts to purify the Latin of his time were so successful that they created a gulf between the speech of ordinary people and the standard tongue. For the first time it was realized that the 'rustica Romana lingua', as the Council of Tours called it in 813, was a language in its own right, and it was certainly no accident that the first text we possess in this idiom, the Strasbourg Oaths, was composed less than thirty years later. The emergence of the French language as an independent medium coincided with the appearance of the first Latinisms. The earliest texts, the Oaths themselves, the *Eulalie* and the rest, already contain a number of words borrowed from Latin, and the tendency became more marked from the end of the eleventh century onwards as the literature in the vernacular gathered momentum. There were several degrees in the assimilation of this Latin material:

(*a*) Some Latin words and phrases were reproduced without any alterations or with only slight concessions to French habits of speech. Such were, for example, *in damno sit* 'may be of harm' in the Strasbourg Oaths;[2] *un grabatum*, from Latin *grabātus* 'small or low couch, pallet, camp-bed', in the eleventh century *Vie de Saint Alexis*;[3] the form *resurrexis*, for Latin *resurrexisti*, in the famous death-scene in *La Chanson de Roland*;[4] *item* and *opium* in the thirteenth century,[5] and others. These 'maximum Latinisms', as they may be called, persist during the Renaissance and even in Modern French: *alibi* and *examen* go back to the fourteenth century, *alias* and *rébus* to the fifteenth, *abdomen*, *errata*,[6] *hiatus* to the sixteenth, *alinéa* 'indented line, paragraph', *angélus*, *ex-voto*

---

[1] 'If you are riding fast, you often feel that it (our language) is languishing and flagging beneath you, and that in its place Latin comes to the rescue, or Greek to others' (ibid., p. 50).

[2] See A. Ewert, *The French Language*, London, repr. 1947, p. 352.

[3] Gougenheim, loc. cit., p. 6.

[4] 'Seint Lazaron de mort *resurrexis*' ('Who made Saint Lazarus rise from the dead') (ibid.).

[5] All the dates and etymologies in this chapter are based on the current (third) edition of Bloch-Wartburg's dictionary.

[6] On the use of *erratum* and *errata*, see ibid. and M. Grevisse, *Le bon Usage*, p. 234. On the plural of Latin words in French, see recently R.-L. Wagner-J. Pinchon, *Grammaire française classique et moderne*, Paris, 1962, p. 61.

to the seventeenth, *maximum, minimum, veto* to the eighteenth, *aquarium, fac-similé, omnibus* to the nineteenth, *moratorium* to the beginning of the present century, etc.

(*b*) A second category of early Latinisms consists of borrowings which were more or less adapted in their form and especially in their ending. On a single page, chosen at random, of the current edition of Bloch-Wartburg's etymological dictionary I have found the following Latinisms of this type which are attested in the twelfth and thirteenth centuries: *secret*, adjective and noun; *secrétaire*; *secte* (about 1300); *séculier* 'secular'; *sécurité* (rare before the seventeenth century); *sédition*; *séduction* (rare before the seventeenth century).

(*c*) A third type of early Latinisms are so-called 'semi-learned' terms whose phonetic shape shows a combination of normal sound-change and the influence of the Latin form. A good example of such a compromise is *siècle* 'century; age, period; the world', a Gallicized reflex of Latin *saeculum*, which emerged in the thirteenth century after long hesitation between several variants: *seule, siegle, secle*. The form *siècle* conforms to ordinary sound-laws in all but one respect: the retention of the *cl* group. If the word had evolved quite spontaneously, it would have given *★sieil*, just as *vetulum*, Vulgar Latin |veklu|, has given *vieil*; if, on the other hand, it were a purely learned borrowing from Latin, it would have developed into *★sécule*, like *véhicule* from *vehiculum* or *fascicule* from *fasciculus*. Other semi-learned terms are for example *charité* in the tenth century and *école* in the eleventh. One can easily see why words for 'charity', 'school' or 'the world' should have been particularly exposed to learned Latin influence.

It is clear from these examples that even before the Renaissance, the French vocabulary had become 're-Latinized' on an appreciable scale. But it was only from the fourteenth century onwards that Latinism grew into a systematic movement, at first mainly in the works of translators such as Bersuire and Oresme, then in the original writings of a whole series of scholars and literary men who deliberately embarked on a major language-reform: the forging of a new French vocabulary from classical elements. Ferdinand Brunot has summed up this change of attitude in the following terms:

'Au XIIIe siècle, si considérable que soit le nombre des termes empruntés au latin, si conscients même que puissent être certains emprunts, on ne voit point d'effort systématique pour naturaliser des mots latins. Or c'est là ce qui caractérise les latiniseurs de l'époque nouvelle. A tort ou à raison, soit éblouissement des chefs-d'œuvre qui leur sont révélés, soit paresse d'esprit et incapacité d'utiliser les ressources dont leur vulgaire dispose, ils se sentent incapables de l'adapter à des besoins nouveaux et ils le déclarent. Ils ont désormais une doctrine et un système.'[1]

In the 'excusation et commendation' with which he prefaced his translation of Aristotle's *Ethics*, Oresme unequivocally stated his views on this problem: 'Une science qui est forte ... ne peut pas estre bailliee en termes legiers à entendre, mès y convient souvent user de termes ou de mots propres en la science qui ne sont pas communellement entendus ne cogneus de chascun, mesmement quant elle n'a autrefois esté tractée et exercée en tel langage.'[2] How conscious and deliberate this attitude was can be seen from the fact that Oresme actually compiled a table of 'strange terms' or 'hard words' (*forsmots*) for the reader's convenience.

This current of Latinism reached its high-water mark in the sixteenth century, not only as a result of the spectacular progress of humanistic and literary activities, but also because of the penetration of the vernacular into spheres which had hitherto been regarded as the exclusive preserves of Latin. The sixteenth century brought two new elements into the vogue of classical vocabulary. Until about 1500, Greek influence, though not inconsiderable, was, as Brunot put it, 'intermittent and indirect', mediated mainly by Latin.[3] Now there began a large-scale influx of Hellenisms into science, medicine and other fields, including even the language of poetry. It is ironical that Ronsard himself, whom we have seen fulminating against the excesses of the new style, could write a line like the famous 'Ocymore, dyspotme, oligochronien',[4] which is made up of three purely Greek adjectives: ὠκύμορος, 'quickly-dying, dying early', δύσποτμος, 'unlucky, ill-starred, unhappy, wretched', and ὀλιγοχρόνιος, 'lasting or living but little time' (Liddell and Scott).

---

[1] 'In the thirteenth century, however considerable the number of terms borrowed from Latin, however conscious certain borrowings may be, one can see no systematic effort to naturalize Latin words. Now it is precisely this which is characteristic of the Latinists of the new era. Rightly or wrongly, either because they are dazzled by the masterpieces revealed to them, or out of mere intellectual laziness and inability to use the resources of the vernacular, they feel unable to adapt the latter to new requirements, and they say so. They have henceforth a doctrine and a system' (*Histoire de la langue française*, vol. I, p. 515).

[2] 'A science which is strong ... cannot be put in terms easy to understand, but it is often necessary to use terms or words peculiar to that science, which are not commonly understood and known to all, especially if the science had not been previously treated and practised in that language' (quoted ibid., p. 516).

[3] Ibid., p. 525.

[4] Quoted by Ch. Bruneau, *Petite Histoire de la langue française*, vol. I, p. 125.

R

The other novelty were the warnings sounded against the indiscriminate use of classical terms; some specimens of these protests were quoted at the beginning of this chapter.

The subsequent history of Latinisms and Hellenisms in French can be summed up very briefly. The seventeenth century, with its ideal of purity and correctness in language, was not in favour of any form of lexical expansion; we have already seen Vaugelas's intransigent principle: 'It is never permissible to coin words' (p. 234). At the same time, writers were anxious to avoid any terms with a technical or pedantic flavour; to Malherbe, the adjective *idéal*, a sixteenth-century borrowing from late Latin, seemed a 'scholastic word', whereas *ulcère*, a fourteenth-century Latinism, was too specialized to be used outside medical contexts.[1] Nevertheless, a number of Greek and Latin terms were introduced into French during this period, such as *armistice, complexe, incendie, magnétique, optique, parodie, précoce, rigidité, télescope*. We have seen how one of these learned formations, *exactitude*, offended the ears of Vaugelas (p. 162); yet this did not prevent the word from giving rise to a further derivative, *inexactitude*, towards the end of the century.

There is no need to trace the diffusion of Latinisms and Hellenisms any further since this is an international phenomenon, even though its range and intensity may vary from one language to another. Modern borrowings from the two classical languages fall into six groups:

1. Words which already existed in Latin: *postulat* from *postulatum* 'demand, request'.

2. Words which already existed in Greek: *stratégie* from στρατηγία 'the office of general, command, generalship'.

3. Combinations of Latin elements: *intercontinental*.

4. Combinations of Greek elements: *télégraphe*, coined by the diplomat Miot in the late eighteenth century.

5. Combinations of Greek and Latin elements: *télévision*.

6. Combinations of classical and modern elements: *bureaucratie*, invented by the economist Gournay in the middle of the eighteenth century.

Before examining the consequences of the vast lexical expansion which took place during the Renaissance, it might be useful to have some indication of the magnitude of the process and of the nature of the terms and concepts with which it has enriched the language. To this end I

---

[1] On the 'purification' of the vocabulary in the seventeenth century, see F. Brunot, *Histoire de la langue française*, vol. III, Part 1, Book II, chs. 2–7, and vol. IV, Part 1, Book IV.

have collected two small sets of data, one from a dictionary, the other from a modern text:

(a) I have compiled a list of all words beginning with *m* which are recorded in the third edition (1960) of Bloch-Wartburg's etymological dictionary as borrowings from Latin and Greek introduced in the fourteenth, fifteenth and sixteenth centuries. Derivatives were included only where they were specifically traced back to Greek or Latin antecedents. The reason for choosing the letter *m* was that, according to the preface to the third edition, it is from this point onwards that the material had been radically revised, in the light of Professor Wartburg's work on the final volumes of his own monumental *Französisches Etymologisches Wörterbuch*. Needless to say, dictionary dates are never definitive, and there are a few border-line cases; nevertheless, the main outlines of the general picture, which emerge clearly and consistently, are not likely to be altered even if some of the details may have to be modified. For this one letter of the alphabet, Latinisms and Hellenisms first attested between 1300 and 1600 total nearly 200. Even more significant than this impressive figure is the quality of the borrowings. A few specimens from each of the three centuries will show that some of the indispensable stock-in-trade of every educated Frenchman entered the language during this period:

Fourteenth century: *machine, maritime, matériel, mélancolique, mental, militaire, misérable, moderne, modeste, modifier, monopole, muscle, mutuel, mystique.*

Fifteenth century: *maturité, médiocre, méditer, minéral* (around 1500), *ministère, mode, monologue, morbide, moribond.*

Sixteenth century: *magie, majuscule, manufacture, manuscrit, médical, météorologie, méthode, méticuleux, mission, momentané, monétaire, monogramme, myope.*

These three dozen basic words, to which many more could be added, will give some idea of the magnitude of the conceptual revolution involved. It should be noted, however, that a new term does not necessarily mean a new concept; as we shall see presently, in a number of cases a learned word simply replaced a native equivalent or sometimes an earlier and more Gallicized borrowing. But while some caution is needed in this respect, there can be no doubt that many of the new terms did denote new objects, institutions or ideas and that, thanks to this huge expansion of the vocabulary, a Frenchman around 1600 possessed an incomparably richer and more refined conceptual apparatus than did his ancestors three hundred years earlier.

(*b*) In order to form some idea of the importance of the Graeco-Latin element in the abstract vocabulary of a modern French writer, I have examined a passage chosen at random from Valéry's *Variété*, which is fairly representative of ordinary, non-technical, French analytical prose style. The passage is as follows:

'Le savoir, qui était une valeur de *consommation*, devient une valeur d'échange. L'*utilité* du savoir fait du savoir une denrée, qui est désirable non plus par quelques *amateurs* très *distingués*, mais par Tout le *Monde*.

'Cette denrée, donc, se *préparera* sous des *formes* de plus en plus maniables ou *comestibles*; elle se *distribuera* à une *clientèle* de plus en plus nombreuse; elle deviendra chose du *Commerce*, chose enfin qui s'*imite* et se produit un peu partout.

'*Résultat*: l'*inégalité* qui *existait* entre les *régions* du *monde* au point de vue des arts *mécaniques*, des *sciences appliquées*, des moyens *scientifiques* de la guerre ou de la paix,—*inégalité* sur laquelle se fondait la *prédominance* européenne—tend à disparaître *graduellement*.

'Donc, la *classification* des *régions habitables* du *monde* tend à devenir telle que la grandeur *matérielle brute*, les *éléments* de *statistique*, les nombres—*population, superficie, matières* premières—*déterminent* enfin *exclusivement* ce *classement* des compartiments du *globe*.'[1]

In this passage I have italicized all words taken over from Greek or Latin as well as those derived from Latin or Greek terms, such as *classement* from *classe*, a borrowing from Latin *classis*. Proper names (*européen*) and loan-words from other languages (*compartiment* from Italian *compartimento*) have not been included. The text contains 35 Latinisms and Hellenisms, and since two of these occur twice (*inégalité, région*) and one three times (*monde*), the actual figure rises to 39.

A chronological analysis of this learned vocabulary is illuminating and helps to place the contribution of the Renaissance in its proper per-

---

[1] 'Knowledge, which had been an article of consumption, now becomes an article of exchange. The usefulness of knowledge makes it into a commodity which is desired no longer by a few very distinguished amateurs but by everybody.

'This commodity will therefore be prepared in more and more handy or edible forms; it will be distributed among a steadily growing clientele; it will become an article of trade, an article which can be imitated and produced more or less anywhere.

'Result: the unequality which had existed between the various regions of the world in the mechanical arts, in applied science, in the scientific means of war and peace—an unequality which was the basis of the predominance of Europe—gradually tends to disappear.

'Thus, the habitable regions of the world tend to be classified in such a way that gross physical size, statistical data, numbers—population, area, raw materials—will in the end exclusively determine the classification of the various parts of the globe' (*Variété*, 42nd ed., Paris, 1924, pp. 29 f.).

spective, even though one cannot, of course, generalize from one sample. The distribution, based on the dates given in the Bloch-Wartburg dictionary, shows the following picture:

Ninth century: 1 (*élément*[1]).
Eleventh century: 2 (*forme, science*).
Twelfth century: 8 (*consommation, déterminer, habitable, matière*[2], *monde, région, superficie, utilité*).
Thirteenth century: 4 (*appliquer, brut, distribuer, mécanique*).
Fourteenth century: 12 (*amateur, clientèle, comestible, commerce*[3], *distinguer, globe, graduel, imiter, matériel, population*[4], *préparer, scientifique*).
Fifteenth century: 2 (*exclusif, exister*).
Sixteenth century: 2 (*inégalité*[5], *prédominance*).
Seventeenth century: 1 (*résultat*).
Eighteenth century: 3 (*classement, classification, statistique*[6]).

Without drawing far-reaching conclusions from this distribution, one cannot help being struck by certain features: the large total of twelve for the fourteenth century; the fact that the twelfth century comes next with eight examples, whereas on the other hand there is only one from the seventeenth and nothing more recent than the eighteenth. Similar analyses carried out on a wide variety of texts would show which features are accidental and which of them form part of a general pattern. Meanwhile, the quality of the learned vocabulary is once again highly significant. It is indeed remarkable, when one comes to think of it, that a twentieth-century author should use classical terms when writing or thinking about such basic notions as 'exist', 'apply', 'distinguish', 'distribute', 'prepare'; 'material', 'gradual', 'scientific', 'exclusive'; 'element', 'form,' 'matter', 'world', 'region', 'science', 'population', 'result', and others.

[1] Tenth century, according to Bloch-Wartburg; but the *Eulalie*, in which the word first occurs, is usually dated from the late ninth century.
[2] Though *matière* is not attested before the twelfth century, its form shows that it must have been borrowed at a very early date; 'it is one of those words which learned circles have always used' (Bloch-Wartburg).
[3] Attested as *commerque* in 1370; the modern form does not appear till a hundred years later (ibid.).
[4] Though *population* occurs occasionally in the fourteenth and fifteenth centuries, it did not become current till the eighteenth when it was reborrowed from English. It should be noted that in Classical Latin, *populatio* meant 'devastation'; the modern meaning is a late Latin development (cf. ibid. and Lewis and Short).
[5] An older variant, *inéqualité*, is found as early as 1290; the modern form has been re-modelled on *égal*, a semi-learned reflex of Latin *aequalis* (Bloch-Wartburg).
[6] Borrowed from German in the eighteenth century; cf. R. A. Barrell, 'Three Philosophical Terms which France Owes to Germany: *Esthétique, Psychologie, Statistique*', *Archivum Linguisticum*, xi (1959), pp. 48–61.

A lexical influence on such a massive scale is bound to have had repercussions in various sectors of the linguistic system. These repercussions fall into three groups: those which concern the form of words, those which affect their meaning and their use, and those which determine their stylistic value.

A. Formal Consequences

1. *Phonetic features.*—Sound combinations which had existed in Latin but had disappeared in French at an early stage tend to reappear in learned terms borrowed from Latin at a later date. Thus, an *l* before consonant has been either vocalized to *u* in French or, in certain positions, has dropped out completely. The sequence *l*+consonant does not therefore occur in any native French word, but it was subsequently reintroduced into the language in borrowings from Latin and other sources. Thus, side by side with the native term *autre* 'other', a continuation of Latin *alterum*, there exists the learned form *altérer*, launched by Oresme. In the same way, *s* before consonant has become silent in ordinary French words but has re-appeared in later Latinisms, so that we have such pairs as *détruire* 'destroy' —*destruction*, *étrangler* 'strangle'—*strangulation*, etc. If one compares *éteindre* 'extinguish' with *extinction*, *mois* 'month' with *mensuel*, *contrainte* 'constraint' with *constriction*, one realizes that, from the point of view of phonetic structure, the learned vocabulary forms a kind of State within the State.

It even happens that the same Latin word has survived in two forms in French, one native, the other learned. In these 'doublets', the phonetic discrepancy is usually accompanied by semantic differences:

Latin *examen* < *essaim* 'swarm'
examen (fourteenth century)

Latin *viaticum* < *voyage* 'journey'
viatique 'viaticum; last sacrament' (fourteenth century)

Latin *rigidum* < *raide* 'stiff'
rigide (fifteenth century)

2. *Spelling.*—During the Renaissance, silent letters were at times introduced into French words so as to bring them nearer to their Latin roots. These embellishments are particularly piquant when they are based on wrong etymologies. Thus a *ç* was added after the *s-* in *savoir* 'to know', in the erroneous belief that the verb was connected with

Latin *scire* 'to know', whereas in actual fact it comes from *sapere* 'to taste of; to have good taste'. This particular error had no permanent consequences; a similar misunderstanding is, however, responsible for the modern spelling of *poids* 'weight' with a *d*. *Poids* comes from the Latin *pē(n)sum* 'something weighed; weight', and was written *pois* until the end of the fifteenth century when a *d* was added because it was thought that the word was derived from Latin *pondus* 'weight'. Elsewhere a letter has been dropped under Latin influence: *cour*, from Latin *cohortem* 'court, enclosure, yard', was originally written with a *t*, as it still is in English *court*, Italian and Spanish *corte*; around the fifteenth century, however, the spelling without *t* was introduced, probably because the word was wrongly identified with Latin *curia* (cf. above, p. 35).

It may even happen that a silent letter perpetuating a false etymology will come to life by a process known as 'spelling pronunciation'. Such a case is the French *legs* 'legacy, bequest', which was originally spelt *lais* and was derived from *laisser* 'to leave'. In the fifteenth century, the spelling was remodelled because people believed that the word was connected with Latin *legatum* 'bequest, legacy'. As a result, *legs* became associated with the verb *léguer* 'to bequeathe', and nowadays it is sometimes pronounced with a |g|.

3. *Gender.*—In some cases, the gender of a French word has been modified under Latin influence. Abstract nouns in *-orem* were masculine in Latin but have become feminine in French: *dolorem* > *la douleur*, as opposed to Italian *il dolore* and Spanish *el dolor*.[1] Even learned words like *la fureur* and *la terreur* conform to this rule. There are, however, two exceptions: *honneur* and *labeur* became masculine during the Renaissance, under the influence of their Latin prototypes.

B. Lexical and Semantic Consequences

1. *Disappearance of old words.*—As already noted, a number of old terms—native words as well as earlier borrowings—were replaced by learned formations during the Renaissance. To take but one example from each century, *mire*, the French descendant of Latin *medicum*, was ousted by *médecin*, a fourteenth-century Latinism; in the same way, the learned *maturité*, first attested at the end of the fifteenth century, has supplanted the older *meürté*, while in the sixteenth century *aver*, the French continuation of Latin *avarum*, was replaced by the classicizing form

---

[1] See recently R. de Dardel, 'Le Genre des substantifs abstraits en *-or* dans les langues romanes et en roman commun', *Cahiers Ferdinand de Saussure*, xvii (1960), pp. 29–45.

avare. Earlier and more thoroughly assimilated Latinisms succumbed to the same tendency: thus the semi-learned *momentain*, from late Latin *momentaneum*, was abandoned in favour of *momentané*, a sixteenth-century form which is closer to the Latin model.[1]

2. *Change of meaning.*—Under classical influence, some French words were given meanings which had existed in Latin but had disappeared in French. Professor Gougenheim has noted several examples of such 'internal re-Latinization' (*gloire, loi, glaive,* etc.); to quote a particularly striking case, when Marguerite de Navarre speaks of 'deux gentilz hommes se deffendans *vertueusement*' 'two gentlemen *courageously* defending themselves', she uses the adverb not in the normal French meaning of 'virtuously', but in the sense of Latin *virtus*.[2]

3. *Homonymy.*—From this point of view, the introduction of learned terms has had both positive and negative effects: it has created fresh homonyms, while on the other hand it has helped to resolve certain homonymic conflicts. An example of the former is the history of the two *gestes*. There was in medieval French a feminine noun *geste* which meant 'exploits' and also a poem about heroic deeds. It had been borrowed from Latin *gesta*, neuter plural of the past participle *gestus* from the verb *gerere* 'bear, wage, perform', which had been erroneously interpreted as a feminine singular (cf. *folium, folia > la feuille* 'leaf'; *gaudium, gaudia > la joie* 'joy'). The eclipse of this *geste*, which now survives only in the expressions *faits et gestes* 'exploit' and *chanson de geste* 'medieval epic poem', was no doubt due to a homonymic clash with the masculine noun *geste* 'gesture', borrowed from Latin *gestus, gestūs* in the late fifteenth century.[3]

In other cases, learned terms have helped to fill gaps caused by homonymic conflicts between native words. A well-known example is the clash between Old French *aimer*, from *amare* 'to like, to love', and *e(s)mer*, from *aestimare* 'to estimate, to value'. This awkward ambiguity led to the disappearance of *e(s)mer* and its replacement by the learned form *estimer*, introduced around 1300.[4]

4. *Elimination of incompatible meanings.*—Learned terms have also provided useful substitutes when there was a conflict between incompatible senses of a native word. Thus French *sevrer*, from Latin *separare*, originally meant 'to separate'; in the thirteenth century, however, it acquired the more specialized sense 'to wean', which made it unusable in

---

[1] For other examples, see Gougenheim, loc. cit., p. 7.
[2] Ibid., pp. 8–13.
[3] Cf. ibid., pp. 17 f., and Bloch-Wartburg.
[4] See especially J. Orr, *Words and Sounds in English and French*, ch. XIV.

the older and wider meaning. The gap was filled by introducing the learned form *séparer* in the early fourteenth century.

5. *Synonymy.*—The influx of Latinisms and Hellenisms has greatly enriched the synonymic resources of the language and has enabled it to express some new and delicate nuances. In many cases, the modern speaker and writer can play on a 'double scale' of synonyms, one native, the other Graeco-Latin: *frêle* 'frail'—*fragile* 'fragile'; *raide* 'stiff'—*rigide* 'rigid; *sec* 'dry'—*aride* 'arid'; *fiévreux* 'feverish'—*fébrile* 'febrile'; *sûreté* 'safety'—*sécurité* 'security', and others. Between such synonyms, the difference may be either semantic or mainly a matter of stylistic overtones. It is semantic in the case of the pair *aveuglement* and *cécité*: since the eighteenth century, *aveuglement*, derived from the adjective *aveugle* 'blind', has become specialized in the sense of moral blindness, whereas physical blindness is denoted by *cécité*, a thirteenth-century borrowing from Latin *caecitas*. One could say, for example, that in Gide's *Symphonie pastorale*, the 'cécité' of the blind girl is paralleled by the 'aveuglement' of the pastor who does not know that he is in love with her.

A case of stylistic rather than semantic difference is that between *pourriture* 'rot, decay' and its learned synonym *putréfaction*, taken over from Latin in the fourteenth century. In a highly rhetorical internal monologue in *Madame Bovary*, Emma asks herself in despair: 'D'où venait donc cette insuffisance de la vie, cette *pourriture* instantanée des choses où elle s'appuyait?'[1] If one were to replace *pourriture* by *putréfaction*, not only the rhythm but the whole tone of the passage would be destroyed, though the actual meaning would scarcely be affected.

6. *Motivation.*—As we saw in some earlier chapters (pp. 9 f. and 67 f.), French has a marked preference for opaque, unmotivated words and tends to use learned Graeco-Latin formations where German, for example, employs a transparent compound or derivative. One can witness during the Renaissance the gradual abandonment of native resources in favour of direct borrowings from the two classical languages. We have already seen how the old word *meürté* was replaced by the purely Latin *maturité*. This change has meant a gain for the unmotivated element in the French vocabulary, since *meürté* was a transparent derivative of the adjective *meür > mûr* 'ripe', the French continuation of Latin *maturum*, whereas *maturité* is opaque and unanalysable: its motivation lies in Latin, not in French.[2] Similarly, *feintise*, clearly connected with

---

[1] 'What was the reason for this inadequacy of life, for the immediate decay of anything she leant against?' (Conard ed., p. 393).

[2] Another transparent derivative of *mûr*, the noun *murison*, disappeared in the same way; cf. Wartburg, *Evolution et structure de la langue française*, pp. 263 f.

feindre 'to feign, to pretend', was ousted by *fiction*; *éteignement*, from *éteindre*, by *extinction*; *accuseur*, from *accuser*, by *accusateur*, etc.[1] In many other cases, there was no earlier term in existence since the concept itself was new, but instead of forming a compound or derivative from French material, people preferred to borrow a word from Latin or from Greek. In this way, the current of Latinism and Hellenism became a potent factor in the preponderance of unmotivated terms in Modern French, as opposed to the more transparent structure of the medieval language.

C. Stylistic Consequences

Since the Renaissance, there exist two 'styles', two stylistic registers in French: one concrete, simple, informal, based largely on native words; the other abstract, literary and erudite, with heavy concentrations of learned terms. In the fifteenth-century *Mystère du Vieux Testament*, Ferdinand Brunot notes some remarkable stylistic contrasts: 'les larrons parlent argot; Dieu, qui ne peut faire moins que l'église catholique, parle à peu près latin en français'.[2] There is a similar contrast between the racy, colloquial language in which Ballaam talks to his ass, and the elegant and polished style of the angels:

BALLAAM: Qu'esse cy?
Devons nous demourer icy?
C'est trop tiré le cul arriere;
Si n'y a il point de barriere
Encontre toy; je n'y vois rien.
Hay, Hay, Hay, Hay! J'aperçoy bien
Que tu es une faulce beste.[3]

AN ANGEL: Souverain roy de la gloire felice,
Que chacun doit en honneur collauder,
Mercy vous rends de cueur sans nul obice,
Pour vostre nom en tout bien exaulcer.[4]

[1] Cf. ibid., pp. 137 ff. and 263.
[2] 'The thieves talk in argot; God, Who could not do less than the Catholic Church, speaks more or less Latin in a French garb' (*Histoire de la langue française*, vol. I, p. 525).
[3] 'What is this? Have we got to stop here? You are pulling too much on your haunches; there is no barrier before you; I can't see a thing. Hey! Hey! Hey! Hey! I can see that you are a wicked beast' (ibid., p. 527).
[4] 'Sovereign king, blessed and glorious, Whom everyone should praise and honour, I thank You from all my heart, without any reservation, in order to magnify Your name in all things' (ibid., p. 528).

It is not surprising that the affectations of Latinizing writers should have lent themselves to parody and pastiche. In his *Petit Testament,* Villon ridiculed the pedantic jargon of the schoolmen, full of erudite Latinisms:

> Et mesmement l'estimative,
> Par quoy prospective nous vient;
> Similative, formative . . .[1],

prefiguring Geofroy Tory and Rabelais, and even Molière's satire of the medical profession and of the language of preciosity; in *Les Femmes savantes,* Bélise actually asks a notary to 'exprimer la dot en mines et talents. Et dater par les mots d'ides et de calendes'.[2] Even in contemporary French, an author can choose, broadly speaking, between two registers of style, with many gradations and a kind of neutral zone between the two. The contrast between the two media is particularly marked in Camus's first two novels, *L'Etranger* and *La Peste,* both of which, it will be remembered, are told by a narrator. Take the opening passages of the two books:

'Aujourd'hui, maman est morte. Ou peut-être hier, je ne sais pas. J'ai reçu un *télégramme* de l'*asile*: "Mère *décédée*. Enterrement demain. Sentiments *distingués*." Cela ne veut rien dire. C'était peut-être hier.

'L'*asile* de vieillards est à Marengo, à quatre-vingts *kilomètres* d'Alger. Je prendrai l'*autobus* à deux heures et j'arriverai dans l'après-midi. Ainsi, je pourrai veiller et je rentrerai demain soir. J'ai demandé deux jours de congé à mon *patron* et il ne pouvait pas me les refuser avec une *excuse* pareille. Mais il n'avait pas l'air content. Je lui ai même dit: "Ce n'est pas de ma faute." Il n'a pas répondu. J'ai *pensé* alors que je n'aurais pas dû lui dire cela.'[3]

'Les *curieux événements* qui font le *sujet* de cette *chronique* se sont produits en 194., à Oran. De l'avis *général*, ils n'y étaient pas à leur place, sortant un peu de l'*ordinaire*. A première vue, Oran est, en *effet*, une ville *ordinaire* et rien de plus qu'une *préfecture* française de la côte algérienne.

---

[1] 'And in the same way the faculty of judgement, by which we form our mental concepts; the faculty of assimilation and formation . . .' Cf. J. Fox, *The Poetry of Villon,* pp. 100 f.

[2] 'Express the dowry in minas and talents, and put the date in ides and calends' (Act V, scene 3; cf. my *Précis de sémantique française,* p. 166).

[3] 'Today mother died. Or perhaps yesterday, I don't know. I got a telegram from the old people's home: "Mother deceased. Funeral tomorrow. Yours faithfully." It means nothing. Perhaps it was yesterday.

'La cité elle-même, on doit l'avouer, est laide. D'*aspect tranquille*, il faut quelque temps pour apercevoir ce qui la rend *différente* de tant d'autres villes *commerçantes*, sous toutes les *latitudes*. Comment faire *imaginer*, par *exemple*, une ville sans pigeons, sans arbres et sans jardins, où l'on ne rencontre ni battements d'*ailes* ni froissements de feuilles, un lieu *neutre* pour tout dire?'[1]

The contrast between the two styles is so sharp that it hardly needs any comment. I have again italicized all the 'learned' words, including such marginal cases as *penser*, which is technically a Latinism but was absorbed many centuries ago into the basic French vocabulary.[2] A glance at the two passages shows that the density of the Graeco-Latin element is very different: in the first, there are only seven learned terms (one of them used twice), not counting the clichés of the official telegram; the passage from *La Peste*, however, which is of almost exactly the same length, contains no less than seventeen Greek and Latin words, again with one repetition. In the extract from *L'Etranger*, all but two of the terms involved are concrete nouns: *patron, asile, autobus, kilomètre, télégramme*; the remaining two are abstract but trivial (*excuse, penser*). This is perfectly consistent with the narrator's personality, with the psychology of the 'absurd' man. Meursault is a man of the here and now, a man of the senses, who records his experiences but does not analyse or interpret them. His vocabulary, simple, limited, concrete and un-analytical, is part of that 'zero degree of style' which we have noted in other aspects of his language.[3]

The lexical texture of the extract from *La Peste* is totally different. One or two of the Graeco-Latin words are concrete nouns, but the great majority are abstract terms of the kind one encounters in ordinary analytical prose. It may be noted that seven of the seventeen learned

'The old people's home is at Marengo, eighty kilometres from Algiers. I shall take the bus at two o'clock and arrive in the afternoon. In this way I can sit up at night, and I shall come back tomorrow evening. I have asked my chief for two days' leave, and he couldn't refuse for such a reason. But he did not look pleased. I even said to him: "It isn't my fault." He didn't answer. Then I thought I shouldn't have said that to him.'

[1] 'The curious events which form the subject of this chronicle took place in 194..., in Oran. It is generally agreed that they were out of place there, that they were somewhat out of the ordinary. At first sight Oran is, indeed, an ordinary town, nothing but a French prefecture on the Algerian coast.

'The town itself, one must admit, is ugly. It has a quiet appearance, and one needs some time to notice what makes it different from so many other commercial towns, in any latitude. How can one imagine, for example, a town without pigeons, without trees and without gardens, where one meets no flutter of wings or rustle of leaves, a neutral place, to put it briefly?'

[2] Cf. W. Rothwell, *Archivum Linguisticum*, xiv (1962), pp. 36 f.

[3] See above, pp. 136 ff., 146 f., 194 f.; on the vocabulary of *L'Etranger*, see also J. Cruickshank, *Albert Camus and the Literature of Revolt*, pp. 154 ff.

words are adjectives. While most of the abstract terms are common and stylistically neutral, some (*chronique, neutre, latitude*) have a distinct evocatory value: they are the language of a cultivated person who expresses himself with precision and sober elegance, and also with an air of detachment and objectivity. In this way, the first few lines of the two novels tell us a great deal, by the choice of vocabulary which is, of course, powerfully reinforced by the syntax, about the personality and attitude of the two narrators and about the atmosphere of the works themselves.

It would be interesting, but would take us too far from our subject, to compare the impact of the classical languages on French during and since the Renaissance with their influence on the English vocabulary during the same period. A detailed comparison would reveal many points of similarity, but also some fundamental differences. In Britain as in France, some Renaissance writers carried the fashion of Latinism to unreasonable lengths; some of William Dunbar's lines, in his *Ballad of Our Lady*, are pure Latin in a slightly Anglicized garb:

> Hodiern, modern, sempitern,
> Angelicall regyne.[1]

In both countries there was a sharp reaction against what were variously described in England as 'hard words', 'aureate' or 'inkhorn' terms. Geofroy Tory's and Rabelais's parodies of these affectations were paralleled by the amusing pastiche, in Thomas Wilson's *Arte of Rhetorique* (1553), of 'a letter devised by a Lincolnshire man':

'Pondering, *expending*, and *revoluting* with my selfe, your *ingent affabilitie*, and *ingenious capacity* for *mundaine* affaires: I cannot but *celebrate*, & *extol* your *magnifical dexteritie* above all other.'[2]

These parodies started the fashion of a linguistic game that has remained popular in England to this very day; to mention but one example, this is how Charles Lamb starts his 'Chapter on Ears':

'I have no ear. Mistake me not, reader,—nor imagine that I am by nature destitute of those exterior twin appendages, hanging ornaments, and (architecturally speaking) handsome volutes to the human capital. Better my mother had never borne me. I am, I think, rather delicately than copiously provided with those conduits; and I feel no disposition

---

[1] Quoted by A. C. Baugh, *A History of the English Language*, p. 224.
[2] Ibid., p. 263.

to envy the mule for his plenty, or the mole for her exactness, in those labyrinthine inlets—those indispensable side-intelligencers.'[1]

Even some of the general consequences of classical influence were closely similar in the two languages. Needless to say, the adoption of hundreds of Graeco-Latin terms introduced countless new concepts into both. In the passage from Thomas Wilson which was just quoted, a modern linguist has italicized all the words which were new at the time,[2] and even this small sample includes a number of valuable terms which were borrowed either directly from Latin or through the medium of French, and which are still part of our abstract vocabulary: *affability* (1483), *capacity* (1480), *celebrate* (1534), *dexterity* (1527), *extol* (1494), *mundane* (1475), etc. Classical influence also had very similar structural repercussions in English and in French: what has been said about spelling, motivation, stylistic differences and other features in French is applicable, *mutatis mutandis*, to English as well.

On the other hand, Latinism and Hellenism in England differed in some vital respects from their counterparts in France. Firstly, the mass invasion of the English vocabulary by foreign terms was no new thing; the current of classical influence during the Renaissance had been preceded by the introduction of a vast number of words from French in the centuries following the Norman Conquest: according to a recent estimate, more than ten thousand were taken over during the Middle English period, three-quarters of which are still in common use.[3] This means that the linguistic situation in England was more complicated: English had, so to speak, to fight a war on two fronts. This is seen, for example, in the system of English synonymy: in addition to the usual pattern of native *versus* foreign (*weak—feeble, deep—profound, hearty—cordial, learning—erudition*), there is also a 'triple scale' where a native term has a French and a Latin or Greek synonym (*end—finish—conclude, kingly—royal—regal, rise—mount—ascend, time—age—epoch*).[4]

A second difference between the two processes was that French, being descended from Latin, was greatly strengthened and revitalized, like the mythological Antaeus, by its contacts with its Roman origins. In English, on the other hand, the new influence simply added a further layer to the mass of foreign material which had previously accumulated in the

---

[1] Quoted by Jespersen, *Growth and Structure of the English Language*, p. 135.
[2] Baugh, loc. cit. The dates which follow are based on the third edition, revised, of the *Shorter Oxford English Dictionary*.
[3] Baugh, op. cit., p. 215.
[4] Cf. ibid., pp. 225 f., and my *Semantics*, pp. 147 f.

language. While French was 're-Latinized', English was merely Latinized. This explains why the French vocabulary, in spite of much in-
coherence and incongruity caused by the influx of classical terms, is
essentially more homogeneous than the English one. It is only more
recently that the indiscriminate adoption of English words into French
has begun seriously to threaten the homogeneity of that language.

A third difference is psychological rather than linguistic. A very
large proportion of Latinisms and Hellenisms in both languages consists
of abstract terms, and the Englishman's attitude to abstract ideas, and
to the words in which they are couched, differs radically from the feelings of a Frenchman. Besides, the abstract and erudite nature of Greek
and Latin borrowings is often underlined by their sheer physical appearance: to many Englishmen, these 'sesquipedalian' words have an affected
and pompous air which is a standing joke in English literature; one has
to think only of Goldsmith's portrait of the village schoolmaster:

> While words of learned length and thund'ring sound
> Amazed the gazing rustics rang'd around,
> And still they gaz'd, and still the wonder grew,
> That one small head could carry all he knew.
> > *The Deserted Village*, ll. 213–16[1],

or of Alice in Wonderland who felt she could safely risk using *latitude*
and *longitude* although she 'had not the slightest idea what Latitude was,
or Longitude either, but she thought they were nice grand words to say'.

This half-amused half-suspicious attitude towards abstract and learned
foreign words has a number of roots some of which go back to the
linguistic situation after the Norman Conquest. Professor Orr has given
a vivid picture of this situation:

'For two hundred years and more, things intellectual, things pertaining
to the spirit, were symbolized by words that had a flavour of remoteness,
of higher courtliness, words redolent of the school rather than of the
home, words that often had by their side humbler synonyms, humbler,
yet used to express the things that are closer to our hearts as human
beings, as children and parents, lovers and workers.'[2]

These differences in the historical background go a long way to
explain why, in spite of many analogies, the vogue of Latinism and
Hellenism produced essentially different results in England and in
France.

[1] Cf. V. Grove, *The Language Bar*, p. 84.
[2] *Words and Sounds in English and French*, p. 42.

Classical influence on the French vocabulary during the Renaissance was without any doubt one of the most significant developments in the history of that language. Its immediate consequences were twofold: it introduced a wealth of new concepts and distinctions and brought about a radical re-Latinization of the French lexicon. This latter process was accompanied by extensive Latin influence on French syntax, which lies outside the scope of the present study. The more indirect consequences of the influx of Graeco-Latin terms were no less far-reaching. There were widespread repercussions in the semantic field, in particular in the synonymic resources of the language, and even the phonological and orthographical system was affected in various ways. Some major structural tendencies of the French vocabulary were either initiated or intensified by classical influence: the predominance of unmotivated words; the fondness for abstract modes of expression; distinctions between delicate shades of meaning and nuances of style. Yet another important result was that French became more cosmopolitan, more easily accessible to foreigners. This proved to be a considerable advantage in subsequent centuries when, for a variety of reasons, French came to be widely used as an international medium in diplomacy, philosophy, literature, social life and other spheres. The peculiar precision, clarity and elegance which are usually associated with the French language, and which are one of the supreme attractions of French style, are intimately connected with the Graeco-Latin contribution to the French vocabulary. As a Swiss linguist declared at the end of one of the most penetrating studies ever published on the structure of modern French: 'Alors que tout se démocratise, il demeure ce qu'il a été depuis l'époque classique: le truchement d'une élite et d'une aristocratie.'[1]

---

[1] 'At a time when everything is becoming democratic, it remains what it has been ever since the classical period: the vehicle of an élite and an aristocracy' (Ch. Bally, *Linguistique générale et linguistique française*, p. 370).

SUBJECT INDEX